The Roar of the Twenties

BOOKS BY JAMES H. GRAY

The Winter Years
Men Against the Desert
The Boy from Winnipeg
Red Lights on the Prairies
Booze

James H. Gray

The Roar of the Twenties

Macmillan of Canada   Toronto

ISBN 0-7705-1276-3

Printed in Canada
for the Macmillan Company of Canada Limited
70 Bond Street, Toronto M5B 1X3

For Sam and Marjory Drache

Contents

List of Illustrations

Preface

As readers will quickly become aware this is much more a memoir than a formal history of the 1920s on the western Canadian prairies. I have used the term "western Canadian prairies" intentionally, rather than Prairie provinces, by way of emphasizing that this is social rather than political history.

Each of us, to make an obvious point, is the product of a multiplicity of influences, of which politics is only one, and frequently a very minor one at that. It is much less important in our lives — and hence in the molding of our society — than our work, our play, our homes, families, and associations, even though politics impinges obliquely on them all. From time to time we are distracted temporarily from such basics as making a living, making love, making mischief, and what used to be called "making whoopee", to contemplate the political scene — even to become involved in it. Both the interest and the involvement pass quickly. We return to the business of minding our own business, which frequently takes the form of circumventing the efforts of politicians to improve our life-styles for our own good. For a few weeks, five or six times during any decade, we become politically conscious. For the other 95 per cent of the time our attentions and our concerns are elsewhere.

This work is a report on some of these concerns. It is an effort to examine the non-political aspects of everyday life on the prairies during the 1920s, to ignore politics where possible in the process of turning over some of the rocks to see what was going

1

on underneath. When we turn to study the daily lives of the people, to contemplate their concerns and their reactions to them, we find there are no simple generalizations—we discover people who were boisterously optimistic and fun-loving, generous, neighborly, and tolerant, and simultaneously funereally bitter, cruel, and vengeful.

Perhaps I can illustrate what I am getting at by using the example of the Manitoba Schools Question. We can bury ourselves in the political convolutions and concatenations of that vexing question, and emerge with little enhancement of our understanding of the forces that molded our parents' lives — that made them behave the way they did. It is only when we ignore politics and go probing into people issues that we begin to understand how complex our heritage is. The Manitoba uproar is politically interpreted as a struggle between advocates of a non-sectarian public schools system and believers in religious schools; as a struggle between the Liberal and Conservative political parties for partisan advantage in federal and provincial politics. It was of course all of those, but only as surface manifestations of a much deeper malaise. When the political aspects are ignored, the fundamental bacterium of the schools question is discovered turning up again and again — in the bitter struggle over Church Union, in the Ku Klux Klan, in the anti-alien hysteria, in the cenotaph controversy, in the bigotry whose roots go back to the Reformation — and beyond.

Politics cannot be completely ignored, for many things that grow up from the grass roots ultimately become political issues. One example of this, and one that I hope will indicate what I am about with this book, is the Progressive movement of 1920-25.

As a journalist I have been more a political animal than most. It is obviously impossible to maintain a detached attitude toward politics from the Parliamentary Press Gallery or as a reporter covering a provincial legislature or a city hall news beat. My immersion in a political environment unquestionably gave me a distorted view of the Progressive movement, for I regarded it as one of the great historical developments of the 1920s. I assumed that relating it to the other upheavals of the decade would be central to the development of this work. It was only after several months were wasted in research that it became obvious that the so-called "Progressive" movement was in reality an exercise in futility, devoid of intellectual content, dominated by such muddle-headed theorists as Henry Wise Wood and such social reactionaries as T.A. Crerar. It pitchforked an assortment of commonplace greenhorns into political office in Manitoba and Alberta where they proceeded to govern with a pathological absence of inspiration. The ultimate impact of the Progressive movement on the future development of western Canada, in the words of Omar via Fitzgerald, was "as much as ocean of a pebble cast".

Out of the same ferment that produced the Progressive movement, however, there arose, almost in spite of the Progressive leaders, the Alberta, Saskatchewan, and Manitoba wheat pools which were the beginning of a revolutionary change in the commercial life of the west. So there is very little about the Progressives in this book and a good deal about Aaron Sapiro and the Alberta Wheat Pool.

For the scholar who may raise an eyebrow, the absence of footnotes is deliberate, because so much of what follows springs originally from personal observance. I was a boy "walking hots" at the old River Park race track when Jim Speers placed his giant brand on horse-race gambling in the west. I was a clerk in the Grain Exchange, standing on the trading floor, the day the price of May wheat took its historic tumble in January of 1925. I was a margin clerk in a brokerage office in 1928 when I.W.C. Solloway made his momentous descent on the west, and was still there when the world ended — financially — in 1929. Whenever Jack Dempsey was involved in fisticuffs, I was an excited face in the crazy crowds in the streets in front of the *Free Press* building. I was, finally, young and eager and ambitious, trying to claw my way upward from the bottommost rung of the ladder at a time of prolonged economic depression, when wage increases were unknown and economic progress was only possible by earning promotions through hard work, or by changing jobs or trades if the promotions did not come.

This work, *ergo,* began with the nudging of dimly perceived memories which had to be fleshed out by recourse to the newspaper files and microfilm of the era. In pursuit of confirmation of times, dates, and places a great many completely forgotten or previously unheard-of high jinks came to light.

Once again I am most grateful to the men and women in the libraries and archives of the west who, not only without exception but with enthusiasm, have gone to endless trouble to assist me in tracking down source material; and to the Canada Council, whose research grant made the tracking down possible. I am particularly indebted to several doctors who trusted in my discretion and reached back in time for details of their ordeals as students at the Manitoba Medical College; to former Ku Kluxers who filled in many a blank spot; to the letter writers who helped to keep the record straight with their personal testimony to events of fifty years ago. Nor would acknowledgements be complete without mention of the diligent research by eager young M.A. candidates whose theses are now assuming a respectable bulk in the archives of the west. Their theses provided clues as to where to look for names, dates, and places long lost to memory. Many of the themes they have been pursuing clearly justify full-dress treatment once they get their professors off their backs. Their work is even replete with themes for the young novelists who need starting points for their great Canadian novel! I hope they all get on with it.

JAMES H. GRAY

Introduction

In the simplest terms, the Twenties on the western Canadian prairies might be said to have begun in February 1920, with the seditious conspiracy trials of the leaders of the 1919 Winnipeg General Strike, and to have ended with the Wall Street crashes of October 1929. But the era was more—a lot more—than a simple transition between a low point and a disaster.

In some ways the decade was almost an anticlimax to the fantastic economic and population boom that had preceded the First World War. At the turn of the century there were barely 400,000 people between the Lakehead and the Rocky Mountains, well over half of them concentrated in Manitoba. In what would become Saskatchewan and Alberta, settlement was so sparse that it recalled John Palliser's description of the area as the northern tip of the great American desert. Then, almost overnight as historic time is measured, the prairies were covered with a seething mass of humanity searching for a place on which to light. In the first decade of this century more than one million immigrants poured in from the United States, eastern Canada, the United Kingdom, and the continent of Europe. Such was the demand for goods and services generated by the influx that men worked from dawn to dark building the instant towns, and the cities with their new railway shops, hotels, massive warehouses, and proliferating subdivisions full of houses and apartment blocks.

This mass migration set off an orgy of real-estate speculation

5

unmatched in Canadian history. So rapidly were the cities and towns growing that no promoter could imagine what the limit of growth would be. Between 1901 and 1911 the population of Winnipeg jumped from 43,000 to 121,000, and Regina grew from 2,000 to 30,000. In the same decade the population of rural Saskatchewan and Alberta increased from 130,000 to 600,000. That was just the beginning. Between 1911 and 1913 twice as many immigrants arrived in western Canada as had come in the previous three years. By the 1921 census there were almost two million people on the prairies—a four-fold increase from 1901. With the beginning of the First World War, the massive influx came to a dead stop.

The war could not have come at a worse time, for it completely disrupted what might be called the shake-down process. These million-odd people brought varied skills and different languages, religions, customs, prejudices, national traits and attitudes, educational attainments, artistic talents, and personality quirks. They came, as well, with different goals in life, with different political, economic, and social philosophies—and with no philosophies at all. The cord that bound them together was necessity—the necessity of making a living, and of finding their way in a new and strange, and sometimes hostile, environment. They were the raw material out of which an out-going and on-going society would be constructed, once the business of living together had been worked on by the leavening influence of time.

The war disrupted everything. It was seen by the Anglo-Saxon majority as a holy crusade to rid the world of the devil incarnate in the German nation. For many thousands of young British immigrants it was also a chance for a free ride back to England and a visit with the folks at home. But for other thousands, who had come to Canada primarily to escape the omnipresent threat of being conscripted into the armies of emperors or czars, it was the end of a dream, and an awakening to the realization that there was no escape — even in Canada.

If the war brought out the best in the human race, in its idealism, courage, and self-sacrifice — and it did — it also brought out the worst of its bigotry, cruelty, and selfishness. As time passed, even Anglo-Saxon idealism began to tarnish with the wartime hardships, inflation, and profiteering, and the mounting toll of casualties. When the war ended, the soldiers came home, not to a land fit for heroes, but to unemployment, miserly pensions, and a land torn by internal strife between employers and labor, between western farmers and the federal government, and between those with jobs and those without. In the midst of social upheaval, witch-hunting, and clouds of uncertainty, there was much harking back to the "normalcy" of the halcyon days before the war. Then capital had flowed in to develop the west and newly created wealth had poured outward from the farms; then there was work for everybody and wages were sufficient for the needs of the wage earners. Out of the disturbed and discouraging conditions of the early post-war years grew a yearning for a return to the good old days of the boom of 1912-13. The yearners, of course, were able to ignore the facts that the boom had run its course in 1913 and that a severe depression had gripped the west in 1914. The good old times never did come back to the prairie farmer in the Twenties, nor to the people of the towns and cities whose livelihood depended on the farmer. Only slowly, and only toward the end of the decade, did a reasonable level of prosperity return to prairie agriculture.

Immigration to the west resumed, but at a rate far reduced from that of the pre-war years. It was immigration with a difference, made up more of wives, children, and relatives coming to join earlier settlers. Though there was widespread unemployment in Britain, there was no rush to join in the assisted settlement schemes sponsored by the Canadian government and the railways. Nevertheless, many thousands of European peasants, caught up in the Russian Revolution and the aftermath of the war, did find their way to Canada. In aggregate, however, the immigrants barely made up for the increasing number of western Canadians who were moving away — mostly to the United States. In the 1920s the prairies did well to maintain the natural population growth.

While the boom times may not have come back, the ingrained optimism and sense of daring that had brought the prairie people to the west in the first place could not remain dormant for long. An insouciant population was soon giving rein to the wild assortment of new enthusiasms being generated by the automobile, the radio, and the electrical and communications revolutions that were soon sweeping across the region like old-fashioned prairie fires.

1. Going for Broke

In searching for an apt phrase with which to label the decade of the 1920s in the prairie west, the professional word-jugglers could have done a lot worse than select "The Gambling Decade". This era did not, of course, actually give birth to the public passion for risk-taking or create a thirsting after "something for nothing". The debris from the shattering collapse of the real-estate gambling orgy of 1910-13 was still scattered across the west, to remain an impediment to progress for thirty years. In that orgy, everybody who could scrape up enough for a down payment on a city lot scraped up enough for a down payment on two city lots. Even the railway shopmen, warehouse clerks, and common laborers, whose sights seldom extended beyond the hope of owning a 25-foot lot on which to build a modest cottage, became infected with the urge to buy the adjoining lots as speculations. Nor did the puncturing of the real-estate bubble curb the public thirst for risk-taking. When oil was discovered in Turner Valley in 1914, the Calgary store-front offices, only recently vacated by defunct real-estate promoters, filled up with oil-well promoters, as the public clamored for a chance to convert hard cash into gaudy oil-stock certificates.

The urge to "go for broke" had been a western characteristic from the days of Louis Riel. In the 1920s it simply veered off in wild new directions, to risk for the sake of the risk rather than investing in land, buildings, and business enterprises. It was one of history's gauche ironies that the force that sent this public

9

passion hurtling away on its new directions was the super-strait-laced and deadly serious One Big Union, whose leaders coupled gambling with booze and religion as opiates of the working classes.

When the One Big Union was formed in Winnipeg after the 1919 general strike, one of the first decisions taken was to establish a newspaper to carry its propaganda to its own members and to the trades union movement at large. The One Big Union *Bulletin* was born on August 12, 1919. Like the O.B.U. itself, the *Bulletin* had to struggle mightily just to stay alive. Replete as it quickly became with stolidly written socialist educational articles and polemics against craft unionism, it had little appeal for a general readership. For two years it limped along on a circulation of around 8,000. Then on December 8, 1921, it launched its first football pool with a modest cash price of $100. That turned out to be the brightest promotional idea in the history of prairie publishing. Within a matter of months, the *Bulletin* could boast that it had the largest mass distribution of any newspaper in Canada.

All the prairie newspapers of the era periodically staged contests to bolster sagging circulation. Usually the vehicle was a simple guessing game based on the number of peas in a gallon jar, the result of an election, or the size of a wheat crop. The O.B.U. *Bulletin* came up with a contest that capitalized on the widespread interest of its predominantly British membership in Old Country football. This interest had made soccer one of the most popular participation, as well as spectator, sports in the west. Organizing a British-type betting pool on British soccer games was a natural to attract public as well as trades unionist attention to the columns of the paper.

A coupon printed in the *Bulletin* listed twelve British soccer matches to be played a week hence. Contestants cut out the coupon and placed crosses in squares opposite each game to indicate whether they forecast a win for the home team, a loss, or a tie. The contest required that each coupon be accompanied by 25 cents for a three-week subscription, and the net receipts each week were to be distributed as prize money the following week. Whichever coupon had the largest number of correct predictions took 50 per cent of the pool, second got 30 per cent, and third prize was 20 per cent.

The contest caught on quickly, and by the end of January 1922 the prize pool reached $1,000. By March it was up to $4,000, and when the football season ended in April readers were contributing over $11,000 a week to the pool. The contest switched to major-league baseball games in the United States and prize money rose to $23,000. By June, when the total reached $47,000 a week, the luxurious new Allen Theatre got into the act. It arranged with the *Bulletin* to announce the winners from its stage on Tuesday evenings, and halted the showing of its feature movie for half an hour to make the announcements.

One of the attractions of the soccer pool, as the prize money sky-rocketed, was the long period of suspense that stretched from Saturday until the following Tuesday. The punters sat on the front steps awaiting delivery of the Saturday newspapers so that they could check their coupons against the published results of that day's games. Then, for the scores of contestants who might have marked 13 out of the 15 correctly, there was the long wait until the ultimate winners were determined by a small army of coupon-checkers who worked in shifts around the clock behind the locked doors of the Plebs Hall auditorium. If there turned out to be a 15-out-of-15 winner, those who had 13 right would have to share third prize and would collect as little as $3 or $4; if the winner had only 14 right they would share second prize and could collect anywhere from $50 to $500 each. And there was always the long-shot chance that their score of 13 would win first prize and a $1,000 to $10,000 bonanza. As long as the contest fever lasted, there was standing room only at the Allen Theatre on Tuesday nights.

The soccer-pool fad never reached the same intensity outside Winnipeg, but in Regina, Calgary, and Edmonton the news dealers got telegraphic advice of the winning scores on Tuesday and posted them on their windows. Nevertheless, as the prize money mounted by the week, interest did spread, and by mid-April a fair proportion of the 150,000 entries pouring into Plebs Hall each week came from the western cities. In addition, the success of the O.B.U. contest attracted all kinds of competition, and soon all the veterans' organizations had pools operating through their papers. But none came close to approaching the *Bulletin* either in the size of the pool or in the enthusiasm of the gamblers. By July its prize money was up to $65,000, and it might have been double that figure if the union, in April, had not moved to severely restrict the number of coupons any individual could send in.

In any guessing games inevitably attract the attention of people who think they can improve the odds. In the early 1920s when the peas-in-the-jar guessing games were at their peak of popularity as advertising gimmicks, hundreds and perhaps thousands of families tried to do just that. They bought duplicate jars, filled them with peas, and then spent hours around kitchen tables counting the peas. When they completed the task at 24,563 peas, winning the prize became simply a matter of putting in enough entries to bracket both sides of the counted number to take into account the variation in the size of the peas. Or so it seemed to the pea-counters. And so it seemed with the soccer-pool players.

In any series of athletic contests there are probable winners and probable losers, and a knowledgeable baseball fan playing the probables might well guess correctly the results of 10 out of 15 baseball games. But 10 out of 15 would never have won a prize in the O.B.U. contests. There it took at least 14 out of 15 to win first prize, and frequently a perfect score was needed. When a score of 14 out of 15 was worth $10,000, however, it was worth spending $25 and sending in 100 coupons with the heavily favored teams all marked to win and the doubtful teams varied. When the O.B.U. contest began getting bundles of several hundred entries from single contestants, and when the names of several people began appearing regularly on the prize list, the managers began to fear that the customers might suspect that the game was fixed. A mere whiff of suspicion could ruin them, so they put into effect a limit of eight entries from any individual.

It all came to a clattering—though hardly precipitous—halt at the end of June 1923 when the Manitoba Court of Appeal decided that the *Bulletin* contest was illegal. The union naturally denounced the decision as discrimination against the working class. It pointed out that there was no essential difference between pari-mutuel betting and soccer pools. Both returned to the players the net amount left in the pool after expenses. Pari-mutuel betting for rich horse-players had been recently ruled to be legal, while soccer-pool betting by the working class was being suppressed. But not quite yet. The O.B.U. had over $70,000 in prize money to return to its players. It launched a series of $10,000 weekly contests in which its readers could compete for free. All they had to do was fill in the coupons in the paper and mail them in.

The decision brought the greatest overnight boom in newspaper circulation in Canadian history. The first issue containing the free coupons sold out in a matter of hours. Newsboys hawking the paper in Winnipeg had to return again and again for wagon-loads of papers as housewives dipped into their cookie jars and teapots for milk- and rent-money with which to buy armloads of *Bulletins*. In some other cities the police departments moved in on the news dealers and prevented the paper from being sold. In Winnipeg the police let the sale proceed and waited for instructions. None came.

For the next issues, the *Bulletin* doubled its price along with its print order and again it sold out. By the end of July it was printing 500,000 copies a week and selling them all. When the free-coupon contests got the surplus prize money back in circulation, the readership boom collapsed as quickly as it had risen. The *Bulletin* revised its contests to get around the law and over the next half-decade ran through half a dozen different contests, from variations on the soccer pools to guessing the weather. As quickly as the courts found one form of pool illegal it set up a substitute. By 1926 it was offering $5,000 a week in prizes for coupon inscribers who came closest to guessing the way the editor marked a list of games. By a coincidence, no doubt, the editor usually marked his coupon the way the games turned out. But as the prize money dwindled, so did the public interest in football pools, and after the excitement of midsummer 1923, public attention turned to other and perhaps more exciting forms of gambling—slot machines, horse races, and the Grain Exchange wheat pit.

The football coupons were a working-class urban diversion, and so in the main were the slot machines. Horse racing was a predominantly urban middle-class attraction, though with rather substantial participation by the farmers and ranchers of Saskatchewan and Alberta. Over long periods the wheat pit was the farmers' monopoly, but when the doctors, lawyers, and other urban speculators went into the market they took over completely. Then, when the urban interlopers lost their margin deposits and went back to work, the farmers had the futures markets to themselves again.

In 1923 the slot machines descended on the west like a grasshopper infestation out of nowhere. In the beginning they were disguised as vending machines for the merchandising of nickel rolls of mints. The customer inserted his nickel and pulled the handle, which set three wheels revolving. If cherries showed up in a line on all three wheels, the customer received four slugs which entitled him to four rolls of mints. Three oranges were worth eight rolls, three bells were worth twelve rolls. If the wheels stopped with the fruit in mixed positions, the nickel was lost, and if three bars came up, the machine spilled the contents of a pot full of slugs into the pay-out tray.

As the mints were almost inedible, the customer would have quickly tired of the game, except for the fact that the keepers willingly exchanged the slugs for nickels. The machines first appeared in poolrooms and cigar stands, and spread rapidly into confectionery stores, corner groceries, and private clubs. They quickly became receptacles for all the loose change in the pockets of passers-by—and for a great deal of folding money converted into change.

Within a matter of weeks the west was awash with slot-machine addicts. Small boys raided their mothers' purses for nickels. Newsboys poured their earnings into the machines. And not only newsboys. Art Serviss's poolroom on River Street in Moose Jaw was a favorite hangout for the railroad crews waiting to check into their jobs at the nearby C.P.R. station. On paydays the running crews waited in line to challenge the one-armed bandits. Serviss had such a play on his 5-cent machines that he sent away for the first 25-cent slot machine in Saskatchewan. When he shut the hall and counted the take from the slot machines over one long-week-end, he had more than $1,000 as his share of the profits from one nickel and one quarter machine.

The proprietor of the Winnipeg Grain Exchange poolroom installed two 5-cent machines. One bookkeeper in particular became fascinated by the whirling wheels and spent a couple of hours every afternoon playing a certain machine. The pool players conceded that it was kind of a nutty way to spend that much time—just standing there pulling the handle and reinserting his pay-outs into the machine. But aside from noting his nuttiness, nobody paid much attention to him until the auditors went through his books. In a matter of weeks he had made away with over $4,000, which he had pumped into the slot machine. The council of the Exchange was suitably scandalized at the defalcation and whistled up the building manager, who ordered the machines removed from the building. Instantly.

In the end the slot machines went the way of all other games of chance, but in the five years which passed between their first appearance on the prairies and their final dispatch they could hardly have extracted less than $50,000 a week from the pockets of gullible westerners, and from many who in every other way were far from gullible.

Psychologists have long noted the ingrained inability of most all-or-nothing gamblers to learn from experience, which supports the old race-track adage that all horse-players die broke. An exception was Robert James Speers, who parlayed a railway accident into a string of race tracks and the overlordship of horse racing in western Canada. Of all the prairie gamblers, none matched the colorful Speers, who rubbed shoulders with race-track touts and consorted with upper-crust Winnipeggers in Manitoba Club poker games with equal zest.

Unlike most other high-stakes gamblers, Speers seemed to

relish the risk more than the stakes. He was equally attracted to
the $1-limit Thursday night poker game at the Manitoba Club;
to the no-limit table stakes Fort Garry Hotel Saturday-Sunday
game with "Squinchy" Loeb, Frank Fowlie, Frank Shea, and Don
Grant; to the kibitzing, joke-telling, wassailing game with Bill
Connelly, Jerry Dohan, and his stockyards cronies in the Empire
Hotel. Intermittently he was involved in inter-city across-the-
table confrontations with W. A. Dutton and Fred Mannix, a
couple of wealthy Calgary railway contractors who thirsted after
Speers' financial hide. It never seemed to matter to him that he
could have bought and sold some of his poker pals a dozen times
over, or that some of them could have done the same to him.

Poker was Speers' enduring passion, but he would gamble on
anything—the wheat market, the stock market, and most of all
on the race tracks, where his coups on a single race often ran into
five figures. This talent probably came natural to a blacksmith's
son who was himself a horse-trader all his life, as natural as it
came for a horse-trader to introduce race-track gambling to
western Canada.

Speers was born in Peel County, Ontario, in 1882 and he first
went west as a harvest excursionist in 1900. From that trip he
developed an aversion to farm labor that lasted a lifetime. He
went home and practised his wiles as an insurance agent for the
next five years. He got married, saved a modest stake, and
migrated to Battleford, where he became involved in the cattle
business, sold real estate, and developed an auctioneering
sideline. By 1908 he was well established in business, owned one
of the best houses in town, had $700 in the bank, and had
become hopelessly addicted to poker. While his wife was off on a
visit to her home in Ontario, Speers lost not only his $700, but his
house as well, in a poker game.

The episode gave rise to a quality that Speers was to hone to a
fine edge in future years. That was his ability to borrow money in
times of crisis. He had more brushes with bankruptcy than a
coterie of Hairsbreadth Harrys, and always there were friends
handy whose resources he could borrow. If he did have to rely
on his own resources in times of financial crisis, he did so with

verve and imagination. When in need of some short-term accommodation, he would draw a sight draft on a relative in North Battleford who was manager of a trust company. It took the draft several days to get there, his cousin would hold it for a day, and then refuse it and send it back to Speers' Winnipeg bank. In the week that elapsed between the drawing and the returning, Speers expected to have time in which to straighten out his account.

Another favorite Speers dodge was to send out unsigned cheques in payment of accounts. When the payee noted the omission and telephoned Speers' office, there would be embarrassed apologies and a request to mail the cheques back for signing. Again, the gambit bought three or four days' respite from financial pressure. If Speers was a lifelong money-borrower, he was also a soft touch for anybody with a sad story, particularly gamblers riding a losing streak. He was meticulous in repayment of debts, in full and on time, and he expected others to behave the same. When they failed, they never got a second chance.

At the very beginning of his borrowing career Speers moved to Wilkie, Saskatchewan, and borrowed enough money to build a grain elevator. In a few months he had a string of six such grain warehouses battening off the farmers. In 1911 he got into federal politics and ran as Conservative candidate in the Trampling Lake constituency. His lavish spending in losing the election cost him his grain business, and he moved to Calgary, where he spent the early war years buying horses for the Belgian government— a business that took him on frequent forays into the United States. On one such trip he was critically injured in a train wreck near Spokane, Washington. He was hospitalized for a year and then he moved to a hotel, where for six months he spent his days playing pool from a wheel chair.

With the aid of Calgary lawyer R. B. Bennett, he was able to pry $40,000 in damages out of the Northern Pacific Railway. After paying his medical and hospital bills he had enough money left to go into the commission business at the Winnipeg stockyards with Jerry Dohan. With Dohan and W. L. Halpenny,

Speers leased the old River Park race track in 1920 and staged a combination trotting and running horse race meet. In 1922 the trio bought a battery of pari-mutuel machines and promoted the first horse races with pari-mutuel betting at this track. So enthusiastically did Winnipeggers take to race-track gambling that Speers dropped his partners and took off on his own in the promotion of the Whittier Park track — with other people's money.

He first leased a 40-acre tract in St. Boniface from the Canadian National Railways in 1924 for $1,000 the first year and $1,500 the second, with gradual escalation until the rent became $3,000 a year after the fifth year. Then he persuaded Gus Creelman, a road-building contractor, to put his equipment to work building the half-mile race track, while a lumber merchant, Dan McDonald, was supplying building material for the grandstand, clubhouse, and stables on credit.

Speers meanwhile was selling memberships in his Manitoba Jockey Club at $100 each to his Manitoba Club and stockyard cronies, and then persuading them to assist in the sales drive. He talked Jack Lee of the Green River Bottling Company into advancing $15,000 as an interest-free loan, in return for the exclusive soft-drink concession at the yet-to-be-built track. In the frantic rush to get Whittier Park completed in time for its opening in 1924, profits from the River Park spring meeting were siphoned off daily to keep construction going at Whittier.

Speers' ability to borrow money was matched only by his penchant for knowing and using the right people. In his suit against the Northern Pacific he retained the only lawyer in Canada who could have arranged a settlement so quickly. He became acquainted with R. B. Bennett in the 1911 federal election, and cultivated his friendship when he lived in Calgary. As the C.P.R. counsel in western Canada, Bennett, from long experience on the other side, knew how to get quick action on a claim against a railway. When Speers was selecting window-dressing figureheads for his jockey clubs, his roster read like the Manitoba Club membership list. For the official opening of Whittier Park he had Lieutenant-Governor Sir J. A. M. Aikins and Premier Bracken doing the honors. He had them both back the following year to assist Lord Byng of Vimy and Lady Byng when the Governor General opened Polo Park.

The six thousand who jammed into the 3,000-seat grandstand at Whittier park for opening day in June of 1924 was the largest crowd to attend any kind of a sporting event in years. On the first of July, a week later, more than 12,000 turned out. With such enthusiasm did the over-capacity crowds pour their money through the mutuel machines at Whittier Park during the two seven-day meetings in 1924 that Speers was well into the black ink when the fall meeting closed. Hardly pausing for breath, he set out to promote a second track, this time on a vacant 80 acres on the western outskirts of Winnipeg. He bought the land with money borrowed for the down payment from Pat and Frank Shea, a couple of wealthy beer barons.

The people who had bought memberships in Whittier Park were invited to buy memberships in Polo Park, but with a difference. In the case of the former, they got common shares in the company along with two free passes to the races. In the Polo Park promotion, Speers kept all the equity for himself. All that the subscribers got were clubhouse privileges, along with car passes through the clubhouse gate and picnicking privileges on the clubhouse lawn.

All this frantic promotion of race tracks, coupled with Speers' expansion into the cattle business, in which he had 1,100 steers on feed in a huge feedlot in western Manitoba, drew baleful stares from his bankers. He was into the Dominion Bank for $100,000 early in 1925 when the bank called a halt to further lending and closed out the loans already on the books. The decision strained even Speers' vaunted borrowing ability. But he tapped the younger Shea for another $30,000, talked the Hon. Robert Rogers out of $10,000, and got to George Atkins, the owner of the Tijuana, Mexico, race track, for another $10,000. With the aid of almost $100,000-worth of on-the-cuff work by Walter Kane, another contractor-crony, he weathered the storm and got Polo Park opened in time for the 1925 spring meet. Then he was off to Calgary to promote the Chinook Park track and talk the Calgary Exhibition and Stampede into giving him the management of its race meets. Contracts to supply horses and provide the management for the Edmonton, Regina, Saskatoon, and Brandon summer fairs followed, and Speers was launched on a horse-racing monopoly that would last his lifetime.

Having had its appetite for betting on horse races stimulated at the race tracks, the gambling public of the west was in no mood to give up the pastime when the horses left town. In all the prairie cities bookmaking services developed for the accommodation of the punters. Bill Borland, a prominent local baseball and hockey player, opened the first Winnipeg bookie joint in a Donald Street store front in the fall of 1924. He pasted the entries from the American tracks on bulletin boards and took bets openly, until the city police pointed out that bookmaking was against the law. Borland and his fellow bookmakers went underground and carried on as before. Sam Pearlman, sports editor of the *Manitoba Free Press,* set up a sub-rosa race-entry-and-result service for the bookmakers, using the information that came in on press association wires. When the publishers frowned on his activities, Pearlman left to establish his own *Sports Digest* and racing wire service, from which he ultimately rose to a high executive position with the *American Racing Form* branch of the Annenberg publishing empire.

Throughout the 1920s a dozen racing books operated more or less openly in Winnipeg, and runners for local bookies haunted the poolrooms in Calgary and Edmonton. Louis Silverman, who ran a Winnipeg financial agency and owned a couple of poolrooms before Speers hit town, got into bookmaking by financing the freight charges on horses coming from California and Mexico for the first race meetings. He paid the freight to bring in the horses and Speers repaid the advances out of the purses won by the indebted horsemen. It was but a short step into the bookmaking business. From this, Silverman expanded into a high-level betting brokerage business in which he laid off the bets for other bookies when too many of their customers bet too heavily on a single horse.

In deference to Speers, the local bookies all took holidays when the horse races came to town. Punters who had become addicted to year-round betting on faraway races were given the cold cure. They could take their money to the local track or keep it in their pockets. Foolhardy bookies who tried to accommodate their customers got special attention from police morality squad raiders. Those who co-operated could expect to be raided only a couple of times a year and to pay fines of $200 in lieu of licences.

R. J. Speers' sensational success in turning Winnipeg on to race-track gambling quickly generated a wave of highly vocal opposition from the retail trade and the moral reform movement. Public interest in pari-mutuel betting built rather slowly in 1922 and snowballed in 1923. The construction of Whittier Park in 1924 doubled the number of racing days in greater Winnipeg, from two seven-day meetings at River Park to four seven-day meets. Then, with Polo Park in operation in 1925, the horse races ran from mid-June till mid-July, shut down for a month, and then spread over another twenty-one days at the end of August.

The flood of money that the huge crowds poured through Speers' machines in 1925 had a disastrous impact on the Winnipeg retail trade. The punters fell behind in their rent and their grocery bills, put off paying their breadmen and milkmen, and postponed the purchase of everything else. When the waves of protest began breaking against the legislature, the Progressive government of Premier John Bracken sat up and paid attention. It then took the only step possible to provide Speers with a lifetime monopoly on racing in Manitoba. It passed a law limiting the number of race tracks to one for each major city, and the number of racing days per track to fourteen a year.

The new law put the Winnipeg Driving Club, which had dropped Speers as general manager in 1924, out of business at the ramshackle old River Park track. It prevented competing promoters of race tracks from ever getting into business, for with Speers in operation in Winnipeg and St. Boniface there was no city left in which to locate a track. Speers had an unshakable monopoly for as long as he lived.

Jim Speers' gambling appetite was whetted, rather than satisfied, by running race tracks and being deeply involved in the
high-risk cattle business. He delighted in master-minding betting coups against Chicago bookmakers when western handicap
horses were shipped to Toronto and dropped into claiming
races. One such coup backfired when the famous western horse
Rochester II won at a handsome price but the Canadian National Telegraphs failed to deliver Speers' telegram to the
bookies before the race was run. Speers threatened to sue the
company to make good his losses, but nothing came of it. When
the horses were away and poker palled, there was always the
Winnipeg Grain Exchange wheat pit, which was never far from
Speers' mind, physically as well as mentally. His cattle-feeding
operation kept him aware of the ever-changing prices of feed
grains. And when the wheat pit was roaring there was no way of
keeping the news from Speers, for it came bouncing through the
windows of his office in the Grain Exchange annex. He could
never resist joining the doctors, lawyers, dentists, businessmen,
and housewives who threw themselves into the boiling maelstrom of the wheat pit whenever action beckoned.

Winnipeg business traditionally lived and died in relation to
conditions prevailing on the farms of the west. A good crop had
the employment-intensive railways working overtime during the
fall and winter. It brought hundreds of farmers to the city every
week to do their winter shopping. The retail and wholesale
business boomed. When the businessmen of Winnipeg, and
Regina and Calgary for that matter, opened their financial
pages, it was the closing prices on the Winnipeg Grain Exchange
to which their eyes first turned. And so an awareness of wheat
prices came naturally to just about everybody in western
Canada. It was an interest, however, that had remained strictly
passive until the dawn of the 1920s and the appearance of some
wildly fluctuating post-war markets.

The Winnipeg Grain Exchange, like everybody else, got
caught up in the pre-war real-estate boom. After making do for a
decade with modest accommodation in the old Chamber of
Commerce building on Market Square, in 1909 the Exchange

moved into its brand-new, seven-storey office building at the corner of Lombard Avenue and Rorie Street, a two-iron shot from the corner of Portage and Main. The move was symbolic as well as physical. It was indicative of the growth of the western wheat economy that the marketing end of the trade could fill a seven-storey building. Yet it had scarcely settled into its new quarters than it was bursting them at the seams. In 1920 an expansion began that extended the building to cover an entire city block, raised the height to ten storeys, and turned it into the largest office building in the British Empire.

Half the sixth floor of the expanded edifice was taken up by the trading floor, which contained not one, but two, pits. The larger was for wheat-trading alone, the smaller for all other grains. The bids, offers, and trades in the pits were instantly transmitted to large quotation boards, and just as instantly flashed by private telegraph wires to the trading floors of the Minneapolis, Chicago, and New York exchanges. At one end of the trading floor, other batteries of telegraph lines connected the floor with similar batteries in all the other exchanges. It took less than a minute for a broker on the floor of the Winnipeg Grain Exchange to send a buying or selling order to Chicago and get a confirmation back that the order had been filled. Similar quick action was possible for brokers in the United States markets who were making trades in Winnipeg.

The Winnipeg Grain Exchange was indeed an integral part of the world-wide wheat-marketing system and its prices reacted quickly to developments everywhere in the world. If the Liverpool Corn Exchange prices rose on reports of a drought in the Argentine, Winnipeg might move in sympathy. When Winnipeg prices dropped as a result of general rains in Saskatchewan, Chicago and Liverpool might also react.

That was the Winnipeg Grain Exchange — a vast agglomeration of interests that included a couple of dozen Canadian country elevator companies, a like number of commission companies, all the flour-milling companies, all the owners of terminal elevators, agents for the Great Lakes shipping companies, a dozen exporting companies, representatives of all the major

United States milling companies, and representatives of the great international trading companies who dealt in commodities of every kind in all the markets of the world.

It also contained the offices of a score of option brokers to whom the wheat pit was a roulette wheel, a slot machine, and a Monte Carlo casino all rolled into one. To wit: a gambling device pure and simple. Whether by accident or design, the option brokers' offices were confined to the first six floors of the Grain Exchange building. There were several of these offices on the ground floor and two or three on each of the next five floors. The offices were made up of boardrooms in which there were up to two dozen hard-seated oak armchairs for the customers. There was a grain quotation-board on which prices, in one-eighth-of-a-cent-per-bushel units, were marked, in large chalk numerals by an office boy who transcribed from a ticker tape from the trading floor. The option brokers were the croupiers of the Grain Exchange casino and existed only as a facility to enable Winnipeg speculators to gamble on the wheat market. They lived off the commissions earned from making trades for the doctors, lawyers, and businessmen taking fliers in wheat.

Anybody with $100 to risk could walk into an option broker's office, deposit the $100, and buy 1,000 bushels of wheat futures on a 10-cent margin. For every cent that the price moved upward or downward, the gambler would gain or lose $10. If the price dropped 5 cents a bushel, the broker might ask him to put up another $50 to maintain his 10-cent margin. If the price rose by 10 cents, he could sell out and pocket $100 in profit, less $2.50 commission to the broker. Or, by using his profit as margin he could buy another 1,000 bushels. Then, as the market rose or fell, he would win or lose $20 for every cent of rise or fall.

It was a process known to every apprentice dice-player in the land as "letting it ride or shooting the works". But craps were different in one important way. At the dice tables the dice-rollers frequently took out part of their winnings and cut back on their stakes. In the wheat market, the reverse happened. For every punter who took his profit and got out, there were scores, even hundreds, who doubled their stakes as the price rose—and they kept on doubling no matter how high it went. The only time most of them retired with a profit was when the market turned so quiet that the game lost its zest.

If gambling in wheat futures had been limited to people with $100 to risk, the general public of the 1920s would have had smaller participation in the game. It was possible, however, for anybody with as little as $1 to get into it. After the regular market closed at 1:15 p.m., a time-out was taken to clear out the debris and a new game was started, called the privileges market. There a $1 bet could be made on what the market would do the following day. A person who expected it to rise could buy options at $1 per 1,000 bushels at a cent or two above the closing price. If May wheat closed at $1.40, the $1 option might be purchased at $1.42. This meant that the purchaser would be the owner of 1,000 bushels of wheat at $1.42 throughout the next day of trading. If the price rose to $1.43 he could sell his wheat and pocket a $10 profit, less commission. If the price failed to reach $1.42, or went down, his dollar would be lost. For those who could not risk $100, or who had blown the better part of their margin, playing the option market — buying "bids and offers" or "puts and calls" it was called—was a popular pastime. This was particularly true in June and July when weather changes frequently produced wide swings in prices.

It was axiomatic in the Grain Exchange that the public seldom came into the market until it had taken off on a wild bull-run. So there were long periods when the option brokerage offices were deserted, followed by periods when all the seats were filled and the dabblers in wheat futures spilled into the corridors and overflowed the visitors' gallery which overlooked the trading floor. Between such periods were the late-fall and winter months, when the farmers of Manitoba would find excuses to visit Winnipeg for a week or so and take what amounted to an annual fling at the market. If a bull market developed while the farmers were in town, the world of wheat went berserk. That happened in the late fall of 1924.

After the bumper crop of 1923, wheat yields in 1924 dropped well below normal in Saskatchewan and Alberta, although there was a good crop in Manitoba. As a result, in the early fall of 1924 wheat prices were fairly stable at around 30 cents a bushel higher than they had been in the previous year. In early September the October future was around $1.35 per bushel, and for delivery in the following May it was 5 cents less. Then the rains started falling in the west to delay threshing and the delivery of the new crop to market. It was not long before the price for October delivery was moving up and down 5 cents a day—down when the sun shone for a few days, up when the rains returned. When reports of failing crops in the Argentine and Australia began adding yeast to the ferment, Winnipeg fluctuations became wilder. By the first week in October the chairs in the option brokers' offices were filled to capacity, and secretaries all over town were keeping hourly logs of the price gyrations in the wheat pit. The greatest speculative orgy in Grain Exchange history was in motion.

And not only in Winnipeg. Private telegraph wires in brokerage offices in Regina, Calgary, and Edmonton gave speculators in those cities instant access to order-desks in Winnipeg brokerage offices. At the country points throughout the west, the agents for the line elevators companies functioned as transmission belts to convey buy and sell orders from their farmer customers to their head offices. Grain price broadcasts at the close of the markets were being made a daily feature of the pioneer radio stations so that the grain-growers could keep abreast of developments on their crystal sets.

In ordinary circumstances the peak activity in the wheat pit occurred during the first quarter-hour after the market opened and in the last quarter-hour before it closed. Then fifty or sixty traders, jammed into an area of 400 square feet, all shouting at once, waving their arms, gesticulating with hand signals, jumping up and down, and running in and out, turned riotous confusion into bedlam. The tumult was punctuated by the piercing falsetto of some traders' voices and the booming basso of others, by the chattering of telegraph-sounders and telephones ringing in the brokers' booths along the walls, by the shouts of messenger boys paging brokers by names, by traders shouting for their order-clerks and order-clerks shouting for traders. Inside this maelstrom, millions of bushels of wheat were being bought and sold each minute.

Normally, after the opening frenzy everything settled down to a more leisurely pace. Once the prices of all the trading months were firmly established and accumulated orders were filled, the atmosphere relaxed. The brokers caught up with their paperwork, gathered in groups to exchange gossip, went for coffee, or retired to the smoking-room for a quick cigarette. As the speculators took control of the 1924 market, the periods of relative quiet disappeared and the wheat pit boiled from opening until closing.

At the close of the market the exhausted traders, their voices reduced to guttural squawks, plopped into the nearest vacant chairs and munched throat lozenges as they dozed, waiting for the clearing house to get a perfect matching on all the trades made that morning. Away from the trading floor the option clerks worked far into the night, and sometimes, during those hectic weeks, right through the night.

The lights blazed throughout the entire building all night long because the fever pitch of trading affected everybody in the business. The line elevator companies, the commission companies with United States and Liverpool connections, and the terminal elevators, exporters, and millers, all had customers with "long" futures accounts. All the individual trades made during the open session had to be posted, by hand in pen and ink, to each individual account and the margins of every account in all the books adjusted each day to the closing price of each futures month. Some of the line elevators companies, which carried thousands of accounts of individual farmers scattered across the west, took rooms at the Grange Hotel across the street so that their harried clerks could catch a few hours of sleep between sessions.

The farmer speculators who stayed home on the farm fared worse than their fellows who watched the trade in the brokers' offices. The latter at least could act quickly to protect their positions when fluctuations got out of hand. For the former, the action was over each day before they became privy to what had happened. Because they were out of instant communication range, their accounts had to be sold out quickly by the elevators companies when a slump in the market dropped their margin deposits close to the irreducible minimum. They could not be notified in time to put up more margin.

When the original trade was made, and the farmer put up 10 cents a bushel as margin on his purchase, the broker would enter a "stop loss" order to sell if the market declined 8 or 9 cents below the purchase price. This was to protect the broker in case a sudden, sharp drop wiped out the entire margin and the broker would have had to absorb whatever additional loss was incurred. As soon as the decline approached the stop-loss figure, the specially identified stop-loss orders were sent to the pit, and the instant the market touched this figure, the trader had to sell. When stop-loss orders flooded into the market they forced the prices still lower, triggering other stop-loss sales and turning bull markets into bear markets.

But all that was still in the future when the great bull market of 1924-5 was pawing the ground to get started. With only short-lived reactions, prices moved steadily upward in October and November, to $1.60, to $1.70, and in mid-December the May future broke through $1.80. By Christmas Day there was hardly a speculator in the market who could not have closed out his account on Christmas Eve with enough profit to spend the winter in California, or to buy some bright new equipment for his farm. But why would anybody sell at $1.80 when it was a universally accepted certainty that May wheat was going to $2.00? Almost without exception, the ten-foot-long charts on the walls of the brokerage offices indicated that the trend was still upward. Instead of selling, the punters used their accumulated paper profits to buy more and more and more wheat on margin. They were as right as rain.

On Friday morning, January 23, the May option broke through the $2.00 mark. "Two-dollar wheat" had been the magical phrase everybody had been intoning from the day, three weeks before, when it had reached and passed $1.75. There were muffled cheers on the trading floor when the first $2.00 quotation was chalked on the board, and for many speculators an eternity seemed to pass before the next quotation—2.00^{1}/_{8}$ —was posted. With so many thousand gamblers holding their wheat for $2.00, what would happen when it got there? Had everybody who had been holding for $2.00 placed orders to sell at that figure? Would a massive accumulation of sell-orders at $2.00 break the market? The market did hesitate at $2.00, but only briefly, and when it closed at $2.02 on Saturday the gamblers confidently set their sights on a new plateau—$2.25 a bushel.

There was every indication, the following Monday, that $2.25 would be quickly reached. Word was flashed that a serious famine existed in Russia, that the Russians had been forced to go into the world market to buy 1,000,000 bushels of wheat, and that wheat-growing areas of the Balkans would also have to import.

The wild gyrations in the wheat pit had long since moved Grain Exchange stories from the market pages of the newspapers to the top of the front pages. This naturally attracted the attention of speculatively inclined readers and each day saw masses of new recruits join the gambling legions. During the week of January 26 prices soared from $2.00 a bushel to 2.20^{7}/_{8}$, the most spectacular rise ever recorded in so short a time. Then came Black Friday, January 29, the most violent day of trading known to the grain trade.

The market opened that morning at $2.20—unchanged from the previous close. The overflow crowd in the public gallery watched the prices being chalked up in anticipation of another new high record being set before the day was out. Instead, buying orders disappeared, and in a matter of minutes the price of May wheat dropped to $2.10 a bushel. In those same minutes the gallery emptied, as its occupants rushed for their brokers to place selling orders of their own. The frenzied pace of the opening trading continued throughout the morning. Buying came into the market at the low, prices bounced back a little, sagged again, recovered, sagged, and closed at $2.14. On Saturday the yo-yoing continued, but within narrower limits, and the May future actually gained a couple of cents at the close. Was the worst over? The next week would tell. There was still time for many of the gamblers to get out at a profit, but even when the price declined below $2.00 there was a mass reluctance to believe that the great bull market had run its course. Those who could hold on, held on. On February 11 the end came for them all when a drop of 12 cents a bushel wiped out everybody who was still in the market on short margins, and launched the legend of Joe Auberge.

Joe Auberge was a French-Canadian farmer from Letellier in southeastern Manitoba who brought his family into Winnipeg on a shopping spree in early September, 1924. While his wife did the shopping Joe went off to the Winnipeg Grain Exchange for his annual fling at the privileges market. He struck it rich. He bought five "offers" at 2 cents above the closing price and the following day the price of October wheat jumped 6 cents a bushel. Instead of taking his profit, Joe held on to the 5,000 bushels and bought five "bids" for the next day at 3 cents below the market, as protection in case the market went down. Instead, it continued to advance and Joe was in the market to stay.

As soon as possible he used his profits to double his holdings, then doubled them again. In the weeks that followed he was in and out of the market like a jack-rabbit. Time after time he would conclude that the top had been reached and would get out. Then he would get back in, always buying to the limit of his margins and always giving the privileges market a heavy play. By the end of December Joe was carrying 200,000 bushels of May wheat on margin and frequently was riding another 100,000 when "offers", bought in $100 lots, were good. Badly bruised by the Black Friday disaster, Joe was wiped out on February 11 when May wheat dropped below $1.90.

Anyone less addicted to the futures market than Joe would have packed himself back to the farm. Not Joe. He gathered up the great pile of purchase and sales slips he had accumulated in his four months as a high-rolling gambler and added up the commissions he had paid the E. J. Bawlf Grain Company. They came to a staggering $10,000-odd on his total of almost 4,000,000 bushels traded. That, he was convinced, made him the most profitable customer the company had on their books. He approached E. V. E. Raikes, Bawlf's office manager, with a proposition.

Joe said that his records demonstrated he had a feel for the market. He had been right on at least forty occasions in getting out and getting in at the right time, and he really had only been wrong once. He was a tremendous money-maker for Bawlf. So how about Bawlf staking him to $5,000 so that he could get back into the market and make him thousands more dollars in commission? Raikes turned down the proposition, so Joe buttonholed Eddie Bawlf himself. The most colorful of all the Bawlfs who were then cutting wide swaths in the grain business, Eddie Bawlf had a weakness for left-footed deals — but not for addicted gamblers like Joe Auberge. Nevertheless, he couldn't help being impressed by Joe's figures of the brokerage he had paid.

"Joe," he said, "I'll tell you what I am prepared to do for you. I'll go in right now and get you a cheque for $2,000 and give it to you, but on one condition. In return I want your written undertaking to go back to the farm and never come into the wheat market again. You had the chance a dozen times in the last month to get out of the market with enough money to live on in comfort for the rest of your life and to provide for your family as well. Time after time we urged you to take your profits and go home. The wheat market is poison in your blood and you'll never be able to get it out. So, if you will get the hell out of Winnipeg and stay out of here, the cheque is yours."

Joe Auberge spurned the offer!

Instead of going back to the farm, he got a job marking a quotation board, lived alone in a furnished room, and scrimped and saved to play the privileges market. Over the next four years wheat prices drifted about in doldrums in which upward and downward movements were of short duration, and always within modest limits. By the spring of 1929 October wheat was $1.00, when the unseasonably hot, dry weather began to cause widespread concern. During the first week in June the *Free Press* published its first crop report of the year, and a spectacularly bullish report it was. In less than a week the price of the October future jumped from $1.02 per bushel to $1.18, and Joe was into the privileges market the day the upsurge began.

By the end of June the price reached $1.28, and Joe was once again pyramiding his holdings and buying "bids" and "offers". The rise naturally brought masses of speculators into the market, and the price moved to $1.40 by mid-July, then to $1.50, $1.55, and $1.60.

On the last day in July the October future reached $1.67 and Joe Auberge had another small fortune dangling before his eyes. He left it dangling there over the long Civic Holiday weekend when the wheat pit was closed. On that first Monday in August somebody pulled the plug on the Chicago market and it dropped 10 cents a bushel. On Tuesday morning Winnipeg followed the Chicago decline, and when it dropped 12 cents under the previous close, Joe Auberge was cleaned out once again, and left without a dollar of the fortune he could have taken four days before.

Joe Auberge went back to marking the quotation board in the brokerage office, to await the outbreak of another wild market that would give him a third chance at a fortune. It never came.

The exact basis in truth of the legend of Joe Auberge is lost to history. Certainly, during the early years of the Great Depression he was pointed out to visitors, as he wandered the corridors of the Grain Exchange, as a great speculator who had ridden boom-markets to disaster in 1924 and 1929. He was not the only living spectre then haunting those marble and glass hallways. Some of the great names of the grain trade of only a decade before were reduced to beggary by the 1930-1 demoralization of the wheat pit.

Gambling on wheat futures was always a sometime thing, an on-again off-again proposition. Horse-race gambling was different. Once it became firmly established it outstripped all other forms of gambling in year-round popular appeal. Poker lost ground steadily to auction bridge and then, as the decade ended, to contract bridge. Floating crap games never really caught on until after the Second World War. The lure of the wheat pit was buried forever beneath the dust storms of the 1930s. But in the 1920s race-track fever, wheat-pit fever, slot-machine fever, and soccer-pool fever, all developed simultaneously to distract public attention from the underlying economic malaise that was a hallmark of the decade.

2. Down on the Farm

The conventional wisdom of the prairies holds that the underlying motivation that drove western farmers into one political protest movement after another was economic. The testimony of the political scientists is all but unanimous that the Progressive movement grew out of refusal of the Conservative-dominated Unionist government to listen to western demands for reductions in the tariffs and in the cost of moving goods into and out of western Canada. Flowing out of that refusal came disillusionment with the behavior of politicians of any and every stripe. This study takes passing notice of all these considerations and gainsays none of them.

Yet a case can be made for the nearly total lack of creature comforts, as distinct from economic discontent, as an equally important underlying cause of the bilious attitude developed by prairie farmers not only toward politicians, the railways, and the Winnipeg Grain Exchange but toward the whole non-farming population. It was a rancor that surfaced in spectacular political form in the 1920s, and kept on resurfacing in the decades that followed. Farm settlers by the tens of thousands were lured to the western prairies by the prospect of a vastly improved way of life. Instead they settled into one which in many ways suffered by comparison with that of European peasants. Not only were living conditions sub-marginal and worse, there was little improvement until the tag end of the 1920s.

For the many thousands of immigrants from Ontario and the United States who had arrived just prior to the Great War, the deprived nature of their environment was underscored every time they visited one of the cities in the 1920s. On these once-a-year visits, usually on fall shopping excursions, the farm families frequently bunked in with city relatives. Within the visiting brood there was the inevitable youngest child who would discover indoor plumbing for the first time. Many a city toilet needed a general overhaul after the country-bred small fry had sated their fascination with water sloshing into, around, and down the bowl. Girls somewhat older could marvel at kitchen sinks where the water came hot and cold from taps and did not have to be lugged in pails from a pump in the yard. Sometimes the city homes even had gas-burning stoves which were both fascinating and frightening. "Oh boy," the girls chortled, "no kindling to split and no woodbox that can never be kept full." And the porcelain bathtubs! Think of being able to have a bath any time one wanted to, simply by turning on the tap and lolling full length at the bottom of the tub!

The discovery of such facilities always led to interminable arguments around kitchen tables about the advantages of city life over farm life. The visitors made so much of the creature comforts of the urban dwellers, compared with their own deprived circumstances, that it could take a host family a week to get over feeling guilty after they left. But such was the ambivalence of the farmers' minds that they were quick to point out they would not trade farm life for city life for "all the tea in China". They abhorred the noise, the hurry, the congestion, and the pressure of city life.

At the end of a week in the city, exhausted by being forever on the go, the visitors were eager to escape back to the farm. The return journey would be made with a reinforced conviction that the cities were bastions of parasites battening off the farm population. All they needed to confirm their belief was to compare the prices they got for the things they grew with those charged in the city stores. They hatched and housed and fed the chickens and were paid 10 or 15 cents a dozen for their eggs. By the time the eggs went through the hands of the middlemen — the hated middlemen — the price paid by city people was up to 45 or 50 cents a dozen. The wheat for which they got 70 cents a bushel on the farm went through a different chain of hands and wound up as a $3.50 sack of flour. And the price of meat! And cans of pork and beans!

The farmer, with considerable justification, had developed a strong antipathy toward the cities very early in prairie history. In the days before Prohibition the cities were regarded as sinkholes of iniquity infested with pickpockets, footpads, and whores, who waited in the railway stations or lurked in the streets to rob the farmer of his hard-earned money. It was an image that persisted in the agrarian mind long after the conditions that produced it had faded from reality. With the coming of Prohibition, the bars that surrounded the railway stations were shuttered and dismantled. City and railway police combined to drive most of the petty thieves from the stations, and the hazards to the pockets of the less sophisticated farm visitors were reduced to such minimal threats as subscription salesmen who worked the entrances to mail-order houses and tractor showrooms. To the farmers, however, the cities were still wastelands of banks, manufacturers, wholesalers, and speculators who grew ever more wealthy on the sweat of the farmers' brows. The antipathy that existed between town and country was a happy hunting-ground for politicians on the make. In Manitoba the Bracken Progressives managed to stay in power for fifteen years simply by maintaining a strong anti-Winnipeg posture in whatever they did.

In the decade before the war the farmers had come to these western prairies by the hundreds of thousands anticipating a land of boundless opportunities. They had come from the United States and Ontario with all the skills and equipment needed to turn these opportunities to their advantage. A widely circulating myth of western history is that the prairies were settled mainly by legions of peasants from Central Europe who were lured to Canada by Sir Clifford Sifton's immigration policy. Sifton was federal Minister of the Interior from 1897 to 1906 and under his aegis the Department of Immigration sent its agents scouring the continent of Europe for the thousands of settlers needed to people the empty western plains.

The fact is that the bulk of the settlers who swarmed into western Canada during the population implosion of 1902-13 came not from continental Europe, not from the United Kingdom, and not even from Ontario. They came from the United States. It was into the United States middle west that the main thrust of Canadian settler-recruiting was directed.

Not only did the Canadian government establish information offices in most of the main U.S. population centres, it flooded the country with promotional literature and newspaper advertising. Its efforts were enthusiastically augmented by the C.P.R., which co-operated fully with American promoters of Canadian land companies. The C.P.R. sent its excursion trains into the middle west to pick up prospective settlers for complimentary junkets to settlement areas. In co-operation with the government it organized cent-a-mile excursions for individual prospects. So successful were these campaigns in arousing interest in Canada that certain U.S. communities saw in them a threat to their existence and counterattacked with barrages of anti-Canadian propaganda. To offset this unfavorable publicity, an advertising campaign, involving the use of several hundred farm-belt papers with a combined circulation of 7,000,000, was launched by Ottawa. The railway organized concurrent junkets for newspaper editors, who were expected to reciprocate by publishing favorable reports on Canada. The editors did not disappoint.

All this came to pass at a curiously favorable time. As Edgar McInnis has pointed out, the American communities of the middle west had passed from the pioneer stage to that of stable settlement. A younger farming generation was having to look farther and farther afield for land on which to settle, and finding it difficult and frequently impossible to locate within the United States. So their attention was directed outward to the Canadian west, just as the attention of Ontario farm boys had been directed to the American middle west two generations before.

From the 1880s, the rapid development of the "bonanza

farms" in the Red River Valley of Minnesota and North Dakota accentuated the problems of land-finding. The Cass-Cheney spread of 75,000 acres kept 30,000 acres in crop, and a labor force of 1,000 men and 800 horses and mules was required to put in and take off the crops. During harvest, a total of fifty-three steam-powered threshers were used to beat the chaff out of 600,000 bushels of wheat. Other bonanza farms were smaller only by comparison. The Grandins owned 62,000 acres, Carrington and Casey had 35,700 acres, and it was estimated that before the turn of the century, there were 2,000 farms in the Red River Valley of more than 500 acres.

No wonder so many farmers' sons of the United States midwest were crowded out of the nest and onto the immigrant trains to Canada. They were joined by many thousands of established farmers who sold their home places at the inflated values then prevailing and moved to homesteads or railway land on the Canadian plains.

How many Americans came to the Canadian west is impossible to estimate with any accuracy. Grant McEwan has estimated that during the first twenty years of the century, 1,000,000 Americans settled in western Canada. Paul Sharp, the Montana historian, is quoted by Douglas Hill as the authority for the estimate that 1,250,000 Americans deserted the United States for the Canadian west.

Almost all of the prairie settlers, whatever their origin, came, not in the covered wagons so popularized by Hollywood, but by train. In many cases the farmers accompanied their equipment and livestock in boxcars filled with "settlers' effects". The railways moved settlers' effects at nominal freight rates and provided the sort of service such rates would justify. A week or ten days en route from the United States middle west to the Regina plains was about the norm for travel time. Their household goods ranged from a bare minimum of chairs, tables, and beds, and crates of pots, pans, and clothing, to furnishings for complete households, including parlor furniture and even a piano or organ. Many American settlers had enough for two carloads, one for household stuff, with bed, table, and chair space for the settler himself, and another for farm machinery, horses, harness, and a cow or two. After the immigrants got their belongings unloaded and transported to their homesteads, they sent for their families, who came by passenger train to the mainline centres and then rode in the caboose of a freight train to the town closest to the homestead. Alternatively, the farmer drove across country to the nearest passenger terminal and took his family home by farm wagon along the prairie trails that crisscrossed the country in lieu of roads even into the 1920s. Occasionally, if the volume of traffic justified it, the railways hooked a colonist car onto the freight train so that the settlers' families could travel from Ontario to the west with their belongings in relative comfort. At the slow crawl of a freight train, of course, but in comfort none the less.

Once on their chosen homestead, because the vital thing was to get the land broken and a crop in, housing was, at best, a secondary consideration. And for many farm families it remained so for fifteen or twenty years. For temporary shelter the wiser settlers built sod houses, in which they could survive in comparative comfort through the worst of a prairie winter. Others could get enough lumber for $25 to put up a two-room frame shack in which they could barely escape freezing to death, even in mild weather. None ever thought of either type of accommodation as other than the most temporary of makeshifts. With the first good crop they would build a proper house.

That happened frequently enough on the Regina plains and in southern Alberta, which seemed to attract American farmers with sufficient cash resources to build substantial homes at the outset. In point of fact the resources needed did not have to be substantial. With the best grade of fir lumber available at $25 per 1,000 board feet, a 16′ × 20′ shack could be completed for $65-$75. It was always possible in most of the newly settled areas to buy enough lumber to build a five- or six-room house for $500. One settler on C.P.R. land provided the company with a breakdown of the capital requirements for getting into the farming business. Of the $1,900 he had spent, $300 had gone for housing. Noting that the house was something less than palatial, he said that it was adequate until they got on their feet. In a brochure advertising its Ready-Made Farms, the railway offered plans for a complete four-room house, 22′ × 25′, which could be built for $900. An even better deal was offered by British Columbia Mills of New Westminster. It was prepared to supply, pre-cut, all the materials needed for a four-bedroom semi-bungalow for $725 plus freight. For an additional $133 it would supply enough 1″ × 3″ "V-joint" to finish all interior walls and ceilings.

For those with fancier tastes, more money, or large families, the T. Eaton Company advertised seventy separate designs of mail-order houses. For $1,000 it offered all the materials for a six-room, two-storey house, 29′ × 30′, with a front verandah, bay window, and third-floor attic. The price included lumber, windows, doors, trim, laths, shingles, nails, and a complete set of architect's plans for erecting the house. There was a small catch to purchasing Eaton houses — who in the context of those times had $1,000 in cash to send along with the order form? Only those rare farmers who raised a bumper crop the year wheat prices reached their historic highs — 1919-20. Nevertheless the pictures of houses, like everything else in the catalogues, must have given farm women anticipatory palpitations for weeks as they pawed endlessly over the colorful illustrations in the bittersweet process of reconciling desire with resources.

Keeping up with the phenomenal growth in its mail-order business forced Eaton's to double the size of that facility in 1921 and to establish its own printing plant to turn out the hundreds of thousands of catalogues that were demanded twice a year. That success engendered a great deal of bitterness among small-town merchants, who complained that the farmers only patronized local merchants when they had no money and needed credit, and bought from Eaton's when they had cash to spend. With their low volume, slow turnover, and credit extension, the country storekeepers had to charge high prices to survive. On the other hand, the farmers themselves could not have survived if they had not been able to take advantage of Eaton's low prices. The Eaton archives are loaded with letters from farmers telling them precisely that.

One explanation for the low priority given farm home improvement and shack replacement may have been that time was more important than money. For farmers to have ordered a mail-order house from Eaton's or British Columbia, for example, would have meant dropping everything else for a week or two while the material was unloaded, hauled to the farm, and erected. House-building was essentially a fine-weather undertaking and there were always three other things that needed doing whenever the weather was favorable. Wells had to be dug, pastures plowed, plows sharpened, machinery fixed, wagons repaired, mud-holes filled. And everything moved at the walking pace of the horse-drawn vehicles.

The development of western Manitoba is a case in point. There lumber was plentiful and handy, yet it was common for farmers to spend a decade or more in their log cabins and frame shacks before they got around to replacing them. Often that replacement came only after a helpful nudge from nature in the form of a fire that destroyed the shack. By the end of the Great War the farmers of western Manitoba were at last getting themselves housed in buildings that did many of them proud. In the rich southwestern section they built substantial brick houses with stone basements and cisterns from which they could hand-pump water directly to the kitchen sink. Here and there the more prosperous farmers were experimenting with Delco lighting-plants which brought the magic of electricity to the farmyard. But all this came only after two decades of putting up with submarginal accommodation.

The trouble with shack houses was that they tended to become self-perpetuating encumbrances to the family farm. Once the shell of the shack was in place the settler was committed to making it habitable. If the wind blew through the cracks, a roll of tarpaper under a sheathing of siding would make it draft-proof. Composition paperboards such as Beaverboard were coming onto the market in 4' × 8' sizes and, where available, were widely used for inside wall and ceiling cover. All this absorbed a great deal of time and effort and gave rise to a tendency to keep improving the shack, adding rooms as the need arose, rather than creating an urge to abandon it to the chickens and build a whole new house.

For the settlers, it was not simply going without creature comforts that were taken for granted in the cities of the west, it was also the immersion in a standard of living that was as tedious as it was laborious; and nothing was as tediously laborious as providing fuel for the winter, for farm homes consumed fuel out of all proportion to their size. Kindling could be bought in town, cut to stove-lengths, and hauled home when cash was available; or it could be harvested by hand from the poplar bluffs that dotted the prairies around sloughs and creek edges. For winter heating, as distinct from cooking, they hauled $9.00-a-ton coal from the nearest coal yard, often ten or fifteen miles away. It had to be shovelled up, over, and into wagon boxes, two or three tons to a load, then shovelled off again at home into a storage bin. Then, several times a day, it was shovelled into scuttles, carried into the house, and converted into ashes, only to be shovelled into scuttles and carried out again. It was a process that was diminished hardly at all by the snow piled around the outer walls halfway to the eaves to insulate the floors from frost penetration.

The interiors of the shack homes were never the answer to a homemaker's dream. Yet the record of what life was like for the farm women of the settlement era is curiously sparse. In the nostalgic euphoria of 1967, many communities in western Canada undertook to publish histories of their areas as centennial projects. Though dozens of these publications were compiled without any central direction, they developed a curious uniformity of format, best described, perhaps, as Doomsday *Who's Who*. They meticulously recorded the dates of arrival of all the settlers for miles around, who married who, and who begat who, when the first school was erected, when the first church was built, the names of the school teachers and members of the school boards. Great blizzards, prairie fires, and crop failures were identified by date. Who bought the first car and first tractor in the district was frequently noted. But of the home lives of the people there was seldom more than such afterthought sentences as:

My mother often told me of that winter. She would go about washing her table after doing the dishes and the water would freeze before she could wipe it up. There was only a wood stove for heating and cooking ...

Or —

Mother played a tremendous part in the pioneer home. It was no small job raising ten children in those days when there were no conveniences. A few tasks were: Carrying water, washing by hand on a scrub board, cooking, cleaning, sewing, mending, gardening, raising poultry, helping with chores and odd jobs ...

Or —

Mother used to help in the fields at harvest time in stooking and hauling grain, as well as cook for the crew at threshing time. There was always cows to be milked, pigs to be fed and a large garden for mother to work in. ...

Mother was not the only one whose work was never done. As soon as the children were big enough to lift a sheaf or hold a pair of reins they too were put to work. When the Great War broke out, it became, for many farm youth, a hatch through which to escape from endless days of walking behind discs and harrows that churned up never-diminishing clouds of nose-clogging dust.

After months when there was never enough time to do half the things that needed doing, the onset of winter put an end to all activity except that of huddling around stoves to keep warm. When the weather turned sour the roads to town became impassable and travel was undertaken only in cases of real emergency—like going for the doctor who lived two towns away. With a minimum of time spent on outside chores, there were days on end when everybody was underfoot and getting on everybody else's nerves. That was particularly true in January and February in areas of Saskatchewan when even the schools were shut down. The farm women, of course, had more than enough to do with their washing, cooking, knitting, patching, darning, and quilting. But for the farmers themselves there were long stretches of sitting and brooding, weighing the prog-

ress they were making and finding the answers wholly unsatis-
factory.

The foundation for social disenchantment had been laid when
the government surveyed the country in square blocks. If it had
gone out deliberately to devise a settlement plan to drive the
farm women up the walls of their shacks it could have hardly
proceeded differently. In Europe the farm people lived in villages encircled by farmland. Thus a community life of sorts was
possible and in many cases the farm men and women worked
their land co-operatively. At the very least, they lived close
enough together that social life was possible and help was always
available when it was needed — and in a matter of a very few
minutes. In the west the country was laid out as if to isolate the
farm families from each other and to make social contact as
difficult as possible. The standard prairie homestead was 160
acres in extent and each homesteader had a right to pre-empt
the purchase of an adjoining 160 acres. This ultimately resulted in many farms of 320 acres being established, or two
farms to a square mile or section. The surveys established
66-foot road allowances between each section east and west and
two miles apart north and south. Houses were usually built
handy to the east or west road allowances, so that in most cases
farm houses were a crow's-flight mile or so from each other.
When the crop was growing, the effective distance became two
miles around if communication was by road.

The system condemned farm women to lives of unrelieved
isolation broken by attendance at church when weather permitted and by occasional schoolhouse dances. In between they
starved for someone to talk to. It was no accident that the top
priority for every farm home in the west was a party-line telephone connection. In 1921 there was one telephone for every
two farms in Saskatchewan, while 25 per cent of the farms in
Manitoba had phones. And they got plenty of use for the telephone provided entertainment as well as communication! Many
a harassed mother, becoming unnerved by squalling offspring,
would blurt: "Oh, for goodness' sake, Georgina, stop that teas-
ing. Go listen to the telephone for a while!"

The isolation was never as oppressive to the men, but there is little doubt that the unhappiness of the womenfolk rubbed off on them. Farmers by the thousands deserted their farms and moved into the towns, to open livery stables, stores, or blacksmith shops, or to get jobs as railway section hands or elevator operators. Between 1911 and 1921, the C.P.R. had to cancel the sales of about a third of the land it had sold. Between 1921 and 1925 it cancelled twice as many sales as it made. During the same period more homesteads were cancelled than were taken out.

During the great settlement surge, there was a great deal of going as well as coming, and many farms passed through the hands of two or three owners before being permanently settled. In addition to the new settlers coming into the country, there were a goodly number who, having given up once and moved into town, could not resist the urge to try again as farmers. No census was ever taken, but many thousands of the settlers were borderline nomads who tried first in Manitoba then in Saskatchewan, then in Alberta, and ended up in the Peace River block of British Columbia. In the interlocking and often contradictory motivations for population movement it would be dangerous to blame farm abandonment in favor of town living only on isolation or a submarginal environment. Poor crops, low prices, and marketing difficulties were also contributing reasons for moving into town. They were, that is, until the production miracle of 1915.

The bonanza crop of 1915 was the bench mark against which all other crops were measured for thirty years. In many places the wheat went 40 bushels to the acre and across the whole prairie it averaged 26 bushels on more acres — 13,800,000 — than ever planted before. When the crop was finally delivered there was money enough for just about everything a farmer's heart could desire. For more land. For the breaking of another quarter section. For the down payment on that most fascinating of all gadgets, the new light gasoline-burning tractor that would pull a three-bottom plow. And so far down on the list that it was lost to sight was a new house, electrically lighted by a Delco plant, and with inside plumbing. At the very top of the list was the purchase of an automobile.

The lifelong love affair of prairie farmers with the internal combustion engine in general, and the motor car in particular, erupted out of nowhere in 1916, and a star-crossed affair it was for the next decade. The choice of makes and models offered the farmers in 1916-17 was bewilderingly broad, but ultimately the Model T Ford became the popular choice, and for a curious reason. It was no more rugged than the Grey-Dort, the Maxwell, or the Chevrolet, which meant that it was barely equal to the challenge of the dirt roads and mud-holes of the west. But when a Model T broke down, the dealer who sold it had a stock of parts needed for repairs, and the parts were cheap. So the down time for the Ford was less than that of other makes, even if some of the other cars cost two or three times the $745 price tag on the 1916 Fords.

It was the automobile, for those who owned them, that put the word "neighboring " into the language of the prairies. On Sunday afternoon after church a family with a car could call on friends ten or fifteen miles away and still get home by milking-time. In the process they could often drop in—"go neighboring" — on other farmers along the way.

By 1921 there were 70,000 cars and trucks in the farmyards of the prairies. The persistent attraction of cars for farmers is difficult to understand in face of their almost total unreliability. They were so hopeless in cold weather that most farmers jacked the wheels up onto blocks in December and left them there until spring. Not only were they difficult to crank into life in cold weather, but radiators filled at the outset with boiling water had a tendency to develop cold spots and freeze solid. Gear grease turned to ice and engine oil congealed. This led to attempts to heat engine blocks with blowtorches — with predictable results. Even when minor miracles occurred and the cars were cajoled into running, it was seldom worth the effort. Not even the isinglass side-curtains could make the open touring-cars habitable in winter. Nevertheless, being able to afford a car became the goal of every farm family on the prairies from 1920 onward.

Regardless of make, the cars they bought were cantankerous, flighty, and frivolous Jezebels that had to be coaxed or threatened into behaving in a tractable fashion. Once started, they ran beautifully in fine weather, and were balkier than a barn full of mules when it rained, snowed, or froze. The cars came with operating and repair manuals couched in unde-cipherable jargon. Driving instruction consisted, at most, of being driven a couple of times around a block by the dealer. The co-ordination required between eyes, ears, hands, and feet was frequently beyond an older farmer's ability to master before he had run his new vehicle through a fence and into a ditch.

Nevertheless, devotion to the automobile forced the infected swains to drastically remold their way of life. For life with their new gadgets to be tolerable at all they had to transform them-selves from stockmen and plowmen into mechanics and grease-monkeys. They had to learn the different functions of the gas lever and the spark lever, and they had to acquire the sixth sense required to release the choke wire at the right frac-tion of a second to prevent flooding and to avoid having a wrist snapped by the crank when the engine backfired. In the case of trouble of any kind, it was every man for himself, with only a rudimentary owner's manual as a guide.

Many of the older farmers, raised with horses, never did master the intricacies of the automobile and remained erratic drivers, at best, all their lives. On most farms responsibility for keeping the automobile running devolved on one or more of the boys—as often as not one who was still a teen-ager when the first automobile was purchased. These younger fry were usually more interested and more adept at keeping the Model T run-ning, and especially with the "binder twine and baling wire" that, legend has it, was a major ingredient in repairs.

Inevitably the infatuation of the farmers with the motor car spread to their sons. Working extra hours on threshing gangs, hauling coal, and cleaning elevators bins were recognizable symptoms of an infection which would abate only when they had raised money enough to buy a second-hand Model T. Then, if the weather co-operated, for the summer months at least they could make forays in search of feminine companionship and other diversions beyond the limits of their own school districts or immediate neighborhoods. Given the precarious mechanical condition of their transport, these excursions were rarely without incident, and few farm boys of the Twenties do not have memories of arriving home from a country dance in the full light of dawn, with scarcely time to change clothes before heading for the barn to begin milking.

The handy-sized gasoline tractors, which came onto the market about the same time as the cars, took years to overcome a well-earned reputation for unreliability. In truth they worked no worse than the cars, and from any standpoint there was more justification for spending money on tractors than on cars in a frontier agricultural economy. It is true that most tractors cost about double the price of a Model T, but both were available for a third down with the balance covered by notes payable when the next crop came off. Yet by 1921 the western farmers had acquired only 35,000 tractors, one for every seven farms, compared with twice that many cars and trucks.

The new small-sized tractors were, of course, unmixed disasters for everybody who bought one. It was a predictable development, for there were more brands of tractors on the market than there were brands of automobiles. In 1920, Imperial Oil was advertising lubricating oils and greases for no less than seventy-five separate makes of tractors in Canada, and several manufacturers had three or four models in different sizes. Almost without exception they had two fatal defects—they lacked the ruggedness required for heavy farm work, and they could not operate efficiently at the very low speeds at which they had to travel. They would do what the manufacturer claimed—pull a three-bottom plow; but at the end of a week a valve-grinding job would be needed along with a new bearing or two for a gummed-up engine. Halfway through the next week the bolts holding the band clutch in place would break and the clutch would fly off into the field. Every town in the west had blacksmiths, hardware merchants, and even, occasionally, insurance agents acting as sales agents for tractors. Nobody, however, stocked parts, so when something broke the machine had to be laid up for a month or six weeks waiting for the parts to arrive from the factory. When they did come, the odds were about even that they would be the wrong parts.

So the farmers were forced back to horse power while $2,000 tractors mocked them from the edges of their fields, and lured them back again and again for one more $300 gamble that they could get it to work. If there was one thing the men wanted more than anything else, it was for tractor farming to work. Not only because a tractor allowed them to sit ahead of the dust kicked up by their machinery, but, more important, if the tractors would only work, they could add a good third to the productivity of their farms. Pastures and hay-fields that were needed to grow feed for their horses could be broken and planted to wheat.

If they would only work! But work they would not, despite hours of tinkering that culminated in explosive rage when nothing turned out as it was supposed to turn out.

Yet there were worse things than tractors that would not work because of cantankerous ignition systems or worn parts. One thing was a tractor that became an orphan. At least 80 per cent of the brand names that proliferated in those years were destined to find their way to the junk dealers when their manufacturers went out of business and parts of any kind ceased to be available. In the decade that followed, a half-dozen successful machines would emerge and, by reason of their improved reliability, become the basis for the mechanization of agriculture that would reach fruition after the Second World War.

The great crop of 1915 was important not only for the flood of purchasing power it unloosened. It was the vindication of the faith of every settler who had put his hand to the plow, and in that crop they could see happy auguries of more great crops to come. Western Canada was indeed the promised land they always knew it would be. Yet almost overnight the gloss began to tarnish, for in 1916 wheat stem rust hit the Manitoba crop and yields in the other provinces dropped sharply back to normal. The decline continued in 1917 and then, in 1918, the bottom dropped out of everything with the poorest wheat crop in twenty years. The crop of 1919 was just as bad. Only the high wartime prices the farmers got for their wheat saved them from what would have been calamitous years. But for the farmers whose crops were wiped out by rust, high prices meant nothing for they had nothing to sell. As a farmer in southeastern Saskatchewan once said, "After what we went through in 1918 and 1919, the Dirty Thirties were pretty easy to take." As its image dimmed with the onsetting disasters, the Bonanza Year lost all resemblance to a wave of the future and turned into a cruel mirage that had raised the settlers' hopes only to dash them into dust.

After five years of watching their worldly hopes turning to ashes it was hardly surprising that, in January 1921, 1,389 delegates representing 29,000 farmers in 598 locals turned up at the United Farmers of Alberta Convention with blood in their eyes looking for somebody, anybody, to blast into the middle of next week. The result of their frustrations was the Progressive movement which shattered the traditional party structure in the west.

Predictably, the political fall-out from the explosion of the prairie farmers was fatal to friend and foe alike. But for the farmers themselves, the more they changed things politically the more everything stayed the same back on the farm. The essentially conservative zealots they sent to the legislatures settled comfortably into administrations of unblushing orthodoxy, impotent to supply solutions to farm grievances. Economically, everything went from bad to worse. The Fordney-McCumber tariff of 1922 in the United States was aimed directly at Canadian farm products. The United States market was shut to Canadian beef producers, and prime steers on the Calgary market were selling for $5 per 100 pounds in 1922. In each of the Prairie provinces, legislative committees began kicking around the problem of farm debt, seeking solutions for the payment, with 60-cent wheat, of debts that had been contracted when wheat was $2.00 a bushel.

For the people on the farms, everything seemed completely out of phase for most of the first half of the 1920s, a fact that was underscored statistically by the snail's-pace movement toward farm mechanization. On the 250,000 farms of western Canada in 1921, there were 35,000 tractors, or one tractor for every seven farms. By 1926, there were 45,000 tractors, or one for every 5.5 farms. In 1921, 86 per cent of the farmers of western

Canada relied exclusively on horse power for farm needs and by 1926 this had been reduced only to 77.5 per cent. During the next half-decade, however, when higher prices for better crops were realized, tractor ownership almost doubled to 81,000 machines in service. In 1927-28-29 the farmers bought 41,000 tractors, more than twice as many as they had been able to afford in the first five years of the decade.

Yet the mode of life on the farms of the prairies changed very little from the first stages of settlement to the onset of the Great Depression. In that catastrophe, the standard of living of the farmers did not really have all that far to drop to touch absolute bottom. Of the 117,000 farms in Saskatchewan in 1926, only 1,334 had water in the house and perhaps half of these had indoor plumbing as well as water in the kitchen. Despite the fact that Manitoba had been settled much longer, its farmers had made no more progress in creature comforts than those in Saskatchewan. On the 53,251 farms in 1926, the census could find only 843 with piped-in water. Alberta did better than the other two provinces; 1,903 of its 77,130 farm homes had water in the house. It trailed Manitoba, however, in farm electrification. Only 1,441 of Alberta's farms had electricity, as compared to 1,525 in Manitoba and 2,331 in Saskatchewan. In the three Prairie provinces less than one farm house in sixty had piped-in water. Nor did things improve substantially by 1931 when the next census was taken. By then the census tables listed two categories of water systems — water piped into bathrooms and water piped only into kitchens. In the three provinces there were just under 4,000 farm bathrooms or, because there were 50,000 fewer farms in 1931 than in 1926, one bathroom for every fifty farm houses. There were another 1,100 homes with water in the kitchen but without bathrooms. A quarter of a century after the homesteading land-rush reached its peak, barely one prairie farmer in fifty had achieved a living standard which every city resident enjoyed and every city government, by the by-laws it enacted, deemed essential to the health of citizenry. On the farms of the west, it would be another quarter of a century before the producers began to catch up with urban levels of creature comfort.

3. After the Strike Was Over

For the working class of the prairies, the 1920s began and ended with the Winnipeg General Strike of 1919. The workers went into that strike more united than ever before, with a leadership cadre unmatched in Canadian history for dedication, intelligence, initiative, and organizational skill. They emerged from it, forty-two days later, in disillusioned disarray, forced back to work on the employers' terms, and with their unity shattered beyond recall. In the Manitoba provincial election in 1920 Labor candidates captured 11 seats in the house of 57. Three of them were strike leaders who were still in jail. Two years later, in Winnipeg alone there were six separate labor parties vying for labor support, and labor representation in the legislature was cut by half. Labor solidarity was replaced by petty jealousy and fratricidal strife that touched bottom in 1923 when the Teamsters Union threatened its members with instant expulsion if they were caught attending amateur boxing matches sponsored by the One Big Union.

In the 1920s all hope of wage increases was abandoned, for it would take most of the decade for the working class to regain the level of income they had achieved prior to the strike. For the working class of the prairies the 1920s was a nothing decade, made so, in part at least, by the viciousness of the ideological struggle between the conservative advocates of craft unionism and the socialist zealots of industrial unionism and the class struggle.

To the radical socialists who led the militant wing of the trades union movement into the 1920s, nothing was further beneath their contempt than "Gompersism" and the craft union movement. They coined the contemptuous phrase "labor skates" to describe the leaders of the Trades and Labor Congress, whom they accused of deserting the workers in the 1919 general strike. These same leaders, they said, had worked hand in glove with the federal authorities to smash the strike and jail the strike leaders. By the beginning of the new decade, the radicals had organized the One Big Union and were hell-bent on the destruction not only of the craft unions but of the capitalist system itself. A primary requisite for achieving these ends was to replace the —to them—archaic and useless crafts with one union which not only embraced all the workers within a single organization but included the entire working class. Never did an organization begin with loftier goals or more vigorously dedicated leadership — or fail more completely, or as quickly.

Sam Gompers was the anti-intellectual lifetime president of the American Federation of Labor and espouser of the "pork chops" or "meat and potatoes" principle of labor organization. To Gompers, trades unions should be exclusively concerned with wages and working conditions and leave politics strictly to the politicians. Some A. F. of L. unions even went so far as to constitutionally interdict the discussion of politics at local union meetings. For almost forty years under Gompers' leadership, the A. F. of L. followed the policy of rewarding its political friends and punishing its political enemies, regardless of their political affiliations. Legislators who enacted laws favorable to organized labor were rewarded with labor votes at election time. Those who supported anti-labor legislation, or opposed measures favored by labor, drew the opposition of labor at the polls.

Otherwise the craft union ideology was politically nonpartisan. The flirtation of the Knights of Labor with direct political action was one factor which led Gompers to withdraw his Cigarmakers Union from that organization in 1886. He also opposed the concern of the Knights with the reform of the banking system, the encouragement of co-operatives, and the support of labor organization by industries instead of by specific

1 & 2. Creature comforts for prairie settlers were few. The primitive and hastily built first dwellings on prairie homesteads *(above)* were only slowly replaced by more substantial houses like this one *(below)* near Richdale, Alberta.

3 & 4. The breaking of the Winnipeg General Strike in 1919 had a profound effect on the labor movement in the 1920s. *(Above)* A group portrait of the Strike leaders, and *(below)* an unemployed veterans' parade in April 1921.

5. *(Below)* Labor unrest would attract little attention from these elegant ladies attending a garden party on the grounds of Manitoba College in June of 1921.

6, 7, 8, & 9. The mansions of the wealthy were obvious status symbols in the prairie cities. *(Above)* One in Winnipeg was the Wellington Crescent home of James H. Ashdown *(right)*. *(Opposite page)* Two interior views of the Ashdown residence reveal the elaborate furnishings and the highly skilled workmanship of the detail finishing.

10, 11 & 12. Each prairie city had its showplace houses. *(Above)* "Beaulieu", the Calgary home of Senator Sir James Lougheed, contained twenty-six rooms. *(Opposite page, top)* The Eugene Coste mansion in Calgary, built in 1914, completely dominated Mount Royal Hill, while *(bottom)* "The Highlands", the Edmonton residence of W. J. Magrath, was particularly noted for the elegance of its interior finishing.

13. The fondest dream of any society hostess of the decade
was to entertain His Royal Highness the Prince of Wales,
photographed here with his brother, the Duke of Kent, on a
trans-Canada tour in 1927.

trades and crafts. In Gompers' view, labor had enough to do just concentrating on improving the wages and working conditions of its own union members through the negotiation of individual closed-shop contracts. When they tried to achieve general gains, like the eight-hour day, through industry-wide strikes they courted disaster. Such things as the Haymarket Square massacre in Chicago in 1886, the Carnegie Steel shooting-war of 1892, and the Pullman strike two years later, led to the passage of anti-union legislation. One way in which labor could be encouraged to mind its own business was through being organized by crafts instead of on an industry-wide basis. Out of this thesis evolved the stance of the A. F. of L. as the bulwark which protected capitalist America from the threats of anarchists, syndicalists, revolutionaries, and, ultimately, Communists.

Under Gompers the A. F. of L. became a federation of autonomous unions patterned after the British unions of the early 1800s. In Britain great emphasis was laid on restricting the number of apprentices in the skilled trades with the objective of increasing bargaining power by preventing surpluses of skilled labor from developing. Surpluses of labor could depress wages. Shortages of skilled labor could force wages up. *Ergo*, the ideal form of union was one which restricted entry into the trade by controlling the number of apprentices allowed to learn it, and which, by means of closed-shops contracts, prevented the employment of non-union workers. That the British theory worked out badly in practice for several generations in the United States did not, however, prevent many of the crafts from improving their earnings in localized categories of employment.

Both the theories and the practices of the A. F. of L. naturally spilled over into western Canada in the 1880s. Because of the seasonal nature of the early construction industry, the first building booms in Winnipeg were staffed largely by tradesmen who migrated north from Minnesota in the spring and went home again in the fall. Or they moved north on reports of high wages and returned south when lack of work or too many craftsmen forced wages down. In early Winnipeg there was a suspicion abroad that building contractors spread false stories

about carpenters earning $3 a day—when the going rate was $2
—in the hope of luring enough tradesmen north to bring wages
down to $1.

Many of the building tradesmen who came north from the
United States in the first Winnipeg boom of 1880-2 belonged to
the Knights of Labor and brought its radical gospel north with
them. When it fell into disfavor the union men who were left in
Manitoba followed their U.S. parent unions into the A. F. of L.,
and by 1890 there were enough unions in Manitoba to establish
the first Manitoba Trades Council. In 1894 the American Society of Engineers and the various railway unions helped to form
the Winnipeg Trades and Labor Council.

A globule or two of the radical ideology of the old Knights of
Labor still lingered, however, for the Winnipeg Labor Party was
formed and elected Charles Hislop in 1894 as the city's first labor
alderman. Thereafter, despite the A. F. of L.'s strong anti-
political-party bias, members of western Canadian craft unions
became permanently addicted to labor parties. The first one did
not last long and was succeeded by the Labor Representation
Committee, which elected A. W. Puttee to the House of Commons in 1900. Then the unionists ran through a half-dozen
movements before labor party candidates appeared regularly on
ballots in Regina, Calgary, Edmonton, and Winnipeg during the
1920s.

By the turn of the century the itinerant construction unionists
had disappeared as a working force of permanent residents
took over. Then came the influx of thousands of British trades
unionists to challenge the Gompers ideology and turn the western labor movement into a battleground of ideas that would lead
to its ultimate destruction as a force to be reckoned with.

By 1900 the labor movement of England had moved far ahead
of the simplistic theories still prevalent in the United States. The
massive spread of machine production had swept away the notion of specialized trades achieving privileged positions above
the general mass of workers. After the dockers' strike of 1889,
the drive to organize all the workers in an industry into a single
union became an irresistible force. The thousands of skilled

British trades unionists — machinists, molders, carpenters, plumbers, steamfitters — who came to western Canada to man the railway shops were vociferous missionaries for industrial unionism.

As they were union men first, and organizational theorists second, they joined the craft unions wherever they found them, but at once set about to remold them more closely to their heart's desire. Not only were they industrial unionists, their ranks included every known variety of radical zealot—anarchists, Owenites, Fabians, and Marxian socialists. At the slightest opening they would turn a routine Trades and Labor Council meeting into a forum for a three-hour debate on evolutionary versus revolutionary socialism. There was scarcely one among them who had gone farther than English grammar school, but they were all graduates of the after-school educational programs of the British trades union movement, and had sharpened their argumentative wits in the lunch-hour disputations of their apprenticeship years.

In Winnipeg there was R. J. Johns, a bantamweight Cornishman and as articulate a spellbinder as ever mounted a socialist soap-box. There were John Queen, Jack Clancy, Jack Blumberg, A. A. Heaps, Tom Flye, William Cooper, native-born George Armstrong who could deliver a two-hour socialist sermon and never look at a note or repeat an argument, Charlie Foster, W. H. C. Logan, and Bob Bray. Across the west, stretching all the way to Vancouver, were other pockets of imported British socialist agitation—Joe Knight in Edmonton and W. A. Pritchard in Vancouver were not only great orators but among the most active minds in the movement. And then there was Bob Russell. Most of all there was Bob Russell.

R. B. Russell was a Clydeside machinist who emigrated to Canada in 1911 and who, with Dick Johns, provided the radical labor movement with the one-two punch that pummelled the solar plexuses of the conservative Gompersites who headed the Winnipeg Trades and Labor Council. Russell possessed the earthiest vocabulary ever heard in Anglo-Saxon Winnipeg. Alan Meikle, the electrical union business agent, once described Russell in anger as pouring forth a stream of invectives that "would have melted the rusted bolts off a Clydeside scow".

Russell seemed to have a tied tendon in his upper lip so that his mouth, in repose, was in a perpetual pout. When he got excited he seemed to be troubled with an excess of saliva so that he occasionally seemed to be almost frothing. Neither hampered him in his ability to marshal an argument that would stir an audience. To write him off as a rabble-rouser of distinction, however, would be to unfairly underestimate his talents. He was the chief tactician of the radical labor movement and it was he who, more than any one man, molded the forces that produced the Winnipeg general strikes of 1918 and 1919. Whenever a voice was needed to put the case for socialism, industrial unionism, or political action, Bob Russell seemed to be first choice —whether the forum was a Trades and Labor Congress convention, a Workers' Party convention, or an organizational meeting anywhere. If his name failed to appear on any list of delegates going anywhere or doing anything in the decade prior to the strike, it was either an oversight or a printer's error.

In a mellowing mood, twenty years later, he delighted in dwelling on the in-fighting in which he had engaged in the prelude to the strikes:

> You hear a lot these days [it was in 1936] about the Commies getting control of respectable organizations by "boring from within". Boring from within? Them claiming they invented it? We invented it right here in Winnipeg long before the Commies ever crawled out from under the rocks. Look, we'd have been crazy to have tried to come here and organize industrial unions to compete with the craft unions that already existed. All we had to do was join them and turn them into industrial unions. It was as easy as taking candy from a baby. Most of us knew the union constitutions upside down and backwards and some knew more about parliamentary procedure than the guy who wrote the book. It wasn't only getting things done we wanted done. There was also blocking things we didn't want done. We always came to important meetings with our motions prepared and we

sometime worked it so one of our guys would move an amendment to our own motion. The opposition would argue like Hell against our motion not realizing the motion itself was a decoy that we were really only interested in the amendment.

We could have taken over the Trades and Labor Council the same way if we wanted to. As a matter of fact we did in 1919. But it was better to have these labor skates of the international unions being front men. We'd pass the resolutions and they would have to carry them out.

All this in-fighting and resolution-carrying, of course, made nary a ripple on the public mind at the time. The newspapers paid no attention to labor news, and a struggle between advocates of clashing theories of trades union organization would have got little space even if they had been interested. The struggle was carried on in the shops, at regular street-corner meetings in the Market Square on Sunday nights, and occasionally in the columns of *The Voice,* the dull-as-dishwater publication of the Trades and Labor Council.

Until the depression of 1913, which brought mass unemployment in the building trades, trades union growth fell far behind the huge influx of population to western Canada. With work plentiful and wages relatively satisfactory the newcomers were under little compulsion to go looking for unions to join. When conditions deteriorated there was a fairly rapid growth in union membership until the war absorbed most of the unemployed. Membership then declined until 1918-19, when prices began to rise and grind down everybody's standard of living.

The agitations within the Canadian trades union movement during the early years of the war indicated how far the Canadian affiliates had drifted from the American Federation of Labor ideology. There was agitation against the war itself, although, curiously enough, the war split the socialists into two irreconcilable camps. One group opposed the war as a capitalist-imperialist conspiracy. The other refused to oppose the war because it was an inevitable capitalist development which would, in the end, lead to the destruction of the system. In the main, however, the radical unionists, whether in Quebec, Winnipeg, Calgary, or British Columbia, spoke out against support of the war — even when it meant going to jail.

In 1916, when the spectre of conscription for overseas service appeared on the horizon, it triggered an intensification of trades union opposition. The national convention of the Trades and Labor Congress itself featured fiery speeches denouncing the war and conscription as a capitalist-imperialist conspiracy against the working class. There was great soul-searching over how the workers could bring the war to a halt. Resolutions were introduced urging the organization of a nation-wide general strike. In the local trades and labor councils of the west, passions were as deeply aroused as they were at national conventions. From the lack of enthusiasm on the part of the general membership for concrete action of any kind, however, it was fair to assume that most union members — as distinct form the radical leadership — supported the war like the great majority of the citizenry.

Just as the Canadian labor opposition to conscription was reaching a crescendo in 1917, the United States entered the war and the leaders of the A. F. of L. outdid the employers in the fervor of their patriotic enthusiasm for the war — including conscription for overseas duty. Sam Gompers himself journeyed to Toronto to keynote a Victory Bond rally and prove his sincerity with the purchase of a $50 bond.

The super-patriotism of the A. F. of L. hierarchy in the United States, and its reflection in their subordinates in Canada, convinced the radicals that the time was approaching when it would be necessary to make a clean break and establish a single industrial union for all Canada, divorced from the A. F. of L. Russell, Johns, Armstrong, Pritchard, and Knight, however, had been coming to the conclusion that even industrial unions were not enough. Strongly organized industrial unions had lost strikes because workers in other industries had stayed at work. Labor's ultimate weapon must be the general strike which would require that all workers belong to one union. Thus, the One Big Union idea was born and a campaign was begun to organize such a union. When the threat of a general strike in Winnipeg in 1918 won the day for the Civic Employees Union, which was striking for higher pay, the One Big Union drive picked up snowballing momentum.

In March of 1919, more than 200 delegates from all the western cities met in Calgary to bring the One Big Union to life in a veritable orgy of far-out speech-making. At a time when the Canadian non-socialist majority was being shaken by the revolutionary currents sweeping the world, by fear of Bolshevism and threats of new wars, the resolutions passed by the Calgary convention could hardly have been more disturbing.

To some delegates, the O.B.U. was to be more than a labor movement; it was to be a replica of the Russian soviet system of government. Resolutions calling for the sending of fraternal greeting to the Russian revolutionary government were passed. The convention demanded the removal of all Canadians from the Allied Expeditionary Force in Russia by June 1 on threat of a general strike. It demanded the release of all political prisoners and, perhaps worst of all, it pledged support to the German Spartacus movement and denounced the murders of Karl Liebknecht and Rosa Luxemburg. To fraternize with Germans of any political stripe was to set a cat among the dovecotes of the prairie establishment. These wildly discordant and disturbing resolutions had greater impact on the establishment mind than the internecine squabbling between union officials over doctrinal differences about the trades union structure could ever have had.

The Canadian trades unions, despite the rigid adherence to autonomous craft unionism by the American Federation of Labor, had been edging toward industrial unionism for many years. During the war, the railway unions had bargained as a group with the railways as a group. In Winnipeg the building crafts were organized into a building trades council which sought to bargain as a unit with the contractors as a unit. The metal trades council, which embraced just about everybody who worked with machinery or metal—from machinists and molders to sheet-metal workers—tried to do the same with the various iron works around Winnipeg. It was the flat refusal of the employers to bargain with either the metal workers or the building trades council that brought on the Winnipeg General Strike of 1919. The fact that the leaders of the strike were also leaders of the Calgary convention which established the O.B.U. resulted in an erroneous impression that the O.B.U. had organized the strike. In fact the new union did not come into existence until after the 1919 strike was over.

Underlying the strike were seething currents of rancorous discontent that touched every segment of western society. Instead of diminishing, the spiralling cost of living increased with the end of the war. The first contingents of returning soldiers came home to discover that there were no jobs for them, that, in some of their minds at least, hated aliens were filling the jobs that belonged to them.

Nor was the frustration with steadily rising prices and the growing anger with governments limited to trades unionists. Everybody who worked for wages was in the same boat. Their mood was shared by the employers, whose costs had been forced upward by increased freight rates and tariffs and who were thus faced with shrinking markets and profit squeezes. Instead of peace bringing a resumption of the building boom, it had brought little but continuing stagnation. The upper-class soldiers coming back from the war were as disillusioned and cantankerous as the working-class soldiers. It was a bilious, distraught, and disenchanted society in which the building tradesmen and metal workers struck on May 1, 1919.

A week later the Trades and Labor Council called for a vote of its affiliated unions in favor of a general strike to support the strikers, and the workers in fifty-two affiliated unions responded with a vote of 11,112 to 524 to strike. Were the workers who voted to strike really determined to strike? Or were they counting on bringing the employers to time simply by making the gesture? That had happened in the west on several occasions during the previous year, when favorable settlements were achieved simply by taking a general strike vote. The most notable example was the Winnipeg Civic Employees' strike, where the threat of a general strike had brought an almost immediate settlement. But 1919 was not 1918, for now there were large numbers of unemployed walking the streets. The strike vote produced no response from the employers, and on May 15, 12,000 unionized workers went on strike. They were followed on succeeding days by thousands of unorganized workers who seized upon the strike as a means of venting their wrath against their own low wages and the high cost of living. Within a week 35,000 workers in a city of 200,000 were off the job.

It was a strike without pickets, without demonstration, and, until the very end, without violence. It spread to other western cities and was broken in the end by the combined efforts of the federal, provincial, and municipal governments, with tacit assistance from the Trades and Labor Congress hierarchy. It was broken, not as a strike, but as an apprehended seditious conspiracy of the radical leaders to overthrow the government and set up a dictatorship of the proletariat in Canada. That was the government's paranoid reaction, which grew out of the rhetoric of Russell, Queen, Johns, Knight, Pritchard, Ivens, and their associates in the months that preceded the organization of the O.B.U. The strike itself lasted forty-two days, from May 15 to June 26, but it was actually broken by the arrest of its leaders on June 16 on charges of seditious conspiracy. Following the arrests all public meetings were banned, and the strike committee ran out of funds and called off the strike on June 26. In the trials that followed, Russell was sentenced to two years in the penitentiary; Queen, Johns, Pritchard, Ivens, and Armstrong were each given one year in jail; and Bray was sent to jail for six months.

The penalties assessed against the strikers themselves were never catalogued. The non-union workers who had joined so enthusiastically in a gesture of solidarity paid the heaviest price. Many of them never got their jobs back. The employees of the C.P.R. lost their accumulated pension rights and their seniority rights. Under the railway's company-controlled pension scheme, this meant that many middle-aged employees would be unable to qualify for a pension before compulsory retirement age. Postal workers and department store and many clothing industry employees simply lost their jobs.

In several coal-mining towns in Alberta, the sympathetic strike in support of the Winnipeg General Strike took the form of a walkout in demand of recognition of the One Big Union into which the miners had bolted from the United Mine Workers Union, District 18. In these towns the strikes were anything but peaceful. The Drumheller mine owners scoured the countryside for returned soldiers and hired them as combination miners and goon squads to terrorize the strikers. Though the miners were mainly aliens who had been hired for the mining skills they brought with them from Europe, their union leaders were mainly Anglo-Saxon. Nevertheless, as in Winnipeg and everywhere else, the media, the governments, and the employers insisted that the miners' strike was an alien conspiracy against Canadian democracy. This made it easy to arouse the hatred of the Anglo-Saxon veterans for the miners who happened to have jobs when they did not. The war veterans, usually led by Drumheller businessmen, were organized into marauding gangs who periodically routed the miners from their shacks and drove them out into the hills. Jack Sullivan, the head of the Drumheller union, managed several narrow escapes from a beating until his luck ran out. Then he and Robert MacDonald were captured by five carloads of vigilantes and taken to the mine at Wayne, where they were beaten, tarred and feathered, set upon the road to Calgary on foot, and warned never to return. Unlike the Winnipeg strike, the mine strike at Drumheller, involving thirteen mines and 500 men, continued throughout the summer. In the end it too was lost; the miners were forced to tear up their O.B.U. cards and return to the U.M.W., which was given a closed-shop contract. The veterans who had conducted the three-month reign of terror suffered the traditional fate of strikebreakers. When the skilled miners returned to work they lost their jobs.

Until 1919, the fight between the industrial unionists and the craft unionists had been waged within the craft union labor temples. The internecine nature of the struggle ended when the O.B.U. came into existence. For a few months it seemed to be carrying everything before it, as it was able to boast a membership of 45,000. But this was an ephemeral splash, a false dawn for the new organization.

Instead of the strike acting as a spark to ignite a new and greater conflagration of proletarian anger and outrage, the failure of the strike only spread a thick blanket of torpor over the working class. For the unorganized workers there was disillusionment with both strikes and unions to add to disillusionment with wars, profiteers, and politicians. Canadian union membership, which had skyrocketed from 160,000 in 1916 to 375,000 in 1919, dropped sharply to 275,000 in 1920. How much of the rise and fall was in the west cannot be ascertained because adequate statistics were not being kept. Even those compiled by the Dominion Department of Labour may well be suspect. They came from union sources and would tend to err on the high side. In any event, when the labor leaders of Alberta tried to mount a one-day strike across the west to protest the jailing of the Winnipeg strike leaders, it fizzled completely. Certainly the organizing zeal of all unions disappeared, along with the will to continue the struggle to improve the lot of the workers.

As for the jailed leaders, only Russell and Armstrong remained active in the labor movement in Manitoba. Russell became the general secretary of the O.B.U., where he remained until he presided at its liquidation. John Queen turned to salesmanship and a long career as a member of the legislature and seven terms as mayor of Winnipeg. While still in jail, Ivens, like Queen, was elected to the legislature, and served there for more than a decade. Dick Johns abandoned trades unionism for a career of distinction in education. Abie Heaps was elected to Parliament, where he served North Winnipeg for almost twenty years.

Aside from the fact that the O.B.U. arrived on the scene twenty years before its time, the causes for its decline were manifold. The drive to raise $50,000 to finance the defence of the strike leaders took all the energy that could be mustered. Because the leaders of the O.B.U. — Russell, Johns, Pritchard, and Armstrong, and fellow travellers Queen, Ivens, Heaps, and Dixon — were all leaders of the Winnipeg strike, the O.B.U. became identified with, and blamed for, that strike. In the aftermath, the craft unions flooded the west with their international officers who succeeded in getting closed-shop contracts from employers who had previously adamantly refused to bargain. They managed to re-establish the Winnipeg Trades and Labor Council with such unions as the printers, carpenters, and others which had saved some of their membership from the O.B.U. With the top leadership of the O.B.U. in jail for the better part of 1920, the new union lacked both the organizing and administrative skill of Russell and Johns, and the enthusiasm of Pritchard and Armstrong.

Perhaps most important of all was the misreading by the O.B.U. leaders of the character of the working class of western Canada. Frank Woodward, the editor of the O.B.U. *Bulletin,* brought everything into focus when he said that the workers of western Canada were forty years behind their British counterparts in the development of class consciousness. Many of the thousands of union members who had come to western Canada came passively, without any burning thirst to liberate the working class from wage slavery. They came with an ambition to escape from their trade into the employer class — to branch out into a business of their own. The examples of those who had done so were everywhere. Jimmy Ashdown had begun as an itinerant tinker and ended as a millionaire. Most of the biggest contractors in the west had started as carpenters, plumbers, or bricklayers. Indeed the ideology of the craft unions was fundamentally anti-class-conscious. To the extent that they achieved closed shops and better wages, they became the aristocrats of the labor movement, who had common laborers to fetch and carry for them.

The O.B.U. leaders erred, too, in over-estimating the capacity of the working class to absorb education. No other organization, short of the school boards themselves, laid as much stress upon the imperative need for the working class to educate itself as did the O.B.U. It moved in on the newly organized Labor Churches which had been set up throughout Winnipeg. On Thursday nights it supplied instructors in public speaking. Friday nights there were classes on economics. On Sundays a class on economics followed one of religious education. In the conflict then raging between science and religion it came down solidly on the side of science. It published long articles in the O.B.U. *Bulletin* attacking Roman Catholic dogma. Bishop William Montgomery Brown, who had been unfrocked by the Episcopal Church of the United States for his defence of communism in Russia, was brought in for a lecture tour of western Canada. It also sponsored the tour of Joseph McCabe, the British rationalist lecturer, who delivered a series of speeches on the theory of evolution. The *Bulletin* acted as distributor for masses of cheap editions of classical works by Darwin, Huxley, Kropotkin, Marx, Engels, Owen, Spencer, Tom Paine, Upton Sinclair, H. G. Wells, K. J. Kautsky, and Jack London. In addition, it carried regular advertisements for the famous Little Blue Books of Haldemann-Julius, which popularized science and history and sold for as little as five cents.

The O.B.U. erred rather seriously in switching its emphasis from industrial unionism, geared to the fundamental standard-of-living problems of the members, to radical socialism. The belief in industrial unionism was still strong, as indicated by the expulsion of the Canadian Brotherhood of Railway Employees from the Trades and Labor Congress in 1921. Under the leadership of A. R. Mosher, this industrial union of the C.N.R. employees outside the brotherhood eventually founded the All Canadian Congress of Labor — one of whose objectives was freedom from domination by American unions.

Finally, the O.B.U. underestimated the recuperative powers of the craft unions, the bitterness of their opposition to the O.B.U., and the animosity of employers to the movement. The craft unionists were content to work alongside non-union members. But, if an O.B.U. member showed up, the business agent would rush to the employer and demand that the man be dismissed. The extent of this pressure can be gauged from the fact that the craft unions in the C.N.R. Transcona shops forced the railway to fire two of the most prominent members of the O.B.U.— Jack Clancy and Charles Foster. Despite pressure from the O.B.U., they stayed fired.

Outside Winnipeg, O.B.U. organizers faced continuing threats of violence. P. M. Christopher was kidnapped by vigilantes in Bienfait, Saskatchewan, beaten up, and taken into North Dakota, where he was released. Some weeks later he suffered the same fate in Drumheller and ultimately resigned as an O.B.U. organizer.

All these factors, however, might have been overcome if it had not been for the steady worsening of economic conditions in western Canada. Winnipeg itself went into a long economic decline. The Panama Canal, which had opened on the day the Germans marched into Belgium in 1914, ended that city's thirty-year reign as the tollgate of western Canada, through which everybody and everything had to pass, both going and coming. Its wholesale district went into a permanent depression as new distribution systems from Vancouver were developed. Expansion of railway shop facilities in other western cities, which was just beginning at the outbreak of the war, drained away employment. Yet none of these developments brought any semblance of a boom to the cities in question, and unemployment was a continuing problem throughout the west for the first half of the decade.

The major construction projects of the decade between Winnipeg and the Rockies could be counted on one hand, if the new railway hotels were set to one side. There was the Eaton Mail Order building and the Hudson's Bay store in Winnipeg, Eaton's store in Calgary, and the General Motors plant in Regina, and that was it. Not a single office building of any consequence was built in western Canada between 1919 and 1930. The statistics for building permits that were issued tell the story of the economic malaise of the prairies as well as anything:

	WINNIPEG	REGINA	CALGARY	EDMONTON
1910	$15,105,420	$ 2,351,288	$ 5,898,594	$ 2,161,256
1911	18,233,550	5,137,615	12,907,638	3,804,794
1912	20,595,750	8,046,238	20,393,820	14,446,919
1913	18,621,650	4,018,350	8,619,653	9,242,450
1914	12,845,050	1,761,875	3,425,350	5,513,277
1915	1,826,300	464,065	150,550	309,825
1919	2,948,000	1,699,020	2,212,000	931,000
1920	8,370,150	2,597,920	2,906,100	3,231,955
1921	5,580,400	2,160,038	2,298,800	1,583,696
1922	6,875,750	1,784,124	3,102,700	2,338,109
1923	4,484,100	1,264,030	821,840	1,488,670
1924	3,187,900	939,785	1,031,420	2,305,095
1925	4,156,690	1,208,304	1,197,475	1,481,890
1926	10,362,600	4,242,511	1,990,408	1,853,735
1927	7,569,300	3,482,090	2,330,131	2,568,565
1928	10,547,400	6,619,216	6,320,142	3,374,971
1929	11,050,250	10,022,631	10,022,631	5,670,185

The west was won with the gigantic real-estate and construction boom that came in the wake of more than 1,400,000 settlers who descended on the prairies prior to the Great War. It was a boom that had been financed in small part by the new wealth being generated in the west, and in much larger part by a veritable flood of outside capital into the west. The real-estate boom had already run out of steam before the war, along with the construction boom. It did not return after the war for several very good reasons. Except for housing, the prairies were substantially overbuilt. Immigration did not resume at previous levels. The westward flow of both capital and mortgage money dried up. In the five years before the war, the four main urban centres on the prairies recorded a total of $195,000,000-worth of new construction. In the five years after the war, the total was no more than $59,000,000. Nor do the figures indicate the full story of the decline, for the post-war figures are in inflated dollars, worth half the pre-war dollars.

The construction statistics are one indication of the doldrums through which the west was drifting. Population figures are another, although the significance of what was happening was unapparent to the people at the time.

In the 1920s it was still a common sight to see newly arrived settlers from Europe, in their funny clothing, trudging the streets around the railway stations of Winnipeg and Edmonton with their wicker baskets and all-steps-and-stairs families. They were bound mainly for the homesteads in the hinterlands, though a good many did settle in the cities. Their presence was noticeable enough to attract the baleful eyes of labor leaders whose unions passed resolutions calling for restrictions on immigration. Some municipal councils did yield to pressure and restricted their hiring to British subjects.

Missing from the equation, however, were the hordes of prairie dwellers who were getting out of the country. Despite the influx to the area, the Prairie provinces were barely able to hold their natural population increase between the census of 1921 and that of 1931. Thus Manitoba, which had a population of 610,000 in 1921, recorded an increase of 90,000 in the decade. If it had simply kept its natural increase, with no immigration at all, it would have risen 116,000. Saskatchewan gained 164,000, while its natural increase was 173,000. In Alberta the figures were 142,000 for population growth and 116,000 for natural increase.

The population boom, which in the pre-war decade had created a rash of new towns, also ended. Between 1921 and 1926, half the twenty-four towns in Saskatchewan lost population and eight dropped below their 1916 census figures.

In Alberta thirteen out of twenty towns lost population between 1921 and 1926, and in Manitoba the figures were ten declining towns out of twenty-two. Because no figures were compiled provincially for migrants entering or leaving, only a rough estimate is possible of what the figures might have been. A conservative estimate might be that the decade of the 1920s saw at least 150,000 new settlers arrive on the prairies to replace a like number who had sampled what the region had to offer and had chosen to go elsewhere.

With the construction industry in a sadly depressed condition, the urban west was largely reduced to living off the wheat crop. How much unemployment there was is also impossible to determine, for the only figures compiled during this era were arrived at by sampling unemployment among the members of selected trades unions. In the winter months of 1920 and 1921, the figures reached 15 per cent. In the main centres, among the non-union majorities, unemployment may well have reached 20 or 25 per cent. Except in Winnipeg, there were few facilities for succoring the unemployed. Winnipeg had a woodyard at which the jobless were put to work sawing up cordwood for use in cooking and heating. Winnipeg, however, delayed opening its woodyard until well on in the winter because it did not want to encourage the harvesters who had come west from Ontario to put down permanent roots in the city. As late as 1926, Calgary was still sending destitute workers, who ate 30-cent restaurant meals that they could not pay for, to jail for thirty days. When the numbers so jailed threatened to overcrowd the pokeys, the provincial government stepped in and freed the prisoners. Some idea of the rudimentary level of social assistance being provided following the Great War may be gained from the system used in Brandon and elsewhere in 1920 to assist the unemployed veterans. The veteran was first required to apply to the Soldiers Re-establishment Board, a Dominion government agency, for a certificate that he was unemployed and that there was no work available for him. He could then take the paper to the Canadian Patriotic Fund, a private agency, and a clerk there would decide how much aid the veteran needed to sustain himself and his family. Many of the veterans who were recovering from war wounds were still unfit for heavy work and the Great War Veterans Association was agitating for disability pensions. It was demanding $100 a month for totally disabled veterans, based on $1 per month for each one-per-cent disability.

The surplus of labor and the lack of jobs reversed the course of trades union activity of a generation. Instead of fighting for higher wages, the unions were reduced to rear-guard action to resist a drive of employers everywhere to cut wages. This campaign was based on the fact that the cost of living, which had risen steadily for a year after the strike, levelled off late in 1920 and dropped sharply in 1921. To western employers, "high wages rates" became the universal explanation for business stagnation. In this agitation the employers ignored a salient fact. The biggest jump in living costs in a decade came after the strike, while wages remained static — at least in the west. For example, the Dominion Department of Labour budget for food and rent for a family of five was placed at $14 a week in 1914, at $23.49 in 1919, and at $26.92 in July of 1920. In February of 1922, the index was back down to $22 a week, and in this month the construction industry council demanded that the building trades accept a 25-per-cent reduction in wages, although the decline in the workers' budget from 1919 to 1922 was less than two index points, or 10 per cent. In Alberta the coal-mine owners shut down the mines to enforce a wage cut of 30 per cent. The miners fought the owners for five months and then went back to work for a pay cut of 15 per cent. Three years later another demand for a 30-per-cent cut resulted in another prolonged strike, which was again lost by the miners.

Some other unions, notably the printers in Winnipeg and the metal trades in Winnipeg and Edmonton, staged prolonged strikes against wage cuts. The printers managed to stave off the reductions, but the metal workers lost almost 20 cents an hour and the miners took some whopping reductions. In general, however, wage-cutting was the order of the day. Wages went down and stayed down for the better part of the decade. The wages of carpenters, plumbers, and bricklayers dropped by 15 cents an hour under collective agreements, but, as time passed, these agreements came to mean less and less. They applied in the main only to the larger construction jobs and government contracts. A great deal of the work on housing construction was done by individual sub-contract. The tradesman would bid to complete the job at a fixed price and his hourly rate could vary from 50 cents to $1.25 depending on his skill, his speed, and the weather. Tradesmen who could not find regular work frequently went into business for themselves as general contractors. In the garment trade in Winnipeg, which enjoyed a mild expansion during the 1920s, many of the employers had been skilled garment-shop workers who had lost their jobs through strikes or lay-offs.

The changes in wage rates reported in the *Labour Gazette* during the 1920s are indicative of a decade of trades union impotency that accompanied a stagnant business climate. The decade began with wages for the skilled trades running at around $1 an hour for 48 hours per week. Bricklayers and stonemasons got 10 or 15 cents more, and painters a dime or so less. As a result of the wage-cutting campaign, the general level dropped to around 85 cents an hour in 1922. There it stayed for the next half-decade, while unions were more than eager to extend the existing agreements for another year or two when they came up for renewal. As the previous table shows, a substantial jump occurred in building construction in 1928-9 on the heels of the big 1928 wheat crop. With the impetus of this mini-boom, wages generally managed to move upward to touch, and then to exceed by a few cents per hour, what they had been at the time of the 1919 general strike. The stonemasons and bricklayers even managed to reach $1.45 an hour, a gain of a full 25 cents over what they had been earning in 1920. Even the building trades laborers were doing better, as they received 60 cents an hour compared with the 50 cents they were getting a decade before. Union membership also recovered, climbing to 320,000 members across the country—still 50,000 less than were enrolled at the outbreak of the 1919 strike.

4. The Rich Were Rich

If the 1920s was a nothing decade for the farmers on the land and the workers in the cities and towns, it was anything but for the affluent minority who battened on their productivity and their labors. It was indeed the age of elegance, in which the "good life" was enjoyed to the hilt by everybody with a predisposition for living it up—and the financial resources for doing so.

The Prairie provinces never did develop a leisure class that devoted itself exclusively to the pursuit of pleasure. Indeed, the work ethic still dominated the lives of employer and employee, rich and poor alike. The sons of the successful who did not follow their fathers into the family businesses, move into the paternal professions, or strive manfully to outstrip their fathers' success, were targets for scorn — when not regarded as being slightly touched in the head. In the urban west there was only one yardstick of status, of success, of personal and community worth. That measure was money. Unusual qualities of mind or spirit brought little recognition outside a small circle of the sensitive cognoscenti. In an environment in which the vast majority of denizens were struggling to claw themselves out of the basic human condition of the frontier, there was little time or inclination for preoccupation with such frilly things. Nor was there much reflected status to be attained from familial relationships. The sons of the successful, though their fathers' money gave them a substantial advantage in launching themselves into business, had to make it on their own before they themselves achieved recognition.

75

Of the western millionaires of the 1920s, it was possible to count on one hand those who brought any important wealth with them to the west. W.F. Alloway married the daughter of an Ontario lumber baron before going west to open his private bank in Winnipeg. James Richardson had inherited the well-established grain business from his uncle when he arrived in Winnipeg to take charge in 1915. R. B. Bennett had come into the Eddy match fortune before he became Calgary's most successful corporation lawyer. And who else?

No matter what the calling, there were examples in all the major cities of people who got rich from a standing start — from makers of harness to makers of candy bars; from shapers of biscuits to shapers of cities; from diggers of sewers to builders of railways; wholesalers, retailers, jobbers, doctors, lawyers, and the occasional thief. There were examples everywhere of Horatio Alger heroes who by dint of hard work, frugality, opportunity, and a touch of luck, had become wealthy. And there were ten times as many who everybody, including themselves, believed were well on their way to making it.

The result was that the prairie cities were cloaked with a hard-to-rub-off aura of opulence, which was altogether attractive because covetousness seldom surfaced among those who were well down the scale. The fact that the people now so securely ensconced in their mansions had come all the way up from nothing was proof positive that the west was indeed a land of opportunity. Instead of begrudging the affluent their success, the trailers in the economic struggle encouraged themselves with the thought that "if he could do it, I can do it."

Without a leisure class there was little preoccupation with what Thorstein Veblen called "conspicuous consumption". With one universal exception — housing. The house and the neighborhood in which he lived was the accepted measure of a man, once he had reached even a modest level of financial competence.

The progress being made by all those with a foot on a rung of the ladder of success could be neatly plotted by their houses and by the neighborhoods they lived in. Thus, James H. Ashdown, the author of the greatest success story of them all, moved three times from his modest diggings in Point Douglas until he settled permanently in his mansion on Wellington Crescent in Winnipeg. His course was repeated by literally hundreds of others.

In Winnipeg the successful developed a curious predilection for huddling together along the river banks. It was started by Sir John Schultz himself, whose castle was the first big house on Armstrong's Point (so called because of the sharp V-turn taken by the Assiniboine River as it approached confluence with the Red River a mile to the east). As the prospering storekeeping class moved toward merchant-prince status, they moved first to the north bank of the Assiniboine. Then they moved into the Armstrong's Point area. Such was the impact of prosperity on Winnipeg that the well-off were multiplying faster than space there could be found for them.

In the 1905-10 era, C. H. Enderton became an overnight millionaire by picking up a quarter section of land across the river from Armstrong's Point and turning it into a landing site for the newly wealthy who were unable to find a place elsewhere. Once he had persuaded Ashdown to build a mansion on a half-acre river lot on Wellington Crescent, Enderton's Crescentwood became Winnipeg's most prestigious residential area. During the rest of the pre-war years, the status seekers tried feverishly to surpass Ashdown in the size and elegance of their housing projects. A dozen of them did.

If some deranged Bolshevik agent or displaced anarchist had decided, in the winter of 1919-20, to take revenge on the Winnipeg establishment, it would have been easily managed. He could have started west along the Assiniboine River from the Osborne Bridge with a sleigh full of bombs. Four hundred yards from the bridge he could have begun lobbing his bombs right and left. By the time he reached the Maryland Bridge, a mile upstream, he would have wiped out the entire Winnipeg establishment and reduced the mansions of fifteen or twenty millionaires, or hoping-to-be millionaires, to rubble.

In Calgary the destruction could have been achieved with a mere handful of bombs. One at the corner of Sixth Street and Thirteenth Avenue would have got both the Lougheeds and the

Hulls, who together had recently owned most of Calgary. A half-dozen more bombs, detonated along the north slopes of Mount Royal, up which the less wealthy were building, would have accounted for most of Calgary's mansion-builders.

The mansions that the Morgans of the prairies built for themselves had, first of all, size: then they had individuality of design, for each was tailored to the tastes of the owner. The idea of building a house with even a remote resemblance to the house next door, or to any within the same block, would never have occurred to architect or owner. As the basic interior design became standardized, great pains were taken with the finishing material in order to camouflage this fact.

Each house was a tribute to the skill of the tradesmen, for the instinct for workmanship was a hallmark of every craftsman who had learned his trade abroad. In any craft, the gulf separating the journeyman from the laborer and the apprentices was unbridgeable. During the great mansion-building boom before the Great War it was still possible to catch a glimpse of an authentic English bricklayer at work. He would be standing at his wall wearing a business suit and bowler hat, with a white shirt and tie and with his shoes neatly shined. The mark of his craft was the machine-like way he laid his bricks. He never varied a centimetre in the depth of his mortar, never splattered or wasted an ounce of material, never laid a single brick a fraction of an inch out of line. An endangered species even then, it is true, but he still existed.

The emphasis on quality in the construction industry was universal. When doubt existed concerning the ability of local artisans to do a job, the owners never hesitated to send away for those who could do it. When Sir James Lougheed was building his mansion in Calgary, he sent clear to Italy for marble-setters to place the marble around the eight fireplaces with which the 26-room home was equipped.

Preoccupation with quality of workmanship came naturally to the thousands of British immigrants who had been immersed for five years in the old-country apprenticeship system. It was a system that laid great stress on doing things over and over and over until perfection was achieved. It was a regimen which was watered down considerably when apprentice training became established in western Canada. Where a British apprentice might have been forced to spend an hour applying three grades of sandpaper to a single piece of wood, Canadian apprentices tended to get a lot more lifting and carrying to do. None the less, if an English carpenter became a public school manual-training instructor he reverted to type with a vengeance. Thus, when F. G. Tipping taught carpentry at the Earl Grey School in Winnipeg, his pupils had to pass a three-pronged exam in wood-sawing. They were handed three boards to be cut along a marked length. On the first cut the pencil mark had to be removed. On the second board the mark had to be left on the off-cut. On the third the pencil mark was left on the measured board.

Carpenters turned out by the system that produced Tipping were considered competent only if they could do every job on a house where wood was required, for no distinction was drawn between rough and finished carpentry or cabinetmaking. The meticulous expertise of the tradesmen was reflected everywhere in the mansions, from the soundness of the stone basements to the straightness of the walls, the perfect laying of the hardwood floors, the hanging of the doors, and the finishing of the underside of the shelving in the butler's pantry.

The competition of the new rich to outdo each other in the size and magnificence of their mansion-building reached its peak in 1912-14. In each prairie city one house so outshone all others that it put an end to the competition. From then on, the upwardly mobile were satisfied to keep their desires within reasonable limits. In Winnipeg, the mansion to end all mansions was built by A. R. Davidson, a real-estate millionaire, not on Wellington Crescent but a block south, on Ruskin Row, where he had half a city block on which to build. The Davidson mansion contained thirty-seven rooms and took two years to complete. It was 100 feet wide and 50 feet deep over all, and with its Tyndall-limestone-and-brick exterior, it was as stately as any of the stately homes of England after which it was fashioned. Its grounds and flower beds would have drawn an approving nod from a critical-eyed English gardener.

The Davidson house was completed in 1913 at a cost of $100,000, a maharajah's ransom in the days when $2,500 would buy a two-storey family home in a less affluent neighborhood. The price of the Davidson place included a 42' × 36' stone garage, with a four-room apartment for the servants on the second floor, and a 28' × 20' stable. The garage boasted the only automobile turntable in western Canada. Davidson's chauffeur could drive the car into the garage and onto the turntable, give it a 180-degree turn, and the car was headed outward in case any of the Davidsons wished to go for a drive. In that event, they could do so without venturing outside if the weather was unfriendly. A 30-foot concrete tunnel, seven feet high, connected the house with the garage.

The residence was unique in one other feature. It contained the only passenger elevator in a house in western Canada. It ran from the wine cellar in the basement to the third floor. The magnificence of the finish of the Davidson house was unequalled. The flooring on the first floor was quarter-cut oak, polished to mirror smoothness. The trim was solid walnut, and the main rooms were panelled in walnut to a height of seven feet, with three feet of plastered wall above. The ceilings were either beamed with walnut or finished with highly decorative plaster cornices. The main staircase had walnut treads and risers and walnut-panelled walls extending to the second floor. The servants' stairway in the rear was finished in oak and maple. A walnut staircase led to a basement dance hall which could accommodate 100 guests and, on a dais, an eight-piece orchestra. There was a billiard room on the third floor. The house contained seven bathrooms, all finished in imported tile, and nine fireplaces with marble and walnut facing.

Housing the servants over the carriage house or garage was common practice where lots were large enough to accommodate extra buildings. Most of them were. The Coste house in Calgary, built by Eugene Coste in 1914, matched the Davidson house in cost, size, outbuildings, and lawns, but not in the magnificence of its interior finish. But it had its points—oak and mahogany wall panelling, and an open stairway that would have carried an infantry charge. It completely dominated the Mount Royal hill, dwarfing and turning its back upon the mini-mansions being built on the slopes below it.

In Alberta, the William J. Magrath house in Edmonton was in a class by itself for sheer elegance of appearance and interior finishing, even though it contained only fourteen rooms. Magrath was a real-estate promoter who struck it rich and poured a soupçon of his wealth, $35,000-worth, into a mansion on the eastern outskirts of Edmonton.* From his front verandah Magrath's view took in the South Saskatchewan River and an unbroken landscape to the horizon. Built in Renaissance style, its verandah ran the full width of the house, with Ionic porticoes at each end and Ionic columns at the front, reaching upward to a balustraded balcony. The massive wood trim of the eaves matched the porticoes and it all glistened white in the sunlight. Inside, the Magrath house was a masterpiece of the carpentering and plastering arts. The ceilings of the main rooms were replete with friezes and cornices and decorative gewgaws. The walls were covered in part with polished oak panelling and in part with rose-patterned silk. In the reception room the rose pattern was repeated in three-dimensional wall boarders, and on the ceiling pink-skinned cherubs floated in a misty sky. The rooms on the second floor were all master-bedroom size, while the third floor contained a billiard room and ballroom.

Edmonton had several houses larger than Magrath's, but none as fancy. The Hon. C. W. Cross, the first Alberta attorney general, built a huge place on Stoney Plain Road that dominated the banks of the Saskatchewan on the west side of the city. The Pearce family erected three tudor mansions on 96th Street, and

---

* Latter-day writers have put original costs of the mansions at upward of $200,000. The assessment records of the City of Winnipeg list the permit for the Davidson house at $100,000. Promotional material published in Edmonton in 1914 contains $30,000 and $35,000 estimates of cost of Edmonton mansions. Carpenters' wages at the time were 50 cents an hour and everything else was in proportion.

Harry Shaw's mansion featured decorative plaster inspired by the mansions of the Renaissance, and wall murals painted by a Russian artist imported from New York for the job.

Clustering around the great houses in each city were the 12-, 14-, and 16-room mini-mansions of the rich brokers, lawyers, and entrepreneurs. Until Coste came along, Calgarians had three houses of almost equal size that they could ogle admiringly. The Pat Burns home, built in 1891-3, was centred in a city block at Fourth Street and Twelfth Avenue, though it contained only fourteen rooms. It measured 90' × 44' and was finished in brick and stone. A block to the west and south was the Lougheed home, built in 1900, with its magnificent sunken gardens, massive carriage house, and conservatory. Built fifteen years later, the William Roper Hull house on Sixth Street also boasted a superb garden covering half a city block, a carriage house, and a conservatory. During the summer, there was a charity garden party in the neighborhood almost every week. When the Prince of Wales toured the Empire in 1919, he was guest of honour at a reception for 100 guests in the Lougheed garden, while several thousand uninvited Calgarians jammed the surrounding streets watching the upper-crust tea-drinkers and, as the newspapers noted, cheering the Prince whenever he came within hailing distance.

In Winnipeg there were scores of houses within walking distance of the Davidson home which, though smaller in size, could almost challenge it in craftsmanship, décor, and sheer elegance. There was Sir Daniel MacMillan's mansion on Wellington Crescent, with its crystal chandeliers, its hall furniture from India, and its great crimson-and-cream Khorbistan carpet imported in 1910 at a cost of $35,000. There was the Bawlf place, and the Stewart place across from Ashdown's. At the end of Wellington Crescent, on Roslyn Road, there were a dozen secluded residences of the rich and the powerful, furnished to match the expensiveness of the taste that their owners had acquired en route to financial eminence. Heintzman grand pianos were as common as ivory-inlaid commodes and rosewood-and-mahogany writing desks.

William Magrath encouraged his wife's shopping tours of Europe, from which she always returned with period pieces for their Edmonton home. On one occasion she retrieved a hammered-brass-and-porcelain fireplace front from a British museum to replace the one already in place. W. R. Hull's home in Calgary tended toward the oriental, and he prized a figured-brass dinner gong which was suspended between two carved ivory elephant tusks. On the occasion of the visit of the Duke and Duchess of Connaught to Calgary, Sir James Lougheed transformed a wing of his mansion into a royal suite, with furniture imported from England for the occasion.

Whether in Calgary, Edmonton, or Winnipeg, the grand homes of the prairies were for show as well as for habitation, and they were on show continually during the endless rounds of entertaining that marked the 1920s. The pace was the most frantic in Winnipeg because the bulk of the wealth of the west was concentrated there. For every rich resident Calgary could boast, Winnipeg had at least five, and the proportion for Edmonton was ten to one. In Calgary the super-social set numbered about twenty. In Winnipeg there were half a dozen such circles on intermixing levels of affluence. This meant that in Winnipeg just about everybody in the Assiniboine River enclave entertained at dinner at least twice a week, and was probably entertained once or twice in turn. A dining room that seated less than twenty was less than adequate, and having 100 guests in for tea was commonplace.

In all the going and coming there was none of the informality of dress that grew out of the Great Depression and the Second World War. Dinner parties at which white ties and tails were not *de rigueur* called at least for tuxedos, as dinner jackets were called. William Klass, owner of the Fort Rouge Cleaners on Osborne Street, grew to affluence on the trade that he developed laundering the formal clothing of the residents of Roslyn Road, Wellington Crescent, and Armstrong's Point. Not too many homes had butlers, but the keeping of several servants was quite common. By the mid-20s, having a Chinese as combination cook and houseboy was not unknown, nor was the practice of "dressing for dinner", even when the family was dining alone.

No social affair, however modest, was ever complete unless a guest list was supplied to the newspapers. The lists were printed in full even if there was a foul-up in the mailing of invitations and nobody came. At the posher affairs the society editors were invited to attend so they could write well-adjectived descriptions of the gowns of the ladies.

It was more than fitting that the 1920s should have been ushered in with a formal ball in Winnipeg to open the newly finished, scandal-ridden Legislative Building on February 20, 1920. Sir J. A. M. Aikins, the Lieutenant-Governor, held the reception, ball, and dinner for 1,100 invited guests. It took three and a half columns of solidly set newspaper type to encompass that guest list. The era itself, as well as the decade, ended on a similar note on December 30, 1929. Then Mrs. H. M. Tucker, wife of the resident grand vizier of the T. Eaton Company, took over the Colonial Ballroom of the Royal Alexandra Hotel and invited 100 guests to a New Year's Eve dinner and dance in honor of her son.

During the height of the winter season the railway hotels in Calgary, Edmonton, Regina, and Winnipeg were hosts to weekly supper-dances. None ever reached the heights of prestige and popularity achieved by the Royal Alexandra. When the demand arose, it could cater to five king-sized private supper-dances at once, and during the winter its vice-regal suite was booked well in advance by the prestige pyramid climbers who were prepared to pick up a $400 tab for dinner for a score of friends served in regal surroundings.

The culinary needs of Winnipeg's upper class were supplied mainly by two Osborne Street merchants, who prospered by providing sustenance for cultivated tastes. Fred Marples was one of a half-dozen brothers who operated butcher shops around Winnipeg, but he catered only to the carriage trade. William Buchanan was grocer by appointment to everybody who was anybody. His Hardy and Buchanan store on Osborne was stocked with out-of-season fruits and vegetables, condiments, and delicacies from all over the world. The grand ladies of the mansions seldom gave an important dinner party without personal consultation with Buchanan. With their cooks in tow, they would descend on his store to talk over menu-planning, to be sure they would not be serving on Tuesday what another hostess had served to the same guests on Monday.

Buchanan might well have concluded that his ladies went out to dinner primarily to make mental notes of the food being served. If they ate something out of the ordinary they would be sure to have it on their own grocery lists for their next dinner party. Conversely, if Buchanan had shipments due in midwinter from his California suppliers, his customers would be alerted so that they could work the delicacies into their menus.

Buchanan did so well as provisioner of the mansions that he opened a second store on Stafford Street to serve the second- and third-flighters. He not only prospered but, like most grocers and butchers who were masters of their business, enjoyed his work to the utmost. There were times, however, when it had its drawbacks. A cook who had failed to put some yeast on her grocery order would hardly hesitate before calling Buchanan at home, long after store closing hours, to get him to rout out one of his clerks to make the delivery. One of his customers became something of a nuisance by calling after hours to have him deliver bottles of vanilla. That ended when her husband telephoned to say that his wife was using vanilla extract as a substitute for Scotch when she was on a binge and ran out of supplies.

In Calgary and Edmonton the mansion trade went largely to the superb grocery departments of the Hudson's Bay Company. The spicy aroma of the grocery departments permeated both stores, and batteries of clerks were kept at order desks taking down orders over the telephone for delivery the following day. All stores provided customers with free delivery service and the individual stores, such as Fairley Brothers in Calgary and Buchanan's in Winnipeg, even had twice-a-day deliveries to ensure same-day service on orders.

Aside from the endless rounds of entertaining and being entertained, the mansion set took their fun where they found it. The women involved themselves in private charities and church work. The men had their clubs—the Manitoba and the Carlton in Winnipeg, the Assiniboine in Regina, the Ranchman's (or as it was earlier called, the Ranchers) in Calgary, and the Edmonton Club in the Alberta capital. All were substantial red-brick structures with billiard rooms, card rooms, lounges, and locker rooms in which members could store their own personal bottles of whisky during the Prohibition era.

The long summer evenings of the prairies lent themselves to all manner of outdoor activity, from a brisk ride at the hunt club to a chukker or two of polo, or, most of all, a round of golf after work. Winnipeg, probably because it was larger, and had a much larger proportion of self-employed merchants, grain brokers, stock brokers, and real-estate brokers in its population, boasted more golf clubs than all the other prairie cities combined. The prestige club was the St. Charles, but there were three other private clubs at Bird's Hill, and the Winnipeg Hunt Club was in the process of being converted into the Southwood Golf Club, while another brand-new club was under construction at Niakwa.

The owning and showing of blooded equine stock had about run its course by the First World War. The horse-show amphitheatre on Whitehall Avenue in Winnipeg was converted into a hockey rink. After its barns were destroyed by fire, the outdoor exercise ring was made into a baseball diamond. In Calgary, the horse was still king, however, and its horse shows attracted entries from across the country. The polo grounds on the south of town were the site of weekly matches, and John Hazza, a theatrical tycoon, established the Rocky Mountain Polo Pony Ranch to supply well-trained riding stock to those who could afford to play the game.

Judging by a reading of the newspapers of the time, going to funerals seemed to be a favorite pastime. This was particularly the case in Winnipeg, probably because it was settled so much earlier and had a much older population. In the 1920s its successful pioneers were dying off at a rapid rate. Funeral procedures made it possible to establish quickly the financial standing or professional status — usually the same thing — of the deceased. The gauge was the column inches of newspaper space devoted to his obituary and the description of his funeral. The standard treatment of a mansion dweller, in all the prairie cities, fell roughly into the following pattern:

If he were big rich, he would merit a newspaper deathwatch and his condition would be reported at intervals. Meanwhile, the newspapers would dust off and update the obituaries they had on file and prepare for the demise. When it came, the deceased would get his picture on the front page—a two-column cut if he were of particular financial eminence, one column if not. A standard list of business associates and local notables would be called upon to express their tributes to the sterling character of the deceased — but only if he were among the financially elite. The tributes could run to a column or so. On the day of the burial it was usual to have two services, with two or three officiating ministers. One would do the service in the home, attended by the immediate family and fifty or sixty close friends and business associates. A second clergyman, assisted by the first, would conduct the church service, which was of course open to everybody. A third clergyman — an archbishop if the deceased was really pre-eminent — would officiate at the graveside. The history of the life of the departed was reproduced in great detail upon his passing, and the highlights were summarized again at the time of his burial. The funeral orations of the reverend clergy were reported *in extenso,* along with the names of all the prominent people at the funeral.

When Sir Augustus Nanton died in Toronto in 1924, his tributes, biography, and funeral story spread over more than five columns. This exceeded the space given to James Ashdown a couple of weeks before, though Ashdown had been a community leader, mayor, financial rescuer of the city's sinking fund, and a generous contributor to local charities during his lifetime. He had also left $380,000 to charities out of an estate of $1,639,000. Nanton, however, was richer, had a knighthood, and only recently had become president of the Dominion Bank, while Ashdown was only a hardware merchant.

Though titles for Canadians would soon be forbidden, there is little doubt that they were highly prized by the mansion set and even respected by the general public. Sir James Lougheed, a senator and a knight, got twice as much space in the Calgary newspapers as William Roper Hull, his neighbor and fellow tycoon. Hull left his entire estate, on the death of his wife, to the orphans of Calgary, and by the time his will was given final probate its worth had risen from under $2,000,000 to more than $6,000,000.

There was an exception to all this. The exception was women. Women of eminence were noted with a small picture and a short obituary—even such women as Mrs. W. F. Alloway of Winnipeg. She, with her husband, had established the Winnipeg Foundation with a couple of $100,000 "seed" gifts. The Foundation was western Canada's first charitable trust, with interest earnings to be used to finance charities that nobody else was concerned about. Over the years it would attract many other large bequests and ultimately would become one of the largest funds of its kind in the country. On her death Mrs. Alloway left her entire estate of $800,000 to the Foundation. She got her picture on the front pages and an obituary notice somewhat larger than that of Ginger Snooks, an eminent city scavenging contractor.

Going to funerals was an accepted custom of the times, on the part of all classes, and an automatic excuse for an afternoon off. When a super-tycoon was buried there wasn't a church anywhere big enough to accommodate everybody who turned out for the burial. Funeral processions could stretch for blocks, and a practice developed of touring the processions past the deceased's place of business so that the skeleton staff on duty could pay its respects to the departed millionaire. As a procession passed along the streets en route to the cemetery, it was considered bad form for pedestrians not to snap to attention and remove their hats when the hearse hove in sight.

Communities short on millionaires, such as Saskatoon and Regina, did their best with what they had. Thus, in Saskatoon, when the owner of the city's largest hardware emporium died, the *Star* and the *Phoenix* gave him a high-status send-off. Not having too much to report on him, they fleshed out the accounts of the funeral service with a half-column of names of all the people who sent flowers and a description of the flowers.

During the late 1960s it was said of the farming population of the prairies that they "lived poor and died rich". The quotation grew out of the fact that, for most of their lives, the farmers did without many of the comforts taken for granted in the cities. These creature comforts came to the farmer of the west late in life. So did a measure of prosperity. Yet, because of the steady increase in value of farmland as a result of better times and inflation, farmers were able to sell out in the late 1960s and retire with more money than they had ever seen before.

It could well have been said of many of the mansion-dwellers of the 1920s that the reverse was true—they "lived rich and died poor". Certainly, many of the Grain Exchange and stock brokers who bulked so large in the Crescentwoods and the Mount Royals and the Highlands in the 1920s lived well up to their incomes, and far above a level which their net worth would have justified. The Ashdowns, Alloways, Allans, Robinsons, Lougheeds, Hulls, Burnses, Magraths, Munsons, Endertons, Gardiners, Rileys, Ryans, McMeans, and the others built the kind of mansions they could afford out of the capital surplus they had built up. As their store of wealth grew they moved into larger and grander homes. Many of the latecomers to the feast were too impatient to do likewise. As quickly as their incomes covered mortgage payments and entertainment costs, they too indulged their taste for high living and moved in as close as they could get to the authentic rich.

When the crash came in 1929, and incomes dropped sharply along with capital assets, they went down like tenpins. Grocery and other bills went unpaid as long as credit was obtainable. As William Buchanan and his fellow merchants tried to collect their bills, they were put off with endlessly replayed promises and sad stories which, however, rang with authenticity. One former high-living woman customer collapsed in tears at Buchanan's demands for payment, and offered to strip the rings from her fingers and give them to him. He refused the offer, but the rings eventually went anyway. One delinquent customer remembered his indebtedness to Buchanan in his will, leaving him an antique chair in payment of his account.

The collapse of the real-estate boom in 1913 was already taking its toll by 1925. William Davidson was forced to sell his Winnipeg showplace in 1924. William Magrath of Edmonton was dead by 1921, although his family stayed in the house until it was lost to a sheriff's seizure of home and furnishings at the onset of the Depression. A similar fate overtook B. A. Holgate, Magrath's partner, who had built an only slightly less impressive mansion 100 yards to the east. Holgate went broke soon after Magrath's death, and his home reverted to Edmonton for taxes and remained empty for years. Harry Shaw, who was Edmonton's largest pre-war employer, was broke by the middle of the decade, and his home also went to the city for taxes.

Eugene Coste, who was demonstrably smarter than anybody else, sold out all his Calgary interests before the 1929 crash and moved with his family to Montreal. He put his mansion up for sale but never got a nibble until a promoter came along with a proposal to turn it into an apartment house. The city refused to permit that and after dunning Coste for several years for payment of his taxes, took possession of the house for $7,000 in back taxes. For a full decade it looked as if Coste had got the best of the deal, for the house remained vacant until 1940. After the death of Senator Lougheed's widow the Lougheed mansion was transferred to the Red Cross. The Pat Burns mansion was donated to the government as a military hospital, and it — ingraciously—named the hospital after an obscure colonel of an earlier time. Many of the other mansions were converted into apartments when maintaining them became too expensive even for wealthy widows to afford.

With the onset of the dry years in 1928, the earth under the foundations of many of the most beautiful Winnipeg mansions began to dry out. The shrinkage caused the foundations to disintegrate, and the interiors cracked so badly that the wreckers were called in and the houses were pulled down. The casualty list of the homes almost matched that of the owners who fell on hard times. As the pre-Great War crop of millionaires died out, the 1920s failed to replace them. Without a steady production of millionaires, mansion building, even on a modest scale, was a spent force. With the spending of that force the age of elegance was over on the prairies.

5. A Golden Age for Games

Someone, probably Grantland Rice, once called the 1920s the Golden Age of Sport. It was certainly that on the prairies of western Canada, though in a context different from the one Rice had in mind. He was thinking in terms of the great sports heroes who emerged to beguile the public and make the sports pages the most exciting, the most colorfully written, in the newspapers. Whether the colorfulness of the sports heroes revolutionized sports reporting, or whether the new trend in sports writing created colorful sports heroes, was arguable either way.

Every sport developed its headline-makers. Boxing had a dozen of them, headed by Jack Dempsey, Gene Tunney, Mickey Walker, and Luis Angel Firpo. Walter Hagen, Bobby Jones, and Gene Sarazen were turning the game of golf into a spectator sport. Baseball's "Black Sox" scandal was quickly driven from the public mind by the hysterically chronicled exploits of Babe Ruth, Hack Wilson, Rogers Hornsby, and Grover Cleveland Alexander. Big Bill Tilden and Rene LaCoste collided in great tennis duels. Red Grange and Knute Rockne were making football history. Howie Morenz, Frank Nighbor, and Nels Stewart made hockey headlines. The miscellany of sports heroes included Man O'War and Reigh Count; Earle Sande and Clarence Kummer; Paavo Nurmi, Jose Capablanca, Willie Hoppe, Peter dePaolo, and Sir Thomas Lipton. That the list is predominantly American is an indication only that the United States was going hog-wild over sports, and that Canadians were paying more and more attention to everything that was going on in the United States.

Frederick Lewis Allen called the 1920s the Ballyhoo Years, and no group contributed more to the ballyhoo than the sports writers with their endless coining of nicknames, including nicknames for nicknames. Thus, George Herman Ruth became "Babe" Ruth before he was re-christened "The Bambino" and "The Sultan of Swat". Nobody ever called "Red" Grange, Harold, when they could call him "The Galloping Ghost". Firpo was "The Wild Bull of the Pampas", Mickey Walker was "The Toy Bulldog", Jack Dempsey was the "Manassa Mauler", Jimmy McLarnin was "Baby Face".

Canadians followed the careers of all of them as avidly as did Americans, not only through the sports pages, but also by way of that other medium then being launched on its own Golden Age —radio, truly the phenomenon of the 1920s. Sports lent itself to radio coverage, and radio was peculiarly adaptable to sports. Even if prairie Canadians had not become inordinately preoccupied with sports in the 1920s, their addiction to radio listening would have made them aware of the sports revolution in the United States.

As it was, the playing of games developed into a prairie passion after the Great War. Here the emphasis was not so much on games as spectator sports as it was on participation. There were opportunities to participate in every game yet devised by man, and everybody joined in the fun, beginning with the elementary grades in public schools. In Calgary physical training had a prominent place in the curriculum. The course included calisthenics, running, jumping, and skipping. At the close of each school year the city schools competed in a physical fitness tournament, at which highly prized shields were awarded to the winning schools.

Track and field sports were part of the high school programs everywhere, and these activities were pursued well into adulthood by both sexes. In Winnipeg the T. Eaton Company established its own athletic facilities for its staff at Sargent Park. The North End Athletic Club, which was devoted mainly to track and field, occasionally produced athletes of Olympic quality. Two of its sprinters, Cyril Coaffee and Laurie Armstrong, represented Canada in the 1924 Olympic Games and made it into the semi-finals.

Athletics, moreover, played an important role in the youth activities of city churches. The Anglicans had their Boy Scouts, while the United Church sponsored the Trail Rangers and the Tuxis Boys. Indoor baseball diamonds and basketball courts were laid out in church basements and in Roman Catholic parish halls. There were church lawn-bowling leagues and tennis leagues, and in Calgary and Edmonton there were church teams in the city cricket leagues.

There were church picnics, fraternal picnics, service club picnics, and just plain picnics, every week of the prairie summer. Some of them, like those of the civic employees in Calgary and the caterers in Winnipeg, attracted an attendance of several thousand. A regular feature of every picnic was an all-afternoon program of track and field events. The programs naturally were well sprinkled with the fun events — fat ladies' races, three-legged races, wheelbarrow races — but many picnics offered handsome prizes for real athletic contests. Boys and girls who excelled in high school competition turned up at picnics to challenge adult sprinters, and frequently encountered just such people as Coaffee and Armstrong.

For the country people, the picnic equivalent was the town fair. Every town in the west held a summer fair of some sort in July or August. They too had their athletic contests, usually topped by a baseball game between the local all-stars and those of an adjacent town, on which substantial bets were frequently laid. The country fairs, however, were mainly for the showing off of livestock and the housewifely arts. So, in fact, were the big city fairs in Brandon, Regina, Edmonton, and Calgary. Here the afternoons were enlivened by horse races and auto racing and the rides and games of the travelling carnivals. In southern Alberta and southwestern Saskatchewan rodeo contests replaced the races. The Calgary Exhibition in 1923 added bronc riding, calf roping, and bull riding to its list of attractions and became the Calgary Exhibition, Stampede, and Buffalo Barbecue. Like the other urban fairs, however, it continued to function primarily as a showcase for field and animal husbandry and farm-based handicrafts. The use of fairground facilities for fun and games was of little consequence.

The popularity of games varied with the region. Curling, for example, owing to climatic variations, was more popular in Manitoba and Saskatchewan than in southern Alberta. The former froze solidly in November and stayed frozen until March. Southern Alberta was occasionally beset with chinooks which, in the days before artificial ice-making, turned skating rinks and curling rinks into swimming pools. As early as 1921 the Winnipeg bonspiel was attracting 250 entries, with 100 of the rinks coming from rural Manitoba and Saskatchewan.

Though golf was confined mainly to Winnipeg, Edmonton, and Calgary, it was by far the most popular individually played outdoor urban game. Winnipeg had one civic golf course in operation and was building another, and there were four other public courses on which the game could be played for 50 cents a round, with a set of $8.95 golf clubs. In 1921 the Winnipeg municipal course reported that 31,000 rounds of golf had been played. Tennis, played everywhere on clay courts, also ranked high, and play was climaxed each year by week-long provincial championships for both men and women.

It may be playing fast and loose with etymological precision to include dancing under the heading of sport. But when the young men and women of the prairies paired off in the 1920s, dancing outstripped every sporting activity in popularity. Dances in the rural schoolhouses were weekly events throughout the winter—weather permitting. Winnipeg had four large public dance halls which filled to capacity on Friday and Saturday nights. Throughout the summer the railways ran nightly excursions to their Lake Winnipeg beach resorts, where dance halls that could accommodate 500 couples provided music for every taste, from traditional waltzes and fox-trots to the Charleston and the Black Bottom.

The most elegant dance hall anywhere in the west was in Moose Jaw, where Calvin and Trudy Temple built the Temple

Gardens in 1921 and operated it for thirty years. It was to the Temple Gardens that Mart Kenney repaired when the Waterton Lakes Lodge closed for the season, and it was there that he built the reputation that made him Canada's most popular musician in the 1930s. With its California-Moorish façade, Temple Gardens was the most distinctive building in all Saskatchewan, and it doubled as a convention centre for politicians and the lodge brethren.

At the other end of the scale from the Temple Gardens was the Belgian Club in St. Boniface. Liquor law enforcement in St. Boniface throughout the decade was, at best, notoriously casual. The Belgian Club was one of the very few dance halls that tolerated open drinking on the premises. In those days it was the sort of place that well-brought-up Winnipeggers visited only on a dare, and never alone. By 10 o'clock the dancers were enthusiastically demonstrating that the large sign above the orchestra was there for purposes of record only, in case the police wandered in. It read "No Rough Dancing Allowed". What went on at the Belgian Club might not have been sport, under a strict definition of the word, but it was certainly a lot more physically demanding, and hence more "athletic", than a lawn bowling set of mixed doubles, or a round of golf.

Monseigneur Jubinville of St. Boniface Cathedral lashed out at the dancers in an angry sermon on December 28, 1925. He deplored the spectacle of "half dressed girls writhing around like snakes" to the "brutal" music of jazz bands. He called their escorts "five cents sports who came to mass smelling of booze, took holy communion and rushed out after another bottle."

The dominance of the British influence in western Canada, despite the preponderance of immigrants from the United States, is seen quite clearly in the games people played. There were flourishing cricket leagues in all the cities, particularly in Winnipeg, Edmonton, and Calgary, each of which had 8-team senior leagues, plus junior leagues for teen-aged boys. Lawn bowling, directly descended from the game Sir Francis Drake refused to interrupt in order to drive off the Spanish Armada, had hundreds of devotees in all the prairie cities. As for the other kind of bowling, Calgary and Edmonton had several busy alleys, there were alleys in Regina and Lethbridge, and Winnipeg, as befitting its size, had half a dozen on which it staged international tournaments.

As for other indoor sports, the west played snooker and English billiards rather than American rotation pool and three-cushion, or balkline, billiards. The Manitoba Billiard Association boasted a membership of 10,000 in 1921, and claimed that 3,000 games of billiards were played in Winnipeg daily. Winnipeg was the only western city with billiard and snooker leagues playing on an organized basis. Within a ten-block radius of Portage Avenue and Main Street, there were a score of billiard rooms, with more than 200 tables. On Donald Street one emporium alone had fifty-eight. Calgary boasted a dozen rooms within a five-minute walk of the Palliser Hotel; Edmonton had as many in and around Jasper Avenue and on Whyte Avenue.

Billiard rooms and bowling alleys, particularly in Manitoba, had to compete in the winter with curling rinks and skating rinks, and even with the wind-driven snow. One of the most popular outdoor winter sports in Manitoba and Saskatchewan was snow-shoeing. There were snowshoe clubs in all the cities and larger towns. There, members of both sexes donned colorful habitant-type greatcoats and tramped for miles along frozen rivers and through parks, regardless of 30-below temperatures. Pleasure skating took over the rinks on evenings when there were no hockey games or speed-skating races. There were hockey teams for every age group up to Allan Cup level, and commercial leagues for hundreds of players who could not make it with other teams.

British rugby had to struggle to survive, but soccer was played everywhere at all seasons, by all ages, and with a high order of skills that enabled prairie teams to lose respectably to English and Scottish teams that made regular cross-country tours. It was by far the most popular participation sport of the public schools, and even the churches had soccer leagues for their Sunday-schoolers. Soccer was not only the prime favorite of the British immigrants, it was the only athletic competition in which recently arrived immigrants from Europe could join with any familiarity.

Competing with soccer for playing room on the athletic fields was the national game of the United States, though baseball never, in any of the cities, rivalled soccer in terms of teams or numbers of active players. In the rural areas, however, where settlers from the United States predominated, baseball was the outstanding favorite. All summer long there was baseball every Saturday at some convenient location. Not only did the town teams challenge each other, they played regular circuits, and the larger towns played host to touring American teams.

Two of the blacklisted Chicago White Sox players, Happy Felsch and Swede Risburg, who sold out the 1919 World Series of baseball to the gamblers, played for Lee Dillage's Minot, North Dakota, team which annually toured the larger towns of southern Saskatchewan. Dillage came to town with his ball club like a maharajah on a royal tour. He was the proud owner of a Duesenberg touring car and it led his motor cavalcade through the town to the baseball grounds, with his outlawed stars ensconced in the back seat. As time passed, and the lustre of the stars dimmed, Dillage shunted them into the secondary vehicles. In their place he parked several of his comeliest doxies from the brothels of Minot, who dropped off at the local hotel and set up as a subsidiary attraction to the baseball game.

Whether Dillage ever paraded his Duesenberg full of prostitutes as far west as Shaunavon, Saskatchewan, is doubtful, given the rudimentary nature of the province's roads. But word of his advertising scheme certainly penetrated the area, for Lola Surtees, who ran the biggest whorehouse south of Moose Jaw, on First Avenue west of Main Street in Shaunavon, adopted his idea as her own. Every Saturday afternoon during the summer months she had the owner of the local taxicab — a Studebaker touring car — call at her brothel. She loaded her staff, dressed in their Sunday best, into the taxi and toured the shopping streets of the town, waving gaily to the farmers and ranchers who were there on their weekly visits. Opinion in Shaunavon divided sharply on the efficacy of Lola's publicity campaign. There were those who allowed that southern Saskatchewan womenfolk had their suspicions so aroused that they took countermeasures to discourage patronage of Lola's institution.

Competing with the Dillage baseballers were two other touring American teams which attracted crowds wherever they went across western Canada. The zaniest was the House of David team of long-bearded semi-pros. The House of David was an off-beat religious order in St. Joseph, Michigan, which was periodically exposed in the more lurid weekly newspaper supplements of the United States.

The House of David was headed by King Ben Parnell, an aging patriarch of a polygamous cult which seemed to have borrowed its tenets from the Mormons, Hutterites, Amish, and Old Testament Israelites. King Ben was alleged to have married a number of widows, who brought their wealth to his management and were content to share him with forty or fifty younger adoptees. The House of David baseball team began as a missionary gimmick to attract attention to the Michigan backwoods cult. Soon there were House of David teams all over the place, though they took care to stay out of each other's way. They survived on their baseballing skills — which were considerable — long after the Michigan authorities put King Ben out of business.

Most skilful of all the touring players were the Negro teams, whose members could well have been major-leaguers had not the color bar been raised against them. The great Satchel Paige once toured the Canadian prairies with Gilkerson's Colored Giants and the Kansas City Monarchs. Black teams always won more games than they lost, even when the locals had been strengthened by imported professional pitchers. Black baseball was sold as much as entertainment as baseball. The teams always carried a coterie of players whose clowning antics — catching pop flies in hip pockets, sliding head first into second base on home runs over the fence, throwing two balls instead of one from the pitcher's mound — were great sources of amusement. The ultimate in zany promotions was achieved as the era ebbed, when a

team of falsely bearded Negroes turned up in Manitoba billed as
— what else — the Colored House of David.

All the city newspapers carried daily reports of big-league
baseball, and when the World Series came around they rigged
up mechanical contraptions on which the play-by-play of the
games could be simulated. These devices, coupled with pasted-
up bulletin service on election nights, made the newspapers the
gathering-point during all big events. The biggest sporting attraction of the decade, bigger for concentrated attention than
the Allan Cup or the Memorial Cup, was Jack Dempsey, who
never got within 200 miles of any major prairie city.

The Dempsey era began with the fiasco at Shelby, Montana, in
June and July of 1923. Shelby was a divisional point on the Great
Northern Railway whose population of 5,000 developed sudden
delusions of grandeur from the discovery of oil in the vicinity.
James Johnson, the president of a local bank, and his rancher
cronies decided that what Shelby needed to put it on the map was
a spectacular, continent-wide attention grabber. They chose the
promotion of a world championship prize fight as the vehicle. In
the spring of 1923 they negotiated a deal with Jack Dempsey to
defend his title against a not-too-distinguished opponent named
Tommy Gibbons for a guarantee of $300,000, payable in three
instalments before the fight.

After sealing the deal with Dempsey and his manager, the
promoters set the date for the fight for the fourth of July and
went home to complete the arrangements. Things started to go
awry from the start. One of their promotional ideas was to get
the railways to run excursions into Shelby and include the price
of a $25 seat in the Pullman fare. In the beginning not even the
railways would take the small-town promoters seriously. For one
thing, it would take 1,000 Pullman cars to move the estimated
crowd to Shelby, and there were not that many cars available in
the whole United States. Even if there had been, the railway
sidings in Shelby could accommodate barely a tenth that
number.

The Shelby promoters had no trouble getting the first

$100,000 together. Banker Johnson simply dipped into his till for it. The second $100,000, however, was anticipated from ticket sales through the railways. When nobody outside the Shelby area bought tickets, the promoters missed their deadline for the second instalment, which created more uncertainty than ever. In the end a couple of bankers came into the promotion and put up the money. Lumber for a 35,000-seat stadium was hauled in, and the promoters once again sat back to await the stampede for tickets.

The only ticket rush that developed was caused by the sports editors of Canadian prairie newspapers, who flooded Shelby with requests for press passes for their reporters to cover the fight. It was the only truly international sporting event that had ever been held within a thousand miles of them, and they were all eager to participate to the utmost. Certainly, in late June of 1923, Canadians were a lot more excited about the madcap promoters of Shelby than were their American counterparts. Cash customers, however, continued to ignore the whole business, and the situation was not helped by Dempsey's manager who, with $200,000 in his pocket, declaimed that there would be no fight until he had the other $100,000 in his hands.

The on-again, off-again nature of the promotion put the kibosh on the by now sadly curtailed plan to move in thousands by railway. It was watered down to overnight excursions from Minneapolis-St. Paul and from Seattle, to arrive before and leave after the fight. On the Saturday before the fight—the fourth of July was on Wednesday that year—word went out that the fight was off, and with it went all the railway excursion arrangements. But by Monday it was on again, and the Canadian reporters were bombarding their offices with stories, while their publishers were preparing to turn the fiasco into home-town spectacles.

Special platforms were erected above the sidewalk in front of all the newspaper offices. Leased telegraph wires were run from Shelby to the newspapers. On the day of the fight a telegrapher typed out the blow-by-blow descriptions as they came over the wire from ringside. The message was then relayed to the platform, where an announcer shouted the words into a huge megaphone hired for the occasion.

The megaphoning of the fight blocked the streets in front of every newspaper in the west. Many, many more fans took in the fight vicariously in front of Canadian prairie newspapers than paid their way in to see it in Shelby. Indeed, listeners at the *Free Press* and *Tribune* buildings in Winnipeg alone outnumbered the 6,000 cash customers at Shelby. The Lethbridge, Saskatoon, Edmonton, Regina, and Calgary papers all had from 2,000 to 4,000 on hand.

For everybody directly involved with the fight — except Dempsey — it was an unmixed disaster. Six thousand people bought tickets but twice as many people beat their way into the fight. Two banks in Shelby closed their doors, though some money was ultimately recovered from the sales of the motion pictures of the fight. Tommy Gibbons took such a beating over the fifteen rounds that his career thereafter was all downhill, and he got a mere pittance for his pains. Shelby itself went into a steady decline that ultimately reduced its population by half.

One Calgarian collected a modest long-term dividend from the ill wind at Shelby. His name was Josh Henshorn and he had gone to Shelby with a load of window cards and other advertisements for the Calgary Stampede. A whole-hearted publicity flack, Henshorn approached the beleaguered promoters with a request for permission to announce the Stampede dates to the fight crowd. The Shelby bankers suddenly realized they had not hired an announcer to introduce the fighters and get their disaster in motion. They made a deal with Henshorn. He could make his Stampede announcement if he would also become the honorary, unpaid official announcer of the fights. Henshorn accepted, and when word of his performance reached Calgary he was launched on a forty-year career as a peripatetic public address system. As "the man who announced the famous Dempsey-Gibbons world heavyweight boxing championship match at Shelby, Montana", Henshorn's services were demanded thereafter wherever a rodeo was held or a horse race run in southern Alberta.

Across western Canada, however, it was a great day for the throngs who played hookey from work to join the crowds at the newspapers. By the third round they were cheering and groaning with each blow and shouting encouragement to their favorites. By the fifth and six round a sharp-eyed observer could spot individual spectators doing shoulder-feints and head-bobs in tune, as it were, with the megaphoned descriptions. The combination of the huge audience and the fight excitement brought out the ham actor in the announcers, and they wrung all the pathos and excitement they could from the words coming out of the typewriters. With the enthusiastic additions and extemporaneous elaborations of the announcers, the fight conjured up in the minds of the beholders at the newspapers was infinitely more exciting than the pedestrian plodding that was taking place under the blazing sun at Shelby.

With their eyes on the main chance — which, of course, was selling papers and beating their competition — the newspapers perpetrated a mildly dirty trick on the captive crowds. As the fight moved into its final rounds they slowed the pace of the blow-by-blow descriptions imperceptibly, so that the fight was over several minutes before the megaphoner reached the judges' decision. By then the presses were revolving inside printing "fight extras" containing a full description of the contest. These hit the streets before the crowd could completely disperse.

The shouts of "Extra!" from the throats of newsboys enlivened the 1920s as they had the pre-war decade. Getting out extra editions to herald the onset of a disaster or the result of an athletic contest was a prestige thing with newspapers, and earned not a sliver of profit. But it added spice to the life of journalism that was lost when radio-listening became so universal that putting out extra editions of newspapers became redundant — the radio listeners had heard all about it long before the extras could hit the street.

Curiously enough, radio did not immediately kill off the interest of the public in assembling in front of newspapers for

broadcasts of far-off sporting events. For a good many years
after the radio was a fixture in most prairie homes, the herd
instinct of the sports fans brought them out in their thousands.
Sitting alone by their radios was a poor substitute for the electric
excitement to be felt by being part of a monster crowd.

The prairie newspapers had an opportunity to improve on
their performance when Jack Dempsey defended his title
against Luis Firpo two months later in the Polo Grounds in New
York. Once again they attracted thousands to their front doors.
The *Manitoba Free Press* claimed 6,000 listeners on Carlton
Street, the *Tribune* had a couple of thousand less on Smith Street,
while the *Calgary Herald* estimated it had 4,000 on First Street
West and Seventh Avenue. This was the less-than-two-round
bout that Grantland Rice called "the most sensational four minutes in the history of boxing". Dempsey knocked Firpo down
four times in the first round, then was himself knocked out of
the ring and pushed back in by the newspaper reporters at the
ringside tables. In the second round Dempsey knocked out his
opponent, after fouling him several times. The Firpo fight made
history because for the first time radio stations took their mi-
crophones to ringside and tried to broadcast from there. It was a
disaster for the broadcasters and the listeners alike, for little, if
anything, could be heard above the noise of the crowd. The
stations that faked it, rebroadcasting the news as it was wired into
the station, got better results, for their listeners could understand what was going on.

Three years later, after marriage to a movie queen and plastic
surgery on his flattened nose, Dempsey returned to the ring in
Philadelphia against Gene Tunney, before the largest sporting
crowd in history — 120,757. He entered the ring a three-to-one
favorite and left it beaten to a pulp by the former marine. This
time the contest was carried by a network of radio stations in the
United States, and many stations in the western cities also subscribed to the service. But still the crowds at the newspapers grew
in both size and volume of cheers as the fight progressed.

The peak was reached in 1927 at the second Dempsey-

Tunney fight in Chicago. By this time the technologists in the radio studios had devised ways of filtering out some of the crowd noise so that the voices of the ringside announcers could be heard. In Calgary and Edmonton the stations combined to bring in the broadcasts direct from Chicago. Yet the real fight fans still made their last great trek to the newspaper offices. In Winnipeg more than 10,000 jammed Carlton Street between Portage Avenue and Ellice Avenue, overflowed down the intersecting back lanes, crowded onto roof-tops along the street, and raised a din that could be heard half a mile away. In Edmonton, 5,000 jammed 101 Street and overflowed onto Memorial Boulevard. So excited did the *Journal* become that it put out two separate extra editions on the fight. During the Dempsey-Tunney fights the newspapers devoted more space and ink to each contest than they had previously thought justifiable for the Tokyo earthquake of 1923, which killed 90,000, or the Florida hurricane of 1926, the most disastrous storm of the century.

From the second Dempsey-Tunney fight onward, it was all downhill for the newspapers as purveyors of sports excitement. Radio slowly and surely took over, until the crowds before the newspapers dwindled to corporal's guards, and as play-by-play equipment wore out, facsimile reproductions of baseball games were abandoned completely.

Though the sports fans turned out by the thousands to the re-creation of major sporting events by the newspapers, they were unpredictably fickle when it came to paying out their hard cash to watch professional and semi-professional sports. The Winnipeg Falcons, fresh from their Olympic victory of 1920, kept interest alive in the Manitoba senior hockey league. But not for long. After that league succumbed to anemic attendance a commercial league composed of teams sponsored by Eaton's, the Hudson's Bay, the C.P.R., and the Grain Exchange filled the rink for a while. It too died of financial malnutrition, as did an ill-starred effort to promote professional minor-league hockey.

The same situation developed in the other western provinces. The Western Canada Hockey League put teams in Saskatoon,

Regina, Calgary, Edmonton, Vancouver, Victoria, and Seattle and stocked them with such superstars as Newsy Lalonde, George Hainsworth, the Cook brothers, George Hay, Dick Irvin, Joe Simpson, Red Dutton, Duke Keats, Frank Frederickson, Slim Halderson, etc. Huge crowds turned up in Regina and Edmonton occasionally, but the league came apart financially and a new one was formed. It disappeared in 1927 when the Patrick brothers sold their teams to the National Hockey League to supply players for the new teams being established in New York, Detroit, and Chicago.

Baseball and soccer fared worse. A professional baseball league of prairie cities lasted a couple of years. It was succeeded by a league of Alberta and British Columbia cities which quit after a year and a half. Soccer attracted crowds to provincial play-offs and visits of international teams. At other times the spectators stayed away in such droves that the leagues expired during the Depression.

The extent to which the radio craze of the 1920s sapped public interest in attending spectator sports is problematical. Certainly radio broadcasting of big-league baseball games was later blamed for cutting disastrously into attendance. The game itself was probably saved from extinction by the development of lighting systems that made night baseball possible. The crowds that came out for Edmonton Grads championship basketball games dwindled notably after the Edmonton radio station started to broadcast the games. Unlike the American radio stations, however, the prairie broadcaster did not turn to sportscasting with all that much enthusiasm.

It may very well be that declining interest in spectator sports was simply an indication that public interest in athletics of all kinds was diminishing, after reaching its peak in mid-decade. With the passing of the decade any number of previously popular participation sports passed into limbo. Tobogganing, for example, which was a tremendous party pastime, fell into oblivion. The snowshoers turned in their charters. Speed skating lost its zest, and forty years passed before anybody thought of doing any barrel jumping after the river rinks closed in Winnipeg. Pleasure skating to music went out with the Charleston and the Black Bottom. The kids stopped playing soccer at school, and lacrosse sticks became museum pieces. Tennis courts disappeared from the cities, the billiard rooms were vacated one by one, and the dance halls went out of business.

It was a strange, almost cataclysmic, way for a golden age to end.

6. The Gospel of Co-operation

The post-Stampede languor was well settled over the newsroom of the *Calgary Herald* when Percy Woodbridge wandered in on a July afternoon in 1923, clutching a newspaper clipping. He walked over to the desk of Charles Hayden, the managing editor, and after an exchange of pleasantries, handed him the paper.

"How," he asked, "would you react to the suggestion that it would be a hell of a good idea for the *Herald* to bring him to Calgary for a meeting and see if we could get something started here?"

The "him" of the story was Aaron Sapiro, and until that moment Charlie Hayden had never heard of him. The clipping was a report of a series of meetings which Sapiro had been holding in the Okanagan Valley on co-operative marketing. The "something" that Percy Woodbridge wanted to get started was a wheat pool, a wheat-owners' co-operative to market their crop as an alternative to the Winnipeg Grain Exchange. It was a proposal that had been kicking around the west since the federal government had closed down the Wheat Board and re-opened the wheat pit in the summer of 1921. Hayden scanned the clipping and rubbed his chin noncommittally.

"Promoting public meetings is outside my field," he said, "but let's bat it up to the Colonel." Together they strolled into the office of the publisher of the *Herald,* Colonel J. H. Woods.

Few more pregnant ideas ever reached fruition in the prairie west, for out of it was to come a whirlwind drive that would revolutionize wheat marketing for all time. J. H. Woods bought Woodbridge's idea with enthusiasm, little suspecting that in doing so he would grease the skids to oblivion for his pet aversion of the moment — the Progressive political movement. The Progressives, of course, would linger moribundly in office in Alberta and Manitoba for another generation, despite Sapiro. But his coming diverted the concerns and enthusiasms of prairie farmers from political action into co-operative marketing economics. Deprived of emotional fervor, the Progressives lapsed into a reasonable facsimile of an ordinary group of office-holders intent on staying in office. Recurrent outbreaks of agrarian anger, which had been blowing up storms for forty years, reached their peak in 1921 with the birth of the Progressive Party. It brought the two-party political system clattering down in ruins, wiped out the Liberals and Conservatives, and replaced them with a phalanx of political greenhorns in Parliament and in the legislatures. They changed nothing.

The rankling gripes and grievances remained largely untreated as the impact of the ever-worsening post-war depression became more sharply focussed on the farm population. Wheat prices on the farms, which brought Alberta growers an average of $2.31 a bushel for their 1919-20 crop, were down to 76 cents a bushel in 1923. The U.S. embargo on Canadian cattle exports had reduced the return for prime steers to a ruinous $5 per 100 pounds at the packers. The inevitable royal commission was touring the prairies, probing into the latest round of charges by farm leaders against the cheating tactics of the line elevator companies.

Thirty years before, the grading and weighing practices of the grain buyers had produced the first great threat of militant farm reprisals. That brought the Manitoba Grain Act into existence, and later led to the establishment of the Board of Grain Commissioners. All such past grievances lived on in memory, if not in fact. When new tribulations evolved, the effect on the farmers' bile ducts was cumulative. It was still an unshakeable article of faith of western farmers that "you always get gypped on the grades!" As deeply held was the conviction that the least reliable pieces of equipment extant were grain-weighing mechanisms in country elevators.

Periodically, when the agrarian unrest became too noisy to ignore, governments bought peace and quiet by appointing royal commissions to investigate current complaints. Whole firms of lawyers in Winnipeg, Regina, and Calgary grew to affluence by following royal commissions around the country.

Not only were the conditions familiar, the attitudes of mind that the farmers brought to bear upon their problems were essentially unchanged from those they had brought with them from the United States and Ontario a quarter of a century before. That was only to be expected, for the farm problems of the west differed very little from those that had prevailed in the middle west of the United States at the turn of the century.

In a general way, American experience anticipated Canadian development by about thirty years. In the decades following the Civil War, vast stretches of the Great Plains were broken to the plow. Wheat production expanded beyond the developed abilities of transportation and marketing to handle it. The breaking of the semi-arid plains in periods of high rainfall led to disastrous crop failures when rainfall returned to normal. Interspersed with these developments were shattering collapses on Wall Street that spread financial panic across the land. In Chicago the savage wars of the bulls and the bears for control of the wheat market caused prices to soar and drop in senseless fluctuations. The railways charged whatever the traffic would bear for moving farm products, and combined with the big elevator companies to circumvent the efforts of farmers to ship their own grain. Eastern U.S. manufacturers, sheltered behind high tariffs, combined to keep prices high.

Parties of protest erupted and subsided in the United States as the Greenbackers merged into the Populists, who disappeared into the William Jennings Bryan free-silver Democrats. Out of all this the American migrants to Canada had absorbed a strong reformist bias. Included in their intellectual baggage was an abiding suspicion, if not a downright hatred, of "eastern financial interests", and an open antagonism toward the railways, the elevator companies, the speculative wheat-marketing system, and tariff-protected manufacturing industries.

To combat such conspiracies against the farm population, the immigrants came loaded with panaceas. To overcome the penchant of railways and banks for corrupting legislators and luring them away from their sacred promises to the electors, they had invented such devices as "direct legislation" and "initiative and recall". Direct legislation meant a system in which, if a fixed number of the electors petitioned for a certain action, the government had to take a referendum and if the electors endorsed the proposal the legislature was required by law to enact it. If an elected member abandoned the platform on which he was elected, certain initiatives could be set in motion and the member forced to resign his seat.

To combat the elevator trust, American farmers turned to co-operative construction of their own elevators. In matters of taxation, many were committed to Henry George and the Single Tax. As cultivators of the soil, they were susceptible to the conviction that, as all wealth derived from the land, a tax on land would tax all wealth at its source and make tariffs and excise taxes unnecessary. While the United States government had been reducing drastically the amount of money in circulation, the farmers were all in favor of steady expansion of the currency supply.

In religion, the mid-western Americans, whether of Anglo-Saxon, Scandinavian, or German extraction, were overwhelmingly Protestant, and generally of a fundamentalist persuasion. Whisky they regarded as distilled damnation, so they were ardent espousers of the cause of Prohibition, in season and out.

The first wave of American immigrants was made to feel comfortably at home with the discovery that most of the problems that had afflicted their parents in the United States were still awaiting solution on the Canadian prairies, or had been only recently taken in hand. Although, as Richard Hofstadter has noted, Anglophobia went hand in hand with anti-Semitism in Populist demonology, the Americans found little to hate and much to admire in the English farmers they found in the west. Generally, the settlers from England and from Ontario at least matched the passions of the Americans for reform. These were no Populist stereotypes of the hated English. They were skilled and successful farmers, well schooled in the co-operative principles of Rochdale and in Robert Owen's philosophy. They had steered their United Grain Growers company into a head-on collision with the Winnipeg Grain Exchange and wrecked its attempt to exclude their co-operative. They had marched on the Parliament at Ottawa in 1910, at the head of a farmers' army 800 strong, to demand the removal of customs duties on farm equipment and the necessities of life. In the election of 1911 the United Farmers of Alberta campaigned strongly on the side of the Laurier Liberals for reciprocity with the United States.

Unhappily for the prairie farmers, many of the reforms achieved under the Manitoba Grain Act tended to wash out, the farther west they went. The universal distrust of grading and weighing by country elevators had led to the struggle that ultimately forced the railways to supply boxcars into which farmers could load their own grain and ship it to market instead of going through the local agent. It was a law that the railways and the elevator companies obeyed only when pressure was continually applied by the farm organizations. In the sparsely settled newer districts of Alberta, the regulations were openly flouted.

All such common grievances as those involving weight, grade, price, and transportation of grain, important as they were in keeping the embers of agrarian discontent glowing brightly, were temporarily submerged by the bitterness of the reciprocity election of 1911. The Liberal free-traders won landslide victories in Saskatchewan and Alberta, and the "Be British: No truck nor trade with the Yankees!" slogans of the Conservatives prevailed elsewhere. As Arthur Morton assessed the situation, it was a bitter and stunning blow to the organized farmers, and became the first act in the agrarian revolt of the west. Disillusionment with both old parties spread far and wide, and led inexorably to the launching of the farmers' own Progressive Party in the federal election of 1921.

Under other circumstances, anger at the defeat of reciprocity might have subsided with time. But the sharp, biting depression of 1912-15, and the crop failures, price collapses, and inflation that followed the war, kept the thoughts of the farmers turned forever in on their own problems. Under other circumstances, too, the bumper wheat crop of 1915 and two intervening years of high-priced wheat might have served as an antidote to outrage. Instead, the consequences of that crop and those prices ultimately made everything else just so much worse.

Between 1910 and 1915, the acreage sown to wheat on the prairies doubled, from 7,867,000 to 13,868,000 acres, with all the expansion taking place in Alberta and Saskatchewan, and 1915 was a phenomenal growing year. The rains came at the right time, there was a notable lack of pests, and an open fall enabled the farmers to thresh the greatest crop every grown in Canada — 360,000,000 bushels of wheat. The previous year, a much smaller planting and poor climatic conditions had produced only 140,000,000 bushels. While the 1915 crop caused a sharp drop in the price of wheat, the decline went largely unnoticed in the magnificence of the harvest.

With the war in Europe creating an unlimited demand for Canadian grain, prices soon improved, from $1.10 a bushel during the 1915 crop year to $2.00 a bushel a year later. At that point the government closed the Winnipeg Grain Exchange futures market and set up a Wheat Board to take over the marketing of wheat for the duration of the war.

The combination of a bountiful harvest in 1915 and the record price in 1916 sent the farmers on a wild spree of land-buying and acreage expansion, particularly in the last frontier area of western Saskatchewan and eastern Alberta. It was a whirlwind-reaping operation. The rains left and never came back. In their place came sawflies and grasshoppers. From 31 bushels to the acre in 1915, Alberta production dropped to 6.1 bushels in 1918, the poorest crop in Alberta history. Saskatchewan production declined from 25 bushels in 1915, to 10 bushels in 1918, and to 8.5 bushels in 1919.

Farmers who had borrowed heavily to buy equipment and

more land in 1915 found themselves with near crop failures at the onset of the post-war inflationary spiral. So desperate did the environmental damage from drought and wind erosion become in eastern Alberta and western Saskatchewan that thousands of settlers simply gave up their homesteads and moved away. By the time the census was taken in 1926, there were 10,000 abandoned farms in Alberta, most of them in a strip along the Saskatchewan border north of Medicine Hat.

In the spring of 1919 the consensus of the experts was that world wheat prices were destined for a sharp decline, and so, when the Wheat Board reached the end of the crop year in July, it was allowed to expire and the trading in wheat futures was re-opened in the Winnipeg Grain Exchange. Instead of dropping, wheat prices rose as a result of famine conditions in Europe. To keep Canadian prices from rising, the government reinstated the Wheat Board as the sole marketer of Canadian wheat.

It established a price of $2.15 a bushel at the lakehead terminals. As this was well below the American price, there was an immediate outcry from the producers. To quiet the uproar the Board issued "participation certificates" along with its cash tickets when the farmers delivered their grain. Most of the farmers had little faith in the participation vouchers, which entitled them to share in any surplus the Board got in excess of the initial price of $2.15. Some were tossed into drawers and forgotten. Others were lost or thrown away. Some were bought up for a few cents a bushel by local speculators. Some elevator agents picked them up for a few cents on instruction from their Winnipeg offices. When the Wheat Board wound up paying 47 cents a bushel for the participation certificates, it was a welcome dividend for the farmers who had preserved them, but for those who had sold or lost them, it was more grist for the mills of disenchantment.

Nothing that happened during the war did other than increase the antagonism of the farmers toward the national government. The bloom wore off the 1915 bonanza very quickly. Prices doubled for everything the farmers bought, and free-trade sentiment naturally doubled with them. Instead of tariff's being lowered, they were raised by 7$\frac{1}{2}$ per cent on American imports and 5 per cent on British goods. Instead of reducing freight rates, the government suspended the low Crowsnest Pass rates on grain and approved a general freight increase. Instead of expanding the monetary supply and easing the interest burden on farmers, it contracted the money supply and interest rates rose. The Unionist government did, however, persuade Thomas Crerar, the free-trader head of the United Grain Growers, to join the government as Minister of Agriculture and this, along with the expansion of patriotic fervor generated by the war, enabled the Union candidates to sweep the west in the election of 1917. But for the Conservatives and Liberals alike it was a Pyrrhic victory. Three separate agitational brush fires were being fanned into flame on the prairies which would ultimately be combined into a single conflagration of angry protest.

Below the border, in North Dakota, a delegation of farmers stormed out of the state capitol in 1915 to declare political war on both Republican and Democratic parties. They had appeared with a bill of particulars against the railway monopolists and the Minneapolis milling combine, and had been told, according to legend, to "go home and slop your hogs". Instead, they formed the Nonpartisan Political League and drew up a platform calling for state ownership of grain elevators, flour mills, banks, and hail insurance companies. They adopted the strategy of supporting candidates of either party who would pledge themselves to that program. In the election of 1916 they scored a sweeping victory, and three years later the state legislators delivered the state bank, a state flour mill, an elevator company, and a homebuilding association.

The N.P.L. campaign was barely into gear before word of it drifted northward and a Canadian Nonpartisan League was organized at Swift Current. It was in Alberta, however, where it made the most rapid strides. Several of the leading farmers of the province took it under their wing. In the provincial election of 1917 two Nonpartisan leaders, Mrs. L. C. McKinney of Claresholm and James Weir of Nanton, were elected to the legislature.

A storm of a different kind was blown up by Henry Wise Wood, a balding Populist Puritan from Missouri. Wood had migrated to Alberta in 1905 at the age of forty-five. An attractive platform presence, wry wit, and puckish sense of humor combined to quickly nudge him into the front rank of Alberta farm leaders. Besides, he was constitutionally unable to resist an invitation to speak, and such was his contribution to the organizing drives of the United Farmers of Alberta that he was elected president in 1916 and held that office until 1931.

Wood thrashed around a good deal before he got his political philosophy straightened out, but when he did, it was a dilly. At first he seemed to favor the Liberals of Alberta. In the 1917 general election he supported the conscriptionist Union government. For a while he seemed to embrace the Populists' idea of getting behind farmer candidates in the established parties. In the end he underwent a conversion to the idea of government by class action, to replace the government parties and opposition parties in parliamentary democracy. Wood's was a religious conversion of a depth and intensity seldom matched since the episode on the road to Damascus.

With his conversion, Wood set out at once to attack the heresies of the Nonpartisan Leaguers, whose strong advocacy of government ownership clashed with his concept of salvation through group action. He wanted the party system replaced by the proportional representation of groups within a legislature, each group representing its own special economic interests and co-operating with all other groups to achieve its, and their, ends. For three years the Nonpartisans and the Woodites warred bitterly within the bosom of the U.F.A. At a time when the economic plight of the farmers worsened as the world turned, this would appear at first glance to be about as irrelevant a controversy as could have been devised. Yet the debate provided growth and vigor to the United Farmers of Alberta, as each faction worked overtime agitating, organizing, and bringing in new members. Wood proved himself to be both the best organizer and the most persuasive advocate. He carried the overwhelming majority of the Alberta farmers with him, but nobody else.

The philosophies of T. A. Crerar and H. W. Wood clashed wherever they touched. Crerar's general economic bent was traditional western Liberal reformist. He opposed protection as the bulwark of the big industrial and financial interests of the east, although he was also a single taxer and an advocate of direct legislation by petition. But he believed in working within the framework of established political parties and within the traditional parliamentary system. When the revulsion of the farmers to the Borden high-tariff budget, which brought about Crerar's resignation from the Union government in 1920, ignited the drive to organize the Progressive Party, a reluctant Crerar was persuaded to be drafted for leader.

The meteoric rise of the Progressives in the federal election of 1921 has been chronicled elsewhere and in depth. It failed, despite its 65 seats in Parliament, to achieve even a modicum of success in redressing farm grievances, but the failure did not dampen Progressive enthusiasm in the boondocks. Within a matter of months the Progressives had destroyed the Liberal party in Alberta and had driven the Norris Liberals from office in Manitoba.

The cream of the political jest was that these Liberal provincial administrations had been, in almost all essentials, farmers' governments, which gave first attention to the voice of the farmers and the back of their hands to the urban citizenry. The Norris administration had passed more advanced social legislation in five years than all the other Manitoba administrations had done since Confederation. The reforms ranged from the adoption of woman suffrage, workmen's compensation, Prohibition, and compulsory school attendance, to the establishment of a comprehensive provincial farm loans agency, a department of health, a department of labor, and a complete renovation of the public schools system, with heavy emphasis on major improvement in rural facilties. Yet in 1922, the United Farmers of Manitoba drove this administration from office and replaced it with a "group government", only one of whose members had ever held public office before.

The developments in Alberta were an almost exact parallel. There, the Liberal administration of Charles Stewart was driven into the wilderness by a legion of spear-carriers for Henry Wise Wood's new religious crusade. So rigid were Wood's ideas on restricting U.F.A. support exclusively to bona fide farmers that he refused to countenance endorsement of any candidates in the cities of Calgary or Edmonton. Alberta, too, got a government of greenhorns without previous legislative experience.

The experience with the Wheat Board of 1919-20 had converted what for many years had been only a suspicion into a firm conviction: farm prices were always low when farmers had wheat to sell, but when drought or hail or rust wiped out most of the crop, prices were high. In short, prices were high only when farmers had nothing to sell. And the futures market system of the Winnipeg Grain Exchange was to blame for this sorry state of affairs.

As a corollary of this conviction, there was a subsidiary theory, held by most prairie farmers, that prices were always forced to unreasonably low levels in the fall, when the farmers were delivering their grain. After the flush flow of wheat to market subsided, prices gradually rose again. Thus, the farmers who sold their grain in the fall lost out to the speculators who bought it and held it until spring. This theory could be demonstrated statistically to be fallacious. In some years the price dropped after the harvest was delivered. But making such a case had little effect on farm opinion, and commitment to the theory kept many western farmers skating near the brink of bankruptcy when they might otherwise have been lolling back in comfortable affluence. They became addicted to gambling on the Winnipeg open futures market.

The futures market of a commodity exchange was far from being as complicated as it seemed at first glance. Throughout the year, anybody who wanted to get into the grain business could do so by buying or selling wheat for future delivery. In August a speculator could walk into a brokerage office anywhere on the prairies, put up $100 "margin", and buy 1,000 bushels of October, December, or May wheat for whatever the price on the quotation board happened to be at the time. The buyer undertook, when the unknown owner of the 1,000 bushels of wheat delivered it in October, December or May, to accept delivery of it and pay the full price stipulated in the trade—$2,000 if the price was $2 a bushel. At the time the speculator was buying his 1,000 bushels, a farmer somewhere in the west was delivering several truckloads to the local elevator, where he was paid for it in cash. To protect itself from loss in the interval between purchase from the farmer and ultimate sale to exporters, the elevator company could go into the market and sell 1,000 bushels of futures for each 1,000 bushels of cash grain it purchased.

In the ethereal mythology of Grain Exchange apologetics, having vast numbers of speculators on hand to buy wheat was the essential virtue of the system. The speculators carried the risk. And because of the steady loss of huge sums of money by these speculators, the farmers got more for their wheat because the elevator operators, with risk of loss removed, could charge less for their services. Without the speculators, the elevator companies would have had to take all the risks and absorb the losses, so they would have paid lower prices to the farmers. The orchestration of this theme was central to the Grain Exchange propaganda concerto during a 30-year season.

In fact, however, the bulk of the speculating public seldom came into the market until after it became highly agitated for some reason or other—frequently by a series of scare stories in early July about impending crop failures. The inrush of speculators always pushed prices higher than they otherwise would have gone. When the speculators were cleaned out as the market turned around, prices dropped below the point they might otherwise have touched. In any event, the farmers railed endlessly against the speculators, and called them parasites whose activities caused violent upward and downward price fluctuations and kept the producers in rankling uncertainty as to when they should sell their harvest.

And who were these speculating parasites? As Pogo, the cartoon-strip character, once phrased it: "We have met the enemy, and he is us." The United States Commodity Exchange administration once made an exhaustive study of the occupations of the grain-market speculators and found that the largest single group was composed of farmers. A similar study in Canada would have produced about the same result. Convinced as they were that wheat prices were depressed at harvest time, and bound to rise, Canadian wheat farmers, when they sold their grain for cash, could not resist putting up part of the proceeds as margin for a flier in May wheat.

They almost always lost, for no matter how right they were or how high the market rose they did not sell out at profit because it was always going to go higher. When they bought their 1,000 bushels of May wheat at $1.25 it was with the firm intention of selling it for $1.40 or $1.50 a bushel. When it reached that figure, instead of selling they would buy more, for by then they had become convinced that the market was going to $1.75. At $1.75 it would be a sure bet to hit $2.00. As the Stamp Commission reported in 1930: "The evidence shows that many farmers and many of the public throughout the west gamble in wheat futures. They go into the market invariably as bulls on a rising market and go out almost invariably as losers. The farmers gamble in wheat more than anything else...."

The United States Commodity Exchange authority went over the customers' accounts of a defunct Chicago brokerage house and examined over 400,000 trades in almost 9,000 accounts. The examination revealed that 6,598 speculators lost over $12,000,000, while the 2,184 winners gained only $2,000,000. The grain brokers themselves did very little better in the wheat market than the farmers, housewives, and ribbon clerks, for 70 per cent of them also lost money. Charles Dunning, the former Premier of Saskatchewan and a farmer in his own right, once summed up the typical farmers' attitude in these words: "Farmers think when grain prices are on the rise that they will keep on rising and when grain is on the drop it will keep on dropping. As a result they hold when the market is rising and sell when it drops."

So for twenty-five years prairie farmers had been damning the Grain Exchange and nursing their wounds, but were unable to resist the temptation to go back again for one more fling. They were as addicted to the futures market as other gamblers were addicted to cards, dice, or marriage. During periods of remorse, however, they yearned passionately for some other system of disposing of their crop. The Wheat Board of 1919-20 suddenly loomed as the solution. And not only because it would establish an orderly market and free them from making the decision about when to sell their wheat. Like the confirmed alcoholics who worked for Prohibition, they saw the ending of the futures market as freeing them from the temptation to gamble on margin on wheat futures.

The farmers of the west had little sympathy with the Wheat Board of 1917 when it was established to prevent wheat prices from rising to the world level. And when it was re-established in August of 1919, as prices again seemed upward-bound, it engendered no enthusiastic arm-waving. But when it closed down and distributed the 47-cent dividend on the participation certificates, the farmers took a second look. As prices continued to drop for the next two years, despite a crop failure in Alberta, the Wheat Board appeared in an increasingly favorable light.

"Why," the farmers asked each other and their leaders, "doesn't that kind of an institution make more sense than the Grain Exchange? What do we need with the futures market? Suppose all the farmers turn over all their wheat to a central selling agency. It could spread the sales over the whole year instead of just over the fall months and pay us whatever they get for it. They could pay just like the Wheat Board did — a down payment in the fall and a patronage dividend when they get all the crop sold. What's wrong with that, can anybody tell me?"

Nobody could. So, from the Progressive Party phalanx in the House of Commons, agitation blazed for the re-establishment of the Wheat Board. The best Ottawa would do, in 1921-2, was to agree to establishing a one-year Board. No farm leaders could be found to serve as directors for such an institution, so nothing came of the agitation. In frustration the farmers turned to arguing for the setting up of their own wheat pool as an alternative to the futures market.

The farm journals went digging for stories on the commodity pools in the United States, where scores of such pools had been organized in everything from tobacco and cotton to fruit and rural telephones. No such story was ever complete without fulsome reference to Aaron Sapiro, who seemed to have developed into a one-man crusade for co-operative marketing.

It was a simple matter for the farmers to sell themselves on the wheat pool idea. But what kind of a wheat pool? A voluntary pool which they could choose to go into or stay out of? Or a compulsory pool in which all the producers would have to deliver their wheat to the co-operative? Could a wheat pool work if farmers could opt in and opt out as they pleased? As interest in the idea mounted, the freedom-versus-compulsion argument diminished in importance, because until a wheat pool of some kind was organized it lacked much relevance. Talk there was aplenty, but that was about all there was, except in the south country, until Percy Woodbridge and Charlie Hayden took their walk into Colonel Woods' office on that July afternoon.

In the pre-oil boom year of 1923, Alberta was the have-not province of the west. Still wholly dependent on agriculture for sustenance, it was living very low on the hog, and seemed destined for a long siege of starvation diets. Because it was at the end of the line as far as transportation costs were concerned, Alberta farmers ordinarily got less for everything they grew than their fellows in Saskatchewan and Manitoba. The low farm prices then prevailing made the higher freight rates even more burdensome. The people of Alberta, urban as well as rural, suffered another disability. They had to pay more for everything they consumed because of the higher freight on incoming goods. Alberta needed high farm prices — substantially higher prices than Manitoba or Saskatchewan — to survive. Instead, farm prices were disastrously depressed. The closing of the American market to Canadian beef was an unmixed disaster for the livestock industry that was centred in Alberta.

The wheat pool idea might not have appeared to be all that attractive, but the *Calgary Herald* had good reason to be worried about its own survival along with that of the business community that lived off the farmers. The time when anybody could afford to pick and choose among the straws to be grasped had long since passed by, on that summer afternoon.

The decision of the *Calgary Herald* to underwrite the cost of bringing Aaron Sapiro to Alberta was unique in more ways than one. Such a thing could have happened only in Calgary. Certainly, no Winnipeg newspaper publisher would have been caught dead in bed with the wheat pool idea. In Regina, when word of Sapiro's coming to Saskatchewan reached the *Leader-Post,* it did a character assassination job on him that resulted in a $50,000 suit for libel. And the *Herald*'s decision must have been the first time in history that a group of city people got so concerned about any farm problem that they seized the leadership of a campaign to solve it.

While Colonel Woods was negotiating with Sapiro, he invited Henry Wise Wood to join in the sponsorship. The invitation was angrily spurned by Wood, who had decided that it was too late in the year to organize a wheat pool to handle the 1923 crop. Wood, that July, could think of a dozen reasons for backing away from organizing a pool for 1923. The farmers would be in the fields with their binders once they got their hay off. There would have to be negotiations with the banks. Deals would have to be made with the elevator companies. Besides, a lot of the steam had gone from the U.F.A. since it had come to power in Alberta in 1921. Its membership rolls had been decimated by non-renewals, and it was $5,000 in debt.

The southern Alberta farmers, nevertheless, were not prepared to wait for Henry Wise Wood to get a provincial wheat pool organized some time in the future. They would go it alone on a local basis. They were about to harvest the best crop in five years and were hell-bent on having some kind of a wheat pool in business to handle it. Their wheat pool organization drive was launched while Wood sulked and the *Herald* pursued Sapiro.

Turned down by the U.F.A., the *Herald* persuaded the Kiwanis Club to sponsor the first Sapiro meeting in Calgary, and before the head-table guest list was completed it read like a *Who's*

Who of Alberta. Long before the meetings could be held, however, the *Herald* got into a long-range shouting match with Henry Wise Wood. In his rejection of the *Herald's* invitation, Wood brusquely invited the paper to stay out of something that was none of its business. The U.F.A. government already had the business of bringing in Sapiro at hand. The *Herald,* he suspected, was just trying to horn into the act to make the farm leaders look bad before their supporters. The *Herald* took after Mr. Wood with all editorial guns blazing.

> There is a great deal of confusion about Wheat Pools in Western Canada and it is a pity that this is so. . . . In Alberta the U.F.A. leaders speak of a Pool to be ready next year. They are, we understand, interested in the Sapiro Plan but have left the bringing of Sapiro to the Alberta Government and the latter does not appear to be working very effectively to get his advice. The Herald would ask the farm leaders in all kindness if it would not be well to end the confusion. If they do not want Mr. Saprio's advice let them say so, and leave it to those who do want it to get it. . . . Let us not have the U.F.A. officers saying 'the government is doing it.' The government is not doing it or else it is doing it in the wrong way.

The *Herald* returned to the attack two days later with another editorial which said in part:

> The Political farmers have let the farmers down. The latter should rely on their own wits, with which they are well endowed, if they would only use them. We have a need of a new spirit in Alberta, an all-Alberta spirit, not a farmer spirit alone. . . . If co-operative marketing of the wheat crop can be made successful let us hear about it. Right now.

Each succeeding day saw the *Herald* giving more and more front-page publicity to the efforts of local farm communities in southern Alberta to organize their own local pools, and columns of space to singing the praises of Aaron Sapiro. It was small wonder that the *Herald* began to get under the skin of Henry

Wise Wood. In an angry letter to Colonel Woods on July 27, he wrote:

> I want a Wheat Pool. The U.F.A. wants a Wheat Pool. The farmers of Alberta irrespective of their organization want a Wheat Pool. Every legitimate interest in the province should want a Wheat Pool and, I believe, will when it is fully understood what it means. The U.F.A. is putting forth its best effort to establish a Wheat Pool. The U.F.A. is sincerely giving what assistance it can to that effort. In all sincerity we do not know what you are trying to do or why you are trying to do it. The Wheat Pool is to be strictly an economic organization without any politics whatever mixed in with it. We have not tried at any time to mix politics with it, or to flavor it with politics. Frankly, I am not convinced in my own mind that you are not trying to mix politics with it. If you are, and you are trying to use Mr. Sapiro to that end, and he responds to your wishes, it is perhaps needless for me to say that neither I nor the U.F.A. can co-operate in such an enterprise. On the other hand, we are prepared to co-operate in every practical way with any interest or individual who makes clear he is actuated by sincere and undivided concern for the organization of a Wheat Pool on a strictly economic basis for the purpose of selling the wheat of this province. . . .

In the end peace was restored. Both Wood and Premier Greenfield attended the Kiwanis luncheon and the latter moved the vote of thanks to the *Herald* for bringing Sapiro to Alberta. While the luncheon audience was composed mainly of Calgary businessmen, their response could hardly have been more enthusiastic if they had been wheat farmers. The speech was broadcast over radio station CFAC, and a farmer who listened on his crystal set described the applause that greeted it as sounding "like a wagonload of bricks".

After the luncheon the U.F.A. leaders shepherded Sapiro to a meeting in the Palliser Hotel's rooftop Sun Room, where they grilled him for the next two hours on the practical details of getting a wheat pool organized. The questions ranged all the way from principles of organization to contract-wording and office management. The fiery-eyed, black-haired little lawyer from San Francisco had convincing answers for every objection, every quibble. Would the pool not require vast sums of financing to carry the crop while it was being sold? No problem. If the Canadian banks would not lend the money, Sapiro could get $200,000,000 for them in a minute in New York. How could the pool operate without elevators in which to receive and store the wheat? Simply make a deal with the regular elevators companies.

The climax of the visit came that night, at the Victoria Arena on the Stampede Grounds. Farmers from all over southern Alberta tracked in, 3,500 strong, and sat enthralled on the hard plank seats for two hours as Sapiro preached his sermon on co-operative self-help. And sermon it was, the like of which Billy Sunday and Aimee Semple McPherson could never have equalled, even by combining their talents. Frank Underhill, who attended one of Sapiro's rallies in Saskatchewan, described him as the best revivalist orator he had ever heard.

An essential ingredient for any successful speech is, of course, a receptive audience, and wherever Sapiro went he was assured of that, in spades. The farmers of the west were desperate for a revivalist's message. For a decade they had been floundering after a succession of false hopes from the Nonpartisan League and the Single Tax to the Progressives. Nothing seemed to work. No matter what they did, they seemed to wind up in the same place, with ruinously low prices when they had wheat to sell, and high prices when they had none. A bumbling stammerer with a message of hope could have held that audience. Sapiro was far and away the most eloquent and effective platform performer Alberta had ever heard. And he came by his talents naturally.

His platform manner, voice control, and projection may well have been the product of the eight years he spent in rabbinical studies at the Hebrew Union College in Cincinnati. But the emotional pitch he attained in preaching the gospel of co-operative enterprise was the visceral product of his six years as one of the smallest boys in an Oakland orphanage.

An orphanage, he once said, was an awful place for any child, but it was sheer hell for the little kids, who were knocked around unmercifully by the more muscular types. Young Sapiro had grown up on the streets of Oakland, peddling papers and matches for the pennies that helped to feed a family of seven, of which he was the second oldest. When his widowed mother could no longer keep her brood together, four of the children were placed in the orphanage. Using his gutter-learned wiles, he organized the little boys into "my first co-operative. Whenever one of the bullies picked on one of us, we would wait for the chance and the whole thirteen of us would lay into him and beat him to a pulp."

The chance to attend the rabbinical seminary came when he was sixteen, and he seized it with enthusiasm. But toward the end of the nine-year course his doubts mounted about the relevance of the position he would hold in the real world of poverty he had known. If he had been a Methodist or a Presbyterian it could have been said that he had become infected by the social gospel. He dropped out of the rabbinical course and went off to work his way through law school. He got his degree in 1911 at the age of twenty-six and, after several years spent in the service of the government of California, was appointed special counsel to the California Market Board, where he represented the vegetable and fruit growers in prosecutions of packing monopolies.

He soon became convinced that the salvation of the farmers lay in the adoption of the tactics he had learned in the orphanage —gang up on the big guys! He became an overnight specialist in co-operative law and soon was making the organizing of grower co-operatives his life work. Within five years he had made such strides in co-operative organizing and reputation building that his services were everywhere in demand. He organized the tobacco growers in Kentucky, the prune and raisin growers in California, the potato growers in Idaho, and the cotton growers in the deep south. He knew how to go about organizing co-operatives, but, perhaps more important, he also knew how *not* to go about organizing them. Most of all he talked the language of the ambitious poor, for it was the language he had learned on the streets of Oakland.

"I don't think of wheat as wheat," he told his farm audiences in Calgary and elsewhere. "Tobacco is not tobacco: fruit is not fruit. These are only other words for boots and shoes and clothes, for education and a share of the better things of life. All you have to do to convert your wheat into the better things of life for yourself and your families is to want them hard enough to go out and organize to get them." He told them how the burley tobacco farmers of Kentucky had been grubbing along on an income of $360 a year until they organized their co-op and raised their income to over $2,000. He went down the list from the raisin-grape growers to the prune-plum growers.

Most of all he urged the Alberta farmers to go out and organize their wheat pool for the 1923 crop. "Don't let anybody tell you it can't be done," he urged. "Get involved! Get everybody else involved! Get your neighbors involved! Get the merchants and teachers and businessmen to join with you! Above all, stop depending on governments to do it for you!"

In Alberta, to the consternation of Henry Wise Wood, and in repudiation of Wood's cherished gospel of salvation through group government, that was what actually happened. The Boards of Trade in Edmonton and Calgary got behind the wheat pool idea. So did R. B. Bennett, K.C., and A. A. McGillivray, K.C., who donated their time and legal advice, and John I. McFarland, the head of the Alberta Pacific Grain Company. Small-town merchants helped distribute contracts for farmers to sign.

Into his highly emotional appeal, Sapiro inserted sharply pitched words of warning: "Avoid cheap help as a plague! Do the same for advice from amateurs! Never settle for less than the top men you can hire! Be prepared to pay the highest salaries to get them!" He rocked his tight-fisted farm audience by reporting that the cotton co-operative paid its marketing manager $60,000 a year and considered that it had got a bargain at that price.

When Sapiro got through, there was no doubt what the Alberta farmers' decision would be. They would organize a wheat pool on the spot, even though the harvest was at hand. Sapiro had set a target of signing up 60 per cent of the Alberta farmers as the minimum required to make the operation viable. That entailed the monumental task of visiting, and getting signed contracts from, almost 30,000 farmers within a three-week period, at a time when the wheat producers were on dawn-to-dusk duty on their binders and bundle racks. Even with the help of just about everybody in sight, they didn't make the 60 per cent, but the sign-up did produce 25,000 members with 2,500,000 acres of wheat, or almost half the total of both in the province. Henry Wise Wood, who had been dragging his feet clear up to his hips in July, leaped for the bandwagon on August 3, and when the campaign took off the next day, he had moved into the driver's seat.

After repeating his performances in Edmonton, Sapiro departed for Saskatoon and Regina to carry the message to the Wheat Province farmers. The impact was the same, if not more so. One group of farmers, who could not get to his meeting, gathered at the home of one who owned a crystal-set radio and took turns passing the earphones back and forth to listen.

Sapiro's crusade to get a wheat pool off and running quickly in Saskatchewan foundered on the embarrassment of riches created by co-operative enthusiasm. There were at least four separate co-operative movements clamoring for farm support, and some farmers belonged to all four. The oldest, and probably the largest, was the Saskatchewan Grain Growers' Association, headed by J. A. Maharg and Alex McPhail. It was being vigorously challenged by the newly formed Saskatchewan Farmers' Union of L. P. McNamee, a rough-hewn prairie Demosthenes *cum* rabble-rouser, and Louis Brouillette, the hardest-driving organizer of the era. The Saskatchewan Co-operative Elevator Company had been organized by Charles Dunning and financed by provincial government loans, and now operated 450 country elevators and two Lakehead terminals. Finally, there was the United Grain Growers, through which the co-operative movement got started in 1901. As the Grain Growers Grain Company, it had expanded its operations in all directions—into the milling, farm machinery, binder twine, and oil businesses.

Across the province the farmers themselves had established co-ops without number. Some were simply groups that got together to buy binder twine in carload lots. Others confined themselves to group buying of barbed wire. Several farm groups set up bulk-oil co-ops when they discovered that the so-called 40-gallon drums of gasoline they had paid for never held, or could hold, more than 35 gallons. Still others got into general-merchandising co-ops. While many succeeded, many of the early efforts also ran out of steam, as the farmers could not resist the lure of the will-o'-the-wisp organizations that were forever spilling over the border from the United States.

As Sapiro viewed the scene in 1923, it was plain that the Saskatchewan wheat pool could not succeed if it became just another farm organization. It would require the united effort of the entire farm movement to bring it off. So, instead of urging the immediate organization of the Saskatchewan pool, he concentrated on getting all the top leaders into a single organization. That meant washing out the hard feeling that had developed between the S.G.G.A. and the S.F.U. in particular. Sapiro brought it off by putting the leaders of the rival groups on a committee to draw up a list of directors for the wheat pool. They came up with ten of Saskatchewan's most successful farmers, who represented just about every crosscurrent in the province. The pool was born with McPhail as president and Brouillette as vice-president. During the winter of 1923-4 the agents of the pool fanned out across the province and came home with 46,509 members who farmed 6,330,000 acres of wheat.

In Manitoba everything took a lot longer. The failure of the Home Bank in 1923 had cast a pall over the Manitoba wheat belt. In 1907, in the midst of the Grain Growers Grain Company's battle with the Winnipeg Grain Exchange, the chartered banks shut off its line of credit and the company was saved from disaster only when the Scottish Co-operative Wholesale Society bought a large quantity of its wheat. The fledging Home Bank then came forward and offered to become the company's banker. In return, the U.G.G. subscribed to a block of Home Bank stock and named T. A. Crerar to its board of directors. Worst of all, the U.G.G. became the agent for selling Home Bank stock to the farmers. Not only did the farmer shareholders lose their money when the bank went broke, but they were faced also with paying double liability of the value of their shares to rescue the depositers from loss. All this added to the difficulty of selling Manitoba farmers on signing five-year contracts with the Manitoba Wheat Pool. Despite the unblemished prestige of Colin Burnell and Donald McKenzie, who headed the drive in the winter of 1923-4, it fell far short of the 1,000,000 acres which would have meant a 40-per-cent sign-up. Nevertheless, the promoters decided to go ahead with the 711,000 acres they could get.

With the three pools in business, the next step was to organize a central selling agency which would handle the marketings of all three. This was completed in August 1924, with McPhail as president, Wood as vice-president, and Burnell as secretary.

Sapiro came back to Saskatchewan in 1924 to help with the general organization and the drafting of procedures to be followed, and to launch his $50,000 lawsuit against the *Leader-Post* for a series of articles in which he was scathingly attacked as a fraud and a double-dealer in his relations with American farmers. Ultimately, although the paper won the first round, it lost on appeal and the suit ended in a stalemate. The fiery American returned for a third time in 1927 to help the leaders of the Saskatchewan Pool in their campaign to turn the voluntary pools into compulsory pools to which all farmers would have to deliver their wheat. Once again Sapiro collided with Henry Wise Wood and this time it was Wood, who violently opposed the compulsory plan, who carried the day.

History, however, was on the side of Sapiro. Operating in tandem with the open futures market of the Winnipeg Grain Exchange, the wheat pools failed to bring the wheat growers the results they had expected. Nor could the Wheat Board, which had to work with the futures market in the 1930s. The compulsory Wheat Board, which became the marketing agency for all the prairie wheat growers in 1943, was freed from competition with the wheat pit. Sapiro's advice ultimately prevailed, almost twenty years after the dust settled on the voluntary-pool *versus* compulsory-pool argument.

From 1924 the road ahead for the wheat pools led through the 1930s valleys of disaster and humiliation but never to despair. First, however, there were five golden years of unbroken success which worked wonders for the self-confidence of the farm population. In the wheat pools' first full year of operation, the farmers saw the price of wheat on the Winnipeg Grain Exchange rocket from $1.25 in September to $2.20 in January. That price rise did more than all the eloquence of Aaron Sapiro to sell the farmers on the virtues of co-operative marketing. The truth was that the price of wheat was propelled upward by a frenzy of speculation set off by serious crop damage in the United States and abroad, and had very little to do with how the farmers marketed their wheat through their wheat pool.

Meanwhile, in Saskatchewan McPhail and Brouillette were busily welding the Farmers Union and the S.G.G.A. into a single organization. The Saskatchewan Wheat Pool absorbed the Saskatchewan Co-operative Elevators. In both Alberta and Manitoba the pools embarked on ambitious elevator-building programs. By 1927, the three pools had doubled their memberships to 140,000 farmers cultivating 15,531,000 acres of wheat.

These were the years in which the foundations were laid for the vast expansion of do-it-yourself co-operatives that would come to dominate the rural economy of the west. As the farmers turned their attention to economic experimentation with service co-operatives, consumer co-operatives, and wholesale co-operatives, political activism lost much of its attraction. The Progressive governments in Manitoba and Alberta settled deeply into their ruts as the "in" parties of the 1920s.

As for Aaron Sapiro, he was off in Dearborn, Michigan, launching a libel suit that would bring the greatest industrialist in American history grovelling to his knees. Henry Ford, who was himself a Wall-Street-hating Populist from the backwoods of Michigan, was the owner of the newspaper *The Dearborn Independent*. From 1920 until 1927 the paper was devoted to stirring up hatred against the "International Jews" with the publication of such garbage as "The Protocols of the Elders of Zion". Its slanders were reproduced in pamphlets and given world-wide circulation. But when it accused Aaron Sapiro of being in league with a group of Jewish bankers to control the food supply of the world, it went too far: "This whole Kahn-Baruch-Lasker-Rosenwald-Sapiro program is carefully planned to turn over to an organized international interest the entire agricultural interest of the Republic."

Sapiro sued Ford for $1,000,000 for defamation of character. The case was halted by a mistrial and was not retried. Out of it, however, came not one but a whole series of Ford apologies to Sapiro and the Jewish community, plus the abandonment by Ford of his newspaper. The Dearborn editor stayed on the Ford payroll, however, and at least two generations had to pass before any Jew in the United States or Canada could feel comfortable driving one of Mr. Ford's automobiles.

Nothing like Aaron Sapiro had ever happened on the prairies before; nor was his like ever to be seen again. Whether his meetings were in the cities or in rural centres, the crowds were immense, and in the main they left convinced that they had got "the word" from the lips of this little spellbinder. Sapiro was the beginning of the wheat pools, and he was also the end of the Progressive movement, though he avoided direct reference to or confrontation with it. It was a spent force in Saskatchewan by 1925, and would survive in name only in Alberta and Manitoba for another decade as socially insensitive administrations of monumental dullness.

7. Back to the Booze

One of the most intriguing "ifs" of Canadian history is: How would the pattern of social development in the prairie west have been changed if the Senate, in June 1919, had passed, instead of rejecting, a government bill to confirm orders-in-council involving the National Prohibition Act?

Between 1915 and 1917 all the provinces in Canada, save Quebec, passed legislation outlawing the sale of all alcoholic beverages within their borders except by medical prescription. In 1917 a federal order-in-council was passed forbidding the transportation of liquor into any province that had enacted such legislation. The same year it put an end to the use of grain in the manufacture of alcohol. In February 1918, an order-in-council was passed establishing nation-wide prohibition for the duration of the war and one year thereafter.

Early in 1919 a bill was passed, with little dissent by the House of Commons, to attach the orders-in-council to the National Prohibition Act which gave federal support to provincial legislation. Quebec, however, had recently opted for the legalizing of sales of light wine and beer. The Senate, under the urging of the Quebec members and with support from some senators from the west, defeated the bill. There then ensued a desultory series of conferences between the two bodies and in the end a compromise was worked out. A law to ban the shipment of alcoholic beverages into any province where Prohibition was in force was agreed to, but only provided a plebiscite was held first to confirm the desire of the electorate to have Prohibition continued.

135

Despite the Senate's rejection of the bill in June, interprovincial shipment of booze was still banned, under the authority of the War Measures Act, until the end of 1919. The federal government, however, put off the date for holding the plebiscites in the west until October 1920, for reasons that were never explained. This created a hiatus between the expiration of the ban on interprovincial shipments in December of 1919 and the holding of the plebiscites—an enforcement void that would not have developed if the Senate had not rejected the amendment in June.

The combination of the Senate rejection and the plebiscite hiatus turned provincial Prohibition laws into enforcement fiascos; undercut the immense social gains that had been made during the Prohibition period; set forces in motion that would, a half-decade later, lead to the repeal of Prohibition; and provided an obscure hotel-keeper in Yorkton, Saskatchewan, by the name of Harry Bronfman, with the opportunity to found one of the great Canadian fortunes, based upon the temporarily legalized interprovincial shipments of mail-order booze.

Conversely, without the Senate action, Harry Bronfman would never have mastered the art of instantly converting straight grain alcohol into Scotch whisky in his Yorkton blending plant, or have devised the fiendishly clever cash-and-carry system of legally supplying American rum-runners with cars, trucks, and ultimately boats full of booze, or have established the string of export "boozoriums" in southern Saskatchewan which provided the grist for the propaganda mills that ultimately scuttled the Prohibition experiment.

The detailed account of the origin, growth, and decline of the Prohibition movement in western Canada is to be found, for those who are interested, in the author's book *Booze*. For these purposes it is only necessary to ventilate a few of the myths that have encrusted the Prohibition experiment.

Contrary to the almost universally accepted legend, Prohibition was not foisted upon an unsuspecting public by a lot of fat old ladies from the Women's Christian Temperance Union. It was not the result of women voters using their newly acquired franchise to shut down the bars while the men were off fighting for freedom in the Great War of 1914-18. In Manitoba, under an exclusively male franchise, the vote was as overwhelming for Prohibition as it was in Alberta, where the women did have the vote. The legend that the vote was some kind of women's-lib conspiracy against the soldiers can be quickly repudiated. Separate polls were taken at the army camps in Saskatchewan. Some 2,000 soldiers in training at six bases voted by better than three to one for total Prohibition. The soldiers, like the rest of the people of the prairies, voted for Prohibition in 1915 and 1916 in simple revulsion against the evil social consequences of untrammelled boozing in the hotel bars of the cities. The vote in Manitoba was two to one for Prohibition, in Saskatchewan it was four to one in favor, and Alberta went dry by a 60-40 majority. In all three provinces the bars were voted out by a majority of 205,000 to 89,000.

With few exceptions, the bars that surrounded the railway stations on all sides were odious entrapments of the working class, frequently infested with pickpockets and thugs who preyed upon the drunks. It was into these "dens of iniquity" that the workers trooped on payday to demonstrate their physical prowess and "real manhood" by "standing" several rounds of rot-gut booze and knocking back rounds bought by their friends. Then they would stagger off home with what was left of their pay, frequently to terrorize their wives, their children and the immediate neighborhood. Booze, as the One Big Union *Bulletin* was later to note, had never been a friend of the working class.

While the vote in 1915-16 in favor of outlawing the sale of intoxicating beverages was overwhelming, it was soon demonstrated that it was an incredibly naive populace who had cast it. So overly concerned were the "Drys" with closing the bars that little thought was given to enforcement of the Prohibition law once it was on the books. The provincial governments gave little more thought to how the local police were to enforce the law than would have been given to the enforcement of a law against tethering goats in cemeteries. The universal assumption was that because the sale of alcoholic beverages was forbidden by law people would automatically obey the law and stop selling booze. And that, curiously enough, was largely what happened. The majority of the hotels shut down their bars and the bartenders went off to the war or to fill job vacancies left by others who had done so. But "largely" was not synonymous with "completely", and the difference soon threatened to burn holes through the intent of the law.

In addition to the hotel bars, all the cities were served by retail liquor dealers who sold whiskies, gins, and rums by the bottle and by the case, as grocery stores sold groceries. In addition, there were large liquor wholesale houses which imported alcohol in large quantities and operated nationwide agencies that supplied the bars and the retail stores. Finally, there were the drug houses which used large volumes of alcohol in their patent medicines, hair tonics, and painkillers. Under the Prohibition law it became illegal for any of these concerns to sell alcohol within the province in which they were situated. The exception was wholesale drug companies, which could sell medicinal alcohol to drugstores for resale under doctors' prescriptions.

The echoes from third readings of the first provincial Prohibition laws were barely stilled before lawyers were discovering loopholes. The most important was that interprovincial trade was still untouched. Residents of one province could send to a liquor dealer in another province for supplies, and it was legal for those dealers to ship orders by express to customers in the other provinces. This loophole was plugged by Ottawa in 1917 and thenceforth, until the end of 1919, prairie drinkers had to depend almost exclusively on the doctors and druggists for their quenching fluids.

In the beginning no restrictions were imposed on the number of prescriptions a doctor could issue or a druggist could fill. Nor was either profession required to keep records of business done. As a result, in all the cities across the west the doctors did a roaring trade, but only with those who could afford to pay $2 for the prescription and $3 to $5 to the druggist for the whisky. The doctor-druggist team-up in Manitoba in particular became a public scandal. At one time all but one of the doctors in St.

Boniface had their licences to practise suspended because of violations of the liquor regulations. In Winnipeg one Portage Avenue druggist and his staff filled 180 prescriptions in an hour. In Alberta doctors signed pads of blank prescriptions and left them with the druggist to complete for customers who simply walked in off the street and bought a bottle across the counter.

All this, of course, was a product of administrative inexperience with unique legislation. As time passed, the doctor-druggist scandal diminished as control of prescriptions was instituted and severe restrictions were placed on the bottle sizes. At the outset, doctors could prescribe a quart of Scotch. Two years later the outside limit was 8 to 12 ounces. An indication of the trend can be obtained from a comparison made in Saskatchewan. There, in January 1917, the doctors issued a total of 29,640 prescriptions for 12- and 26-ounce bottles. In 1922 the number was down to 7,760 bottles of 8-ounce capacity.

In the controversy over the effectiveness of Prohibition some statistics, striking at first glance, got bandied about. Toward the end of 1921, the Alberta government revealed that doctors in that province, who by then were limited to 100 prescriptions per month, had issued 137,547 orders in ten months. This figure was seized upon by the "Wets" to indicate the Prohibition was a sour joke; that anybody with $5 could get a 12-ounce bottle of booze. The Drys however claimed that the figures proved the success of the experiment. The Dry argument went: The 474 doctors in Alberta could have issued 47,400 prescriptions each month. They issued only an average of 13,755—barely a quarter of their permitted limit. On the basis of 12 ounces per bottle, Albertans consumed 164,000 ounces per month, or about one ounce of prescription whisky per month per adult Alberta male.

There was, of course, a good deal of illicit distilling carried on in the hinterlands and part of this production flowed into the prairie cities. Moreover, some hotel owners built themselves secret storage facilities and stocked up with liquor before the Prohibition deadline. Many years later, and after several changes of ownership in the interval, renovators of the Balmoral Hotel in Yorkton discovered underground caverns in which several thousand gallons of liquor could have been stored.

Other hotels, which kept their bars intact, ostensibly for the sale of 2-per-cent Prohibition-strength beer, installed some imaginative plumbing so that they could switch their taps back to weak beer from strong beer if the liquor inspectors hove into sight. The prairie breweries all stayed in business throughout the era, making and selling strong beer that was shipped out in the guise of Prohibition beer. There were suspicions, as well, that the breweries were also marketing substantial quantities of alcohol which they recovered in the process of boiling strong beer down to weak beer.

There is therefore no doubt that anyone with a thirst to be slaked could get the job done fairly easily during the Prohibition era. All he needed was money to spend and the time to go through all the motions required to obtain his supplies. But that has been true of all contraband throughout history, and is irrelevant in any assessment of the failure or success of Prohibition. By far the most important fact about Prohibition on the prairies was this — it shattered, although it did not completely destroy, drinking habits which had been case-hardened through steady usage over a period of thirty years.

Before Prohibition, getting through the central core of any prairie city without being lured into the omnipresent bars was like running the gauntlet for anybody with even the mildest kind of drinking problem. Winnipeg in 1912 boasted no fewer than sixty hotel bars, most of them within Nicklaus-Palmer range of Main Street, between the C.P.R. and C.N.R. stations. The railway stations were the hubs of Brandon, Regina, Moose Jaw, Saskatoon, and Calgary, and each was encircled by beckoning bars. Not only were the bars handy to the stations, but to everything else in town, from livery stables to brothels to theatres to poolrooms. Indeed, many of the hotels tried to have part of all the other action. Some of them had poolrooms attached to the premises; some permitted a whore or two to operate upstairs. In one Edmonton hotel the clerk always handed the guest his room key with the comment that "the girls are in the room on the left at the top of the stairs."

For thousands of unattached males who poured into the west with the turn of the century, the hotels were the first port of call, for information about job opportunities and for transient accommodation, as well as for drinks. As the flow of immigrants increased, living space within the downtown rooming-houses became unspeakably congested, frequently with several men to a room and sometimes two men to a bed. Nudged out of their rooms by the heat of summer and the odors of winter, the single settlers repaired at their leisure to the only social centres available to them — the bars, the poolrooms, and the brothels. A stag night on the town — women never entered the bars, not even the prostitutes — usually began at a bar, because the bars were the most convenient of meeting places.

The bars became a habit for married as well as single males. They were places to drop into for a drink while waiting for a streetcar, and above all they were places for cashing pay cheques on fortnightly paydays. The ritual of cheque-cashing always required that the customer buy at least a drink for the bartender and usually a round for his workmates. Nobody got very rich running hotels in the west during the pre-Prohibition era, although according to J. R. Boyle, the Attorney General for Alberta, bar trade in excess of $1,000 a day was by no means uncommon. At 25 cents a drink, with only a modicum of $2 bottles taken home for Sunday drinking, the $1,000-a-day bars certainly kept their bartenders busy.

The coming of Prohibition changed everything. It broke everybody's established behavior patterns — the habit of dropping in for drinks en route home from work, of cashing cheques on paydays, of using bars as convenient loafing and meeting places. Most of all, it removed the temptation to drink from those who in later years would be described as alcoholics or people with incipient drinking problems. From being everywhere available, booze suddenly became hard to get, and adult males could get from home to work and back again without ever being tempted to drink. Where going on the wagon had once been an insuperable challenge to the willpower of any

drinker, the disappearance of the bars gave such positive rein-
forcement to the habit of not drinking that bouts of sobriety
became longer and longer.

In every city there were hoteliers who were tempted to do a
little bootlegging. But it was by nature a highly selective trade,
with known customers. A sure way of attracting the unwanted
attention of the law was to permit obvious drunks to lurch in and
out of the premises. So, while moderate drinkers might have
found hair available from the dogs that had bitten them, a
confirmed alcoholic had to go to a great deal of trouble to
indulge his addiction.

The impact of Prohibition on the lives of the people was
important in many other aspects. Drunkenness ceased to be a
factor worth noting, as the drunks disappeared from the streets
and the police-court statistics. Crimes associated with booze
dropped to near nothing, and crimes of all kinds were reduced
by as much as two-thirds. Manitoba closed two provincial jails
and Saskatchewan one, for lack of miscreants to incarcerate.
Savings accounts doubled; bailiffs sat in idleness as their business
dropped off. Absenteeism ceased to be a problem in business
and industry. Men stopped beating their wives, and children
stopped going shoeless to school. The Winnipeg General Strike
of 1918 passed off without a single important scuffle, let alone a
major riot, a fact that labor leaders were quick to attribute to the
closing of the bars. The more explosively prolonged strike in
1919 was likewise notable for its lack of violence, until the very
end when nerves on both sides had rubbed raw.

By 1919 most of the people of the Prairie provinces seemed to
be becoming reconciled to life in a Prohibition era. An exception, perhaps, was in Greater Winnipeg. St. Boniface, the
French-Canadian enclave across the Red River form Winnipeg,
had voted solidly against Prohibition in 1916 — one of the few
communities in the west to do so. The notoriously lackadaisical
St. Boniface police department paid scant attention to liquor law
violations and from the onset of Prohibition till the end of the
1920s "going to St. Boniface" was a Winnipeg euphemism for
visiting a booze-brothel combination. Enforcement of the liquor
laws in Winnipeg itself was never notably vigorous or consistent,

mainly because the provincial government pocketed the fines assessed against violators and refused to share the cost of liquor-law enforcement in the city.

Enforcement everywhere in the west was impeded by overlapping as well as walled-off jurisdictions. The Mounted Police were responsible for the suppression aspects of Prohibition that came under federal law. Some provinces had both provincial police forces and special liquor inspectors on the prowl for law violations. In addition, responsibility for suppressing the operation of illegal stills was allocated to the enforcement branch of the Dominion Excise Service. A provincial liquor inspector was powerless to interfere with the operation of a still if he blundered onto one, while an excise officer had no power to deal with ordinary bootleggers.

A regular feature of each provincial legislative session was a prolonged debate over lack of diligence by the attorney general in enforcing the Prohibition law. It was seldom indeed that either the law itself or the concept of Prohibition was attacked. Instead, and particularly in Saskatchewan, the opposition accused the government in power with being suspiciously soft in suppressing the liquor traffic. There is little doubt, however, that as time passed, both governments and populace gradually settled more comfortably into a Prohibition environment. Then came the 1920 hiatus and nothing was ever the same again as interprovincial shipments of booze were resumed.

The controversy over the traffic in mail-order booze was not something that blew up out of nowhere, like the Regina cyclone, with the arrival of boxcars full of booze on Harry Bronfman's Yorkton doorstep at Christmas 1919. Bronfman had been into the mail-order booze business briefly late in 1916. While he was surely not alone in thus obtaining an appreciation of the profit potential of the trade, he was alone in western Canada in taking all necessary measures to ensure that he would be first in business with the largest stock of wet goods the day the ban on interprovincial shipments came off.

In the beginning, the general public took little notice of the resumption of cross-border shipments. For one thing, the traffic was very slow in developing. Before they could get into business at all, the mail-order entrepreneurs who followed after Bronfman had several legal hurdles to get over. Ottawa insisted that mail-order booze had to be stored in bonded warehouses, and would only issue such licences with the prior approval of provincial governments. Bronfman had already wrangled three such approvals, two for drug warehouses and one for a general bonded warehouse, before his future competitors discovered that local approval was essential. After the others obtained provincial approval there was the usual delay in Ottawa, and when all the paperwork was complete there was still a stock of liquor to obtain. Because his Yorkton inventory was the handiest available, the mail-order houses in Calgary and Edmonton turned to Bronfman for supplies. Manitoba alone refused to approve applications for bonded warehouses, so no mail-order export houses were established there.

The controversy over booze, which was eventually blown up into a public scandal by the newspapers in Regina and Winnipeg, developed slowly because the trade itself failed to come with a rush. The workers who had once dallied in the bars, or jammed into them on paydays, were caught in the main crunch of the post-war inflation and had more than enough trouble stretching their pay cheques to cover the necessities of life. They might have squeezed enough for a drink or two if the opportunity arose, but finding $4 for a bottle of Scotch or $7 for a two-gallon tin of alcohol was simply out of the question. Misreading the temper of the times, the Dominion Express Company expected a rush of booze business to develop immediately and opened a special office in downtown Calgary to handle the rush. It never developed and the office was shut when the lease expired.

The most important contributory factor in the controversy was the fact that the mail-order business enabled everyone with an urge to do a little bootlegging to lay in a supply of booze at reasonable prices. The brothels which were operating with impunity in Winnipeg, Saskatoon, Moose Jaw, Lethbridge, Calgary, and Edmonton no longer had to pay the doctor-druggist premium prices for medicine bottles of whisky, or rely on lower-priced but throat-burning home-brew. As supplies increased, so did bootlegging, and so did prosecutions for drunkenness. The apartment building blind pigs became as numerous in the main cities as the old hotel bars had been. So, while the hiatus made law enforcement more difficult, it also increased the volume of criticism against governments for not enforcing the law.

This criticism, however, was very low-key compared with the crescendo that developed over the export houses which were established in the border towns of Saskatchewan to service the American market. By midsummer 1920 most of the small towns along the U.S. border sported at least one newly opened export store. Some like Govenlock, Estevan, and Bienfait had two or three. In, the main they were opened by people out to make a fast dollar, who lacked the wits to develop a necessary network of customers in the United States. Instead of a steady stream of regular customers coming in convoys to take back 100- and 200-case shipments, they attracted only small patronage and the attention of stick-up artists rather than customers. Within a matter of months many of them closed for lack of business, or were taken over by Bronfman's gradually developing monopoly of the export trade. He, of course, did have the wits to have the American outlets all arranged before he opened his first store. Bronfman even took out a charter for an interprovincial trucking company to carry his liquor before there were any interprovincial highways.

There were enough world-shaking or Canada-shaking things happening in 1920 to keep things in perspective, and to make any fuss over Prohibition seem pretty small potatoes. The Borden-Meighen Unionist government was on its deathbed, the prairie farmers were frantically hammering the new Progressive political movement together, business was stagnant, and newspaper advertising columns were full of foreclosure notices and tax sales of urban property. Unemployment was serious, but not nearly as serious as the high cost of living. And for those who could spare the attention, there was the revolution in Russia, chaos in Germany and Austria, the red-scare panic in the United States, and warlordism in China.

Nevertheless, as the October 25 plebiscite approached, the seamier side of Prohibition got increasing attention in the press. An occasional burglary of a liquor store, coupled with the high-jacking of a load of booze, became a crime wave. The impact of all this, however, showed itself far more in delayed action than in immediate action. In the plebiscite campaign itself, voices were raised here and there attacking Prohibition as such, but nobody was listening. Far from giving rise to the full-dress campaign of 1915-16, the 1920 vote generated only a minimum interest among either Wets or Drys. Aside from the usual temperance sermons in the Presbyterian and Methodist churches, and the sending of moral-reform speakers on casual tours of the country-side, the Drys mounted no campaign. They assumed that the argument was over and that the people would troop to the polls to again cast a substantial majority against the demon rum. The results confirmed that assumption. Despite a severe storm that isolated much of rural Saskatchewan and kept thousands of farmers at home, the Dry vote held solid, though the margin over the Wets narrowed considerably, as will be seen from the following comparative table.

| | 1916 | | 1920 | |
	DRY	WET	DRY	WET
Alberta	58,000	37,000	63,000	44,000
Saskatchewan	95,000	24,000	87,000	55,000
Manitoba	52,000	28,000	59,000	46,000
Total	205,000	89,000	209,000	145,000

The decline in the Dry majority from 116,000 in 1915-16 to 82,000 cannot be attributed to any weakening of enthusiasm for Prohibition after almost five years of experience on the part of the people. The Dry vote, it will be noted, actually increased slightly. Rather, the explanation is to be found, as later events were to demonstrate, in the return of the soldiers from overseas. They had gone off to the war, many thousands of them, as callow youths devoid of sophistication. Those who returned had been matured beyond their years by their experiences on the killing-grounds of Flanders. But when they got together, as they frequently did, in a comradeship no secret society could ever match, their "remembering when" turned not to the battlefields but to the joyous hours they had spent in the pubs and brothels of London and the bistros of France and Belgium.

Even the confirmed drinkers among them, men who had served their drinking apprenticeship in the bars of the urban west, had never known anything to match the British pubs. No meeting of any of the veterans' groups that sprang up after the war was ever over without a nostalgic reference to the pleasures of the pub. There a man could sit around with his friends for hours on end, nurse a couple of beers, and depart at closing time as sober as a judge. What a travesty it was that Canadian veterans, who had fought for freedom, were denied the freedom to quaff a bottle of beer in their Army and Navy clubrooms! There was a good deal of phony rhetoric in the veterans' posturing because they did in fact have beer in their clubrooms illicitly. But when they lurched home drunk and the neighbors complained, the veterans' clubs were raided by the police like common bootleg joints. And so when the chance came to express an opinion on October 25, they voted strongly against the system.

Nothing much might have come of the protest vote had it not been for the British Columbia plebiscite. It was held a week before those on the prairies, and in it the government gave the electors the choice between all-out Prohibition and the sale of liquor and beer in sealed packages by a government-owned monopoly. The vote for government sale carried by 25,000 votes. The situation on the coast had no counterpart on the prairies. The long coastline made the province vulnerable to liquor smuggling. Little effort was made to enforce the law against downtown clubs, which operated without restraint. The chief liquor commissioner himself was accused of making off with seventy-five cases of whisky. Such things combined to raise doubts among the less dedicated Drys, and the trick was turned for the Wets by the organization of a Moderation League headed by the Mayor of Vancouver and a covey of prominent Tory policiticans. It was financed by the breweries and strongly supported by the war veterans. Yet it was even stronger in its denunciations of the open bars than some Prohibitionists had been. Its main argument was twofold: Better a law that could be enforced than one which demonstrably was not; if the vast profits being pocketed by the bootleggers were diverted to the government, taxes could be cut and budgets balanced.

The result in British Columbia had little effect on the prairie voting. But it demonstrated to the prairie Wets a foolproof way of getting rid of Prohibition—not by a frontal attack on the idea itself, but by encirclement, as British Columbia had done. Within a matter of months all the prairie provinces had Moderation Leagues in operation and petitions in circulation demanding another plebiscite similar to the one in British Columbia. The Moderation Leagues were all headed by retired army colonels and majors. The breweries supplied the financial sinews to get unemployed war veterans circulating petitions.

While the names were being collected, the image of Prohibition was being badly tarnished. An outbreak of bank robberies in 1921 and 1922 was blamed on the rum-runners and bootleggers. Substantial leakage developed from the export stores, both before and after they were moved out of the small towns into the major cities. A great deal of export booze consigned to the United States disappeared into the domestic markets before it reached the international boundary.

The use of automobiles and trucks to carry liquor from Canadian stores to the United States was judged to be legal very early in the Prohibition era. From late 1921 onward there was an epidemic of lost sense of direction among prairie rum-runners. Drivers with cars loaded with booze documented from Regina to Estevan (in the southeast corner of the province) were sometimes spotted heading west between Moose Jaw and Swift Current. When news was scarce in Winnipeg, it was always easy for the newspapers to document stories of liquor being shipped from Regina to the United States and diverted into Manitoba via the back roads to Brandon.

About this time the federal government increased the excise tax on alcohol from $2.25 to $9.00 a gallon. This was followed by a big increase in the number of illicit stills being operated. Mostly they were the so-called "tea kettle" stills made from washtubs and a coil of copper tubing, with a capacity of a gallon or two a day. Other elaborate small-scale distilleries could turn out several hundred gallons a day. The increase in the excise tax raised the price of illegal booze to a point where the risks of heavy fines and jail terms for keeping stills became worth taking for the financial reward that could be gained from a few weeks of operation. When stills were raided there was usually a newspaper photographer along to snap pictures for front-page reproduction. In 1922, the *Winnipeg Tribune* ran a series of exposés on the Bronfman operations in Saskatchewan. It included a detailed explanation of how Harry Bronfman was turning thousands of gallons of straight grain alcohol into bourbon, Scotch and rye whiskies, gin, and rum by the simple addition of water and flavoring. The *Regina Morning Leader* spread a crusade against the chairman of the Saskatchewan Liquor Commission across its pages over several weeks, and wound up in a libel suit.

The continual publicizing of the minor shortcomings of Prohibition had the same effect on the prairies as it had had in British Columbia. It was easy for the brewery-funded Moderation Leagues to sell the public on the notion that there was a better way of handling the liquor problem. Each province in turn held its own plebiscite — Manitoba in June and July 1923, Alberta in the following October, and Saskatchewan in July 1924.

For the first time since the arguments started, the Wets had someone out front for them besides the bartenders and employees of the booze business. The Moderation Leagues were all headed by enough military brass to stock a battalion. The Conservative Party leaders rushed to let themselves be counted on the side of moderation and government ownership of a liquor monopoly. Their names appeared in newspaper advertisements along with those of recently unjailed labor leaders from the 1919 strike. The stance of the Conservatives was perhaps natural enough, for the Progressives and their Liberal predecessors had all been staunch Prohibitionists. Indeed, in the Manitoba campaign Premier John Bracken was a strong and very active participant on the side of the Drys.

The issue of the plebiscites was neither political nor alcoholic, it was financial. The case for repeal of Prohibition and the substitution of government sale was that it would enrich the provincial governments and make it possible for them to assist their nearly bankrupt municipalities. The Moderationists in Manitoba put the government's take at at least $3,000,000 a year. In Alberta they were talking of $10,000,000.

Two developments of the repeal plebiscites indicate the depths of the public's opposition to wide-open boozing. The first occurred in Manitoba, where there were two separate votes. On the first question the voters were given a simple choice. They could reaffirm their support of Prohibition, or they could vote for sale by government monopoly. They voted 84,000 to 54,000 for the latter. But how would the sales be handled? On the second ballot two weeks later they had to choose between the selling of all alcoholic beverages through the monopoly, or having the hotels serve wine and beer. Such was the prejudice against public boozing that they voted down beer and wine by the glass by 64,000 to 27,000. Even Greater Winnipeg, which had provided most of the 30,000 majority for government sale in the first vote, reversed itself and rejected beer and wine by a substantial majority.

In Alberta, the *Edmonton Journal,* which in 1915 and in 1920 had strongly supported the Wet cause, changed its mind. Prohibition, it said, had never been given a fair trial. Nevertheless, the social gains scored during the eight-year dry spell had convinced it that the experiment should continue. It argued that since the resumption of beer-by-the-glass sales in British Columbia in 1922, drunkenness had substantially increased on Vancouver streets and crime of all kinds had risen rapidly. As elsewhere, however, money talked in Alberta and the electors voted 93,000 to 62,000 for a government monopoly and sale by hotels of beer by the glass. Saskatchewan joined the trend the following year but it, like Manitoba, rejected beer by the glass.

14. Dancing outstripped every sporting activity in popularity.
Dance halls were filled to capacity by couples like this who,
though apparently in some sort of costume, seem to be about
to embark on an exotic tango.

15 & 16. The dance craze was catered to by elaborate dance palaces like this one *(above)* at Winnipeg Beach. This group of more orthodox sportsmen *(below),* at the St. Charles Country Club, Winnipeg, in 1926, found golf more to their liking.

17 & 18. In the early Twenties there were leagues for practically every amateur sport, and no doubt this ladies' baseball team from St. John's Presbyterian Church in Winnipeg belonged to one. *(Below)* The start of a snowshoe race at the Winnipeg Winter Carnival, February 1922.

19 & 20. Speculating on wheat futures was a major outlet for
the gambling instincts of prairie residents. Its focal point was
the Winnipeg Grain Exchange *(left)* on Lombard Street.
(Above) The trading floor of the Exchange, as seen in later
and more tranquil years, does not reflect the frantic buying
and selling that took place in the 1920s.

FIRST GENERAL MEETING OF DELEGATES — SASKATCHEWAN WHEAT POOL — REGINA, FEB'Y 26-27, 19

21 & 22. Aaron Sapiro *(left),* who
brought the gospel of co-operation to
the prairies, was the most eloquent
platform speaker the west had ever
heard. From the wave of enthusiasm
he created came the formation of the
wheat pools. *(Above)* The delegates to
the first general meeting of the
Saskatchewan Wheat Pool in Regina,
February 1925.

23 & 24. Entertainment for the prairie farmers was scarce, and they and their families turned out in great numbers to attend the travelling Chautauqua lectures such as those at Deloraine in 1920 *(below)* and at Manitou Lake in 1922 *(above)*.

At this point the question posed at the beginning reappears for attention. Would the prairie provinces ever have found their way back to unrestrained boozing in public bars if the Senate had not created the hiatus of 1920 which derailed the Prohibition experiment? It is at least arguable, as the *Edmonton Journal* argued in 1923, that on the ground of social gains alone it merited a much longer trial. And this argument was made in spite of the difficulties created everywhere by the interprovincial mail-order trade. It was the Senate refusal to pass the government bill that created the hiatus extending from the end of 1919 until the middle of 1921, and further extended in attenuated form until the end of 1922. Every argument that was used to bring back booze had its origins within that period. Without the hiatus there would not have been an argument that bootleggers were reaping millions in profits which could be diverted to the coffers of the provinces and cities. Without the hiatus there would have been no massive increase in the volume of booze made available to bootleggers. Without the hiatus there could have been no argument that Prohibition spawned violent crime and tended to create a lawless society. In point of fact, none of these arguments were made during the 1920 plebiscite, or if they were, no attention was paid to them.

If it had not been for the Senate, it is conceivable, although hardly likely given the rapid urbanization of society after the Second World War, that the habit of not drinking might have become as strong as the habit of drinking did become. In any event, one thing is certain. If the hiatus had not intruded in 1920-1 and set so many arguments in motion, the return to wide-open boozing on the prairies would have been ever so much longer delayed.

8. Remember the Night They Robbed the Bank?

An outburst of bank robberies in 1920, '21 and '22 marked the end of the almost total isolation of small-town life in western Canada. The change was brought about, of course, by the automobile, and it occurred even before there were highways over which the cars could travel. There were only country roads, from nowhere to nowhere, graded occasionally and sprinkled lightly with gravel if there was a supply handy and the community had been sufficiently foresighted to have elected a member of the right party to the legislature. Horses and buggies and horses and wagons still provided 90 per cent of the motive power for moving about on the prairies. Mud holes, which would become impassable for cars and trucks, were no impediment to teams and wagons. They simply veered off and went around them.

The farm towns of western Canada were railway towns. The railways located their townsites every eight or nine miles as they extended their main lines and branch lines across Palliser's Triangle. Settlement, as W. A. Mackintosh has pointed out, followed the railways, although during the great immigration waves prior to the Great War the settlers frequently anticipated the extension of rail lines and took up homesteads near where they estimated that the railways would be located. The location of stations was based on a calculation of the limits to which farmers could reasonably be expected to haul their grain. It was arbitrarily decided by somebody in Montreal that farmers would hesitate to haul their grain more than ten or twelve miles to the railways. By spotting their stations eight miles apart, the railways assured themselves that most of the land ten miles distant on either side of the road would be taken up by settlers.

The railway lines were laid out with the intention of providing their owners with monopolies in moving grain and livestock to market, and in bringing in all the equipment and supplies required by the farmers. Branch-line tentacles were extended out from Winnipeg, Brandon, Regina, and Moose Jaw, in generally westerly directions. In creating their freight and express monopolies the railways also created passenger monopolies. Because few of the market towns were served by both railways, it was often easier for a country resident to get to a city 75 miles distant than to get to another town 20 miles away. Indeed, if the towns 20 miles apart were Lampman and Stoughton in Saskatchewan, a traveller had to take the C.N.R. all the way into Regina from Lampman, switch over to the C.P.R., and make a 90-mile return trip to Stoughton. Such a journey might well entail a two-day layover in Regina, for branch-line trains seldom operated more than two or three times a week, and no railway ever arranged its schedules to accommodate passengers from a rival railway.

Roads were developed, if at all, to enable the farmers to get to the nearest towns, not to provide communication between towns. In short, highway networks had not yet been invented at the dawn of the 1920s. Until then they were not needed on the prairies, for automobile ownership was only emerging from its novelty stage. In 1921 the Brandon Board of Trade decided it would be a great stunt to sponsor an automobile caravan to Jamestown, South Dakota, a distance of 300 miles. The *Brandon Sun* published a detailed map of the roads to follow to get to the border and thence through North Dakota. The journey took a week to complete, and as the weather was fine there were no delays because of muddy roads.

Wherever the railways spotted a station, that was automatically the focal point for a town to be established. Usually there was a spur track at the station for the servicing of grain elevators, which were erected by grain companies to handle the farmers' wheat. The main street of the town usually paralleled the railway tracks, sometimes on the station side, sometimes across the tracks. The nature of settlement and the 8-mile spacing doomed most of the towns to a decidedly marginal existence.

Each town served an area of about 150 square miles, on which an average of perhaps 200 families would be settled. The town itself would quickly develop a hotel, a general store, a blacksmith shop, a combination barber shop and poolroom, a branch of a chartered bank, a telephone office, a butcher shop, a hardware store, a drug store, an implement dealer or two, a livery stable, a post office, a Chinese restaurant, a school, a church or possibly two, and a doctor's office — often a room in a private home where the doctor from the next town saw patients once a week or fortnightly. In addition to the families of the merchants, the populations were swelled by the families of the elevator agents, station agents, and coal dealers, and by sundry building trades-men, section hands, school teachers, and occasional government employees. Most towns depended for their existence wholly on the service they supplied to the farm community. In other words, the fifteen or twenty businesses lived off no more than 200 to 250 farmers. On the basis of numbers alone it had to be a pretty thin living at the best of times.

As the endless flood of settlers was hitting the west, the town-folk tended to get carried away with their estimates of the amount of services the farmers would be capable of absorbing, and paying for. But by 1921 most of the farm towns were long since past their population peaks, and those not suffering seri-ous declines were barely holding their populations. Whether a town held 200, 300, or 400 people, it was pretty much like any other town. In a great many cases, if one had seen one of them, one had seen them all. Save for an irresistible urge to break the monotony of small-town life, there was little reason for any resident of one town to go barrelling down the road to the next town on the line.

If the towns were all so very much alike, so were the people. They were frugal, hard-working, and honest to an unbelievable extreme. One obvious characteristic of small-town people was that they trusted each other. In the unlikely event that they would lock their doors when they left home on any local errand, the key would be left under the doormat. Except during the harvest season, strangers were sighted infrequently in the towns, and it would seldom occur to the townsfolk that any of their neighbors had designs on their property.

Trustfulness sometimes got carried to outlandish extremes. When the Alberta Provincial Police from Lethbridge arrived at the hamlet of Foremost in southeastern Alberta to investigate the robbery of the bank, their first call, naturally, was at the bank to talk to the manager. They walked into the bank through the unlocked front door and found it deserted. The manager had gone down the street on an errand and hadn't bothered to lock the door before leaving. It was, the gendarmes reported to the head office of the bank, a strange way to run a bank.

Serious crime of any kind was unknown in the villages of the Canadian prairies. The town of Oxbow, for example, had a population in excess of 600 before it got around to employing its first policeman in 1921. Like his brother officers in the other towns, he functioned more as a town caretaker than as an officer of the law.

Most towns quite early in life got around to adopting some rules for communal living. Throwing garbage into the streets was frowned on, and people who kept cows were required to keep them tethered. Children running at large were not permitted to raid neighbor's gardens. Pigs were not allowed to roam around unattended. Children of school age were required to be in school. The superintendent of the Alberta Provincial Police summed it up quite accurately in his 1921 annual report. Most town policemen were of little use when an important crime was committed because they were largely untrained handymen who always had a lot of other work to do. The horse was still very much king of the road in the early Twenties, but the automobile was beginning to press a small challenge. The leading undertaker in Brandon, for example, was advertising that his clientele could have a choice between a horse-drawn and a motorized hearse. And it was a poor and miserable town indeed that could not boast at least a small handful of motor vehicle owners, counting the owners of trucks, of course.

There was an axiom in Alberta in the 1960s, when Indians discovered the joys of car-owning, that "nobody has ever seen just one Indian, and nobody has ever seen an Indian car loaded to less than capacity". White car owners of the 1920s yielded nothing to Indians of the 1960s when it came to gregariousness and the desire for company when they went car-riding. People with new cars tended to become instant explorers and to blaze trails to the homes of friends in localities far beyond the restricted range of horse-drawn vehicles. And they always went with the car fully loaded, possibly — for one reason — to always have someone on hand to do the pushing if the car became stuck in the mud.

The hiring of the policeman at Oxbow, after the town had managed without one for twenty years, underscored the emergence of the automobile as a disturbing new force in society. If the rutted roads of the countryside did not always lend themselves to trying out the speeds of the cars that were being sold in steadily increasing numbers, there were always the smoother streets of the towns. Oxbow had tolerated the nuisances created by pigs, cattle, and wandering horses, along with litter and occasional noise-making. It was the speeding cars on the main street of the town that ultimately tilted the scales in favor of hiring a policeman. Nobody seemed to have asked how a lone policeman, on foot, could have been a match for the gay-blades tearing through town at forty miles per hour. As it turned out, he would have been more than a match.

Cars were not yet so plentiful that a local policeman could not quickly identify car and owner on sight and haul the owner before a justice of the peace when the joy-ride was concluded. Even in Winnipeg, which by this time had more than 15,000 car and truck owners within its environs, there were no traffic jams, and a couple of traffic cops on point duty at rush hours managed to keep traffic flowing. The Chief of Police of Minot, North Dakota, who was being troubled by a gang of car thieves who were selling their stolen cars in Canada, visited Winnipeg to investigate reports that it was a prime dumping-ground for stolen and smuggled cars. In a newspaper interview he said that he had been able to identify five cars, stolen from his city, on Winnipeg streets. So, appointing a speed cop who worked on foot was not as far out as it appeared at first glance.

The behavior for which small towns hired constables as deterrents was nuisance creation, not crime. It was well that this was so, because it would be difficult to imagine any self-respecting crook being deterred from law-breaking by one of the middle-aged and slow-moving plodders appointed to keep the prairie peace. Nor would the presence of the provincial police forces have been any more deterring. In none of the three provinces were the provincial police spread thickly enough to have any noticeable presence. In 1921 the Alberta Provincial Police had 185 men, sixteen cars, and two boats to police the province—or about one policeman for every 1,000 square miles of settlement. The same general ratio applied in both Manitoba and Saskatchewan. The chance of a provincial policeman being within fifty miles of any town when a need arose for his services was at least ten to one against. That need seldom arose, for the word for the small towns of western Canada as the 1920s broke over them was: QUIET.

For the prairie towns adjacent to the United States border this quiet was shattered by the refusal of the Senate, in June 1919, to extend the existing prohibition of interprovincial shipments of liquor until the provinces held plebiscites confirming their desire for the continuation of total Prohibition. The hiatus thus created, between the end of 1919 and the holding of the plebiscite in October 1920, brought all the mail-order booze dealers from 1916-17 back into business. But with a difference, because a new ingredient had been added to the booze business.

The United States completed the last hurdle to the constitutional amendment to bring in nation-wide Prohibition on January 16, 1919, and it became an established fact a year later. So instead of concentrating their stores in remote areas like Edmonton, Calgary, Saskatoon, and Kenora, the dealers set up shop in the small towns adjacent to the U.S. border, to serve both illicit markets in the United States and legal markets in Canada. Not only did U.S. Prohibition provide the Canadians with a large potential market, it also provided the Canadian dealers with an unlimited supply of primary alcohol at a time when Canadian supplies were at a low ebb as a result of wartime distilling regulations.

Throughout 1919 American distilleries operated intensive sales campaigns to get rid of their liquor supplies, not only to domestic drinkers financially able to store the stuff but to export markets as well. Yet by January 15, 1920, when export sales became illegal, there were still 67,000,000 gallons of whisky and grain alcohol, 1,500,000 gallons of gin, and 1,200,000 gallons of brandy, in U.S. bonded warehouses.

How much of the original stock of alcohol bought by the prairie dealers in December 1919 and early in 1920 came from the United States and how much came from Scotland cannot be determined. In Yorkton, from which Harry Bronfman launched the world's greatest whisky empire, the legend is that the carloads of whisky that rattled into town during Christmas week, 1919, were from Scotland. That legend holds that the Hon. J. A. Calder, a Unionist government minister from Saskatchewan, while on a journey to London, managed to snip through some red tape and get a large quantity of Scotch whisky released to Harry Bronfman. Although his home was in Regina, Calder represented the Saltcoats constituency in which Yorkton was located. The story may well have arisen from the fact that Harry Bronfman's unquestioned influence within the Liberal Party of Saskatchewan was an almost automatic door-opener into cabinet offices in Ottawa as well. Harry Bronfman himself insisted that his first substantial sales were of high-quality imported whiskies. His story was undoubtedly true as far as the early business was concerned, for his customers testified that "Bronfman whisky was good whisky". Such testimonials undoubtedly made it easier to sell huge volumes of homemade Scotch, bourbon, and Jamaica rum when he began running straight grain alcohol through his vats and bottling plants in Yorkton and Regina.

An alternative story, for which there is some corroborative evidence, is that much of the original stock was bargain-basement alcohol purchased from Kentucky distillers in the fall of 1919, when the Americans were unloading everything they could sell. By this time the Bronfmans had parlayed the Yorkton hotel into two hotels in Winnipeg and one at Port Arthur. Harry, himself, was one of the biggest real-estate operators in Yorkton and owned the town's largest car agency, plus a local trust company. In 1919 he had a line of bank credit with the Bank of Montreal of $50,000 — an impressive amount for any small-city entrepreneur. He was able to go to Montreal and arrange for an increase to $300,000 with which to buy all the alcohol he needed to launch the combination liquor blending and mail order business at Yorkton. Certainly the carloads of alcohol that poured into Yorkton in December 1919 swamped the storage facilities of the town. The Royal Commission on Customs and Excise, some years later, estimated that during 1920 Harry Bronfman imported more than 300,000 gallons of straight grain alcohol from the United States.

When and how the main thrust of the mail-order houses was diverted from interprovincial business to the American market are questions unlikely ever to be answered. Whether the Americans came looking for supplies, or whether Harry sent his brother Sam on brush-beating excursions in search of customers, is likewise unknown. But by early summer of 1920 connections had been made, not only by the Bronfmans, but by two dozen other enterprisers who had rushed into the mail-order booze business on the prairies and had established boozoriums in most of the conveniently located towns in southern Saskatchewan. There were two each in Gainsborough, Carnduff, and Carievale, one each in Assiniboia, Estevan, Tribune, and Bienfait, and, farther west, two each in Moose Jaw and Govanlock.

The Gainsborough and Carievale stores served customers in Manitoba as well, but all the others were established for the American trade, and soon the Americans were buzzing northward into the liquor stores like bees into hives. Their coming and going, stealthy though it invariably was, added touches of excitement to the lives of the townsfolk that they had never enjoyed before.

In the beginning the stores depended mainly on the Minot, North Dakota, and Minneapolis-St. Paul bootleggers for their sales. It was, of course, a seasonal business; when the roads became impassable in winter the American trade dried up. This gave the boozorium operators a chance to make sales-development trips through the United States. Thus, in December of 1920 the *Oxbow Herald* noted that Louis Barnblatt, who operated a liquor store and hotel at Oxbow, had returned from an extensive sales tour of the United States, 380 miles of which had been by airplane, a mode of travel he found most exciting.

The traffic in booze from Canada to the United States was overwhelmingly an American-dominated business. The Americans came north in their Hudson and Studebaker and Buick touring cars with back seats removed and springs reinforced, and loaded them with up to thirty-five or forty cases of whisky.

Usually the Americans came in after dark, drove right into the liquor warehouses where their cars were loaded in semi-darkness, and left quickly and quietly for the United States. From the hills south of Carievale the farmers could follow the progress of the incoming cars. The reflection of their headlights on the clouds would become apparent soon after a convoy of rum-runners crossed the border into Canada. Their course could thus be followed as they zigged to the west, zagged north, and zigged west again along the country roads that divided the surveyed sections of western Canada. Then the reflections would disappear because the cars shut off their headlights as they approached town.

Driving in the dark without lights when they had to was no problem for the rum-runners, for the country roads were easy to follow in the moonlight. The real hazards were farmers going home late at night with their horses and buggies. A homeward-bound rum-runner, speeding down a country road, would have nudged many a farmer and his horses into eternity if the hearing of the horses had not become quickly attuned to the sound of faraway engines of destruction bearing down on them. When the horses started to balk and pitch, it was a signal to their driver to get well off the road and get a sure grip on his reins against the moment when the speeding car roared past.

As Harry Bronfman had had the foresight to organize the Trans-Canada Transportation Company, and had obtained common-carrier status for it, there was really no reason why the Americans had to come in for their booze at night. The courts had established that it was as legal for a common carrier to move liquor by highway as it was to move it by rail. When the rum-runners loaded their cars with Bronfman booze they received documents stipulating they were under charter to Trans-Canada Transportation Company. They also were supplied with all the documents needed to prove that they were carrying their loads to destinations in the United States via the nearest United States customs entry port. On the unlikely chance that they would ever be stopped by a member of the Royal Canadian Mounted Police or a provincial policeman, they had all the documentation needed to prove their right to innocent passage to their destination. In addition, all the runners had to do to protect themselves from any other Canadian law when they entered the country was to report to Canadian customs offices and get a visitor's permit.

There was nothing even remotely illegal about what the Americans were doing. Still, to them Canada was very much a foreign country in which it was unwise to take chances. Besides, as the greater risk to their cargo was not from Canadian authorities but from high-jackers in the United States, travelling at night was a precaution against being robbed on their homeward journey. On that account alone, travelling without lights was a wise precaution.

On one occasion in 1920 a gang of American high-jackers threw up a roadblock on the Canadian side of the border. When the rum-runner came to a stop, a gun-fight ensued in which one man was seriously wounded. The high-jackers withdrew to North Dakota, but were identified to Canadian authorities by the rum-runners. Extradition proceedings were launched, the gunmen were tried and convicted at Estevan, and sentenced to ten- and eleven-year terms in the penitentiary. The severity of the sentences may well have persuaded the Americans it was worth going to a lot of trouble to avoid being caught red-handed above the Canadian border. At the very least, driving with head-lights out prevented high-jackers from being forewarned of their approach in time to set up their roadblocks.

Nevertheless, American hoodlums were abroad in sufficient numbers in daylight to discover the peculiarity of Canadian small-town life. They discovered that the boozoriums func-tioned with as little evidence of security as grocery stores. No-body carried guns, the windows, while barred, were hardly burglar-proof. But most interesting of all were the banks. What was to prevent a couple of safe-crackers from coming into town after dark, kicking in the front door of the bank, blowing the safe, and escaping with its contents? In these isolated-from-each-other, policeless towns of the Canadian west, the answer was nothing, and nobody.

Contrary to the widely held illusion that gangsterism and racketeering originated with Prohibition, being held to ransom by organized criminals has been the lot of American cities for generations. Lincoln Steffens was building a national reputation as an "investigative reporter" of urban crime at the turn of the century. He noted that some cities, notably St. Paul, Minnesota, sought to insulate themselves from the depredations of itinerant gangsters by giving them shelter from the law. They provided havens for criminals from other cities on the understanding that the crooks would refrain from all criminal activity while in tem-porary residence. Minot, North Dakota, according to contem-porary journals, had gone into that business on a small scale and had succeeded to the title of Crime Capital of the North West. It was through Minot that much of the liquor from Canada found its way to consumers in the adjoining states. Naturally, the word about the vulnerability of both the banks and the boozoriums got bruited about in the small talk of the Minot underworld. It was from Minot that the safe-cracking gangs debouched for their raids on Canadian banks. But before they got around to bank robbery, the Americans took several practice spins by robbing the liquor stores.

The liquor store at Tribune, Saskatchewan, a hamlet halfway

between Weyburn and Williston, North Dakota, was a sort of convenience-outlet branch of a large Regina export house. Early in November 1920, a posse of robbers from Williston turned up, and escaped at gun-point with two carloads of booze. A couple of weeks later one of the stores at Carnduff was knocked over and $4,000 worth of booze was taken. The Carnduff robbery was done in the best movie tradition. Four masked men burst into the store with guns in each hand. The employees were forced to lie on the floor while one gunman stood guard. The others loaded their cars with liquor. A pedestrian on his way to a Loyal Orange Lodge meeting in a hall next to the boozorium became curious about the proceedings; a gun was poked in his ribs and he was invited inside to join the employees on the floor. When the cars were loaded and ready to leave, the robbers bound the prisoners and took off in the general direction of North Dakota, scattering tacks and bent nails in their wake to discourage pursuit. They got clean away, of course, which was more than could be said for any natives who tried to burglarize the boozoriums the following year.

After the plebiscites of October 1920 the importation of liquor into Manitoba, Saskatchewan, and Alberta was prohibited, effective on February 15, 1921. Exports from one province to the other were likewise banned, except to British Columbia, which had opted for government stores. So the boozoriums were thenceforth to be restricted in their sales of exports to the United States and British Columbia. It could have been a shattering blow to the business, but Harry Bronfman, who was then busily buying out most of his competitors, had confidence in his ability to survive. His confidence was firmly based. During the hiatus period his sales had been running at better than 10,000 cases a month, which at an average of $50 a case produced a gross revenue of $500,000 and net profits of $391,000 a month. The largest portion of the business was done within Canada — perhaps in the ratio of two or three to one. But the "one" that would be left after the end of interprovincial trade would be profitable enough, in view of the fact that export sales brought $65 a case compared with the domestic price of $35. So between the taking of the vote and the official end of imports, the export houses loaded their premises to the rafters. So, of course, did all the drinking westerners who could afford to have cellars or garrets filled with liquor.

The small-town drinkers, who were always in the minority, were a real nuisance to the boozoriums. If the employees of the export houses were caught bootlegging to the local drinkers the entire stock of the store could be confiscated. Since the wholesale profits were so immense, the store owners were quite strict in their efforts to prevent leaks from their stores. But leaks there were, and the existence of the stocks of booze almost within reach was a challenge to the small-town thirsty. It was a challenge that increased when the stores were overloaded with supplies in January of 1921.

When the Bronfman store at Gainsborough ran out of storage space inside the well-secured store premises, it packed the surplus away in an adjacent storage shed. It was quickly looted by a group of local people, who carried better than $1,000 worth of liquor down to the States and sold it. Unfortunately, too much of the balance was sold locally without reasonable prudence. A group of Oxbow teen-agers turned up stone-cold drunk at a skating rink, blew the whistle on the sellers of the booze, and the entire Gainsborough caper ended in disaster for the culprits.

While the American gangsters continued to knock off the liquor stores when favorable circumstances arose, the robberies dwindled as boozorium security increased in 1921 and the gangsters turned their attention to the banks, standing everywhere so defenceless that they almost pleaded with somebody to rob them.

Bank-robbing in the Canadian west lasted for a period of no more than thirty months, and while most of the robbers came from the United States, their depredations bore little resemblance to the classical American frontier pattern of outlawry. In the United States the robber gangs descended on the towns at high noon, robbed the banks and express offices, and roared off at a gallop with all guns blazing. In Canada they came in the dark of the night, robbed the banks at their leisure, and made off with their loot with no more noise than the muffled exhaust of their getaway car! Or, on the testimony of a hundred silent movies, the American banditti robbed trains and bushwacked stage coaches and settlers' caravans with equal enthusiasm for fistic violence and gunplay. On the Canadian prairies, they left the trains strictly alone, save for rare prove-the-rule exceptions.

While it was happening, nevertheless, the wildness of the Canadian west was more concentrated in time than anything the United States experienced, even in the days of the James brothers, Cole Younger, and Bill Quantrill. Moreover, it was totally different from their type of banditry, inasmuch as in Canada nobody ever got badly hurt, at least not intentionally. The open season on Canadian country banks extended from the onset of harvest in late August until the first major snowfall immobilized the countryside for the winter. It first broke out in 1920 with a few rather tentative forays, approached epidemic proportions in 1922, and then tapered off into nothing of much consequence for the balance of the decade.

In addition to having a season for robbing banks, the Canadian experience was unique in other ways. As a general rule the robbers seldom ventured farther than forty miles from the United States border. Once, when a gang of burglars got their directions reversed and wound up in Regina, they set off an old-fashioned shoot-out in which guns blazed from cars speeding up and down the main streets of the city. Another strange feature of the Canadian robberies was their one-town, one-bank, one-robbery pattern. No matter how easy the robbery or how rich the haul, the looters seldom repeated their raids.

The first raid was an almost classic example of how to rob a bank in a Canadian small town. Some time well after midnight on October 13, 1920, five gangsters in two big cars coasted into the town of Winkler, Manitoba, for an assault on the Union Bank. A thriving Mennonite centre twelve miles from the border, Winkler proved a handy and profitable target. Before tackling the bank, the robbers went first to the railway station and cut the telegraph wires. Then they located the telephone office and applied their wire-cutters there as well. An armed guard was posted outside the bank while one of their number climbed through an open window and aroused a bank clerk who was asleep on the premises. The clerk came down, opened the door, and let the robbers into the bank proper. The clerk opened the main vault for them but did not have the combination to the safe in which the bank's money and securities were held. That constituted no problem. They tied up the bank clerk and turned their attention to preparing the door of the safe for a charge of nitroglycerine. When the clerk realized their intentions he almost collapsed with fright. He explained that he was a shell-shocked war veteran and feared the explosion would blast him into a nervous breakdown. His plight evoked a most sympathetic response from the robbers.

"We're veterans ourselves," the robbers told him, and explained that they were reduced to robbing banks for a living because the United States government was refusing to pay them the bonus they so richly deserved for their part in winning the war. They retrieved a blanket from the clerk's bedroom, wrapped it around his head to filter out the noise, and carried him out to the back yard, as far away as possible from the explosion. Then they fired their charge of nitroglycerine.

The door withstood the first blast, so they readied it for another charge. Meanwhile, the explosion awakened a local citizen who had been asleep in the livery stable across the street. When he rushed outside and spotted the lookout standing in front of the bank, he quickly concluded that foul deeds were afoot and started to trot to the fire hall to sound the town alarm. The fifth shot from the lookout caught him in the leg and the would-be town-arouser bit the dust, where he pondered the wisdom of further action. Thinking better of it, he returned to the livery stable, nursed his wound, and left the robbers to their business.

Winkler, with a population of 700, had a full-time policeman — of sorts. He and his wife had been to a dance at Morden and got home only shortly before the assault on the bank began. Both were awakened by the first explosion, and the policeman was out of bed with the sounds of the shots being fired.

"Sounds like the bank is being robbed," he said, reaching tentatively for his trousers.

"It sure does," said his wife, "and what do you think you are going to do about it?" Her voice took on a querulous tone as it rose in pitch.

"Well, I'll have to go and investigate, won't I?"

"You'll do nothing of the sort," his wife screamed. "Here the town is full of bank robbers and maybe murderers and you are prepared to leave me alone in this house while you go off risking getting killed yourself! I won't have it. I won't stay alone in this house with those men in town!"

The town constable of Winkler opted for discretion over valor and went back to bed. And not only the policeman. The combination of the first explosion and the shooting had awakened just about everybody in town, and several citizens got up, dressed, and went out to investigate. All were ordered back into their houses by the lookout, and they all went. Those who had an unobstructed view watched proceedings from behind their blinds without hazarding a step out of doors. Nobody in the whole town, so far as could be discovered, even considered taking a pot shot at the lookout or at the bandits when they emerged from the bank.

The first robbery revealed a striking contradiction in the character of the people of the small towns. They were meticulously honest and profoundly respected their neighbors' property. A prowler carting away any of their neighbors' chattels would undoubtedly have had them to reckon with. But about the bank they could be utterly objective and dispassionate, because nobody in western Canada ever regarded a bank as a neighbor. After all, it was only the bank's money that was being stolen! So, purely as spectators, they watched for a while and went back to bed.

The Winkler robbery yielded over $19,000 and was the biggest bank robbery in Manitoba up until that time. In recognition of the occasion the *Manitoba Free Press* chartered an open-cockpit airplane—there was no other kind—and flew Cecil Lamont, its star reporter, to Winkler for a first-hand report of the event. He reported, among other things, that the town of Winkler was somewhat disenchanted with its police department and talk was spreading that a replacement was needed.

The pattern of safe-blowing used by the Winkler robbers was repeated time and again during the next two years. Now and then the more venturesome even chose to try robbery by daylight. When they took the precaution of cutting communications with the outside world, these robberies went off without a hitch. At Ceylon, Saskatchewan, a trio of hold-up men turned up at noon to rob the Bank of Montreal branch there. They apparently had become quite familiar with the town, for one of them went to the home of the local policeman with the idea of taking him hostage while the robbery was carried out. However, that worthy was in the midst of his afternoon nap and his wife said he did not like to be disturbed. "That's all right," said the robber, "just let him sleep and I'll come back and see him in an hour." He went off to rob the bank. While the operation was being carried out one of the men acted as lookout on the sidewalk outside. His rather jittery behavior was noted by several local citizens who watched from across the street. Asked later why they had done nothing to forestall the robbery, they had a perfect answer. Nobody they knew owned a gun. The Ceylon robbery was specially noteworthy because the robbers not only took off with all the cash on hand, they also took a large folder filled with promissory notes, mortgages, and sundry other securities for debt. It was the greatest single debt adjustment act in Saskatchewan history, for it reduced the indebtedness of the entire community to zero.

The skill and expertise of the North Dakota bank robbers became the more impressive when it was occasionally placed in contrast with the ineptitude of the natives who tried to emulate them. In August of 1921 a quintet from Winnipeg decided to rob the Banque de Hochelaga at the hamlet of Elie, Manitoba, and set out for the job in a taxicab, planning the project en route while the cabby listened. Some twenty miles out of Winnipeg and about halfway to Elie, they stopped the car, tied up the driver, and tossed him into a ditch. Then they got lost en route to the bank and had to make several detours before reaching the town. The cabby meantime worked himself loose and managed to hop aboard a passing freight train which carried him to the next town, where he was able to sound the alarm, not to the bank in Elie but to the police in Winnipeg. While the bandits were robbing the bank of $1,000 the Winnipeg police were organizing a posse to take up the pursuit. They came upon the bank robbers a few miles out of Winnipeg, sitting disconsolately in the taxi which had just broken down and run into the ditch.

All this was but a prelude to the epidemic of bank robberies that hit southern Alberta, Saskatchewan, and Manitoba during the summer and fall of 1922. After successfully robbing half a dozen small-town banks in southwest Manitoba, and emboldened by success, the thieves ventured as far north as Moosomin to pick up an $8,000 bonanza for a night's work. By mid-October panic was gripping the towns along the border. The "what-do-we-care-it's-only-the-bank" attitude was being replaced by growing fear that sooner or later somebody was going to be killed, for guns were being fired with increasing frequency. The Saskatchewan government announced that it was sending two cars equipped with machine guns to patrol the back roads in the vicinity of Estevan and to arrest suspicious strangers on sight.

At Pilot Mound in Manitoba and at Estevan and Oxbow in Saskatchewan, the citizens organized night patrols who went about armed with hunting rifles. Near Oxbow the vigilantes set up a roadblock one night, lay in wait with their car lights off, and caught a group of errant duck hunters in their sights when they switched on their lights. The Pilot Mound group was the largest and most vigilant that was organized anywhere along the border. It split up into small cells, which not only patrolled streets and alleys at night but kept track of the movement of strangers in town. One night its patrollers spotted a foreign car with five passengers pulling up, with lights dimmed, before the telephone office. The posse rushed to investigate and so startled the occupants of the car that they roared out of town and didn't stop until they got to Manitou, fifteen miles away, where, the coast seeming to be clear, they stopped and blew the safe in the post office.

Whether the banks were being robbed by one gang or by many was never determined, and a great chance to find out was blown by the Manitoba Provincial Police. A tip was received that a gang was going to blow the safe in the bank at Pipestone, and an ambush was organized. Instead of trapping the robbers in the bank, however, the police set up a roadblock outside of town. An elaborate system was organized to warn the roadblockers when the robber car would be approaching. Unhappily, the ambushers let off a volley of shots before the robbers got within easy range. The robbers veered around the blockade and escaped, with rounds of shots fired both from the car and from the police. None of the shots hit anything, not even the fleeing car. When it turned out that the Provincial Police had neglected to notify the R.C.M.P. of what was afoot, despite the fact that the Mounties had detachments in the area, heads rolled in the Provincial Police Commission office.

If there had been a modicum of co-operation between the governments of Saskatchewan and Manitoba and the government of North Dakota, some of the robberies might well have been solved. North Dakota, however, took the dimmest view of the string of boozoriums Saskatchewan had permitted along its borders. In addition, because the Canadian government did almost nothing to prevent the smuggling of stolen cars into Canada, North Dakota was happy to let the Canadians stew in their own juices.

In Alberta, however, things were different, and the difference paid off. The biggest bank robbery in Alberta took place at the hamlet of Foremost in August 1922. Five men blew the Union Bank safe and escaped with $121,000 in cash and $75,000 in bonds. When the bonds started to turn up in New York, the Alberta government sent a Provincial Police inspector down to the States to hire the Pinkerton and Burns detective agencies to trace the robbers. A year later they came up with three suspects and extradition proceedings were started. To everybody's surprise, one of the suspects was prepared to confess in return for a light sentence. A deal was made, convictions were obtained, and the confessor even added an unexpected fillip. He escorted the police to Stanley Park in Vancouver, got his bearings from two marked trees, took the required number of steps, plunged a shovel into the turf, and dug up several glass jars containing the securities looted from Foremost as well as from several American banks.

In the early stages of the bank robbery epidemic, there was a general tendency to blame the robberies on the rum-runners. That theory, however, was rendered untenable by the march of events in 1922. The government of Saskatchewan closed the small-town liquor stores in June of that year and confined the export business to cities of 10,000 population. This did not completely dry up the traffic, but it did drastically reduce it and concentrate it at two or three railway points near the border. In Regina the Bronfman-Natanson-Chechik combination quickly devised a system to circumvent the new regulations. They turned the railway stations at Bienfait and Estevan into liquor warehouses by simply consigning shipments of their best Yorkton Scotch or bourbon to John Doe, Minot, North Dakota, in care of the express agent at Bienfait or Estevan. The Americans met the Bronfman agent at the railway station, paid for the booze, and took delivery of it as ordinary express.

So the business went on. But the robberies that created the sensations all took place after the border liquor stores were closed, and none was at a point where a liquor store had been located. There were no liquor stores in Manitoba and it was the Manitoba towns that were hardest hit by the bank robbers. There had never been a liquor store anywhere near Foremost, Alberta. On the other hand, there had been liquor stores in a dozen towns very handy to the border where banks had not been robbed. That the robberies ceased with the passing of the rum-running era was probably coincidental, explainable at least by the possibility that the American gangsters had turned to more lucrative income sources closer to home, or had been removed from circulation by American authorities.

For the residents of the small Canadian towns, the bank robberies provided a time meridian against which they measured all other events, clear into their old age. The bank robberies were for them what the 1915 crop was for the farmers, what the 1919 general strike was for organized labor, what the Wall Street crash was for economists and historians. The bank robberies were what popped into memory whenever it became necessary to locate some other occurrence, and they did so because each had the essential uniqueness to mark meridians in time.

Who, in the town of Melita, could ever forget the Saturday night in September 1922 when six gangsters robbed the bank of $7,000 in cash and bundles of Victory Bonds. A progressive town of 700, Melita was one of the first to install its own gasoline-driven electric plant to provide it with street lighting. After the robbers had cut the telephone and telegraph wires, they noticed an engineer at work in the plant which was opposite the bank. They went in, bound and gagged him, and took him over to the bank with them. Then they awakened two junior accountants, got them to open the bank, and left them tied up in their pyjamas in the back yard.

The safe in the Melita bank was more resistant than most and it took four separate charges before they got the door off. The explosions roused the town from its slumbers, and when the fourth went off, the Rev. Thomas Beveridge, who doubled as the editor of the *Melita Enterprise*, decided there might be a story in what was going on. He high-tailed it for the bank where the robbers, then busily loading their loot and preparing to flee the town, tried to persuade him to leave. When he refused they started shooting at his feet. Whether by accident or design, one bullet struck home, and the Rev. Beveridge hastily retreated. As he did so, another citizen, aroused by the shooting, ran to the fire hall and began pulling the alarm bell. That was the end of sleep for everybody in Melita that night. When daybreak came they organized a posse and took off after the robbers. Newspaper reports noted that they had been able to follow the tracks of the bandits' car clear down to the U.S. border, twenty miles away. The robbery car, it was explained, was equipped with U.S. cord tires which left distinctive tread marks on the dusty road.

Or who within twenty miles of Moosomin could forget four nights later when another gang blew the safe in the bank?

Moosomin, a town of 1,100, was the largest community hit that fall. In addition to cutting the telephone and telegraph wires, the five bandits took the precaution of cutting the rope on the town fire-alarm bell. The night telegraph operator was trussed up at the station and taken along to the bank. The bank accountant and the teller were routed from their beds in the bank building and bound and gagged with the telegrapher. After working on the safe for seventy minutes and using several large charges of explosive, which did more damage to the interior of the bank than to the safe, they eventually got it opened. The loot was disappointing—only $3,500. The unique feature of the Moosomin robbery was the enthusiasm it aroused among the citizenry to share the news with the entire countryside. When the telephone line was repaired, party lines began to ring all over the place. Soon Moosomin came to resemble any town on the First of July, as curiosity seekers rushed in from miles around to see the bank that had been robbed and get the details first-hand from the residents.

Or how about the little town of Altona where a couple of weeks later four bandits held up the bank at noon, locked the bank manager and his assistant in the vault, and made off with $2,500 in cash? They too were traced to the United States after the bank employees succeeded in attracting the attention of a customer who managed to manipulate the lock on the vault.

These were the once-in-a-lifetime explosions which shattered the all-pervasive somnolence of small-town life on the prairies. But the shattering was as ephemeral as it was unique, for if, like the Regina hurricane of 1912, nothing like it had ever happened before, nothing like it ever happened again. The word for the small towns of the west went back to being: QUIET.

It was, that is, until that second week in June 1927 when an itinerant rapist set off the greatest ever manhunt on the prairies.

Hitch-hiking, which would ultimately be developed into a fine art *cum* nuisance, was almost unknown on the prairies in the years between the wars. And with good reason—highways had not yet been invented, though the word was being used to describe gravelled roads between Winnipeg and Emerson, Regina and Moose Jaw, Edmonton and Calgary. Inter-city bus and trucking companies were operating along these roads, which became dust-choked in dry weather, pot-holed in wet weather, and bone-shakingly corduroyed all the time. Drummers for Winnipeg, Regina, and Calgary wholesale houses were already covering their territories by car during the summer months, but ordinary motorists seldom embarked on long-distance touring save in well-organized safaris. Transients who moved around the west did so mainly by railway freight train. Yet it was a pioneer hitch-hiker, Earle Nelson by name, who brought on the greatest seizure of mass hysteria in all prairie history.

If all the excitement of the small-town bank robberies could have been condensed into a single action, with a couple of routine manhunts and a sprinkling of urban robberies thrown in, the amalgam would have perhaps equalled the excitement of a single day in the week-long saga of The Strangler. It monopolized the 8-column, front-page headlines of the newspapers from Fort William to Edmonton. This was an era in which the Canadian papers were becoming increasingly preoccupied with everything American, from baseball heroes to movie heroines, from mass murders to union derbies, from lynch mobs to ticker-tape parades. But on the day of the greatest emotional binge in American history, when more than 1,800 tons of ticker tape was being showered on Charles A. Lindbergh on his triumphal return to New York from his flight to Paris, the story was buried under a one-column head on page eight of the *Manitoba Free Press*. It devoted its prime front-page space to reportage of the fruitless search for The Strangler, who overnight had become the "Gorilla Man" of the headline writers.

The Strangler, Earle Nelson, was an escapee from an American mental institution who had been wandering through the United States middle west. He had hitched a ride to the Manitoba border south of Winnipeg with an American farmer. At Emerson he was given another lift by a Canadian couple who deposited him on Portage Avenue in Winnipeg in the early afternoon of Wednesday, June 8, 1927. A few minutes later he was knocking at the door of a nearby Smith Street rooming house — a shabbily dressed, avowedly religious little man, seeking a quiet room where he could spend his after-work leisure in pious meditation. He paid the landlady a $1 deposit on a $3-a-week room on the second floor, with a promise to pay the balance the next day. On Thursday morning he made his bed, straightened up his room, and left for the day, seemingly for work. When he returned in the late afternoon he had a small conversation with the landlady about paying the $2 he owed her the next day and retired to his room. Early Friday morning he left the house as quietly as he had entered, and never went back.

A couple of miles away, across the Red River in Elmwood, William Patterson returned home from work on Friday evening to discover his wife inexplicably missing and his two small children being cared for by a neighbor. When inquiry in the neighborhood produced no word of his wife, who was seven months pregnant, Patterson became alarmed and called the police. In a search of his home he discovered that his Sunday-best suit was missing and that someone had broken into a suitcase and stolen the family's $60 nest egg. Then his eyes caught sight of the corner of his wife's coat sticking out from under the bed. It covered the body of his wife Emily, who had been strangled, bludgeoned over the head, and raped.

The Saturday morning *Free Press* carried the first of what would become daily 8-column front-page headlines. In announcing the murder of Mrs. Patterson the paper also carried a warning from the Acting Chief of Police George Smith to Winnipeg housewives to keep their doors locked and beware of strangers. The methods used by The Strangler were identical with those described in police circulars from a dozen United States cities stretching between San Francisco and Philadelphia.

On Sunday afternoon, while the police were combing the city for the killer of the Patterson woman, a lodger in the Smith Street rooming house glanced through the door of the room Nelson had vacated. There, on the floor under the bed, was the nude body of a 14-year-old schoolgirl. Her name was Lola Cowan and she had gone into the house on Thursday evening selling artificial flowers. Like Mrs. Patterson, she had been strangled and raped. The discovery of the dead girl's body so unnerved the lodger that he tore down the stairs shouting incoherently, and rushed out of the house and down the street to a telephone to call the police. In his excitement he had ignored the hall telephone in his own lodging house.

The discovery of the second murder brought extra editions of the *Free Press* and the *Tribune* to the streets on Sunday afternoon. The next morning the *Free Press* added a new and sinister subheading to its 8-column streamer.

Second Murder in City by the Same Man

Girl of 14 is victim of strangler
believed notorious killer wanted
for 20 similar murders in U.S.

An all-pervading panic gripped Winnipeg that Monday and spread rapidly through western Ontario, rural Manitoba, and across Saskatchewan into Alberta. Winnipeg housewives, almost to a woman, stopped answering their doors to anybody, even to milk and bread delivery men they had known for many months. Some of them even stopped answering their telephones for fear it might be The Strangler probing for another victim. Some kept their children home from school and in the house. Canvassers, bill collectors, vegetable peddlers, and door-to-door salesmen found the distaff security utterly impregnable and took the rest of the week off. Hardware stores were quickly cleaned out of padlocks and door chains by nervous husbands who rushed home during the noon hour to install them.

If the wanted man had deliberately set out to put the police on his trail he could hardly have left more clues. At the Patterson house he had changed into the husband's suit, which fitted him badly, and left his old clothes behind. At a Main Street second-hand store, he swapped the Patterson suit for one that fitted, stopped at a cigar store for a pocketful of cigars, called in at a barber shop for a shave and a haircut, and garrulously entertained the barber and his customers with a non-stop tale of wandering through the United States.

Midway through Friday afternoon, having committed two murders within twenty-four hours, he had boarded a Portage Avenue streetcar heading west, got into a casual conversation about religion with a couple of passengers, left the car with them at the end of the line, and helped them hitch a ride with a passing motorist to the town of Headingly, twelve miles west of Winnipeg. He parted with them there, and by the time the second murder was discovered on Sunday he was in Regina.

Routine police work picked up his trail on Saturday when the Patterson suit was located in Waldman's Main Street clothing store. Waldman recalled Nelson's inquiry about a barber shop, for he had given him some direction. The barber easily recalled him as the talkative customer who had some strange scratches on his head, who had left a 50-cent tip—something unheard of in Main Street barber shops—and who had given the shoeshine boy a cigar for the whisk job he had performed. Farther down Main Street, a haberdashery clerk recalled having sold the wanted man a champagne-colored fedora hat with a brightly colored band.

Nevertheless, the Tuesday morning paper reported in its main front-page story that The Strangler had completely hidden his trail. The radio, which was just beginning to compete with the newspapers and the party-line telephones as a spot-news purveyor, spread The Strangler story, and the panic, across the west. The description of the wanted man was given wide circulation. Unhappily, it was a description that fitted most of the five-foot-sixers in the land. Between Fort William on the east and Elbow, Saskatchewan, *ad hoc* vigilante groups and provincial and local police rounded up every transient in sight who remotely resembled the fugitive. The *Winnipeg Tribune* later guessed that during the manhunt more than 1,000 wayfarers had been taken into custody for identification, more than 100 of them in Winnipeg alone. The police in Winnipeg, Portage la Prairie, Brandon, Regina, and Saskatoon were besieged with calls from alarmed citizens reporting sightings of the wanted man. Far from resenting the plethora of calls and false alarms, the police urged the public to even greater vigilance, as they worked without sleep checking every report that came in.

The manhunt reached a climax of sorts on Tuesday afternoon, when the Regina police reported that Nelson's presence in that city on Monday had been definitely established. This eased the panic in Winnipeg momentarily, until the police urged an intensification of vigilance because of a pattern established by the American Strangler, who frequently circled back to the scene of his crimes. That Nelson was either heading back to Winnipeg or cutting for the United States was confirmed early Wednesday morning when he passed through Arcola in southeastern Saskatchewan. The Manitoba and Saskatchewan police forces both dispatched reinforcements into the south country but failed to pick up his trail. As it turned out, he was riding eastward with a scrap-iron buyer who was canvassing the farms off the beaten paths of southern Manitoba.

He had sold his fancy hat in Regina on Tuesday, and swapped his suit for a pair of overalls and a khaki shirt. At Boissevain, Manitoba, he parted from the junk collector and was picked up south of town by a local farmer, who recognized his passenger's clothing from the description of the wanted man, found a pretext to turn at a road intersection, and let the man out. He rushed back to Boissevain and notified the police, who called Brandon and Winnipeg for help. None could be given immediately because an all-day rain had made the roads impassable throughout southern Manitoba. Nelson, meanwhile, was making his way slowly southward and reached the hamlet of Wakopa, five miles from the U.S. border, around supper time. He bought some cheese, biscuits, and a bottle of pop in the James Morgan general store and resumed his journey on foot, but this time with a bevy of Morgan's neighbors trailing him from a distance. Morgan had recognized the fugitive at once, and had slipped out of his store to persuade several friends to follow Nelson while he tried to get through on the party line to the Provincial Police office at Killarney, a dozen miles to the north.

The phone call brought a Provincial Police constable slithering through the mud from Killarney. He picked up Morgan at Wakopa, made a couple of wide detours to get ahead of the fugitive, and arrested him without a struggle as he was walking down the railroad tracks. Nelson had registered at the Arcola hotel as Virgil Wilson, a name he had used many times in the United States. Nelson denied ever having been in Winnipeg and willingly accompanied the policeman to Killarney. The constable fed the suspect at a local restaurant, lodged him in a jail cell in the basement of the town hall, and went off to write his report. The town policeman who took charge of the prisoner did so with reluctance because he would have to spend the night on guard. He relieved Nelson of his shoes, secured the cell bars with a pair of padlocks, and went off to stock up on pipe tobacco for the night. He was away, by various newspaper estimates, somewhere between ten and thirty minutes. When he got back Nelson was gone. He had picked both padlocks and the jail door with a rusted nail-file he found on the floor of his cell.

Nobody in southwestern Manitoba got any sleep that Wednesday night. The town constable sounded the tocsin that brought the entire male population to the fire hall on the run. A posse of 200, variously armed with shotguns, .22 rifles, and ax handles, was quickly organized. The party lines spread the alarm and soon search parties were sloshing through the mud and rain into every imaginable hiding place within a radius of twenty miles of Killarney. For the first time within living memory, every town in the area with a lighting plant kept the plant operating and the street lights burning throughout the night.

In Winnipeg the Provincial Police Commissioner, despairing of ever getting to Killarney by road, rounded up a contingent of provincial and city police and dispatched them westward by special train. While all this was going on, Nelson was sheltering himself from the rain in sheds and outhouses in Killarney. In one shed he found a pair of skating boots that fitted him, so he tore the skates off and put on the boots. Eventually he found his way back to the railway station and hid under the freight platform for the night. Shortly after daybreak he emerged from his hiding place and headed down the track. But his luck had run out. An early-rising housewife spotted him and called the police office. The main body of the posse was located, and it rushed back to surround a bush east of town. Unfortunately for the manhunters, the housewife had got her directions mixed; Nelson had gone west instead of east. As the special train was heard whistling for a crossing east of town, the townsfolk hurried from whatever they were doing to the station. Nelson also heard the train whistle and, assuming it was a freight train going through, emerged from hiding just west of town to jump aboard as it passed. Instead, as it came to a halt at the station, Nelson was spotted on the tracks and was quickly captured and taken aboard the train.

Still protesting his innocence, Nelson chain-smoked his way to Winnipeg, regaling his captors during the four-hour journey with a steady flow of dirty stories, interspersed with periods of sphinx-like silence and immobility. The word of his recapture was flashed to Winnipeg by extra newspaper editions and radio newscasts, and Winnipeggers turned out by the thousands at the several points at which the special train was rumored to be scheduled to unload the prisoner. The biggest crowd of all, variously estimated at from 1,000 to 4,000, gathered at the Rupert Avenue police station. Only those within a few feet of the doors of the police garage got a glimpse of the prisoner as the police cavalcade moved quickly through the crowd and into the station.

The hysteria that had gripped the prairies with the strangulation murders lifted as quickly as it had come. The front pages of all the Manitoba Friday newspapers were devoted to the arrest stories and the replaying of Nelson's crimes. But by Monday the city was back almost to normal, and Nelson was shunted aside as the papers returned to their preoccupation with the civil war in China, the threat of war in the Balkans, the shouting war between Britain and Russia, violent crime in the United States, transatlantic stunt flying, and the resumption of the election campaign in Manitoba—a preoccupation that had been brought to a dead halt by The Strangler.

In the weeks that followed his arrest, Nelson's name cropped up frequently in a minor way, as law enforcement officials from American cities found in him an excuse for a vacation trip to Winnipeg, bringing along fingerprints and descriptive material that provided positive identification of Nelson as the man wanted for some twenty-odd strangulation-rape murders. That he was a certifiable lunatic seemed clear enough, for he had been in and out of the asylum at Napa, California, several times over the previous decade. At the age of thirty he had never held a steady job, and his behavior when at large was obviously psychopathic.

Nevertheless, having been convicted of the Winnipeg murders by the newspapers at the outset of the manhunt, Earle Nelson was brought to trial at the fall assizes of 1927, convicted officially, and hanged by the neck until he was dead in the Vaughan Street jail yard on Friday, January 13, 1928. Even in death Nelson's fascination for Winnipeggers diminished hardly at all. During his trial the corridors of the Law Courts were jam-packed with hundreds of spectators seeking entrance to a courtroom that could accommodate barely 150. On the night before his execution, several hundred curiosity-seekers hung around the walls enclosing the scaffold, waiting for nobody knew quite what. They only dispersed when told The Strangler's body had been transferred to the nearby Barker's Funeral Home to be prepared for shipment to California.

One of the largest crowds ever to attend a funeral in Winnipeg turned up at the undertaker's long before the doors opened for public viewing of the body. During the two-hour viewing period upward of 1,500 trudged through the undertaker's for a quick glimpse of the Gorilla Man who had terrorized the whole western countryside for that week of June 1927.

9. A Blow for Women's Lib

The staff of the Inland Shipping Company at 647 Grain Exchange in the fall of 1922 was made up of the manager, an office boy, and two stenographer-bookkeepers — a rather homely older woman and a vivacious younger woman in her early twenties. In the early part of December the girls were frequently seen whispering together, breaking off whenever a third party came within hearing distance. Vivian Maw, the younger woman, was clearly having difficulty making up her mind about something and was being egged on by her companion. As days passed it became apparent that something more important than Christmas shopping was under discussion. Three days before Christmas a decision was taken. During her lunch hour Vivian Maw went out and got her hair bobbed.

The news of her decision was carried through the building by telegraph messengers and until the office closed for the day there was a steady inflow of both men and women to inspect the first female bobbed head in the Winnipeg Grain Exchange. Statistically it was not all that significant, for there were probably less than a score of women employees in the whole building at the time. Nevertheless, it did something for her personality; made her almost schoolgirlish in demeanor. A couple of weeks later the other woman took the same step and had her hair cut. Her personality, too, changed for the better. She seemed much more inclined to smile than before, though that might have been a self-conscious reaction, indicating she was not quite comfort-

183

able with what she had done. Her bob, unfortunately, exposed a too-long stretch of rather scrawny neck which very soon became prickled with unsightly, coarse neck-hair. Within a few more weeks half the women employees in the building had followed Vivian Maw's blow for women's liberation and had bobbed their hair. That really was what hair bobbing was, an historic, if not a giant, step for womankind away from her subservient role in human society.

Vivian Maw was not the first woman in Winnipeg to bob her hair, but the time she took to make up her mind was indicative of the inner turmoil that women were experiencing as they contemplated actions unprecedented in the history of their sex. That so simple a decision as having one's hair cut could create such hesitation was a measure of the distance women's liberation still had to go in 1922. Nevertheless, it was more important, as an historic bench mark, than the fact that women were at work outside the home doing jobs once done exclusively by men. In those jobs they were part of a social change dictated by men. The Great War drained so many men into the armed services that women had to be recruited to fill their jobs. Going to work was partly patriotic and partly an economic necessity for women in wartime, a result of both male encouragement and male pressure. Cutting one's hair was an act of personal feminine decision, as dancer Irene Castle had demonstrated almost a decade before.

If Vivian Maw was a pioneer in women's liberation, so was her fellow-worker, in a very different and perhaps more significant way. She was a married woman whose husband was quite capable of supporting her, yet she was fully employed outside her home. That made her the rarest of rare pigeons, for a working wife of an employed husband was almost unheard of in 1922.

With the coming of peace and the return of the soldiers from overseas, a spreading stigma became attached to the employment of women. Veterans frequently were unable to obtain employment of any kind, yet the stores and offices were full of women who had been recruited in wartime and were still "doing a man's work". The presence of women in the labor force was viewed with a bilious eye by organized labor and veterans' groups alike. Women were an ever-present threat to the standard of wages the unions had achieved through bitter and prolonged struggle.

The objection was soundly based because employers had discovered during the war that there were many jobs women could do as well as men, and they could be hired for a third less wages. That was particularly true in the retail field, where employment of women snowballed. On the other hand, despite the financial advantage, substitution of women for men in clerical jobs was strongly resisted in railway offices, in the civic service, and in provincial government offices. Openings there were for stenographers, and women gradually came to monopolize the craft, but in the bulk of the other clerical positions men still dominated. Even in the banks, which were genteel sweatshops by long tradition, the junior jobs from which promotions were ultimately earned were filled exclusively by males.

As a general rule women were used to fill out staff shortages rather than as full-scale replacements. In the department stores women employees always worked under close supervision of male employees. Even in millinery establishments men still made the decisions. And that seemed to be the dividing point—where decisions were made. In a society so dominated by men, anyone who expressed an opinion that a woman could ever develop "a head for business" would be marked for demotion to the stockroom and a job befitting his retarded mentality. With the end of the war there was a general assumption that everything would revert to the *status quo ante*, that women would return to their kitchens, and that men would take up where they had left off in the business offices of the land.

Two factors derailed such assumptions. The first, of course, was money. Employers had discovered that women would work for less and could do certain jobs as well as men. The second was that the women liked their new way of life — being out in the world, and earning money of their own that they could spend as they liked. But here a split developed within the ranks of working women. Working wives became subjected to criticism and even abuse from all sides, from women as well as men.

During the war many married women, particularly the wives of soldiers, had been forced into the labor force to survive and to feed their families. The state provided nothing in the way of financial assistance to soldiers' dependants except to forward the soldiers' assigned pay to them. Soldiers' wives with small children had to depend on private charities and patriotic funds for support. Those who could work and hesitated to do so were strongly pressured by the charities. For many, wartime employment was not much better than charity, for wages were frequently disgracefully low — $8 and $10 a week was common in many jobs. Nor did things improve much for the families when the soldiers returned and got their old jobs back. Such was the impact of post-war inflation that even when both husband and wife worked there was little surplus available to make up for the wartime losses in family income. But with so many veterans out of work, the employment of wives of any kind, veterans' wives or civilians' wives, was generally frowned upon, and not only by the veterans.

The war had brought a brand-new factor into play. It had opened up new fields of employment outside the home for girls leaving school in their teens. Once employment had been limited to nursing and teaching for those of higher intelligence. For the balance there was housework and the laundries. In the 1920s the girls emerging from school had seen their sisters in all kinds of other seemingly interesting and well-paying (compared with housework or laundry) jobs. They wanted part of that action. Their parents supported their desires because there was not a working-class household that did not need extra income. But there was more to all this than crass material considerations. For those whose inclinations were still pointed toward matrimony, a business career came to be regarded as a desirable preliminary. Becoming employed in an office or store widened the field of choice. Certainly a girl would meet a dozen times more eligible bachelors in a business office or a department store than she would teaching school or nursing. A quick glance at the spinsters drying on the vine of both professions was all the proof they needed of that. When the girls surveyed the employment scene and found it peopled with married women, they became the most vocal agitators against their sisters under the skin. There was no doubt that in their criticism they represented the vast majority of both male and female public opinion.

Once a single woman married it was universally assumed that she would quit work and assume the role of wife, and ultimately of mother, in the home; husbands who permitted their wives to work after marriage were usually regarded as being greedy beyond reason, suspected of "not wearing the pants in the family" and of being a bit queer into the bargain. In most large establishments, women automatically left their jobs with their marriage. Department stores generally followed the practice of not hiring married women.

There was one exception. During the Christmas rush married women by the hundreds moved back into the labor force as extra sales help in the retail field. In the commercial areas, as the practice of permitting employees a week or two of summer vacation became entrenched, stenographers who had married and retired were called back to fill their old jobs when their successors went on vacation. These were merely minor ripples on the social tides of the times but they were an indication of an important fact: once the girls had sampled the fruits of gainful employment they never lost their taste for it. Indeed, as time would ultimately prove, that taste could develop easily into downright addiction.

All this would come later. For most of the 1920s, women's liberation was a matter of adding a small liberty here to a small liberty there. Fittingly, it was bobbed hair, more than anything else, that came to symbolize the 1920s in the world of women. Bobbed hair was always given precedence over short skirts, cigarette smoking, and gin drinking when the professional viewers-with-alarm mounted their pulpits to denounce the behavior of the "modern women" of the 1920s. It was, for example, intransigently opposed by the Catholic Church.

One of the bitterest strikes in Calgary during the decade was precipitated in March 1926 when two student nurses at the Holy

Cross Hospital defied the hospital rule against short hair and crossed the tonsorial Rubicon. Their instant dismissal was followed by a hair-cutting orgy in the nurses' dormitory as thirty nurses cut their hair. Then the authorities cancelled the weekly leaves of the nurses for three months while their hair grew back to acceptable length. The thirty quit in a body. The hospital then demanded that those who remained sign a pledge not to cut their hair while employed in the hospital. Instead, sixty more nurses cut their hair and made bobbed hair practically unanimous at the Holy Cross. With that, the authorities backed down and tolerated what they could not suppress. It was many months before the morale of the nursing staff returned to normal. A year later the girls working in the St. Paul's Hospital in Saskatoon became restive under the no-cut edict the hospital had imposed. They managed to get the order lifted without a confrontation. The girls agreed to do the cutting with discretion and the hospital took down its restraining order. Of the 108 nurses on the staff, 96 were in bobbed hair within a week.

Prairie women plunged less precipitously into other overt assertions of independence than they did into cutting their hair. The move toward shorter skirts and more comfortable clothes was marked by hesitation and timidity. The ankles, which could have been exposed to masculine sight with the raising of the hem of women's dresses, remained encased in high-buttoned shoes until 1922 or thereabouts. It was only with the invention of fine-spun rayon stockings that above-the-ankle shoes were replaced by low-cut slippers and shoes to provide men with ten inches of calf at which to gawk. By 1924 the hemline reached the mid-calf, at which point the New York fashion designers ran amok, dropped the line to the ankle, and hobbled the women in skirts that reduced the length of a woman's step to a foot or less. It was a short-lived disaster few prairie women would tolerate; by 1926 the hem was up to a point where it exposed the knees when sitting, and it stayed there until 1929.

The fashion in haircuts dictated ever-shorter tresses, until the boyish bob was reached in 1927, along with the peek-a-boo hat and the ever-lighter dress fabrics, and the flight of women from identifiable femininity in the traditional sense became a stampede. As their hair got shorter and shorter, and women came to look more like men, they abandoned modesty, tradition, and conformity in a whole-hog drive to look even more masculine. Curves, wherever existing, were de-emphasized in favor of a flat chest and square hips. Dresses were designed to hang rather than cling. Corsets which had encased the feminine figure in iron and bone were abandoned in favor of elastic girdles, which were abandoned by some in favor of mere garter belts. Underdrawers were discarded for step-ins, and the word "bloomers" lost its unmentionable status as it came to be used to describe what women wore when they took up baseball, foot-racing, and other manly sports. And that is what they were doing with a vengeance.

Elsewhere in the world women were challenging, if not the men, then the games that men had developed for masculine amusement and recreation. If they did not play polo they were at least riding to hounds and over jumps in horse shows — and riding astride in jodhpurs instead of side-saddle. Suzanne Lenglen had achieved world fame in tennis and Helen Wills was on the threshold of an even greater career. Dorothy Campbell and Joyce Wethered dominated the women's world of golf. Annette Kellerman not only startled the world in her one-piece bathing suit, she transformed mere bathing into the sport of swimming for thousands of women. But in Canada it was a girls' basketball team in Edmonton that proved there were few games that men could play at which women could not excel.

The Edmonton Grads, who brought world fame to the Alberta capital in the 1920s, were themselves a product of the emergence of women into the commercial world. They were all graduates of a commercial college whose principal, J. Percy Page, was a basketball buff who coached them in dribbling and lay-ups as well as in shorthand and typing. By 1920 the Commercial Grads had run out of competition in Alberta and had to look farther afield for teams worthy of their skills. In 1922 they challenged a girls' team in London, Ontario, for the Canadian championship, which they won easily. A rematch was held in

Edmonton in 1923 and in a two-game series the Grads won by 51 to 28.

The victory over London led to the world championship match two weeks later against the Cleveland Favorite Knits, a professional team sponsored by an Ohio manufacturer. The series was played in the Edmonton Arena and the Grads packed it with more paying spectators, 6,000 according to the *Edmonton Journal*, than any male athletic event had ever drawn in the city. Such was the interest in the second game that local theatre owners arranged to have bulletins flashed to their audience by special telephone lines from the Arena. The Grads won the first game 34 to 20 and the second by 19 to 13, with several of its spares playing.

The Grads demonstrated in the Cleveland game, as they would demonstrate many times over the two next decades as they ruled the world of basketball, that they were superb athletes "even if they were women". It was a team on which everybody was a star. In one game centre Connie Smith might be outstanding, in the next it would be Dorothy Johnson or Winnie Martin. Then one of the guards, Mary Dunn or Eleanor Mountiford, would take her turn at leading the Grads to victory. From their victory over Cleveland the girls went off to Paris in 1924 to demonstrate the game to the Olympic officials, and they defeated the best of Europe with ridiculous ease.

The Edmonton Grads were unique in Canadian sports history. But on the prairies women were honing their skills in just about every sport one could name except soccer, lacrosse, and cricket. Basketball never caught on elsewhere as it did in Edmonton, though it was played at the Y.W.C.A.s and in high schools.

The introduction of five-pin bowling across the prairies was the signal for the women to flock to a sport they had avoided when ten-pins, with the heavier ball, was the vogue. Soon there were scores of three-men, two-women teams competing in commercial five-pin bowling leagues. A half-dozen girls' softball teams played a regular schedule in Winnipeg. Women took to golf and tennis in such numbers that many clubs had mixed-doubles competitions on weekends.

In track and field events at outdoor field days in the 1920s, the girls' events were always well filled. They could never quite outrun the men sprinters, but they could outrun any man who was not in prime physical condition. In Edmonton at the Victoria Day track meet in 1923, Florence Crang ran 100 yards in 12 seconds, compared with 10.6 seconds for the fastest male sprinter at the meet. Neither time would have won an Olympic medal, but four years later Fanny Rosenfeld, Ethel Smith, Jane Bell, and Myrtle Cook did win a gold medal for Canada in the 400-metre relay. They were Ontario girls. The highlight of that Olympiad for the west came when Ethel Catherwood, a Saskatoon high-school girl, became the best girl high-jumper in the world.

While women were embarking on a wide-ranging muscle-building program on the athletic fields, their married sisters were concentrating their attention in the opposite direction — reducing the muscular expenditure required in keeping house. Before the Great War, the dividing lines between the urban classes ran right through the kitchens. The kitchen of an upper-crust home contained a gas-fired range capable of cooking 30-pound roasts. It might also contain a smaller stove, or one- or two-burner grills for preparing snacks or tea. It contained a cold pantry — which was really a super icebox that was loaded with a couple of 100-pound blocks of ice twice a week — and a butler's pantry where the food was gathered and distributed onto plates for serving. The kitchen might even contain a butcher's block and a marble-topped table for pastry preparation. Its sink could accommodate mountainous piles of dishes, and it was served with hot- and cold-water taps. A middle-class home had a 25-pound-capacity icebox instead of a cold pantry, and a Hoosier kitchen cabinet which doubled as a food storage cupboard and a preparation centre. It came equipped with a porcelain-covered table-top which could be pushed back into the cabinet when not in use. Cooking was done on a fancied-up nickel-plated kitchen range which sometimes had demountable gas jets in the firebox. These could be removed in winter when the range functioned as an auxiliary space-heating unit. Middle-class houses built during the real-estate booms in the cities had attached woodsheds off the kitchens. The sheds were unfinished on the inside, and in the summer many families dismantled the kitchen stove and moved it into the woodshed, in the interest of making the kitchen habitable during the summer torrid spells.

The dungeon-like basements of all houses contained a coal furnace in the centre, a large coal bin in one corner, and a cistern into which rain water was diverted by downspouts from eaves-troughs, with a hand pump at the kitchen sink to bring up the water. If the home was on a street served by a gas line, it might contain a hot-water tank with a gas-burning attachment. Otherwise, there would be a "jacket heater" fired by coke to supply the house with hot water.

The working-class kitchen differed very little from the middle-class. If it had an icebox at all it would be much smaller. The kitchen cabinet, if there was one, would be an Eaton Mail Order type rather than the more expensive Hoosier. Cooking was done on a wood-fired range the year round. While there was probably a soft-water pump at the sink, there would be but a single tap — for cold water. When hot water was needed it was obtained from a tank attached to the stove or by heating on top of the stove. While most city homes had bathrooms, those at the bottom of the economic pile carried up their hot water in pails.

One facility was alike in both working-class and middle-class homes. The laundry was done in the kitchen in two round galvanized tubs. One contained a corrugated washboard for scrubbing the dirt from the clothes; the second was for rinsing. Both tubs contained rain water pumped from the basement cistern and heated in the kitchen in a huge copper boiler. Middle-class homes and working-class homes differed in one important way — in who did the work. Middle-class women had regular washerwomen, usually immigrant women, invariably pregnant, who came in every week and did the heavy washing. Working-class women did their own.

It took no blinding stroke of genius for the entrepreneurs of the time to discover that there would be a tremendous market for washing machines if they could invent one that would work.

They invented scores of them, some of which worked after a fashion. In essence they were round wooden washtubs, ribbed around the inside and lidded. From the centre of the lid a sprocket of sorts extended downward. Either the sprocket revolved to rub the clothes against the ribbed side of the tub, or the tub was turned back and forth while the sprockets remained stationary. The most popular type contained a hinged lever attached to a bar on a ratchet atop the centre sprocket. Pulling the lever handle by hand and pushing it by foot made it possible to wash the clothes from a sitting position.

After about the third washing of the family bedding in a July heat wave, there was never any doubt what the item atop every new bride's shopping list would be—a washing machine. But for those who were able to make the purchase, the gloss wore off quickly. None of the machines could equal the grime-removing ability of the old scrubbing-board, soap, scrubbing-brush, and elbow grease. In addition, operating a washing machine manually was not so much easier than scrubbing clothes on a board. Clothes frequently became entangled in the sprockets and had to be wrestled free. Completing the wash with a machine often took twice as long as a vigorous hand-washing would have. Even with washing machines, an immense amount of hand-laundering had to be done to achieve satisfactory results. The early washing machines turned out to be more of a snare and a delusion than a solution for washday miseries.

Happily, with the invention some years earlier of the small-horsepower electric motor, someone got the idea of attaching an electric motor to a washing machine. Just as the early mechanics had built their cars by putting an engine on a wagon, the electric-washing-machine developers began by attaching a motor to the wooden-ratchet machines. The improvers had only to look at these makeshift monstrosities to see there had to be a better way. They threw away the wooden tubs and started over, with metal tubs and attached wringers. By 1922 the inventors had a dozen machines on the market that more or less served their purpose. But they started no kitchen revolt because the price—$115 to $130—was far beyond the means of most urban families, even with the usual easy terms. The big breakthrough came in Winnipeg in 1924 when the City Hydro included an electric hot-water heater with the washing machine and offered both with a down payment of $15 and the balance over two years.

Until that time, a year had been the outside limit for instalment selling. The two-year payment period moved so many washing machines into Winnipeg kitchens that the utility began selling electric stoves the same way, extended the payment period to three years, and added everything to the monthly light bill. As the Winnipeg plan was widely adopted in the other cities, washday lost its terror for the housewives of western Canada, and the washerwoman's occupation became the first redundancy of the electrical age.

With an electric washing machine, an electric stove, an electric water heater, and an electric iron, a reasonable imitation of the millennium arrived for the housewives of the prairie cities. They now had time, halfway through their mornings, for a leisurely cup of coffee and a cigarette. But not many cigarettes, because smoking caught on very slowly in the west, where the men were only beginning to switch to cigarettes from pipes and cigars. In the retail trade, men who smoked did so only in the back of the store, never in the presence of and seldom within sight of the customers. Women, if they had acquired the habit, never indulged it in public, least of all in the business offices where they worked. Nevertheless, the smoking habit was being formed increasingly by younger women, mainly on the anything-you-can-do-I-can-do principle, but the decade was over before there were many women who looked comfortable while smoking a cigarette.

The last bastion of male dominance that the women cracked was addiction to alcohol, and they made little headway there during the 1920s. In the welter of agitation over Prohibition the rights of women to equality with men in the consumption of booze was never thought of, let alone raised in public. The universal assumption was that consumption of alcoholic beverages should remain what it had always been—a male monopoly. If they thought of it at all, the men would have said that by doing so they were protecting women from themselves, that booze was inimical to female health and morals. From the inseparable association of booze with prostitution in the brothels of the west, it was a fair male conclusion that a cause-and-effect relation existed between the two. In any event, women could not abide the taste of whisky or beer, so why consider them? They couldn't stomach the stuff themselves and didn't want anybody else to have any! Did they not vote overwhelmingly for Prohibition?

The truth was that women were not all so teetotal as men liked to assume. For forty years they had been imbibing vast quantities of alcohol in an infinite variety of nostrums and patent medicines advertised to alleviate the special afflictions of women. While the man of the house was knocking back a shot or two of whisky en route home from work, his wife would be taking her egg-cup full of Tanlac, Burdock's Blood Bitters, Lydia Pinkham's Vegetable Compound, Wincarnis, or Parry Davis's Tonic. All were loaded with medicinal alcohol. On the other hand, the booze sold across the bar was usually diluted and adulterated several times before it reached the customer. So the odds were that the housewives were getting more alcoholic content in their tonics than the men were in a couple of shots of bar whisky. It was only to be expected that the tonics, on an empty stomach, gave the women a noticeable lift toward the end of a labor-filled day.

That women might conceivably be interested in the consumption of beer was conceded only in Alberta after the repeal of Prohibition in 1924. On the principle, no doubt, that if farmers' wives went with them when they dropped into a country beer parlor, the men would leave while they could still walk, Alberta permitted mixed drinking in some country hotels. However, in the cities the beer parlors were for men only, although parlors could be set aside exclusively for women if hotels wished to apply for a licence. Few did. All other beverages were available only through government stores.

It was the severity of the government regulations which, ironically enough, opened the bottle for women imbibers. In all three Prairie provinces the consumption of hard liquor was confined strictly to the home. Regulations were most rigid in Manitoba. There a drinker first had to appear at a government liquor store with two letters of character reference along with a one-dollar fee. He was then issued a permit that entitled him to buy a maximum of a two-weeks supply of liquor—twelve bottles. The purchase was marked on his permit and the order, paid for in cash, was then delivered to his residence a day or two later. He could not take it with him. In Alberta and Saskatchewan liquor could be bought by the bottle, but regulations required that it be taken to the purchaser's home unopened and consumed there. Stiff penalties were provided for anybody found with an open bottle of liquor "in other than a private dwelling".

In neither Manitoba nor Saskatchewan was public boozing of any kind tolerated. It was not until 1928 that beer parlors were permitted in Manitoba. In that year hard liquor sales were also permitted on a cash-and-carry system, with the limit of one bottle per day. Saskatchewan did not get around to permitting beer parlors on a local option basis until 1934.

The repeal legislation on the prairies stood the entire system of alcoholic consumption that had prevailed prior to the Great War on its head. Then, the drinking was done at the public bars and only the high and the mighty kept wine cellars in their homes or did much drinking there. After repeal, the homes became the locale for liquor consumption. When liquor was being imbibed, no matter how temperately, it was available for the women as well as the men. Legend has it that cocktails were developed in the United States during Prohibition to disguise the harsh taste of bootleg booze and make it palatable to the female taste, as women were beginning to tipple with men in speakeasies. The whiskies and rums consumed in western Canada after repeal were of impeccable quality but, when taken undiluted, had a bite that only an acquired taste could accept. There is no reason to assume that many prairie women did not learn to enjoy a quiet drink or two via the cocktail route.

Consumption, however, is a function of availability; while the law made the purchase of hard liquor possible, economic reality kept availability to a minimum. A 26-ounce bottle of standard

Canadian rye whisky in 1925 sold for $3.50 to $4 a bottle, while imported Scotch cost $6 to $7. Relative to the income level of the working class of 1926, this meant that it took the better part of a day's pay to buy a bottle of rye, and a full day's pay for the best-paid union tradesman to acquire a bottle of Scotch. Even the closing hour of the liquor store was loaded against the working class, as labor agitators frequently pointed out. The stores closed at 6 p.m., so railway shopmen, retail clerks, etc., would have to take time off from work in order to get into the stores before closing. Though professional men and businessmen could afford to develop the habit of a couple of drinks before dinner and a liqueur afterward, and find the money to order a dozen bottles at a time, hard liquor was a luxury for everybody else. A glance at liquor sales statistics demonstrates that.

Liquor sales in Alberta in 1926-7 were $4,268,000, or roughly $6.50 per capita. On a family basis, that worked out to about six bottles of rye a year, or about enough to lubricate a couple of anniversaries, Christmas, and New Year's if guest lists were kept to an irreducible minimum. Sales in Manitoba, with its home-delivery regulations, were even more modest. In 1926-7 the total was $3,793,000, or $5.80 per capita. Clearly this was not the kind of volume that could give rise to a generation of gin-swilling flappers of the genre popularized by John Held, Jr., in the United States. Liquor was carried in flasks and "mickeys" to supper dances in the hotels and to the other dances that filled the nights with music all over the prairies in the 1920s. But it all came out of the figures quoted above. In the nature of things, the volume that disappeared down female gullets had to be minuscule. The best, or the worst, that could be said of the female assault on the boozing bastion of mankind was that they got the tips of their dancing pumps in the door when Wall Street crashed and booze went out of reach of everybody on the prairies, men and women, until the outbreak of the Second World War.

10. Almost United

Just when the rising tide of Protestant ecumenism reached its crest is probably beyond precise determination, and in any event it is of less than pressing importance to what follows. It began to flow with the unity of purpose reflected in the growing vigor of the Prohibition campaigns in the west in the 1890s, increased in power with the enactment of the Lord's Day acts of 1902 and 1906, and plunged forward with the outbreak of the passion for social reform that brought in Prohibition in 1916. Prohibition was the primary issue on which the Protestant reform movement focussed, but in achieving it they were able to gain an imposing measure of reform legislation in all the Prairie provinces.

The Prohibition crusade was the solvent which, over a quarter of a century, melted the barriers that had divided Presbyterians, Methodists, Congregationalists, Baptists, and the Salvation Army from each other. Social barriers were broken between laity and laity, clergy and clergy, laity and clergy. For the first time in many of their lives people found themselves working together for a common cause without regard for differences in creeds. Such was the euphoria the experience created that common causes seemed to rain down upon each other as social horizons expanded. And as each new cause was added, the bonds of fellowship seemed strengthened. It was hardly surprising that the concept of a United Church that could become the spiritual home of all Protestant Christians gradually became envisioned as a reachable goal.

If the Presbyterians, the Methodists, and the Congregationalists could conclude overwhelmingly that the things that united them were infinitely more important than the doctrinal differences that had divided them in the past, then there was room under the United Church umbrella for everybody. Yet, far from being the signal for a mass movement of Protestant Christians into a single church, this concept signalled the opening of an era in which sectarianism would run rampant, accompanied by a withering away of religious conviction and the erosion of interest in religious observance. Church union itself, rather than bringing in the brotherhood of man, set brother against brother, ended lifelong friendships, and brought explosions like that of an outraged father in Carnduff, Saskatchewan, when his children broke the news that on the following Sunday the Presbyterian Sunday School would become the United Church Sunday School. The blood of his Convenanting Scottish ancestors boiled to the surface and he exploded: "From this day forward I dinna care where ye worship. Go to the Catholic church for all I care. Or go with the Baptists. But if I ever catch you associating with those atheist Methodists I'll skin ye alive!"

The Carnduff Calvinist belonged to an almost infinitesimal minority on the prairies where *de facto* Protestant unity was already established in a thousand communities. To the overwhelming majority of the settlers, organic unity of the denominations was just elementary good sense. The settlers on the frontier had great difficulty supporting a single church in their market towns, let alone two or three. Such was the shortage of ministers, moreover, that no denomination could have met the demands for clergymen if it meant supplying one for every potential congregation.

In countless communities it was the settlers themselves who cut across denominational lines. In most areas of new settlement, the first priority for community action was the erection of a school, sometimes in town and sometimes between towns. Until churches could be built the school became the meeting hall for all religious groups. Once the population reached a point at which a church could be contemplated, a community church building was erected in which denominations might take turns holding services. Or the Methodist minister might serve one set of towns and the Presbyterian another. It was common practice for a preacher to hold a service in one town in the early morning, drive eight or ten miles to the next town for an afternoon service, and finish at a third town late at night.

For the settlers themselves, and particularly the farm women, it was *going* to church and not the church itself or its denomination that was important. For farm women, Sunday was as close to a day of rest as they ever got, and going to church was a welcome escape from the isolated drudgery of farm living. For many thousands of pioneers, denominational allegiance dwindled into secondary importance, as it was dwindling for many church leaders. It had become, for the leaders, downright embarrassing in the field of foreign missions. How could the gospel of Christianity be other than puzzlingly unconvincing to Chinese and Africans when they were asked to choose between the 130 separate brands being offered? So when the bitter opposition to church union blew up in the Presbyterian congregation it caught everybody on the prairies by surprise. That only went to show that nobody had been paying much attention to church history, particularly to the very recent history of the Presbyterian Church of Scotland and its incredible struggle with the "Wee Frees". That battle was destined to be repeated on the Canadian prairies, and over precisely the same issues — doctrine and property.

The "Wee Frees" in Scotland, who had fought against the establishment of the United Free Church of Scotland in 1900, were the hard-shell guardians of the purity of John Calvin's doctrines. This handful of zealots insisted that they alone represented the Free Church of Scotland, not the overwhelming majority of their fellows who had united the United Presbyterians and the Church of Scotland. As such, they claimed title to all the property of the Church, including its colleges and endowments. They carried their case to the House of Lords and won. It took an act of Parliament to sort things out and divide up the property between the majority and the minority.

The history of Presbyterianism, more than that of any other Protestant denomination, had been the history of long and bitter strife over doctrinal differences. Nobody should have taken the Presbyterians for granted, least of all other Presbyterians. Nevertheless, by the end of the Great War the differences dividing Presbyterians from Methodists and Congregationalists in Canada had become thickly papered over by the emergence of the social gospel, or the "social passion" as Richard Allen has called it. It, as noted, had grown out of the common cause which the Protestant denominations made against the ever-present menace of booze and brothels to the morals of their parishioners.

The campaigns for Prohibition failed repeatedly, but the Protestant efforts to legislate morality on other fronts fared better. The federal Lord's Day Act, with supporting provincial legislation, turned the prairies into a Sabbatarian wasteland. All work was forbidden on Sundays save that of mercy and necessity. All railway transportation stopped except through passenger and freight services. No branch-line train could move on Sunday. No streetcar could run. All buying, selling, and delivering of anything and everything was forbidden. Farm work, except the feeding of livestock and the milking of cows, was against the law. All this was the result of Protestant clergymen banding together into the Lord's Day Alliance, as they had banded together in the cause of temperance.

As the clergymen poked around in the side-effects of unrestricted boozing in the cities, they discovered all manner of social and moral problems that needed attending to. There was poverty, mistreatment of wives and neglect of children, and a total lack of protection for women and children, industrial workers, the halt, and the blind. As wave after wave of immigrants hit the west with the turn of the century, all these deficiencies multiplied. In an effort to treat them the Methodists organized their Social and Moral Reform Society and the Presbyterians put together their Temperance and Moral Reform Society. From the beginning it was the Methodists who concentrated most on social improvement. They launched J. S. Woodsworth on his career as a social activist, opened settlement houses, and brought the spotlight of publicity to bear on the dark side of the social fabric. The Presbyterians tended to worry more about moral than social problems.

In November 1907, under the leadership of the Rev. J. G. Shearer of the Presbyterians and the Rev. S. D. Chown of the Methodists, a large conference was organized in Winnipeg to discuss moral and social problems. All nonconformist groups were invited and took part, along with business leaders, labor representatives, and even a sprinkling of Anglicans and Roman Catholics. The primary purpose of the convention was to launch an all-out campaign to banish the bars, but it also worked over all the festering social sores of the time. Out of that meeting the Social Service Council evolved, and under the driving leadership of Protestant clergymen, it became a potent force for social progress in the land. The social passion was a force, however, from which the Anglican Church remained aloof and in which the Roman Catholic took no interest. But it brought the Presbyterians right up with the Methodists in commitment to improving the standard of life of their parishioners.

In the previous quarter of a century the preoccupation of many Methodist clergymen with social problems had raised doubts in Presbyterian minds of the depth of Methodist commitment to "Christian Principles". Presbyterian divines like the Rev. F. B. DuVal in Winnipeg might rail against prostitution and the booze trade but theirs was umbrage based on moral rather than social considerations. To the Presbyterians, the sinful lives of prostitutes were easily squared with the doctrine of predestination. The emphasis of people like DuVal was not on redemption of sinners but on driving the sinners off so they would not threaten the everlasting souls of the faithful. Though the Methodists seemed to share that general concept they were developing an awareness of the part played by poverty, drunkenness, and slum environments in the production of prostitutes.

Regardless of its origins, distrust of a rival denomination was far from a Presbyterian monopoly. All denominations looked askance at all others. With Presbyterians it tended to run a little deeper when Methodists were involved. Just as, among all Christian sects, the word "Jew" has been synonymous with hard bargaining, the Presbyterians had a phrase that gained wide circulation outside the fold. When they wanted to describe an underhanded action they called it "a dirty Methodist trick". Nevertheless, the Winnipeg conference of 1907 marked the end of Presbyterian disdain for social issues as they joined the battle with enthusiasm, even if the doubts many Presbyterians held about Methodist convictions were slow to dissipate.

After the Winnipeg conference the Presbyterians set up their Moral and Social Reform and Evangelism Department under the Rev. G. C. Pidgeon, the Rev. C. W. Gordon, and the Rev. J. G. Shearer. Two years later it was reorganized on a permanent basis as the Social Service and Evangelism Department to, in Dr. Gordon's phrase, "take up the study of problems too long neglected by the church. It sought to bring the church face to face with great national questions as temperance, social vice, industrial and labor problems and the problem of the city."

Writing in 1913 Dr. Gordon noted, in the chapter on Presbyterianism that he prepared for the *Makers of Canada* encyclopedia:

> With such vigor has the board . . . conducted its operations that its annual expenditures have risen in four years from $5,000 to nearly $50,000 and while, in 1910, there existed in Canada not one [Presbyterian] institution devoted to the cause of social service, in 1912 there has been established six social service houses connected with the work of social redemption and three social settlements holding property worth about $150,000 and necessitating the employment of some thirty expert workers and a host of volunteer assistants. The significance and rapid development of this department of the church's work lies in the quickened conscience of the church in regard to the responsibility and the opportunity for ministry not only in word and doctrine but in matters that have an immediate bearing on the material, social and religious well being of the people. And there is no doubt that by the return to the methods and ideals of the

apostolic church the modern church will discover unsuspected powers of service and will recover apostolic power to serve and bless the people of the land in which she is established.

On the theme of church unity, he continued:

It remains to notice the rise of a movement which it is believed may issue in the disappearance from the roll of Christian churches in Canada the name and the outward form of the Presbyterian Church and by the union with the Methodist and Congregational churches may establish a great church which will embody in itself all that has made the history of Presbyterianism in Canada radiant with the glory of heroic courage and adventurous faith.

Dr. Gordon went off to the war as senior chaplain for the Canadian forces in Flanders, and therefore missed the successful culmination of the Prohibition crusades of 1915-16. This surely was one of the many bench marks of the Protestant United Front, which achieved not only Prohibition but woman suffrage, compulsory school attendance acts, workmen's compensation acts, mothers' allowance acts, child protection legislation, dower rights, and wide-ranging health services. In all of these causes the Presbyterians, Methodists, Congregationalists, Baptists, Salvationists, and many of the evangelical sects marched to the tune of social reform. It was a tune in which there was no place for discordant notes of doctrinal differences. But doctrinal differences there were, and they emerged with shattering impact when the liberal, social-gospelling Presbyterian clergymen tried to convert their unity in pursuit of social reform into an organic union of the Methodist and Presbyterian churches. To hard-core Presbyterians predestination and the tenets of Knox and Calvin were not mere gewgaws to be abandoned lightly at the behest of the church elders. The "Wee Frees" of Canadian Calvinism might have entered into fraternal bonds with Methodists in the Masonic order, the Loyal Orange Lodge, the Knights of Pythias, and the other secret societies which abounded in Canada. But to meld their church organically with the Methodist? Never!

After the church leaders had drawn up their Basis for Union in 1908, and it had gained quick approval from Methodists and Congregationalists, it was submitted in 1912 to a vote of the Presbyterian congregations. Out of a membership of 287,944, the vote was 106,755 for and 48,278 against union. Dr. Gordon saw in this vote cause for great optimism. The negative vote was only 17 per cent of the congregation and the general feeling of the Presbyterian leaders was that time should be taken to try to persuade the minority to change its mind. In the meantime the drafters of the Basis of Union went back to work to reword the document in the hope of overcoming the minority's objections. But that minority was beyond appeasement. The new draft was submitted to the Kingston Assembly in 1915 and carried by 368 delegates to 74. But when the question was again submitted to the congregation it was discovered, to the chagrin of the leaders, that the negative vote had increased by 46 per cent. The count was 106,000 in favor of union and 69,913 against.

No argument the leaders could advance made the slightest dent in the minority, and by the dawn of the 1920s the patience of prairie people was becoming a bit ragged. They already had 1,000 communities served by union churches, some ministered to by Methodists and some by Presbyterians. It was a thoroughly acceptable but untidy situation, for it caused problems over ministerial succession and the status of ministers within their churches, and raised questions of property ownership. So while the prairie sentiment was overwhelmingly for union, the Presbyterian leaders held back until 1923, when the majority lost patience with its intransigent minority. They called in the lawyers and joined with the Methodists and Congregationalists in drafting a bill for submission to Parliament and to the provincial legislatures in 1924 to have the United Church of Canada take over the three denominations. Legislative action was necessary in order to overcome problems with property, trusts, educational institutions, etc.

The system of government for the new church drew heavily on the Presbyterian policy, which laid great stress on the parity of the ministry with the congregation and on the rights of the individual members. Prof. J. W. Falconer, in his summary of the government and doctrine of the new church, wrote in the *New Outlook*, June 10, 1925:

> The system is the logical result of the Presbyterian doctrine of the Church as a fellowship of all believers and not a federation of officials, and it is difficult to imagine a more workable system by which a community can guide itself. History seems to confirm this. Prof. Heron writes: "It is a simple historical fact of deep significance that wherever the Reformation had free course, wherever it was permitted to shape itself spontaneously after Scripture and without external interference, it assumed a Presbyterian form." The general principles of government, therefore, as thus outlined, have naturally become the ideal of polity in the United Church and under these enlarged conditions it will continue to develop a deep love for freedom and a resourcefulness of character.
>
> A system of Doctrine. The Presbyterian Church has adhered to the Calvinistic theology, but of recent years most of the different branches have modified their Confessions in the direction of a softening of the emphasis on the doctrine of divine election. Professor Curtis, of Edinburgh, writes: "It may be added that recent changes in the theory and standards of Calvinism have for the most part been in the direction of a tacit compromise with Arminianism."
>
> While it is impossible to define absolutely the tendencies of each of these communions and to give the exact contribution which each brings into the United Church, the following analysis may contain a fair measure of truth.
>
> The Congregationalists (1) have never abandoned their conviction as to the rights of each individual community, (2) yet they have increasingly felt the need of a larger fellowship and a more representative government, (3) and in their religious life there is much stress made upon social and missionary labors.

The Methodists (1) have never forgotten that their denomination grew out of a personal religious experience and
they have accordingly made their appeal to the individual
soul, (2) have refused to place limits on the divine grace and
have emphasized the responsibility of each person to accept
the offer of a salvation open to all, (3) have moved away
from their limited monarchical rule towards a more adequate form of representative government.

The Presbyterians (1) have sought to render increasingly
complete their polity of limited republicanism, (2) have
never abandoned the Genevan ideals of the educated ministry, (3) but have been modifying their theological standards
in the direction of less extreme Calvinism.

The Congregationalists and Presbyterians have thus been
approaching the doctrinal positions of Methodism. The
Congregationalists and Methodists have been advancing
towards the Presbyterian form of government. The
Methodists and Presbyterians have increasingly recognized
the democracy of the Congregationalists and the rights of
each community. But these are not the determining influences that have brought about the great Union, for the real
dynamic is the common religious experience of salvation
through Christ. Christ is the heart of Christianity, and as
members of the Church which is His body we are inevitably
impelled to study everything that makes for the common
good. Christian unity is not a mere option but it is a noble
obligation due to the constraint of Christian love, which by
its very nature strives towards the removal of all barriers
that stand in the way of complete fellowship.

Perhaps the most astounding aspect of the whole controversy
was the misreading by the union leaders of the depth of the
convictions of their opponents regarding Presbyterian doctrine.
People like C. W. Gordon, Leslie Pidgeon, F. W. Kerr, W. J.
Clarke, and Clarence MacKinnon came from long lines of devout Presbyterian ancestors. They had imbibed the doctrine of
predestination, severely interpreted, from birth. They of all
people should have been aware of how deeply Presbyterian

convictions could be held. Once predestination was accepted it was easily possible for the devout to convince themselves they had been chosen by God for ultimate salvation, if they did nothing to change His mind. To the zealots, the Presbyterian Unionists were doing just that, abandoning the true faith.

For those less concerned with doctrine, there were more down-to-earth reasons for objection to union, like bringing a bunch of Methodists into the largest and most prosperous church in town — theirs. Finally, from a moderate wing which supported everything except organic union, there was the argument that greater ultimate good was being achieved by co-operation without amalgamation. This was the position of the Rev. D. G. McQueen of Edmonton, who in the end came out against union.

Underlying the "even-if-it-was-good-I-wouldn't-like-it" position were all manner of anti-union rationalizations. There were some who insisted that a delaying vote at an Edmonton Assembly in 1912 promised there would be no union without complete unanimity. The record fails to support such a contention, though the word "unanimity" was used. There was a complaint that the pro-union forces were bringing large numbers of adherents into the churches to swamp the communicants with their "yes" votes.

When the United Church bill came before Parliament in 1924 it was attacked as unfair, abhorrent, obnoxious, and an infringement upon the religious liberty of thousands of Canadians. After prolonged and acrimonious debate it passed, overwhelmingly, as it did in all the prairie legislatures.

Far from being intimidated by the action of the legislators, the anti-unionists mounted a vigorous campaign to carry their case to the members when the final referendum was taken. Over most of Canada the vote of the Presbyterian faithful was held in the individual churches during the winter of 1924-5. A battery of anti-union speakers descended on the west from Ontario. Wherever they could organize a meeting they blistered their opponents for deserting their faith, for abandoning the Westminster Confession and the shorter catechism, for subscribing to a doctrine that contained not a single biblical quotation, for restricting the rights of the churches to "call" their ministers, and for making no provision for policing the doctrinal orthodoxy of the ministers once they were ordained. All the new ministers would be required to do, they said, was promise to abide by the Bible. The Baptists, Mormons, and Seventh Day Adventists all claimed that that was what they were doing.

The pro-union supporters replied in kind. They accused the dissenters of being more concerned with the Westminster Confession than with the Bible which was the rock on which the Christian Church was founded. They answered concern for the purity of Presbyterian doctrine by noting that in six Canadian colleges out of eight, Presbyterian divinity students were already taking scriptural instruction from Methodist professors, and *vice versa*.

The liveliest debates were in Winnipeg, whose Presbyterian divines had been among the earliest and strongest proponents of union. Teams of anti-unionists arrived from the east to challenge the supporters on their home grounds. The Rev. W. G. Brown of Red Deer, who led the opposition in Alberta, checked in to take up the fight when the easterners went home. The ensuing debates filled the churches to capacity, but the result was a foregone conclusion. In Winnipeg as well as in the country churches the congregations without exception followed their pastor's lead. This, in fact, was what happened almost everywhere else. While all the Winnipeg churches voted overwhelmingly for union, a small church in the suburb of Weston, where the pastor opposed union, recorded a large negative vote. In Edmonton the congregation of the largest Presbyterian church in the city voted against union by better than two to one after its pastor, Dr. David McQueen, preached a strong anti-union sermon. The other churches in which the ministers favored union voted for union. In Calgary the pattern was the same, as only Grace Church, the establishment church, gave a negative vote following a strongly negative sermon. Over Alberta as a whole, the churches opted for union by better than five to one. In Saskatchewan the ratio was more than fifty to one.

But far from ending the argument, the vote of the Presbyterians served only to intensify it. In every city the minorities that were left without churches vowed to remain true to the faith of their fathers and to carry on with services in rented halls until they could get new churches built. In the meantime there ensued an unholy argument over property rights. The minorities demanded that the union acts be reopened to force the United Church to disgorge some of its surplus church property to the minority. As the Attorney General of Manitoba noted, it seemed only right that the majority, which emerged with more churches than they could use, should turn one or two over to the minority which, in the aggregate, bulked fairly large in all the cities. The majority showed little inclination to do so, and so deep did the bitter feeling run that the unionists even tried to prevent the dissenters from using the name Presbyterian. The rows over property kept the factions at loggerheads for months that stretched into years. Bills to reopen the United Church Act were introduced in the legislatures and voted down. The row over property lasted for three full years in Saskatchewan, with the attitude of the majority being denounced as "vicious, pernicious and iniquitous" by the spokesmen for the continuing Presbyterians. In the end committees were put together in Alberta and Manitoba to work out compromises, and in 1927 the government of Saskatchewan agreed that a joint committee of the legislature should meet with representatives of both sides to try to bring some Christian charity into play in an issue that was gnawing at the innards of Protestantism in a dozen Saskatchewan communities.

Aside altogether from the unsettling effect the storm over church unity had on the Protestant community, it came at a time when the cause of social reform could ill afford to become caught up in crosscurrents. And crosscurrents there were in abundance. The aftermath of the Winnipeg General Strike, which saw the election of 11 labor members and 12 farmer-Progressives, reduced the Manitoba legislature to nullity. When the Manitoba and the Alberta legislatures were taken over by the Progressives, dwindling interest in social legislation was reinforced by penny-pinching administrations with a passion only for balancing budgets, not for social advancement. In any event, the Protestant social reformers were running out of ideas as well as steam, and as the breweries got their anti-Prohibition campaign into high gear the social reformers were reduced to fighting rearguard defensive actions for which they were ill-equipped.

The extent to which the row over church union contributed to the downhill slide would be difficult to assess, but of this there can be no doubt: it engendered within the Protestant ranks a seething bitterness where there had previously been only amity and co-operation. It ultimately degenerated into arguments over who rightfully owned framed pictures of departed divines; into secretaries squirrelling away records and minute books while their spiritual leaders were pleading for tolerance and the avoidance of bitterness.

It was a sad denouement of the ecumenical vision of all Protestant Christianity finding a oneness with God within the United Church of Canada. But it was a flawed vision from the beginning, due to other reasons besides doctrinal differences. The drive for church union had political as well as religious motivations, for many of the unionist leaders were as dedicated to the cause of anti-Catholic and anti-French politics as they were to Protestant unity. Canada, to these unionist-Orangemen, was an English-speaking, Protestant, British Dominion which had had the bad luck to have acquired a French Catholic minority along the way. A United Church, more numerically equal to the Roman Catholic, could speak to governments with a more powerful voice than could a segmented collection of spokesmen. The message of the unionist-Orangemen to governments was that no concessions of any kind to the French language or the Catholic Church would be countenanced. Nor would the mongrelization of the prairie population by an influx of central Europeans be tolerated.

The mass influx of central Europeans had been viewed with a jaundiced eye from the beginning. But the reality being that several hundred thousand of the undesirables had already settled, it was assumed that the Ukrainians, Poles, and Germans could be transformed into English-speaking Protestants. To speed that process the Home Missionary Department of the Presbyterians in particular directed its efforts to converting the immigrants to Protestantism and the English language. But to people accustomed to the colorful and mystical rites of the Greek Orthodox and Greek Catholic churches, the austere Protestant practices had little attraction. Nor was there any hope for converts among the tens of thousands of Mennonites, Hutterites, and Doukhobors whose motives for coming to Canada were based on religious conviction. At the time of the Methodist-Presbyterian courtship, Protestant Christianity in the United States was flying apart in all directions. People who had undergone religious conversion to Christian Science, Spiritualism, Mormonism, Pentecostalism, Russellism, etc., and who were also migrating to western Canada by the thousands, would hardly be regarded as prospective converts to the United Church. The vision of a British people united under the United Church was punctured forever by the realities of the demography of prairie settlement.

Outside the ambit of the church's internal problems, a wave of disenchantment with all religions was sweeping the world. The belief in an all-seeing, all-powerful, and merciful God was shaken by the realities of the Great War with its 37,000,000 casualties and more than 8,000,000 dead. Confidence and faith were further impaired by the Russian Revolution and by the inability of any of the western powers to solve the grave social problems that arose from the war. When the churches stood on the sidelines, or sometimes actively supported the employers, in the widespread industrial disputes that followed the end of the war, large bodies of the working class were alienated. As a result Labor churches sprang up in Winnipeg, Calgary, and Edmonton. But the gospel being preached was not salvation by faith in Jesus Christ but salvation through socialism, although whether it was best achieved through Marxian or Fabian socialism was beginning to be argued about. In the beginning there were no less than six Labor churches operating in the halls around Winnipeg. The number dwindled until a single church was being supported in each of the prairie cities — and not too well supported at that.

The truth seemed to be that public opinion was dropping out of step with austere Protestantism. Cracks began to appear in the Sabbatarian dikes. Corner stores began to open on Sunday morning for the sale of milk and then stayed open to sell ice cream to the kids. Newsstands in hotels opened for the sale of papers and cigarettes. Sunday streetcars were running to the parks, and military bands frequently turned up to put on Sunday concerts. In the predominantly Roman Catholic communities like St. Boniface and Gravelbourg, baseball was even permitted on Sunday afternoons. It was all accompanied by protesting sermons from the churches, but more and more the protests were ignored.

The super-strict Sunday observance laws that had been fastened on the prairies from the first days of settlement gave the region an image of religiosity it did not in fact deserve. Drunkenness and gambling, pay-day debaucheries, and widespread cheating at weights and measures were endemic in the cities. Save for short sieges of quiescence brought on by periodic outbreaks of moral indignation in the pulpits, boisterous red-light districts were tolerated, if not encouraged, by the urban police departments. But when it came to cracking down on violators of Sunday observance laws, the full force of the law was exerted against even minor breaches. This came about in all probability through the meeting of minds of the leaders of the labor unions, such as they were, with those of the Presbyterians who dominated the legislatures.

At a time when clerical and manual workers put in ten hours a day, six days a week, anything that would provide a respite from work was welcomed by the unions. The federal and provincial Lord's Day acts did that, so they passed without a murmur of opposition from the unions. When enforcement was carried to extremes in the Prairie provinces, there was a good deal of public grumbling. But why anybody should have been surprised is hard to understand in face of the puritanic reputation of the Scots. The lugubrious Sabbatarianism of the Scottish Presbyterians provided newspapers with the raw material for an endless

Manitoba Free Press

OL. 52—NO. 296   FORECAST—Fair and warm.   WINNIPEG, WEDNESDAY, JUNE 15, 1927   Price 5c per Copy. Edition with Comic, 10c.   26 PAGES

STRANGLER TRACED TO SASKATCHEWAN

RO RUSSIAN NOTE POLAND WILL TAKE TURE OF ULTIMATUM

Demand Expulsion Within ated Time of Russians Agitating Against Soviets

Number of Executions in tion for Execution of Volikoff Now Exceeds 100

Police Chief Who Failed to Run Down Counterfeiters Found To Be Head of Gang

ASSERTS "STRANGLER" IS MORAL IMPECILE

SUCCESSFUL IN IRISH ELECTIONS

Man Wanted for Winnipeg Murders
Last Seen in Regina on Monday

Established Beyond Doubt, Says Chief Bruton, Wanted Man Was in Regina Monday

Winnipeg Police Officers Satisfied Gorilla Man Was the One Seen in Regina Over Week-End, But Are Not Relaxing Vigorous Search in City and District—Suspect Given Ride From Kemnay to Alexander on Saturday.

Manitoba Free Press

L, 52—NO. 297   FORECAST—Warm, becoming unsettled.   WINNIPEG, THURSDAY, JUNE 16, 1927   Price 5c per Copy. Edition with Comic, 10c.   28 PAGES

STRANGLER CAUGHT AND ESCAPES

PECIAL TRAIN CARRIES OUT POLICE FROM WINNIPEG

-POWER WARNING I RUSSIA TO CEASE OPAGANDA POSSIBLE

LINDBERGH'S RECEPTION AT WASHINGTON

Locked Up in Killarney Jail,
Picks Lock and Gets Away;
South Country All Aroused

Arrest Made at Wakopa, Five Miles From International Boundary, by Provincial Policemen on Information Supplied by Farmer at Whose Place Man, Closely Answering Description of Murderer, Had Stopped For a Meal—In Double-locked Cell, Approximately Fifteen Minutes, When He Picked Lock and Escaped, Leaving Boots Behind—Whole Country Aroused.

Manitoba Free Press

OL. 52—NO. 298   FORECAST—Scattered showers, mostly fair.   WINNIPEG, FRIDAY, JUNE 17, 1927   Price 5c per Copy. Edition with Comic, 10c.   28 PAGES

STRANGLER POSITIVELY IDENTIFIED

MUCH WANTED MAN RETURNS TO WINNIPEG

Witnesses Connect Man Arrested
In Killarney With Murders Here

Prisoner is Identified by Portland as Adrain Harris, Wanted There for Murder

Police Confident Chain of Evidence Which Will Lead to Conviction Is Complete.—Recaptured at Killarney Just as Police Special Pulled in Yesterday Morning, Strangler Is Brought Back to Winnipeg, Taken From Train at Outskirts, and Rushed to Back Entrance of Police Station.

Sallow Strangler Suspect Greeted by Seething Crowd

Manitoba Free Press

VOL. 52—NO. 299   FORECAST—Scattered showers, cooler   WINNIPEG, SATURDAY, JUNE 18, 1927   Price 5c per Copy. Edition with Comic, 10c.   44 PAGES

NELSON HAS JAIL AND ASYLUM RECORD

Manitoba Free Press Second General Crop Report for 1927

The Weather During the 20 Days Since Last Report Has Been Generally Favorable to Growth. — Seeding of All Coarse Grains With the Exception of Some Flax and Oats for Green Feed, is Completed.—Considerable Areas of Wheat Have Been Seeded Between the 10th and 15th of June.—Winter Rye Generally a Good Crop and Much of It in Head.—360 Points Queried—340 Heard From.

Name Given by Man in Prison Here
Well Known by Police in California;
Photo Identified by Attacked Woman

SMITH IS CONFIDENT OF NELSON'S IDENTITY

Wanted on a Number of Charges in Pacific Coast Citie —Arrested in May, 1921, at San Francisco for A tack on Woman—Committed to Insane Asylu

---

25. For a week in June of 1927 the search for "The Strangler" — Earle Nelson — was page-one headline news in every western newspaper.

26 & 27. *(Above)* Following the discovery of the bodies of his two latest victims in Winnipeg, a massive manhunt was launched for Earle Nelson. *(Right)* Following his capture hundreds gathered to catch a glimpse of him as he left the train bringing him to a Winnipeg jail. The head with a circled X is Nelson.

28, 29 & 30. *(Above)* The Edmonton Grads ladies' basketball team of 1923, at the outset of a career that would make them — and their successors — the most widely known women athletes of the 1920s. *(Below)* Radio was one of the marvels of that marvellous decade. Pictured is the equipment for demonstrating the first radio loudspeaker, set up in Winnipeg's Capitol Theatre in April 1920. *(Right)* The old and the new — washing clothes by hand while listening through the earphones to one of the early radio broadcasts.

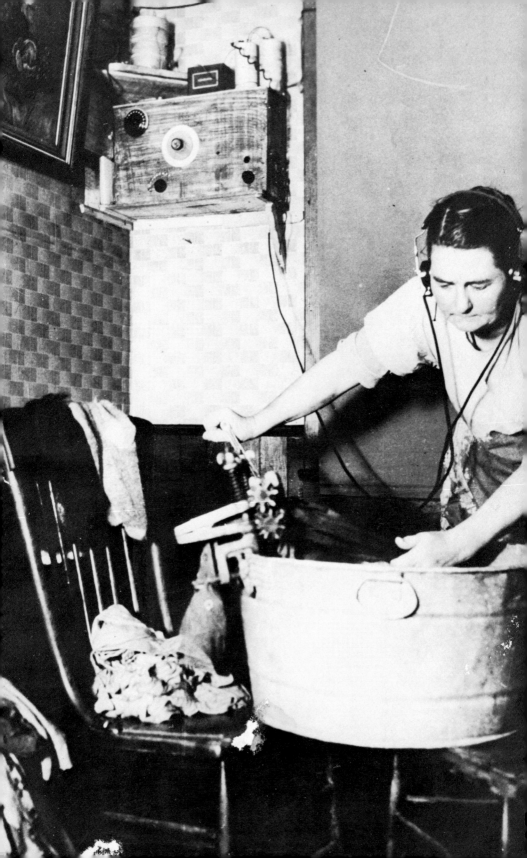

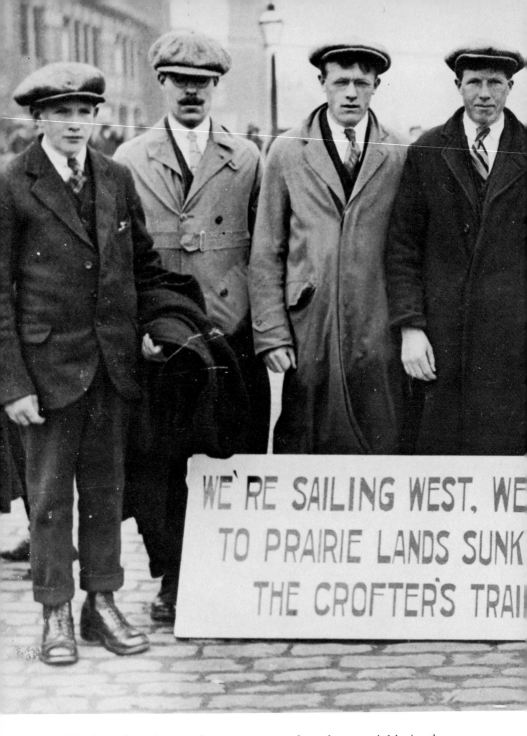

WE'RE SAILING WEST, WE
TO PRAIRIE LANDS SUNK
THE CROFTER'S TRAI

31. Immigration to the west was reduced to a trickle in the
1920s compared with the millions that flooded in prior to the
First World War, but the lure of the new land still attracted
some newcomers like this group of Scots shown on arrival at
Montreal.

GUARD OF HONOUR TO
H.R.H. PRINCE OF WALES.

32 & 33. (Above) The Winnipeg
Police Force was dominated by Scots.
Every member had to be at least six
feet tall. At an even six feet, the
sergeant of this guard of honor is
the shortest of the group. *(Right)* The
Rev. Charles Gordon was a leading
Presbyterian clergyman in the
struggles for Prohibition and church
union, but he was even better known
as the popular author "Ralph
Connor".

stream of ethnic jokes on the Scots. To wit: "Have you heard the one about the Scottish minister who got fired from his pulpit in Edinburgh? One of his leaders caught him smiling at his baby daughter in her crib on Sunday!"

Over a twenty-year period, when the Presbyterians accounted for barely a fifth of the population, they held almost 50 per cent of the seats in the prairie legislatures. When joined by their allies, the Methodists, they had an absolute majority in all three houses. In 1921 in Saskatchewan when there were only 10 per cent more Presbyterians in the province than there were Roman Catholics, the former had twenty-four members while the latter had only four. In Manitoba the representation was always more in balance with proportions of population, but where one group was imbued with a feverish zeal and the others cared little one way or the other, it was the zealots who carried the day, particularly when no one was prepared to argue the case for the opposition. To have questioned the virtue of a puritanical Sunday, moreover, would have put the quibbler in the position of challenging the authority of Holy Writ.

All this changed with the decade and the election to the legislatures of independent labor members and farmer-Progressives whose interests were economic rather than religious. Their presence produced the first break in the Sabbatarian dikes when they voted to allow trains to run to the Lake Winnipeg beaches on Sundays.

Prior to the war the railways in Manitoba had established summer resorts along the beaches of Lake Winnipeg. The C.P.R. had a whole string of resorts on the west side of the lake between Selkirk and Gimli. There was a road of sorts between Winnipeg, Selkirk, and Gimli, but as few Winnipeggers had cars the great bulk of the traffic to the beaches was by train. The trains, however, did not run on Sunday. People who had been able to afford to build cottages at the beaches could take a train down Saturday evening and return before work on Monday morning. But the lack of train service kept the overwhelming majority of the working class from enjoying a day at the beach on Sunday.

"Sunday trains to the beaches" became a major labor cause

after the 1919 strike. While resolutions calling for Sunday trains were voted down by the Winnipeg City Council, the labor members of the legislature eventually managed to obtain an amendment to the Lord's Day Act that specifically exempted beach trains from its provisions. The Lord's Day Alliance cried "Foul!" and attacked the amendment in the courts, carrying their case clear to the British Privy Council which, in December 1923, sustained the Manitoba legislature, and Sunday trains to the beaches became a reality.

The breaching of the blue laws for the bathers naturally set off a chorus of demands from others. Cricketers wanted the right to play in the parks on Sunday. The right was denied. In Winnipeg the City Parks Department, which operated a public golf course, found a gimmick to beat the law. It sold tickets during the week that entitled golfers to play on Sunday. No action taken before or since did more to popularize the game, for it opened golf playing to all the store clerks and industrial employees who still worked on Saturdays. The lawn bowlers, many of whom played on lawns manicured for them by the City Parks Department, began playing on Sunday afternoons, though they closed down early so as not to conflict with evening church services.

The practice of twice-a-day church attendance was rapidly falling out of favor in the cities. Sunday was the best night of the week on radio as "listening in" to Marconi's gift to the world quickly developed into an universal pastime. Given the winter climate of western Canada, it was a lot easier for everybody to stay within the warmth and comfort of home than fight their way through cold and storm to a church service at night. The radio provided an irresistible excuse to do so. It was not long before the clergy were giving sermonial attention to the absentees who were taking their religion via the air-waves from that newest of phenomena, the radio preacher. Unhappily for the orthodox practitioners, the protests went unheeded, perhaps because of a growing public disinclination to pay serious attention to anything the clergymen were protesting against.

On the other hand, a good deal of attention was being paid to the popularizers of the rationalist case against revealed religions.

The revolutionary changes taking place in every branch of natural science were replacing certainty with uncertainty, and dogma was becoming encrusted with doubt. The impact of the popularizers of the new science was being felt even in western Canada. The educational system and the labor unions were placing increased emphasis on adult education. The Haldeman-Julius Company of Kansas City, Missouri, achieved continent-wide popularity with their "Little Blue Book" library of condensations of classical and popular works of science and fiction. The books were widely advertised and were on sale all over Canada for from 5 to 25 cents a copy. Evolution was being taught in the Manitoba schools in the early 1920s, and when the Conservative leaders in the legislature discovered that fact in 1926 they tried to shut off grants to the schools until the subject was removed from the textbooks. The effort failed. Evolution was a subject that frequently got popular treatment in the columns of the One Big Union *Bulletin*. The Union also became a sponsor of lecture tours by two of the most famous heretics of the times.

Bishop William Montgomery Brown retired from the Protestant Episcopal Church of the United States for reasons of health in 1912. At the time he was Archbishop of Arkansas. Whether as the result of retirement or of reading, Brown's health showed remarkable improvement in the next decade. With the onset of the Russian Revolution he became interested in and then converted to communism. His book *Communism and Christianity* gave the Apostles' Creed such a working over that he was charged with heresy in 1924 and banished from the church. The O.B.U. brought him to Winnipeg for a series of lectures in 1926, and while he was more scholar than rabble-rouser his meetings attracted capacity crowds to the Pantages Theatre. For the next decade, Brown turned out about a book a year under the general heading of "The Bankruptcy of Christian Supernaturalism from the Viewpoint of . . .". The viewpoints included astronomy, biology, geology, psychology, and the Bible.

A greater impact across the west was made by the O.B.U.-sponsored tour of Joseph McCabe, one-time rector of

Buckingham College and England's most noted heretic in two centuries. McCabe abandoned the Catholic Church in 1896 and for the next thirty years devoted himself to writing and lecturing on rationalist subjects. He contributed a regular column to the O.B.U. *Bulletin* from its inception, and in 1928 the paper underwrote his tour of western Canada. McCabe was a pleasant little fellow with a fine sense of humor who specialized in enumerating reasons why a belief in evolution was incompatible with adherence to the Christian religion. Churchmen generally tended to give McCabe a wide berth, but in Saskatoon he managed to lure the Rev. A. J. Donnell, a United Church pastor, into debate. The debate not only packed the biggest church in town, it set off a controversy that raged for weeks in the letters column of the *Saskatoon Star*.

The spade-work done by the O.B.U. *Bulletin* made it possible for Winnipeg to become the only North American community with a full-time year-round atheist-in-residence. He was Marshall J. Gauvin, an Acadian refugee from a carpentering career in New Brunswick. Like McCabe, Gauvin was a Catholic dropout and had grown up in an atmosphere of religious disputation. His father was a convert to the Baptist religion, while his mother remained true to the faith. As a result, life in the Gauvin home evolved into a constant struggle between the two to lasso the children for their churches. Young Gauvin remained a Catholic until he came under the spell of a Billy Sunday-type revivalist whose hellfire-and-damnation thundering scared him clear out of Catholicism and into the Baptist baptismal tank. It was a conversion, however, that did not take.

During his interlude as a Baptist, Gauvin all but committed the New Testament to memory. He accomplished the trick, ingeniously, by tearing out a couple of pages of text each morning and taking them to work with him. At his carpenter's bench he folded them into his left hand and memorized them while he hammered and sawed. The trouble with a computer-type mind like Gauvin's was that what went into it one day from the Bible began clashing with what had gone in the week before. When he tried to get his pastor to iron out the conflicts and contradictions between the gospels, he struck mud. About the time his bafflement reached its peak he went for a visit to Boston and blundered into a Rationalist Society lecture series in the Thomas Paine Memorial Hall. That not only ended his commitment to the Baptist faith; it infected him with an incurable urge to become an anti-religious missionary.

It was an ambition that took him twelve years to realize. He returned to the Intercolonial Railway shops in Moncton and spent the next ten years working by day and studying by night. This time, instead of the Bible, he was committing the entire body of the higher criticism to memory, along with new theories of science then raining down from the think-tanks of the world. Once asked about his educational background he facetiously described himself as a "doctor of philosophy from the Intercolonial University". Halfway through his course, in 1906, he started giving rationalist lectures on Sunday in Moncton while still working as a carpenter.

Having honed his oratorical style to a point at which he was swaying his audiences satisfactorily, and wanting easier access to the flood of new books then coming onto the market, he moved to Toronto, hired a hall, and set himself up again as a combined carpenter-lecturer. Gauvin's Toronto mission lasted for ten months before he moved on to Indianapolis and later to Pittsburgh. When the United States entered the war it put an end to his rationalist society and he was without an audience until the magazine *Truth-seeker* raised a fund by public subscription to send him on a tour of the United States. He settled in Minneapolis in 1920 and was lured to Winnipeg by the O.B.U. in 1926-7.

He leased the largest theatre in the city, and his Sunday afternoon lectures quickly became the liveliest show in town, mainly, in the beginning, because they attracted the attention of every Protestant zealot within miles. Gauvin customarily spoke for an hour, caught his breath while the collection plate was passed, and then answered questions for another hour. It was during the question period that the believers sought to confound Gauvin by quoting the scriptures in rebuttal of his theses. It was a fatal mistake.

Gauvin was blessed with a trick memory that gave him almost

total recall of everything he had read. He combined it with
speed-reading that enabled him to plow through batches of
books at a sitting. He had not only committed most of the New
Testament to memory, he could also reel off most of the Old
Testament, including, if he put his mind to it, great gobs of the
begats. The breadth of his biblical knowledge was described in
an article in the *American Mercury* by George Siebel, literary critic
of the *Pittsburgh Sun-Telegraph*. "Gauvin," wrote Siebel, "is the
best Rationalist lecturer on the continent today. He knows his
Bible better than any bishop, can turn instantly to any passage
without a concordance and can argue the Ur-Marcus with
Schmiedel and distinguish the Elohist text from the Jehovist text
as definitely as Paul Haupt."

Against Gauvin, the Christadelphians, Mormons, Baptists,
and Plymouth Brethren were massively undergunned. But they
persisted, and the Winnipeg working class flocked to Gauvin's
lectures in steadily growing droves. As time passed, most of the
attackers quietly gave up the struggle. All except a lay preacher
named J. N. Sturk, who challenged Gauvin to a debate. This
debate in February 1929 marked the high point of Gauvin's
fifteen-year Winnipeg career. To accommodate the crowd two
theatres had to be hired — the Walker Theatre, which filled to
capacity an hour before starting time, and the Garrick Theatre
down the block, where the overflow listened to the debate by
remote control. They missed the real spectacle.

Professor Frank Allen of the University of Manitoba physics
department was the chairman. When he was settled on the stage
he called the Rev. Sturk, who came out with a Bible under his
arm. Then came Gauvin, followed by a couple of assistants with a
heavy oak table. They left and returned with their arms full of
books. They left and returned again with more books, all
marked for instant reference, all from Gauvin's own immense
library. The sight of so much stacked reading matter must have
unnerved Sturk. As he went through his speech he kept glancing
at the books and as he worked toward his climax his whole
argument came unstuck and he became hopelessly entangled in
a torrent of words he seemingly could not stop.

When the audience voted overwhelmingly in favor of Gauvin, Sturk decided he had been jobbed, that his opponent had packed the meeting and kept Sturk's supporters from getting into the Walker Theatre. However the vote over at the Garrick Theatre was even more decisive for Gauvin, by about 1,000 to 40. Sturk decided on a repeat performance, but with himself as the only debater. He rehired the Walker Theatre for an evening of his own and repeated his side of the question of whether scientific evolution or revealed religion offered mankind the best explanation for existence. At Sturk's debate he declared himself to be the winner by a clear majority of those present.

The next year the fundamentalists returned to the attack. This time they imported the Rev. J. F. G. McKnight from the Pittsburgh Theological Seminary for a debate which was held in the Olympic Hockey Rink. Jammed as it was with Gauvin's supporters, the audience was about four to one in favor of the local champion when the vote was taken at the conclusion.

Aside from the debates, Gauvin rapidly assumed the role of full-time gadfly of the Christian clergymen. As members of the modernist school of Protestant theology began to edge away from the fundamentalist position that every word of the King James version of the Bible was the revealed word of God to be accepted literally, Gauvin exhorted them to come all the way over to the rationalist position. He attended their services, made copious notes of their sermons, and then advertised in the newspapers that he was replying in his own lectures. His favorite targets were J. S. Bonnell and Professor F. W. Kerr, and in the end he got so under their skins that they delegated themselves to appeal to the newspapers to boot Gauvin and his advertising off the church pages. The *Manitoba Free Press* and the *Winnipeg Tribune* yielded to the pressure and Gauvin was shunted to the theatrical page. All that, however, would come later.

Gauvin got his greatest satisfaction from baiting the visiting revivalists who were in and out of the west in a never-ending stream in the 1920s. In addition to his oratorical style, which any of them would have envied, Gauvin was a natural-born mimic. His imitations of their eye-rolling, arm-throwing styles rocked the theatres with laughter. And yet, like a comedian yearning to play Hamlet, Gauvin was always frustrated in his ambition to get away from religious argument and devote his lectures to the popularizing of science. When he scheduled a series on scientific topics the collection seldom paid the rent. But when he took out after fundamentalist revivalists or local clergymen he played to overflow congregations.

Marshall Gauvin's path never crossed that of William Aberhart, the millennialist prophesier who was to Alberta believers what Gauvin was to the Winnipeg agnostics. By the time Gauvin got to Winnipeg, Aberhart was already a household idol throughout rural Alberta as well as in Calgary. He had delivered the first radio sermon in Canada from Calgary in 1923 and from then on was a regular Sunday feature on station CFCN. Not only did Aberhart have Albertans' ears glued to their crystal sets, he had them taking pens in hand to write glowing letters of approval, accompanied by generous cash donations. In such volume did the cash flow that Aberhart was soon able to buy up some prime Eighth Avenue land in Calgary and erect his Prophetic Bible Institute. None of Aberhart's prophetic visions of the Second Coming materialized, but he was able to combine the use of the Prophetic Bible Institute and the radio to launch the Social Credit crusade that carried him to political power in Alberta in 1935.

The prairies in the 1920s were happy hunting grounds for anybody with a message — spiritual, profane, uplifting, or iconoclastic. Ida Tarbell, whose *History of the Standard Oil Company* had set forces in motion which brought about the breaking up of the Standard Oil trust, delivered a series of talks on trusts. Emmeline Pankhurst provided personal details of struggle for the emancipation of women. The Chautauquas brought music, culture, and entertainment to the smaller cities with week-long stands each summer. There was something for everybody twice a day under the Chautauqua big-top tents—fine musical programs, variety entertainment, and above all, the most eloquent speakers to be found. They ranged all the way from humorous monologuists to returned explorers, astronomers, and uplifters with messages of inspiration and enlightenment.

Arthur Conan Doyle came through with his exhibition of spurious photographs of spiritualistic seances in which entranced mediums had been caught vomiting "ectoplasm". Judge Rutherford and his deputies regularly attracted throngs with the predictions, in 48-point type in full-page newspaper advertisements, that "millions now living will never die".

Holy Roller revivalists had susceptible youths rolling off benches into the aisles in fits that culminated in awakening orgasms. Aimee Semple McPherson made her debuts in Winnipeg and Lethbridge in 1920. She returned several times before she reached the pinnacle of success in Los Angeles that brought her sexual and financial adventures to the front pages of the newspapers. Like all the revivalists, Aimee climaxed her ministry with healing sessions, although in the beginning her claims were modest. And thoroughly practical. Like the time in Chicago when she fell and broke her ankle en route to one of her services. Instead of calling for an ambulance she called on God to heal her so she could get on with His work. Her ankle got instant divine attention and she got up and walked to the service.

The biggest crowd-attracter and crowd-pleaser of them all was the California spellbinder Dr. C. S. Price, who had his greatest success in Alberta. In September of 1923 he opened a seven-day revival in the Calgary Arena and filled it tighter than it had ever been filled before. In a building with a seating capacity of less than 4,000, Price frequently had up to 6,000 hanging on his message. That message was the quintessence of primitive fundamentalism, which seemed to have a curious attraction for the country dwellers who flocked into Calgary and Edmonton.

Price had no time for the ethereal claptrap of the modernists who talked about a "spiritual" heaven and earth. Price's hell was real and full of fire, brimstone, and legions of sinners suffering eternal torment. Heaven was just as real a physical city as Calgary or Edmonton, with streets and buildings and mansions in which the saved were to enjoy lives of bliss everlasting. Price's forte, however, was faith healing, and after each sermon the sick and the crippled came forward, dropped their crutches, and stood erect. The newspaper gave Price columns of space, written mostly in a vein that would have done his paid publicists proud.

Indeed, when the touring evangelists hit Lethbridge, the *Herald* there let the promotional flacks write the news reports, running their fulsomely approving stories under the heading of "contributed".

Toward the end of Price's 1923 Calgary performance, the Alberta Medical Association decided that things were getting out of hand. A warrant was sworn out charging Price with practising medicine without a licence. Then the Association hired a hall for a public meeting at which one of its leading lights Dr. D. R. Dunlop, was delegated to demolish Price's claims to achieving cures. Such was the temper of the times, however, that Dunlop managed to attract only a few hundred compared with Price's thousands. The Calgary Ministerial Association also went into special session over the Price performance. It, however, voted to give its approval to the Price ministry. So, apparently, did the local magistrate, who found a technical flaw in the charge against the faith healer and acquitted him.

11. The Sting of the WASP

To be British and Anglo-Saxon and Protestant on the western prairies at the onset of the 1920s was not only the best thing. To be British and Anglo-Saxon and Protestant was the only thing.

The whole visible spectrum of human activity was dominated to the point of monopolization by the British Anglo-Saxons. In politics; in business, transportation, and industry; in banking, insurance, and financial promotion; in manufacturing and wholesale and retail merchandising; in trades unions of whatever stripe, and employers' associations; in the arts and sciences, such as they were; in education and the professions without exception; in farm organizations and chambers of commerce, and in polite society; in the provincial and municipal civil services; in newspaper publishing; in moral reform and social betterment crusades—in all these areas the British Anglo-Saxons held a monopoly.

Here and there, in rural areas where there was no one except European immigrants, a Ukrainian or Icelandic name might turn up in a roster of reeves and municipal clerks. That accounted for a small handful of Ukrainian and Scandinavian officials in Manitoba's 180 municipalities. Manitoba even had two Ukrainians and a Scandinavian among its 240 police magistrates. By tradition, Manitoba always found a place for one French Canadian and one Irish Catholic lawyer in its superior courts, but in Alberta and Saskatchewan the rosters of judges and court officials of all kinds, save interpreters, were unalloyed

Anglo-Saxon. So were the universities of all three provinces, with only a rare exception for a foreign professor of mathematics or chemistry. In the University of Manitoba there was one lonely Jew hived away in a chemistry laboratory.

French-speaking Canadians were an insignificant minority who stayed sequestered in their own communities and were neither seen nor heard except at election time and during tiresome arguments over the language of instruction in the schools. English-speaking Catholics, who viewed the educational privileges gained by the French Catholics with jaundiced eye, surfaced briefly on St. Patrick's Day and quickly dropped from sight again.

In the census of 1921, the Bureau of Statistics for the first time accepted "Canadian" for the citizenship of the Canadian-born, though it would be twenty years and more before the United States immigration officials would accept other than "British subject". That Canadians were British subjects was hammered into young Canadian heads from all sides. Every schoolroom in the land had a Mercator projection wall map on which the world was dominated by the red patches of the British Empire on which the sun never set. The biggest red patch of all was Canada, though India and Africa from the Cape to Cairo also were impressively eye-catching.

The rites of spring in prairie schools prior to Victoria Day featured the singing of "Land of Hope and Glory", "Rule Britannia", "Men of Harlech", and "Tipperary", and committing "The Charge of the Light Brigade" and "The Burial of Sir John Moore" to memory. The overview that prairie school children got of the world was British, Anglo-Saxon, and Protestant —the British of Raleigh and Drake and Clive who carried British arms to the farthest reaches of the earth and sea; the Anglo-Saxon of intrepid settlers and missionaries carrying the white man's burden to the benighted savages of the Americas, Asia, and Africa; the Protestant of the heirs to Henry VIII, Knox, Wesley, and William of Orange who had variously led the struggles against the knavish conspiracies of the latin Popes and their French and Spanish allies.

No nonsense was taught about a "British connection" because

third-generation Canadian teachers considered themselves as British as the English, Scots, or Irish. When the Empire went to war in South Africa, Canadians automatically rushed forward to take part in the action, as they did when the German attack on Belgium opened the Great War. Prairie children learned of the relief of Mafeking, the horrors of the Black Hole of Calcutta, and the glories of Trafalgar, Waterloo, and Blenheim, long before they were introduced to anything Canadian. It was hardly an accident that Canadians, no less than the English, admitted to no feeling of self-righteousness in their casual use of such terms as British pluck, British justice, British fair play, British decency, etc., as synonyms for the best there was. Conversely, the worst that could be said for anything was that it was un-British, which in fact was what the Wets were saying of the Drys in the 1920 Prohibition plebiscite. The slogan of the opposition was "Be British—Vote No".

In prairie newspapers, developments in the United Kingdom frequently made more headlines on front pages than Canadian happenings, except, of course, during political crises at home. Alberta newspapers carried special pages of news from Britain in their Saturday editions. Editors commented on British issues as if they were domestic Canadian issues. Even the reverend clergy sometimes felt compelled to intervene vocally in British politics. Thus, in March 1922 the Rev. George Laughton of the Central Congregational Church in Winnipeg devoted a sermon to an attack on the British government for appointing Lord Reading, the Lord Chief Justice of England, as Viceroy of India. Lord Reading was a Jew and hence, according to Laughton, lacking in qualifications for the office. What India needed was an administrator who understood Christian principles. In the then-prevailing time of trouble, Laughton argued, India also needed a strong hand at the wheel. The One Big Union *Bulletin*, which itself watched British development carefully, found Laughton's concern for India less than persuasive. Where was Laughton, it wondered, a few short years before when the British army had turned its guns on a peaceful demonstration at Amritsar and left many hundreds dead in the city square?

The west, in all its outward trappings, was Sir John A.

Macdonald's kind of country, the kind of country he must have visualized when he said, "A British subject I was born—a British subject I will die." By 1920, however, Sir John A.'s vision had become fatally flawed by the immigration policies of the Laurier government which had inherited his mantle, though the pro-verbial man-from-Mars could still have contemplated the scene in blissful unawareness of the existence of the 300,000 central and northern Europeans who were hidden away in the cultural and commercial underbrush of the rural prairies.

They were drawn to the prairies by the twin magnets of free land and freedom from military conscription. They had first come as unskilled laborers to build the railways and dig the ditches of the cities and towns, to earn money with which to bring out their families. Or they had come as families of peasants in rough clothes, eager to carve homesteads out of the bush of Manitoba and Saskatchewan; as Jews fleeing the pogroms of eastern Europe; as Poles fleeing the Germans and Russians; or as Ukrainians in flight from the peonage of Austrian, German, and Russian landlords. No massed brass bands blared them welcome, for their coming was viewed with choleric disdain by the British who preceded them. Rather, they were accepted as an unhappy second choice.

Instead of attracting a huge influx of British settlers, as antici-pated with the completion of the C.P.R. in the 1880s, the west settled into a ten-year depression. Even the influx from Ontario dried up. It became plain that if Macdonald's dream of a domin-ion from sea to sea was ever to be achieved, thousands more people producing millions more bushels of grain were required. Sir Clifford Sifton launched his great drive to attract armies of strong-backed peasants with equally strong-backed wives and children, who were accustomed to lives of privation and hard-ship. It was they who would provide the country with a viable agricultural economy. They came, by their tens of thousands in the years before the Great War, and were swallowed up by the homesteads in the parklands that rimmed the western prairies. The minor fraction which splintered off in the cities disappeared into the developing slums on the wrong side of the railway tracks.

Little was done to acquaint any of the prospective immigrants with the conditions they would find in Canada. If they had been so many consignments of cattle the authorities could hardly have taken less interest, or handled them differently. None of the Canadians they encountered knew or cared anything about the ethnic backgrounds of people like the Czechs, Poles, or Ukrainians who had struggled for a thousand years to retain their identities under a succession of tyrannies determined to destroy them. Thus the Ukrainians from Austria, Germany, Russia, and Romania were variously identified as Ruthenians, Silesians, Bucovinians, Austrians, Russians, Galicians, and Moldavians. It took the Dominion Bureau of Statistics thirty years to get the Ukrainians properly sorted out.

In the countryside the settlers did their own sorting the hard way. The general policy of the immigration department was to direct newly arriving settlers into areas previously settled by people from their particular homelands. This enabled the homesteaders to cope with the language problem while they were getting settled. But when Austrian families were inadvertently placed in Ukrainian settlements, or Poles were mixed in with Germans or Russians, peace, quiet, and the king's order were disrupted and were restored only when somebody left. The racial, religious, and national prejudices and flaming hatreds which the people of eastern Europe had acquired through a thousand years were not something to be sloughed off in a trice during their journey to western Canada.

As long as the country boomed, and everybody was working too hard and too long, or doing too well, to be bothered with what other people were doing, these prejudices of the centuries, which everybody brought with them in such abundance, were fairly well sublimated. Far from being marked by rancorous eruptions of bigotry, the formative years of the west were periods of neighborliness run riot. People went far out of their way to help other people and because the herd instinct kept bringing like into contact with like, the mixed bag of immigrants became segregated and compartmentalized, rather than coalescing into homogeneity.

The Slavs and Germans from eastern Europe, repelled by the desert-like emptiness of the treeless plains, took to the bush of the eastern and interlake country of Manitoba and the park belts of western Manitoba, Saskatchewan, and Alberta. There they threw up log cabins and often moved into them with their pigs and chickens while they began the back-breaking chore of clearing their land. Each wave of settlers looked to their countryfolk who had come before for advice and assistance, and it was freely given. In the cities, two or three families of any ethnic group became a nucleus of an ethnic ghetto into which hundreds of newcomers would tumble pell-mell in Winnipeg, Regina, Lethbridge, and, to a lesser extent, in Edmonton.

All incoming foreign immigrants followed the pattern established by the first Jewish settlers in Winnipeg. Fleeing the pogroms of czarist Russia in the late 1880s, the Jews came by the score to Winnipeg. These first families were barely settled in makeshift housing before they were playing host to fellow Jews who trickled into the city on every other train. First, the earlier arrivers provided the newcomers with temporary living space, even if it meant crowding ten people into a couple of rooms and sleeping in relays. Then they helped them to find jobs, and to obtain clothing and food, and, hopefully, rooms of their own. When that was achieved, the newcomers were expected to reciprocate by doing the same for the next wave of countrymen who landed in town.

This Jewish regimen became the established pattern for everybody else, and even spread to the English, Scots, and Irish. It enabled the thousands of immigrants pouring into the cities and out onto the homesteads to put down their roots with a minimum of privation. It also produced indescribable urban congestion and turned quiet streets of single-family houses into teeming slums, as J. S. Woodsworth discovered in 1910. And it slowed the assimilation of the foreigners into the Anglo-Saxon milieu to the pace of a child on an unpleasant errand.

A Ukrainian or a Polish family that settled into an English-speaking community would have been forced to learn to speak English simply to survive. But when they settled in ethnic blocs, there was no such compulsion, and a few words of English were all that was really necessary. When schools were established in the foreign settlements, it was easier to conduct classes in Ukrainian than in English, so that was what happened. Teachers capable of performing in Ukrainian were so scarce, however, that standards of teacher qualification were allowed to deteriorate. As a result, the quality of education being provided on the pioneer fringes suffered seriously.

In the end the provincial educational authorities adopted a hard-line, unilingual English approach and found themselves involved in a four-way controversy with the German Mennonites, the French Catholics, the Irish Catholics, and the Ukrainian immigrants. The insistence of Manitoba and Saskatchewan on unilingual schools drove thousands of long-settled German Mennonites into migrations to Mexico and South America. For the Ukrainians, being forced to learn and speak another language was what their ancestors had been resisting for 1,000 years in Russia. The retention of their language had been the last line of Ukrainian defence against the determination of their conquerors to destroy them as a people by compelling them to adopt the language of the conqueror. So while their children were being force-fed English, the feeding unified the Ukrainian parents into a temporarily indigestible bloc.

As devout a people as ever hit the prairies, they had vacillated between the sundry doctrines being forced on them from without. Archbishop Langevin of St. Boniface was trying to find a way of winning the Ukrainians not only to the Roman Catholic Church but to the French language as well. He bombarded his superiors with appeals for Ukrainian-speaking Roman Catholic missionaries, and got nowhere. The rival Ukrainian Greek Orthodox authorities could not find any missionaries to spare for western Canada either. The Presbyterians, who were already there, worked hard to convert the newcomers to their anti-Roman faith, and for some years enjoyed some success, since the choice for the Ukrainians was between Presbyterian services and nothing. In the end they backed away from both the French Catholics and the Protestants, and united under the onion-dome and spire of Ukrainian Orthodox and Catholic temples, where the colorful rites of their religion could be performed in the Ukrainian tongue.

If retention of their native language meant more to the Ukrainians than it did to the other settlers, it did not follow that they were alone in reverting to their first language as the family tongue when in company with fellow nationals. It was this fact which brought the animus of the Anglo-Saxon majority down upon them when the Great War and the post-war depression focussed the attention of the self-styled "white people" on the strangers within their gates.

That process began with the anti-alien hysteria whipped up by the newspapers across the west during the war. It was marked by the firing from their jobs of Germans and Austrians, even many who had obtained Canadian citizenship. Calgary fired a tele-phone operator whose father, a German, had served with the British army in South Africa. Poles who had had the misfortune to be born in Germany instead of Russia lost their jobs, as did Ukrainians born in Austria. In the labor unrest that grew out of the war, strikes were blamed on alien agitators despite the fact that all the trades unions were led by Anglo-Saxons. When scapegoats were needed for an economic and social malaise of the urban west, the foreigners were available, visible, audible, and odiferous. Most of all they were audible and odiferous.

To the British of western Canada, as elsewhere, the people of the world were divided into two groups — those who spoke English and those who did not. Which was to say — those with a high order of intelligence and those of demonstrably low levels of intelligence. Not only was inability to speak English proof of downright stupidity, it was also regarded as bordering on sedi-tion. Professional patriots in Winnipeg, Calgary, and Regina made no effort to hide their displeasure when they got within earshot of foreign-language conversations on Selkirk, Ogden, or East Regina streetcars. "You'd think if the country was good enough to give them a living it would be worth learning its language, wouldn't you?" became their litany, usually intoned in a voice heard the length of the car.

The "whites" in Winnipeg seldom rode the Selkirk streetcars that traversed the main street of Winnipeg's North End. The foreigner laborers came to the public transport with their clothes reeking of the railway shops, the abattoirs, and the dust from the streets. Once aboard they exhaled a garlic-laden fog that would collapse Anglo-Saxon olfactory receptors at a dozen paces. If their public use of their native languages evoked the umbrageous comments of the Anglo-Saxons, their incurable addiction to the use of garlic in their cooking drove them to distraction. "Cooking with it? My God, they couldn't stink like that just from cooking with it! They'd have to bathe in the stuff!" Eaton's shopgirls, claiming the odor of garlic clung to their hair, would walk blocks in sub-zero weather to avoid riding on Selkirk and Dufferin streetcars. Their sisters in Edmonton and Regina ducked behind clothes racks in the Hudson's Bay and Simpson's to keep from waiting on foreigners during the annual Christmas shopping congestion. Not even martyred saints could have survived the combination of the Great War, language, and garlic, and it was inevitable in the 1920s, when British Anglo-Saxons felt compelled to refer to the immigrant population, that they would do so in pejorative terms of which "goddam hunkies" and "lousy bohunks" were the softest.

Lower in the scale even than the despised Galicians were the Jews, who were at the rock-bottom of the Anglo-Saxon pecking order and would have been so without either the language or the garlic problem. The Jews wrestled with the English "th" sounds with more success than the Slavs, and unlike the latter they gave learning English their best efforts; they even worked overtime on it, for the binding mortar of Judaism was religion, not language. And it was Judaism that gave Roman Catholics and Protestants of all shades their one common denominator — anti-Semitism.

By the end of the Great War, the Jews of the 1890s were poised for a mass breakout from the ghetto they had developed hard by the C.P.R. tracks in the North End of Winnipeg. While the incoming Slavs opted for homesteading, by seven or eight to one, the bulk of the Jewish refugees who came west got as far as Winnipeg and no farther. The city's Jewish population touched 1,000 by 1900, then zoomed to 9,000 in the next decade and was reaching for 14,000 by 1920. There were then more Jews in Winnipeg than could be found in all the rest of the three Prairie provinces. Barred as they had been from ownership of land, and driven from one country to another, they had been forced for centuries to live by their wits. In the process they had developed sharply honed talents as traders, artisans, money-lenders, and business managers. Booming Winnipeg and the opening west was truly the Promised Land of Opportunity for the Jews, and they made the most of it.

By 1914 scores of Jewish immigrants were well established in business, every kind of business. Main Street, Selkirk Avenue, and Dufferin Avenue were dotted with Jewish grocery, meat, furniture, clothing, and liquor stores. They were well established in the ownership of hotels around the C.P.R. station. They were into the wholesale district and were edging into the garment manufacturing industry. Here and there a Jew was struggling with the complexities of running a tinsmith shop, a plumbing enterprise, or a drugstore. They were beginning to dominate the produce business and were getting a foothold in the jewelry and grain businesses. In short, wherever there were opportunities, there were Jews grasping them.

As they prospered they quickly followed the Anglo-Saxon predilection for turning houses into status symbols. As their resources permitted, they escaped from the cramped quarters of the Selkirk-Dufferin enclave to the tonier St. John's College area, a mile north. Or they followed the southbound Anglo-Saxons into Fort Rouge, and one Jewish family, the Frank Druxermans, made the biggest leap of all, from North Winnipeg clear over to 2 Ruskin Row, next door to the fanciest mansion in the whole of western Canada.

It would be easy to exaggerate the importance of the Jews in the commercial life of Winnipeg, but by 1911 they were at least making their presence felt. Like the Slavs, Scandinavians, and Czechs, the Jews, from the beginning, took the promise of free-

dom and opportunity in Canada seriously. Long before their
numbers might have justified it, they were into civic and provincial politics. In 1895, Louis Wortheim ran unsuccessfully for
alderman; Moses Finkelstein won a city council seat in 1904; in
1910 Samuel Hart Green, a New Brunswick-born lawyer, was
elected Liberal member of the Manitoba legislature.

　Though the Jews were becoming highly visible in Winnipeg in
business and politics, what was happening in the schools of the
North End was far more important. The Canadian-born Jewish
students were beginning to turn the St. John's Technical High
School into a recognizable imitation of a Jewish folk-schule. It
was all very well for Jewish fathers to prosper in business but
Jewish mothers, to a woman, wanted something better for their
sons. They wanted doctors and lawyers first, then more doctors
and more lawyers, then pharmacists, dentists, professors, and
rabbis. Two thousand years of Jewish preoccupation with schol-
arship, with education, with the veneration of learning, reached
its fullest flower in North Winnipeg. In the process it turned
family dinners into monthly battlegrounds at school-report
time. It also threatened to make nervous wrecks of half the
teen-age Jewish population. In an ordinary 35-pupil class in
which half the students were Jewish, it was mathematically impossible for seventeen students to come first. Yet nothing short
of coming first in class would satisfy the parents of the seventeen,
not even an average of 85 per cent if it was worth only a tenth-
place class standing. So, while the Anglo-Saxon kids chased their
footballs, hockey pucks, basketballs, and baseballs, the Jewish
kids were hitting their books, never allowed to lose track of the
family goals — respected professional callings for all the male
children of the family.

　They did not make it, of course—not by a long shot. But while
most of the Anglo-Saxon students slipped into the commercial
stream out of high school, an extraordinary number of Jews
headed for the universities and entry into the professions. And
because they were Jews, and only because they were Jews, they
found the doors closed against them. They were not alone.
When the second-generation Slavs began arriving on the door-

step of the Anglo-Saxon world a generation later, they too found the door barred against them because they were Slavs, and only because they were Slavs.

The door that was barricaded most securely and for the longest time was the one through which Jews and Slavs wanted most to pass — that into the medical profession in Manitoba. How the quota system came to be established, and precisely when, is lost to history, but it was in working shape very early in the 1920s. It did not, however, become formalized until toward the end of the decade. When the University of Manitoba took over the privately operated Manitoba Medical College in 1922 and made it a faculty of the university, the change was in form rather than in substance. It continued to operate as it had in the past, as the private preserve of the medical profession.

To gain admission applicants were first required to complete a two-year pre-medical course at the university, followed by five years of medicine and a year of internship in an approved hospital. There was no problem getting into pre-medical courses. Everybody who had the required matriculation standing was accepted. When the graduates presented themselves to the medical school, however, they were immediately caught up in a system of selection which, though never strictly defined, seemed to have the following constant qualities: first preference went to sons and nephews of practising physicians and surgeons. The next favored group were Anglo-Saxons, broadly defined to include Icelanders, Dutch, and Mennonites. In these groups marks did not matter so long as passing grades were obtained. The university, on bringing in the medical college, placed a limit of seventy students on its annual enrolment. If there were any vacancies left after all the first two groups were accepted, they were filled with Jews, other foreigners, and women, according to grades and to the whims of the selection committee. In the first years there was room for most, if not all, applicants. But as the flow of Jews and Slavs out of the North End increased, a strict quota was established. Under it the Anglo-Saxons, regardless of scholastic standing or numbers applying, were given the first fifty-odd places. The rest were allocated to Jews, Slavs, and women. Those in the favored category were grouped into "A" class and all the others were in "B" class for lecture purposes.

The quota system resulted in only a small minority of the Jews, and later of the Slavs, who passed through pre-med getting into the college, regardless of scholastic attainment. Those rejected frequently reapplied a year later or applied to the University of Alberta or McGill, and some even took their training in England. Some enrolled in pharmacy, some took dentistry in Toronto, some opted for law instead of medicine. One Ukrainian student, who passed his pre-med course near the top of his class, worked as a sign painter for three years before his application was accepted. Others, who lacked his determination to wear down the opposition, simply gave up and went into business.

Those who were accepted soon had cause to doubt the wisdom of their choice. The hazing of the medical initiation ceremonies was as brutal, physically and psychologically, as warped imaginations could make it, and was ultimately abolished by the university. That step came after an upper-classman who protested to the college against the brutality of the initiation was tarred, feathered, and beaten so badly he was hospitalized for some weeks. Fifty years later, those who experienced the initiation, even before it got out of hand, remembered it with shudders and grimaces of distaste. As the initiation approached, the upper-classmen increased the tempo of the preliminary psychological warfare being waged against the freshmen. With nudges to each other while the freshmen looked on, they selected excised organs of cadavers along with buckets filled with specimens from the pathology laboratory, "for the you know what". Anatomical tidbits were saved in special jars. A group of seniors secretly kneaded limburger cheese into cigar shapes which were then cut into one-inch lengths and placed in the laboratory incubator to ripen odiferously.

On the night of the initiation, the freshmen were taken to the Arena rink, stripped naked, blindfolded, and required to run the gauntlet of 200 upper-classmen armed with paddles for vigorous application, particularly vigorous application in the case of the easily identifiable Jews, to the posteriors of the freshmen. They were next required to roll the over-ripe cheese along the floor with their noses, eat peeled grapes otherwise identified, and careen down a children's playground slide into a tank full of blood and guts from a nearby abattoir into which the pails of laboratory specimens were dumped. After an hour of such horseplay the freshmen were washed down by a firehose and ultimately allowed to get dressed, in clothing pre-treated with itching powder. Then, with the downing of a tumblerful of medicinal alcohol, they were welcomed into the Hippocratic fraternity.

The ceremony was more hypocritical than Hippocratic, for it ushered the minority students into a regimen in which bigoted lecturers never allowed the students of the group "B" class to forget that they belonged to inferior and unwanted races of mankind. An eminent surgeon recalled:

> On our application forms we had to list such things as occupation of our fathers along with their birthplaces and religion. When I handed my application to the registrar, he glanced at it, noted that my father was a manufacturer's agent and wholesaler. "Ha," he said, "another Jew. And how many fires has your father had this year?"—a reference to the widely held belief that all Jews were arsonists and no Jew ever had a fire he had not set to collect his insurance.

Designing examinations which minority students would be unable to pass frequently taxed the imagination of the examiners. One orthopedist set a test for knowledge of bone structure by inviting the class to look at three bone fragments as he tossed them, juggler fashion, in his hand at the front of the class. Then he pocketed the chips and asked them to identify and describe their position and function in the bodily structure. Another specialist, at the conclusion of a series of lectures on the heart, confined his examination questions to those relating to the circulation system of the calf and foot.

Students who failed such tests were required to repeat the course the following year. If they failed any course a second time they were dropped from the college. One student from the North End who was flunked in surgery was told by the specialist not to try again because he would be failing him the second time. The student refused to take the advice, re-did the course, and was on the brink of being failed again when he discovered the instructor was a political bedfellow of a candidate then courting the Slavic vote in the Winnipeg North federal constituency. Apprised of the situation at the medical college, the candidate intervened to warn the surgeon that if the student was failed unfairly it would destroy the party's credibility among the Ukrainian voters. The surgeon relented, the student got his degree, and his office became a Selkirk Avenue haven for the sick for the next forty-five years.

After one surgeon failed the "B" class in surgery in the mid-Twenties, Dr. Olafur Bjornson, who taught obstetrics, took countermeasures by giving special tutoring to the "B" group so they could stay in college. He was one of a small handful of opponents of the racial quota system.

Nor were the troubles of the minorities over when they graduated. There was then the internship hurdle to overcome, and it proved vexatious indeed. The best experience was obtained in the large municipal general hospital. It selected interns from the group "A" students and excluded those from group "B", except for women graduates. One of the first Jewish interns accepted by the Winnipeg General Hospital in 1931 was taken aside by the chief of the medical staff who explained that he had been chosen only because of his fraternal connections and should consider himself a very lucky fellow. The religious orders operating Roman Catholic hospitals varied widely in their attitudes. One large Winnipeg Catholic hospital refused to have a Jew or a Ukrainian on its staff. Another accepted Jewish and Ukrainian interns and doctors without discrimination. Another picked and chose, depending on the size of the "charitable" donation an intern's father could afford. This left the veterans' hospitals, mental hospitals, and the odd private institution to which the minority-group interns could gain admission. But none of these could offer the required exposure to surgery, so many Manitoba graduates had to complete their apprenticeship in the rural hospitals of Saskatchewan and Alberta.

As the 1920s passed into the Great Depression the quota

system became increasingly restrictive as the surplus of applicants over openings in the medical college increased. In the end, it became such a public scandal that the university, in the fourth year of the war against Hitlerism, outlawed it completely and made academic attainment alone the basis for admission. The first year that admittance was based on academic standing there was such an entry rush from the backlog of quota-barred Jews that Jewish students accounted for 30 per cent of the enrolment. In May 1946 this brought a protest from Dr. H. Bruce Chown, the chairman of the committee on admissions to the College of Physicians and Surgeons of Manitoba:

> This fact has been brought to the notice of the Faculty by the Dean. It is a fact of which we must take cognizance. We have not progressed so far in this country, or in this community, that our Jewish citizens are completely amalgamated and looked upon simply as Canadians. We still mark them off as a semi-separate group. This is an unhappy fact but it is a fact. Personally I have as high a regard on the average for my Jewish confreres as for my Gentile confreres, and a warm affection for many of them. I know that their position in this community is a difficult one. I know that many fields of activity are closed to them and there is therefore a tendency to concentrate on those fields that are open. Medicine is, within limits, such a field.
>
> Personally I feel very unhappy about this situation. I cannot help but feel that concentration, such as is taking place in Medicine, can only lead to more, and more bitter, animosity.

The University of Manitoba refused to allow the racial quota system to be reimposed. But abolition of admittance quotas did not bring the acceptance of foreigners into the fraternity of healers. No "foreigner" was admitted to any important position in the Winnipeg Medical Society until a generation after the quota system was abolished. The medical society was exclusively Anglo-Saxon. Its members met from time to time to socialize and discuss new trends in medicine and in surgical procedures.

When the Jews became numerous enough to have one, they established a professional society of their own — the Simon Flexner Society, named after the director of the Rockefeller Medical Centre. The same thing happened in law. The Anglo-Saxon lawyers had the Blackstone Club, from which Jews were barred. The latter formed their own professional society, the Jessel Club.

The situation in the medical college, while it was the most glaring case of racial discrimination, was far from unique. The chartered accountants, for example, could boast in 1920 that there was not a single Jewish or Slavic chartered accountant in the whole of Canada. That exclusive status was attained by restricting admission to those who had trained under members of the Canadian Institute of Chartered Accountants, and refusing to accept Jews or aliens as trainees. Lawrence Tapper became the Jackie Robinson of chartered accounting when he broke the "color bar" in 1921 with the aid of two large Jewish business concerns. They exerted enough pressure on the firm that audited their books to get young Tapper enrolled as an apprentice.

Outside the professions, discrimination against Jews and foreigners in employment was almost universal. So far as could be discovered, the only Jew or central European on the staff of any branch of a chartered bank in western Canada was in the Dufferin and Main branch of the Royal Bank in Winnipeg. A Jewish manager who could speak some Ukrainian and Polish was a necessity in a branch whose clientele was overwhelmingly foreign-speaking. The Winnipeg Stock Exchange specifically excluded Jews from membership, although several Jews got into the securities business by purchasing gentile companies and hiring the previous owners as front men. There were few explicit restrictions against central Europeans. It was just that nobody would hire them for any position above the janitorial level.

The life, casualty, and fire insurance companies, without exception, drew the line at hiring Jews and refused to retain Jewish legal firms to draw up their mortgages or handle their legal cases. Provincial governments shovelled out King's Counsel honors with a lavish hand, but the awarding of a K.C. to a Jew or a central European was such a rarity that it sent shocks of surprise through both the profession and the ethnic community. Jewish or Ukrainian appointments to provincial judgeships were even rarer, as rare as appointments to federal courts — of which the first would not be made for thirty years, despite the many hundreds of Jews practising law in Canada.

Irksome as it indubitably was for those who suffered it, economic discrimination was occasionally less traumatic an experience than social ostracism. In the schoolyards of the cities, Anglo-Saxon children were quick to make sport of the clumsy attempts of the immigrant children to participate in Canadian games. They were always the last to be selected in the choosing-up of sides for team games, and were frequently run off completely with some such jibe as "we don't want no hunkies on our side."

As people who had lived with racial discrimination for hundreds of years, Jewish and Slavic mothers could cope with the tears of children running home after being barred from gentile games. By the time they were halfway through public school, the children themselves developed their own defence mechanisms. It was nevertheless a sad experience for eager young commercial college graduates to discover that entire categories of employment opportunities were closed to them because of their racial origin. But they learned to roll with those punches too. They broke through the department store barricades by simply changing their names, sometimes officially, sometimes on the spur of the moment.

There is an after-the-fact school of thought among the ethnic population of the prairies that holds that economic discrimination was really a blessing in disguise. Because they were pushed around and barred from entry, the new Canadians had to try much harder to succeed than did the Anglo-Saxons. The pressure brought out a strong competitive response, both mentally and physically. In support of this theory, they point to the many hundreds of immigrants who achieved eminence in every line of human activity. And they notice how a decline in the drive set in with the third generation, who were free of the pressures their forebears experienced.

It is certainly true that by the mid-1920s the immigrant population was making its way as farmers, merchants, professional people, and entrepreneurs. But socially they were making it anonymously, totally ignored by the Anglo-Saxon world. Social acceptance lagged far behind economic and political progress. There simply were no Jewish or Slavic names on any private club rosters or on anybody's invitation lists, and there would be none for thirty years.

When the Lieutenant-Governor of Manitoba, Sir J.A.M. Aikins, threw his famous party for 1,100 to open the Manitoba legislature in 1920, the invitees included all the banking, commercial, professional, judicial, and political establishments. There was a token sprinkling of French Canadians from St. Boniface. Representatives of various religious denominations were invited, but no Jewish rabbis or Greek Orthodox bishops. T. D. Ferley, the first Ukrainian elected to public office in the west, got in with the other members of the legislature. That put the Ukrainians one up on the Jews, who did not get a single invitation.

At the next mass soirée held at Government House, for the Willingdons in March of 1929, things perked up for the Jews but deteriorated for the Slavs. There was no room for anyone except the *crème de la crème* of Anglo-Saxon Winnipeg at the dinner for seventy. However, at the reception for 250 afterwards, Max Steinkopf, a widely respected Winnipeg lawyer, was allowed in as honorary vice-consul for Czechoslovakia, along with a handful of other consular representatives. By then there were one Jewish and three slavic members of the legislature. None of them made the guest list.

The racism of the prairies, mild as it was in many aspects, virulent as it was in others, was an amalgam of many ingredients. One of these, curiously enough, was as innocent in intent as Christian charity. It originated not in animus toward anybody but as a subversion of the spirit of mutual assistance, of the getting-togetherness which was so much a part of everybody's immigrant years. In its basic form it can hardly be described as discrimination at all unless it is defined as discrimination for, rather than discrimination against. In face of the numbers of immigrants descending on the west, it was early recognized that something more was needed than individuals helping individuals. That awareness spawned a whole raft of mutual welfare associations that functioned to preserve the cultural inheritance of the immigrants as well. It was a poor and unthrifty community that reached 1,000 population without the establishment of such associations as the Sons of England, the Sons of Scotland, the Caledonian Society, St. Andrew's Society, St. David's Society, St. Patrick's Society, or Burns Society. Nor did they stop there. The Scots broke down into a dozen county groupings like the Ayr-Lanark Association and the Argyle-Sterling Association. Even the settlers from Ontario had their Peel County Association and Dufferin-Simcoe Association. As mutual benefit associations they more than justified their existence.

The early arrivals naturally kept in contact with families at home, so it was a rare Englishman or Scot who arrived in the west without names and addresses of earlier arrivals from his home district. It was universally taken for granted that those who had become established would help newcomers to find jobs and "get on their feet". Any Englishman who got a job as a civil service clerk would naturally try to locate similar jobs for recently arrived Englishmen who made his acquaintance. When staff vacancies developed he would look around for Englishmen to fill them. Being a natural-born Englishman opened the door to places on civic and provincial payrolls everywhere in the west, and by the 1920s, as job opportunities diminished, sons and daughters of the original Sons of England were getting the preferences.

The Winnipeg police force, which supplied the foundation stock for the police departments in the other western cities, had two qualifications for applicants. The first was to be Scottish, preferably by birth though acceptable by ancestry. Outlanders who wandered in looking for jobs would likely be told there were no vacancies. Scots would be told the same thing, but they would be allowed to put an application on file if they seemed to comply with the second requirement. That was to be six feet tall. In case of doubt the applicant was paraded into the deputy chief's office to stand at attention at a point at the wall where the six-foot height was marked in heavy pencil. If the deputy chief could see the mark above the hair of the applicant, he was rejected on the spot. If not, his application went on file to await a vacancy. Since Winnipeg served as training ground for the chiefs of police of the other western cities, the six-foot-Scot rule became almost universal.

The English were natural-born shopkeepers, meticulous in their handwriting and account-keeping. Their manners alone would have given them a decided edge over anyone else in retail clerking. An English immigrant in a position of authority would have cared nothing for the height of a man, but everything for his penmanship and attitude. No one thought much of the fact that hiring on the basis of penmanship and attitude led naturally to the monopolization of the civil service, at all levels, by English immigrants. But it did.

In the business world, national affinity came into play in the choice of the grocers, butchers, clothiers, and druggists with which one dealt. If the Scots gave as much of their trade as possible to other Scots, so the Jews, Germans, Ukrainians, and Poles dealt with their own people. In many of the central European concentrations in the country, the first general storekeepers were frequently Jews who were skilled in trade and could speak Ukrainian and English. But as quickly as the young Slavs mastered the language and established a competing enterprise they would capture most of the trade and the Jews would retreat to the cities.

So great was the impact of the mutual aid groups on employment and in business that the only group on the outside was that composed of second- and third-generation Canadians. Scots were helping Scots, Englishmen helping Englishmen, Jews helping Jews, Ukrainians helping Ukrainians, and Masons, Orangemen, and Elks helping Masons, Orangemen, and Elks, but nobody was looking out for Canadians, least of all other Canadians. The inevitable happened in 1927. The Native Sons of Canada was organized in Vancouver to do just that, and although it enjoyed a half-life across the country for a decade or so, it never really became a force to compare with the others.

If it could be conceded that "discrimination for", as an outgrowth of mutual benefit, was a constructive force in the immigrant years, it must also be conceded that it became a destructive force when it evolved into "discrimination against". The antipathy which the Anglo-Saxon Protestant majority developed, during the hysteria of wartime, against all other breeds of humanity might well have evaporated during the decade that followed, if the good times had only come back. Instead there was a decade of business stagnation, a cessation of population growth, and a drying up of urban employment opportunities coupled with serious agricultural depression. It was in this environment that the central Europeans began to make their presence felt in non-commercial aspects of prairie life and unpronounceable Ukrainian names began to appear on local and provincial election ballots. T. D. Ferley won the North Winnipeg seat for the Liberals in 1915, and in 1920 two other Ukrainians, Dmytro Yakimischak and Nicholas Hryhorsczuk, won election to the Manitoba legislature. William Fedun became a Progressive member of the Alberta legislature from 1921 until 1926. He was joined by Mike Chornohus in 1923. All were members of the Ukrainian élite in that they had obtained some education in Russia prior to coming to Canada. Almost 40 per cent of the immigrants were illiterate and had to start their education from scratch in Canada. Some who did made surprising progress. George Mihalcheon, who came to Canada as a boy of seven in 1901, was eighteen when he enrolled in an Alberta school for the first time. He graduated from high school four years later, took teacher training, and was elected to the legislature in 1926.

Though the anti-alien agitation became quiescent, it never really subsided completely during the decade. The trades unions were against immigration. The farmers favored immigration of farm labor. The Anglo-Saxon zealots opposed foreign immigration and demanded increased British immigration. Ottawa, trying to please everybody, tightened regulations, and then could find few British immigrants interested in Canada. Throughout the decade all that was needed to get a lively controversy going in the newspapers was a letter from a reader commenting pro or con on foreigners.

In 1928 the federal government hit upon the idea of bringing in 5,000 unemployed British miners to assist in harvesting the record wheat crop growing that year. At the back of somebody's mind was the idea that the miners might take a liking to the country and become permanent settlers. Nothing worked out as expected. The miners proved less than ideal harvesters. The high wages they expected did not materialize. Most of them returned home in a disgruntled mood, and complained to their local papers about foreigners in Canada undercutting their wage rates, and of being fired in favor of foreigners who turned up where they were working.

Their complaints naturally got an airing in Canada in the form of criticism of aliens by the professional Anglo-Saxons like Bishop Lloyd of Saskatchewan. One of those criticized answered in kind in a letter to the *Calgary Herald* in March of 1929. He charged that Englishmen were never satisfied unless everything was handed to them, and defended the contribution foreigners had made to the country by the efforts they had expended. In turn, he complained that the British immigrants had succeeded in garnering 85 per cent of the city jobs in Calgary to the disadvantage of all other Canadians. Predictably, his letter produced an angry response, particularly from war veterans who, a full decade after the end of the Great War, were still complaining about the aliens who had "stayed comfortably in Canada" while they were off fighting for democracy and the Empire.

In Alberta and in southeastern Saskatchewan, anti-alien resentment was kept high by the repeated strikes of the coal miners against wage reductions. Ukrainian and Polish leaders were beginning to emerge within the ranks of the miners' union to focus attention on the ethnic make-up of the locals. The miners, moreover, were the only militant unionists left in the west. Not

only were they militant, they were radically militant and given to
sending messages of solidarity to their fellow workers in the
Soviet Union.

Perhaps more important than anything else in keeping the
foreigner issue boiling was booze. Harry Bronfman's organizing
genius gained for him a near monopoly of the liquor export
business in western Canada between 1920 and 1924. As he put
that monopoly together by buying out his competitors, he did
what any Jew would naturally have done in expanding his operations. He hired Jewish employees and he went into partnership
with other Jews. When Paul Matoff, a Bronfman brother-in-law,
was murdered and robbed of $6,000 in Bienfait in October 1922
while making delivery of a shipment of whisky to American
rum-runners, it gave the Protestant Prohibitionists a three-
pronged argument: the Jews were to blame for the breakdown
of Prohibition, they were obviously getting rich—for $6,000 was
a huge sum of money for anybody to be carrying around in 1922
— and they were bringing mob violence to Saskatchewan.

Among some of the Presbyterian clergy, it was a moot point
whether their angry criticisms arose more from antipathy to
whisky than from ordinary ingrained anti-Semitism. The Rev.
R. H. Glover, who was organizing western Manitoba for the
Prohibitionist forces in September 1920, charged: "With the
removal of wartime restrictions, a group of American Jews,
assisted and abetted by certain prostitute gentiles whose God is
the dollar, have succeeded in debauching Canada from ocean to
ocean."

The Rev. E. H. Oliver, Principal of the Presbyterian Theological College at Saskatoon, and the Rev. H. B. Johnston of Assiniboia, in a letter to the *Saskatoon Phoenix* in November 1921,
opened with this suggestion: "There are certain Jews in this
province engaged in the liquor trade who could make a great
contribution to this province by leaving it at once."

Col. J. P. Rattray, head of the Manitoba Provincial Police, in a
speech to a Winnipeg service club, charged that 95 per cent of
the big bootleggers in Manitoba were Jews, and most of the
smaller bootleggers were foreigners. And it was all a part of an
international conspiracy against Christianity. There were, he

said, three great races of the world which had sprung from
common stock but which had been separated for 2,000 years.
They had now come together in the twentieth century in a
unified campaign against everything Christianity stood for.
These races were the Jews, the Japanese, and the Prussians.
Those who bought liquor became the tools of a force that was
trying to destroy the morals and character founded on the
teachings of Jesus Christ. The service club gave Rattray its rapt
attention. So did the Jewish Anti-defamation League when they
heard about it. They formed a delegation to protest to the
Manitoba government against such inflammatory statements
from the head of the government's own police force. The government listened but did nothing until six months later when
Rattray was fired, not for rabble-rousing but for incompetence.

That Rattray's assessment of the criminal population was
common in the west is indicated by an earlier statement in
Brandon by Chief Justice C. J. Mathers of the Court of King's
Bench. Noting a light docket, he said the explanation was quite
simple. The reason there were so few criminal cases in Brandon
was because it was a predominantly Anglo-Saxon area. Elsewhere in Manitoba he noted that the majority of persons
charged with criminal offences had unpronounceable names.

There is no doubt that the enforcement of the Prohibition law
produced the kind of statistics Rattray quoted, even if his were
exaggerated. Throughout the west, Prohibition existed in almost an enforcement vacuum. The era was almost over before
the provincial governments put even half-adequate forces together to cope with violations of the liquor laws. The force which
Rattray headed in Manitoba was no more, though hardly less,
inept than that of Saskatchewan or Alberta. In Winnipeg, the
city police did as little as possible about enforcement of the liquor
act because of a bitter dispute between the city and the province
over who paid the piper. That little was done in the area well
north of the corner of Portage Avenue and Main Street. In
short, enforcement was concentrated in the slum area in the
general vicinity of the Canadian Pacific Railway tracks into
which the immigrant population was crowded.

Bootlegging became almost endemic in downtown Winnipeg

when Prohibition was repealed and a government monopoly was established in 1924. Because the sale of all alcoholic beverages was by cash in advance followed by delivery to homes, bootlegging was given an irresistible boost. The two-day delay between purchase and delivery to the buyer's home created an impossible situation for a man who had developed a sudden thirst. On the other hand, a bootlegger could order a dozen bottles at a time and have a supply on hand for anybody who would pay an extra $2 to have a bottle delivered immediately to his office. Failing that, there were few offices in the downtown business section of Winnipeg more than five minutes' walk from an apartment in which girl bootleggers combined prostitution with liquorselling. To patrons of either service for whom price was a factor, the old brick terraces on Smith and Garry streets had whoresin-residence who were prepared to undercut the regular bootleg price of $1 a drink for booze and 50 cents a bottle for beer.

Drinking businessmen who could afford to get their supplies a dozen at a time were soon keeping a bottle stashed in bottom desk drawers, along with glasses and corkscrews. In the Winnipeg Grain Exchange, where after-the-market drinking became something of a ritual, one vessel broker installed an electrical refrigerator to get around the bothersome business of chipping ice from the block in the water cooler. Some brokers installed plate-glass covers on their fumed-oak desks to prevent the discoloring of their desk tops by spilled booze. Members of the city detective detail and the morality squad were frequently welcome guests at the after-the-market uncorkings.

Whether the drinking was done in the apartment-block brothels, in the rooming houses, or in the offices, emphasis everywhere was on decorum. Customers who began to get noisy were shushed vigorously by both the madams and their companions, and if they failed to pipe down they were requested to leave. In Winnipeg and Regina at least, the drinkeries were quite literally speakeasies. It was only rarely, when things got completely out of hand, that the police intervened, and then only when cries of help went up from the neighbors.

In the north end of Winnipeg, in the west side of Saskatoon, and in the east ends of Calgary and Regina, working-class immigrant wassails tended to get out of hand. Among the immigrant populace, traditionally distilled liquor from the pot stills of the farms was still preferred to the milder and more expensive Liquor Commission merchandise. The increase in the excise tax on distilled spirits from $2 to $9 a gallon brought a rapid rise in the market for homebrew and a steady increase in the number of illicit stills in the back country. And not only in the back country. They were frequently discovered in urban warehouses, and according to Calgary legend an imaginative caretaker of the 1920s once located his still in the belfry of the First Baptist Church.

Because homebrew was obviously not purchased through the Liquor Commission, there was a compulsion on its users to finish a bottle to get rid of the evidence of illegal purchase. That, coupled with the congestion in the North End rooming houses, tended to intensify consumption to such an extent that drunkenness frequently resulted. Drunkenness, regardless of nationality, was a natural precursor to brawling, which brought the police, and the paddy wagons, and police court dockets overflowing with, in the words of the Manitoba Chief Justice, unpronounceable names.

The highly selective enforcement of liquor laws naturally produced distorted statistics. Judge L. St. George Stubbs once called liquor enforcement in Winnipeg a colossal farce and an insult to the courts. There was, he said, too much discrimination in the enforcement of the act. Some places were allowed to run wide open and others were raided. The police raided the third-rate hotels for selling beer but ignored the Royal Alexandra and Fort Garry hotels. The newspapers of the era reported frequent police swoops on Ukrainian weddings that got out of hand. A raid on the Royal Alexandra Hotel at the tag end of the Policemen's Ball or Burns Night festivities would have collected a much bigger bag of rowdies, including a full complement of drunken policemen. No such raid was ever staged, nor were the drinking rooms of the railway hotels ever visited during the Saturday-night supper dances patronized by the upper crust of the western cities.

The extent to which racial prejudice permeated public thinking on the liquor question may be illustrated by the fact that, fifty years after the border towns of Saskatchewan broke out in a rash of export "boozoriums", residents were still remembering the operators as "the Jews". Yet nobody ever took the trouble to note that the purchasers of the liquor were non-Jews, almost to a man. The same was true of all the doctors who ladled out whisky prescriptions to the drinkers, and of the overwhelming majority of the druggists who filled the prescriptions. None of the breweries of western Canada which were let off time after time with nominal fines for violations of the Prohibition acts were owned by Jews or central Europeans.

No such opprobrium as attached to the Jews and foreigners ever touched the Anglo-Saxon brewers who flooded the country with their illicit brew, indemnified bartenders who occasionally went to jail for selling it, financed the Moderation Leagues which mounted repeal campaigns, and were still welcomed as communicants in the Prohibitionist Protestant churches. That was just part of being British, Anglo-Saxon, and Protestant on the prairies in the 1920s.

12. The Battle of the Winnipeg Cenotaph

The Battle of the Winnipeg Cenotaph will never find its way onto any list of the 100 most significant brouhahas in Canadian history. By itself it was only a festering pimple on the body politic which would neither respond to treatment nor go away of its own accord if ignored. It should not, however, be taken by itself, for it was a manifestation of a poison that infected the whole of prairie society, a poison of many labels and disguises—nativism, racism, racial prejudice, national prejudice, religious prejudice, bigotry.

The western prairies had been ablaze with religious prejudice from the first days of settlement. Militant Protestant organizations devoted their attention to keeping the Roman Catholics in their place—well down in the pecking order. Prior to the Great War, as Sir Clifford Sifton's agricultural settlement program began to take hold, Anglo-Saxon Protestants began to regard the influx of central Europeans with mounting concern. Sir Rodmond Roblin, the Conservative Premier of Manitoba, was an outspoken viewer-with-alarm of the prospect of the despised "Galicians" taking over western Canada. In the pre-war agitation that was developing against foreigners, two groups were noticeably exempt—the Scandinavians and the Germans. The latter, with their notable frugality, industry, and conservative cast of mind, were generally regarded as just about ideal as settlers, next of course to fellow Britons. Indeed, if they thought of the country at all, the first-generation British in the west might well

253

have regarded Germany as a sort of honorary British dominion. Queen Victoria herself was half German; she had married a full German and that made the British royal family three-quarters German. As she was marrying off her daughters she turned, whenever possible, to royal princes of Germany.

At the outbreak of the Great War, the Germans were regarded by many as the west's most-wanted settlers. Within a matter of months they were to find themselves the least-wanted people on the face of the western prairies. The change set in when the war stopped being regarded as a lark that would be over in a few months and turned into the human slaughterhouse on the killing-grounds of Flanders. Gradually, as Canadian casualties mounted, and the newspaper front pages increasingly became propaganda instruments for the war effort, the word "German" disappeared from the papers. It was the "Huns" who were shooting hostages, slaughtering civilians, enslaving women and children behind the lines, resorting to the use of poison gas on the battlefields, and torpedoing unarmed merchant vessels on the high seas. As the war continued, the horror stories increased. The bestiality of the Hun was given increased home-front circulation by junketing lecturers from the war zones. It was probably inevitable, in the nature of things, that the horrors of the war in Europe would come to be identified with Canadian settlers of German extraction. Whether inevitable or not, it happened, and in western Canada patriotic Canadians took what revenge they could on countrymen of the Huns who fell into their hands.

In Calgary in 1916 a group of soldiers destroyed a restaurant and a dance hall on the false rumor that the owner had fired a returned soldier and given the janitor's job to a German. Next day another group of soldiers wrecked a hotel and looted its bar and cigar counter under the mistaken impression it was owned by a German. Prairie cities fired their German employees, and Calgary went all the other communities one better. It fired all its Polish employees who had been born in Germany. Several thousand German immigrants were seized and hauled off to concentration camps. The publication of all foreign-language newspapers was forbidden, many other papers were banned, and anybody caught with an old copy of a banned paper in his possession could be given, and in fact was given, a long prison term.

As the war ended and mankind began to assess the appalling cost — over 8,000,000 dead and 20,000,000 wounded — the clearly etched images of heroes and villains began to fade. The idealism that had buoyed up the western world for four years dwindled into disillusion and spreading cynicism as peace came and the soldiers came back to homelands riven with dissension, profiteering, corruption, and widespread unemployment.

The 60,000 Canadians who died in France came from all parts of the country, and it was a mean and inconsequential hamlet in the west that had no war dead to mourn, just as it was a poor excuse for a town that did not set about designing and erecting a monument to those of its young men who had given their lives. It was a sincere, serious, and patriotic undertaking in which no one really had to be asked to participate. It was, that is, except in Winnipeg which, over the next ten years, managed to reduce the whole business of honoring war dead to a travesty, a burlesque, and an absurdity.

It began in June of 1921 when a meeting of the Soldiers' Relatives Association struck off a committee to organize a campaign to raise funds for a war memorial. The city had erected a makeshift memorial at the corner of Portage Avenue and Main Street in 1920 to serve Armistice Day wreath-laying ceremonies. However, it was on a triangle of the sidewalk owned by the Bank of Montreal. When the bank decided it wanted a permanent memorial of its own on the site, the city's memorial had to be removed.

In due time the bank's local management sent off the appropriate requisition forms and an eight-foot bronze statue arrived. Somewhere in the higher reaches of the Bank of Montreal things seemed to have gone awry. Traditionally, memorials tended to glorify the common soldier, without whom armies could not exist. The bank memorial took the form of an officer, complete with Sam Browne belt, side arms, binocular case, and gloves. It occasioned a good deal of grumbling in the veterans' canteens, for there were those who argued that, in addition to depicting an officer surveying a battlefield, the figure was that of an American officer to boot. What, the old sweats wondered, was a Canadian bank doing glorifying an American officer? Particularly in 1923, when Canadians were boiling over at Americans' boasting that they had won the war?

The fund-raising efforts for the city's memorial by the war widows and other patriotic groups produced only a disappointing trickle, for Winnipeg in the early 1920s was sunk in the post-war depression. The committee turned to the city council for help and was brushed off. In the end some of the higher service echelons got interested and in 1924 a city-wide campaign was mounted under the chairmanship of one of the town's most distinguished citizens—the Hon. R. D. Waugh, a former mayor who had recently returned from a tour of duty as the League of Nations Saar Valley Commissioner. On June 14, 1924, front-page splurges in the newspapers announced the decision to erect a $25,000 memorial, and that a canvass for the money would get under way at once.

Despite a fanfare of optimistic oratory and the employment of all the artful dodges of the service clubs, the campaign for funds failed — dismally. When the books were finally closed the take totalled scarcely 20 per cent of the quota, and this was made up largely of 5- and 10-cent donations from the schoolchildren. The city council in the end agreed to foot the rest of the bill, and the committee crashed the front pages again a year later with an invitation to Canadian artists to submit designs for the memorial. The designer of the chosen model would receive an honorarium of $2,500 to supervise the erection of the memorial.

The committee appointed a board of nationally known artists and architects to judge the designs submitted. The chief assessor of the five experts, J. H. G. Russell, was nominated by the Royal Architectural Institute of Canada. In order to guarantee impartiality the committee instructed the judges to have all identifying marks removed from the models and numbers substituted before they began their assessment.

The conditions governing the contest were given wide publication and forty-eight designs were received from all parts of the country. Despite this imposing array of entries, the judges came to a quick and unanimous decision on November 11, 1925. They declared that not only was the model of Emmanuel Hahn of Toronto outstanding, it was one of the finest examples of that type of art it had ever been their privilege to behold. Said they, in part, in their report to the committee:

> The outline is of great dignity and picturesque effect. The sentiment is simply and directly expressed in a manner about which no doubt can be felt and no questions need be asked. . . . In the shaping of the shrouded figures on the sides of this rectangular, tapering design great prominence is given to the tragic aspect of war, too apt to be forgotten in times of peace. . . . It has fine architectural and decorative qualities! [And so on, through two closely spaced pages of praise which concluded,] This board feels that the highest respect is due to the power this designer exhibits in setting forth his fine idea and [that] in carrying out his work on a full scale will develop his thought in a still higher degree.

The ultimate accolade for the design came not from the judges but from Hahn's fellow designers in the competition. Several of them said, upon seeing his design, that they agreed that the judges had made the only possible choice. A model of the memorial was put on display in the City Hall and attracted widespread public approval.

It was unfortunate, for the sake of Winnipeg's civic dignity, that the award of the judges was not confirmed by the committee at once. But, at the time it was announced, a Dominion election was waxing bitter and a quorum of committeemen could not be mustered until it was out of the way. The interval provided the professional patriots with the opportunity of mulling over the name of the designer.

"Hahn? Hahn? Sounds like a German name, does it not? No, it can't be. No heinie would have nerve enough to put in a design for a Canadian cenotaph. Probably a Belgian or a Hollander, those foreign names all sound alike anyway. Still he might be at that. It wouldn't do any harm to find out. Let's call up the Free Press, just for fun like." They found out. Hahn was of German birth, having come to Canada thirty-eight years before as a boy of seven.

The publication of Hahn's biographical material might ordinarily have been expected to put an end to any questioning of his fitness to design the memorial. A member of a family of distinguished artists and musicians, he had attended the Toronto public schools as a boy, and after receiving all that Canada had to offer in the way of artistic training, he proceeded to Europe where he spent three years pursuing his studies in the art capitals of the Continent. He then returned to his home in Toronto and at the time in question was head of the sculpture department of the Ontario College of Art. One-time assistant to W. S. Allward, designer and supervisor of the great Canadian memorial on Vimy Ridge, Hahn had earned a wide reputation as a designer of war memorials, no fewer than nine Canadian cities having chosen his work.

That he had applied for his citizenship papers on his twenty-first birthday, that he had lived in Canada for thirty-eight years, that he had made a distinctive contribution to Canadian culture, made not the slightest difference. He was a German, with a German name. That was enough. The veterans' groups met in special sessions to denounce the sacrilege of having a German design a memorial to Canadian war dead. One patriot crowed that, far from lifting his hat as he passed the memorial, he would be inclined to spit upon it. An outfit called the Grand Army of United Veterans denounced the award to Hahn as an insult to the Canadian dead and demanded that designs be restricted to those by British subjects of Canadian birth.

During the early winter of 1926, all other veterans' groups checked in with resolutions in opposition to the Hahn design. They were seconded by the I.O.D.E., the British Empire Service League, and, perhaps most important of all, the Winnipeg Board of Trade, whose secretary, Arthur E. Parker, became the spokesman for the extremist opposition. He not only denounced the award to Hahn, he also attacked the notion that naturalized

Canadians could achieve equality in patriotism with natural-born citizens. Mere naturalization, he insisted, did not make a good Canadian. Look at Popovich, he challenged. (Matt Popovich was a small-bore radical labor leader who had made a few ripples during the 1919 general strike in Winnipeg.) Parker's impugning the loyalty of Canada's naturalized citizens led the debate into much muddier waters. His position was attacked by both the *Free Press* and the *Tribune*, and the static from other incensed citizens, crackling around the Board of Trade, nudged Parker into a denial that he had aimed his brickbats at the naturalized citizenry. Parker continued to insist, however, that Emmanuel Hahn's selection to design the memorial was an insult to the war dead. To ask a man who was German-born to build such a monument, he said, was like asking the relatives of a murdered man to accept a memorial by the cousin of the man who committed the murder.

The argument simmered throughout 1926, drifting occasionally into disputes over whether the body of an unknown soldier should be retrieved from France and buried in the base, and where the monument should be erected. A group of city aldermen, who had earlier been selected to choose a site, had opted for an open spot on the spacious grounds of the Legislative Building. The committee rejected that choice and called for suggestions from the citizenry. Just about everbody with a vacant downtown lot for sale came forward with offers neatly calculated to make patriotism pay a cash dividend.

At the onset of the uproar Hahn offered to ease the embarrassment of the committee by withdrawing his design. The gesture was refused, but in the end the name of Hahn, the German immigrant boy, proved too much for the committee. It paid him off with the prize money and called for a second contest. This time eligibility was confined to "Canadian citizens born in Canada, elsewhere in the British Empire, or in any of the late allied countries". This decision provoked a hassle with the Royal Architectural Institute, and the two architects on the original board of judges resigned in protest. The architects claimed that the decision violated an undertaking given to the board of

judges that their selection would be final. To avoid such a mis-
understanding the second time round, contestants were notified
that the committee reserved the right to sever connection with
any winner, if it so decided, on payment of $500. If it accepted a
design, the winner would be entitled to a fee of $2,500 to com-
plete the job.

The second contest attracted only twenty-five designs compared with the forty-eight that were received for the first. On
Armistice Day, 1927, the judges unveiled their unanimous
choice as winner of the second go-round. It was an entry by
Elizabeth Wyn Wood of Toronto, of which the judges said:

> The winning design, in our opinion, is remarkable for its
> originality and by its heroic proportions is bound to attract
> the attention of the passers by. . . . It avoids the similarity of
> so many war memorials already erected. The rugged execu-
> tion of the dominant figure (a muscular young man stand-
> ing erect, stripped to the waist) is outstanding, breathing, as
> it was, the spirit of the West with its strength and confi-
> dence, and at the same time a memory of the dead em-
> blematic of those who answered their country's call.

The judges did not add that, more important than providing a winning design of great artistic merit, they had come up
with a winning name with an authentic Anglo-Saxon ring to it.
Elizabeth Wyn Wood! There was a name that could be rolled
resonantly over any British tongue!

Then came the deluge!

Their curiosity piqued by a woman's walking off with first
prize in a field of art that was almost a male monopoly, the
newspapers went probing into the background of Miss Elizabeth
Wood. They discovered she was the recent bride of Emmanuel
Hahn! Perhaps naturally enough, the veterans of the previous
campaign rushed to the conclusion that they were being gulled
by Emmanuel Hahn; that the prize-winning design was his and
had simply been entered by Hahn under his wife's maiden
name. The likelihood that the two outstanding designers of war
memorials were to be found within a single Toronto family was
too remote a possibility for serious consideration. Who would

believe that a 23-year-old woman, only lately graduated from art school, could produce such a spectacular work of art? It would have taken more omniscience than any of the professional patriots of Winnipeg possessed to recognize that this was the Elizabeth Wyn Wood who was on the threshold of one of the most successful careers in Canadian sculpture.

Unlike the opposition to Emmanuel Hahn, which built slowly over many weeks, the oppugnancy to the Wood design grew quickly as all the veterans of the first campaign re-enlisted in the second. Unlike the first struggle, in which they had a specific issue on which to focus—Hahn's birth in Germany—the opposition to the Wood design had nothing more to go on than Miss Wood's questionable choice in husbands. And it could hardly reject her entry on that ground. Nevertheless, by the end of November opposition to the design was crystallizing around such nebulous criticism as that expressed by the War Widows Association, that "the design did not adequately portray what the boys died for."

When a nit-picker from the artistic cognoscenti opined that her design was, in fact, not a cenotaph at all, it gave the committee a quick out. On December 5, 1927, it convened for the last time. It rejected Miss Wood's entry and fired off a cheque for $500 to her, which it hoped would rid it of the Hahns, provided there were no cousins lurking in the gallery waiting to bushwhack it with another prize-winner if it held a third contest. It neatly side-stepped around any such hazard. It passed over the second-place award winner, A. M. Eadie of Toronto, and bestowed what was left of the honor of designing Winnipeg's cenotaph to a local English-born architect, Gilbert Parfitt, who was employed by the Manitoba government. No one would ever be able to say that he had not submitted a cenotaph, for his was almost text-book classic in design.

In an effort to dampen the uproar, Chairman Waugh wrote a long letter to the *Tribune*, defending his colleagues, attacking Miss Wood's design, and praising the final choice of his committee:

There has been so much deplorable controversy, some sensible, some useless, about the Memorial that Winnipeg has been trying for the past nine years to erect to the men and women of our province, who gave their lives in the Great War that I have hesitated to send this letter to the press, but I feel it is my duty to do so in justice to the War Memorial committee.

The design of Miss Elizabeth Wood, of Toronto, was discarded by the committee because it did not convey to the relatives of our boys and girls who made the supreme sacrifice, that indescribable feeling which touches our hearts, that choking, heart gripping feeling of grief, pride and gratitude which only those who have suffered can understand. Miss Wood's design may have been a fine bit of artistic work (I don't pretend to have the keen sense of perception that some of the critics of the committee seem to possess, and therefore cannot speak so positively on this point). The outstanding fact is, that Miss Wood's design made no appeal whatever to the bereaved relatives, and therefore, was a complete failure as a suitable memorial.

What our people want is a simple monument, impressive, substantial and enduring, such as the Cenotaph in Whitehall or the plain Tablet to the Unknown Soldier in Westminster Abbey. We don't want something that requires to be explained or squabbled about to the continued disgust of the relatives of those whom we will commemorate. Mr. Parfitt's design meets with the very general approval of all war veterans' organizations and the War Widows Association, and it has the practically unanimous approval of the War Memorial committee. I have had a storm of protest against Miss Wood's design, and nothing but approval of Mr. Parfitt's design, and that approval has come from those who should have the most to say about it. Both the site and design are now decided. Why this continued controversy? Surely we have had enough of it in the past; let us get on with the work far too long delayed.

In her reply to Mr. Waugh, Miss Wood neatly demolished the

argument for rejection of her design because it was not a cenotaph. The conditions of the contest, she pointed out, unlike those of the first one, made no mention of a "cenotaph". In four pages of instruction, the word was not mentioned once! Those conditions, she wrote, began:

> "The Winnipeg War Memorial committee conditions of competition for the selection of the design for an erection of a war memorial for the city of Winnipeg, Manitoba".
>
> Throughout the four pages of conditions and instructions that followed, there recurred many times, the words "war memorial" and "monument". At no place was the word "cenotaph" used or implied.
>
> Proceeding from these conditions, I considered the subject-motif of my design and arrived at a plan of simple symbolism.
>
> A long low base of granite rises from the ground, from the very soil of Canada, its line sweeping forward at a gentle angle. At the front it ends abruptly forming an invulnerable wall. Standing firmly on this is the heroic figure of Canadian Youth. He is not aggressive; he is protective. He holds behind him, clasped in his hand, a great branch of maple, symbol of the far-flung Dominion he has been aroused to guard. I have felt the spirit of the Canadian soldier. He went out there not merely to die but to serve his country and to protect his homeland. He gave his strength and the best years of his youth.
>
> All of the men made sacrifices, many of them made the supreme sacrifice.
>
> So I designed a monument to stand as an eternal memorial to the noble spirit of these men. Engraved upon the steps, where the granite rises from the ground, are the words,
>
> "SERVICE AND SACRIFICE"
>
> The side of the granite carries the names of the honor roll. Below are carved the Canadian emblems, Maple and Pine, and the names of the battles in which Canadians took part. On the front is a quotation from the British soldier-poet,

Rupert Brooke. In his poem "The Dead", written shortly before his own death, he says:

"We have gained a peace ... forever".

Rupert Brooke refers to the Peace of the Dead, of those who fought and died on the stricken fields of war.

ELIZABETH WOOD, Sc.

Toronto, Dec. 5.

At the time the site was selected, the town-planning craze was running amok in Winnipeg. The Hudson's Bay Company had recently completed its $5,000,000 retail store on Portage Avenue between Vaughan and Colony streets. To provide South Winnipeg residents with direct access to the store, the city was busy constructing a curved extension of Osborne Street around the old Manitoba University Broadway Campus to link up with Portage Avenue and Colony Street. Some time in the future a Memorial Boulevard would run directly from that intersection along the west side of the new store to the front entrance of the Legislative Building, half a mile away. The cenotaph was erected on a triangle of land between Osborne Street and Memorial Boulevard, midway between Portage and Broadway.

In 1928, however, the future was still very much on paper. A hundred-odd feet to the northeast were the backyards of a dilapidated string of row houses. The same distance southeast was the provincial jail, surrounded by a twelve-foot, weather-beaten, unpainted board fence. To the southwest was an antediluvian university building, also with its hideous board fence. And hemming it in on the west and north was the dirtiest twenty-thousand square feet of vacant space in the city, mostly quagmire. A chance visitor to the town might have mistaken it very easily for the city dump, for it was littered from end to end with old rags, discarded boots and auto tires, bottles, newspapers, tin cans, and old clothes. Between the mounds of mud, left by the excavators of the street were scatterings of refuse salvaged from nearby garbage cans by stray dogs. This was the site, aptly described by a local dignitary as "the frog pond underneath the scaffold in the back yard of the jail", on which the cenotaph was erected. With the exception of building a barbed-wire fence around the muck-heap, no effort was made to improve the grounds until eighteen months later. The committee had escaped to a welcome oblivion and the efforts to have the grounds cleaned up were made exclusively by those whose business took them past the site.

These efforts, sporadic at best, accomplished nothing. But, in the fall of 1929, ex-chairman Waugh became embroiled in a newspaper argument with the civic finance committee chairman about who was responsible for the sorry state of the plot, and this controversy served to revive the interest of the patriots. The city council, motivated largely by a desire to get rid of their noise, agreed at length to foot the bill for cleaning and sodding the grounds. This was done in 1930.

13. Jimmy Gardiner v. the Ku Klux Klan

An unlikelier inheritor of the mantle of the Temperance and Moral Reform Societies of the prairies than the Ku Klux Klan would be difficult to imagine. Yet when the moral reformers rested on their oars after the great drive that united all the Protestant denominations behind the Ban-the-Bar crusades, the Klan provided the loudest voice, indeed the only voice, raised in the west on behalf of moral reform.

Once Prohibition was achieved, and a whole catalogue of social legislation had been carried through the legislatures on its coat-tails, as it were, interest in the elevation of public morality fizzled out. Here and there a local clergyman or alderman thundered mildly against prostitution and the proliferation of bootleg joints which occurred with the repeal of Prohibition. In Winnipeg, Saskatoon, Lethbridge, and Edmonton there were occasional cries for a clean-up of the brothels and boozeries. The impact of such protests was as ephemeral as the effect of a Sunday sermon. The Klan, however, fixed shortcomings in community morality squarely in its sights and warned the authorities that if they did not clean up their red-light districts the Klan would take matters into its own hands. Idle threats of two-bit rabble-rousers? The facts lend a strange aura of authenticity to the claim of the Klan that it was indeed a force for moral reform and civic rectitude.

The first and largest Ku Klux Klan Konclave ever held in Canada took place in Moose Jaw on June 7, 1927. After two hours of spellbinding oratory it was climaxed by the burning of a 60-foot fiery cross at the top of Caribou Street. More spectacular than the cross was the size of the crowd — more people, in all probability, than had ever been gathered together in Saskatchewan before. The newspapers put the outpouring at 10,000, so the actual count would probably have exceeded 7,000. The Klansmen came to Moose Jaw from all over Saskatchewan — North Battleford, Indian Head, Portal, Prince Albert, Yorkton, Saskatoon, and all points between. More than 400 were hauled in by special train from Regina alone, to be met at the station by 100 car-owning local members who taxied them to the cross-burning. The local gentry became so excited about the gathering that they were parading to the site three hours before festivities were scheduled to start. The occasion set an all-time Moose Jaw record for traffic jams, for it seemed as if every car and truck in southwestern Saskatchewan was parked around the gathering, and it took more than an hour to get the traffic sorted out after the event.

The human traffic jam in front of the speakers' platform was horrendous. The invention of electrical voice amplifiers was still some way off and so only a small portion of the huge throng could ordinarily have hoped to get within range of the speakers. On this occasion, however, the platform was graced with several proprietors of voices that had been well trained for long-distance vociferation. They included the Rev. T. J. Hind of the First Baptist Church, the Rev. David Nygren, a visiting evangelist from Chicago, and Francis Hugh Emmons, who was then "flagging" under the pseudonym of P. F. "Pat" Emory. His job was to deliver the message while others sold memberships and collected donations. The message was that River Street should be cleaned out and Moose Jaw made safe for Anglo-Saxon Protestantism and all those who were devoted to "One flag, One language, One race, One religion, Race purity and Moral rectitude".

"I know the River Street gang is out to get me," Emmons screeched, "but if they do I want you to use my hide as the skin of a drum to beat it loud and long as you march along down that sinful street of depravity!"

That was too much for the Rev. Hind who shouted that Pat Emory was too valuable a man to be lost to the Klan, that he, Hind, would forfeit his life to enable their leader to survive and carry the Klan message to Saskatchewan. None of the pimps, bootleggers, or low-lifers from River Street came forward, however, so neither supreme sacrifice had to be made.

The worldly wise Moose Jaw residents, who had been living with River Street and its whorehouses, dives, and joints for a decade under the benign administration of Chief of Police Walter Johnson, might have been pardoned a cynical smile. River Street had demonstrated time without number that it was invulnerable to any and all kinds of threats or moral suasion. So was Johnson, who went quietly about collecting his weekly tribute from the denizens of the street as he kept the rest of the city clear of vice in all its forms.

Any head of a police department who could survive the break-in scandal of 1924, in which he had to arrest his entire force for breaking into and looting the stores they were paid to protect, was obviously a man of considerable staying power. River Street, like Annabella Street in Winnipeg, Sixth Avenue in Calgary, Third Street in Lethbridge, Avenue C in Saskatoon, and Kinistino Street in Edmonton, lived mainly off the transient trade — the harvesters, the homesteaders, the railway train crews, and the commercial travellers. The street itself intersected Main Street, the retail street of Moose Jaw, at the entrance to the C.P.R. station. No other red-light district in the west was more conveniently located. Any harvest excursioner could be off the train and into a River Street bed in three minutes flat. River Street was separated from the main residential areas of Moose Jaw by the business district; so as long as it was kept under reasonable control, respectable citizens of the town ignored its existence.

River Street tended, however, to be difficult to ignore. Whenever a celebration took place that attracted over a couple of hundred visitors, River Street was usually brought into the act. Then carousers from the parlors of pleasure spilled over into Main Street to the embarrassment of the merchants and their strait-laced customers, reminding all and sundry of the existence of River Street. Neither Chief Johnson nor Tony Townsend, his robust, bully-boy deputy chief, evinced any burning passion to act as spoilsports during such festivities. Occasionally public clamor would nudge the city aldermen into prodding Johnson to more vigorous action. But Johnson had been running Moose Jaw long before any of the aldermen were elected and was confident he would be doing so long after their retirement. So, regardless of a gradual trend toward greater decorum around the railway station, River Street remained the refuge of as colorful an assortment of whores, madams, gamblers, pool sharks, loafers, and con men as could be found on the prairies. So invulnerable was River Street to moral reformers that one surge of reform after another broke harmlessly over it until the reformers at last lost heart and gave up.

They did, that is, until the Ku Klux Klan hit town. Within a month of the burning of the fiery cross the police commission met in secret session and demanded Johnson's resignation. When he refused to resign he was fired on the spot, along with his deputy, and given a month's pay for his twenty-odd years of service.

The Klan did not hit Winnipeg until a year later. When it failed to interest Winnipeg authorities in doing anything about Annabella Street and its score of competing brothels, the Klan turned its attention to St. Boniface, which throughout the decade boasted of forty houses serving the drinking and libidinous appetites of gay blades of Winnipeg. A month later a reform upsurge voted out of office the St. Boniface aldermen who came up for re-election. The new council fired the chief of police and launched a clean-up campaign of the city's dives, some of which were actually put permanently out of business.

It may well have been that Chief Johnson in Moose Jaw and Chief Joe Gagnon in St. Boniface were living on borrowed time, and that both communities were at the end of their patience. It may have been there was no causal relationship between the arrival of the Klan and the dismissal of the officials. It could have been mere coincidence at work in both cases. Still, no Klan emerged in Calgary or Lethbridge and their brothels ran full blast without interruption well into the Dirty Thirties.

There may be a significant footnote in the fact that the only violent episode in the three-year existence of the Klan on the prairies was morally inspired. A blacksmith in Lacombe, Alberta, who had a wife somewhere else in the province, was squiring a local schoolgirl around, much to the displeasure of his fellow townsmen. One dark night he was waylaid by five alleged Klansmen and taken some distance out of town where he was stripped, beaten, and then tarred and feathered.

The Ku Kluxers made their routing of the forces of evil on River Street an essential part of their rabble-rousing in the other cities of the west. The truth was that it was as short-lived a triumph as was ever scored on the morality front. Under one temporary and two permanent successors to Chief Johnson, River Street survived with only slightly reduced bawdiness until the Great Depression wiped out the sex-for-pay industry all across the prairies. Indeed, there was even evidence that at least one River Street businessman had added sex as a sideline. A harvester complained that he had gone into a shooting gallery to practise his marksmanship and had been sidetracked by a prostitute-in-residence, who had light-fingered his summer's wages when his attention was elsewhere.

The Ku Klux Klan reached the Canadian prairies like bobbed hair, short skirts, cake-eater clothes, and the blackbottom dance — as a slop-over from a craze in the United States. The Klan began life as an instrument for terrorizing the Negroes after the American Civil War. Following the Great War it was reborn in the northern and corn-belt states, where it expanded both its activities and its concerns in all directions. As lynching nightriders-in-bedsheets the Klansmen's animus was directed first against the black population. When they were sufficiently cowed the Klan turned its attention to the "white trash" and burned crosses on the lawns of philandering husbands, wife-beaters, and whites suspected of consorting with Negroes. If the warning was ignored, tarring and feathering followed.

The anti-alien hysteria that swept through the United States under the aegis of Mitchell Palmer, Woodrow Wilson's Attorney General, provided an atmosphere highly conducive to the revival of the Klan. It provided the nascent racists with a whole list of eligibles from which to select an appropriate scapegoat to blame for the economic and political travail through which they and their communities were struggling. The blacks were still number one on the Klan hate list, but for prospective members who might not have been able to work up much dudgeon against Negroes, they offered a choice of aliens, Catholics, Chinese, Jews, Mexicans, radicals, and rapists — not necessarily in alphabetical order, and not restricted to a choice of only one. In short, anybody who hated anybody or anything could find shelter under the white robes and masks of the Ku Klux Klan.

Within months after the signing of the armistice, the United States was becoming infested with bigotry promoters intent on turning the animosities of their fellow citizens to a profit. The Ku Klux Klan not only arose from the dead, it spread throughout the northern states where it had previously been regarded mainly as an aberration of the poor whites of the south. A booming market developed for Klan charters, and the Atlanta, Georgia, office of the Imperial Wizard, Invisible Empire Knights of the Ku Klux Klan, worked overtime parcelling out territories and appointing King Kleagles, Grand Dragons, Exalted Cyclops, Grand Kligraps, etc. Soon every northern state had its Imperial Wizards and Grand Dragons superintending the selling of memberships, pocketing most of the proceeds, and sending a rake-off to Atlanta. By 1926 the K.K.K. boasted a membership of 5,000,000 and had reached such potency in politics that it could name governors and major office holders of such states as Indiana. Eventually the American Ku Klux Klan degenerated into a struggle over money and power in its higher echelons, while its bloody record of lynching and of racial and religious violence created the inevitable backlash of public opinion that led to its general decline. It was a decline accelerated by the action of several states that made it a felony to wear masked costumes in public.

The first report of the presence of the Ku Kluxers in the west came as a brief news item in the *Calgary Herald* in 1924. It noted that the Klan was being organized in Calgary and was claiming a membership of 400. The report evoked a mild response by the

Herald editors who wondered in print what conceivable reason the Klan could have for coming to Alberta, and what excuse any Calgarian could have for joining such an organization. No answer was forthcoming to either question and nothing more was heard of the Klan in Canada for several years. In the interim the violent behavior of the Klan in the United States frequently made the front pages of Canadian newspapers. Its lynchings, floggings, and involvement in political corruption caused it great notoriety in Canada. As a result, when the American missionaries for the Klan did arrive they had to devote a great deal of effort to demonstrating that the Canadian Klan had no connection whatever with its American counterpart. With that caveat entered, they then embarked on a crusade of arousing racial hatred and religious bigotry that was indistinguishable from the American brand.

The Canadian Klan — Invisible Empire Knights of the Ku Klux Klan of Kanada — established an Imperial Palace in Toronto in the mid-Twenties under Imperial Wizard C. L. Fowler, who had been expelled from both the Baptist Church and the Ku Klux Klan in the United States. Fowler had done some organizing in the Maritimes without much success, and late in 1926 he recruited Lewis Scott, a fellow Indiana Klansman, to become King Kleagle of Saskatchewan. How the Indiana Kluxers settled upon Saskatchewan, rather than Alberta or Manitoba, remains a Klan secret. But for the Klan, the decision turned out to be the most favorable it could have taken. Scott was big on organizing but rather small potatoes in the field of rabble-rousing. He needed a first-string platform performer and managed to persuade Hugh Francis Emmons, whilom Exalted Cyclops of the Indiana Klan, to go with him to Saskatchewan. Emmons was an unordained revivalist preacher who had used his fundamentalist spellbinding to energize the Klan's "propagation" department in Indiana. But he said he had become disillusioned with the violence and brutality of the Klan. He had lately spent some weeks exposing its secrets to a U.S. Senate committee which was then launched on a nation-wide investigation of political corruption involving the Klan.

Emmons, according to his own later testimony, at first resisted Scott's blandishments. He had had enough of the Klan, he said, to last a lifetime. In the end Scott persuaded him that in Canada the Klan would be a super-Christian endeavor, cleansed of all the foul characteristics of the American Klan. The argument convinced Emmons, whose Klan activities were making it difficult for him to find a job in South Bend, Indiana. So, in January 1927, he and Scott took off for Saskatchewan. En route Scott persuaded him that he should change his name to Emory for appearances' sake, as his connection with the U.S. Klan might prove embarrassing if the word got bruited about. As for Scott, nothing much is known about him except that he took off with Emmons at the end of 1927 with whatever money they had managed to raise from the 12,000 to 20,000 Klansmen they had recruited in Saskatchewan at $13 a head. Scott disappeared forever into the American underbrush while Emmons was brought back from Indiana to face two charges of fraud. He was quickly acquitted on both counts.

The campaign for memberships in Saskatchewan went very slowly at first, probably because of the secretive procedure adopted by Scott and Emmons. Emmons was a compulsive joiner and had belonged to a raft of Protestant secret societies in the United States—the Masons, Oddfellows, Knights of Pythias, etc. It is presumed that in Regina contact was made with lodge brothers and lists of names of live prospects for Klan membership were obtained from them. Their next step was to go around slipping Klan pamphlets under the doors of the prospects, inviting them to write to a Regina post-office box if interested. Two very live specimens dropped into their nets, the Rev. William Surman of the Cameron Memorial Baptist Church in Regina, and the Rev. T. J. Hind of Moose Jaw.

Surman was one of the most thoroughly dedicated and useful members ever recruited in Saskatchewan. His faith never wavered, even after the departure of Scott and Emmons, and he was the "big name" Canadian who helped get the Klan into business. He acted as chairman for a widely advertised and largely attended rally the Klan staged in Regina in February

1927. With that meeting the Klan in Saskatchewan was off and running, although at a jog trot rather than at a fast sprint. Though inquiries came in from around the province, memberships sold rather slowly.

To be eligible for membership, applicants had to be Protestant, above all else, and Anglo-Saxon, which was broadly defined to include Scandinavians and German Lutherans. They had to be willing to donate $10 to the Klan and pay $3 in advance dues for three months. Of the $13, Emmons was to keep $8 while Scott was given the balance. Out of their shares the pair had to pay the cost of getting the Klan into business. In the United States the Klansmen paid $6.50 for their robes and $1.50 for their hoods. Both were supplied by national headquarters, which paid local promoters a small commission. No record exists of the price of robes in Canada because the promoters in Saskatchewan could not make up their minds whether robes were a good idea or not. At some early meetings in Regina the ushers did wear robes. M. J. Coldwell, who was a city alderman in Regina at the time, recalled seeing people wearing hoods at later Klan meetings in the City Hall. In the end, bedsheets were officially abandoned, probably to de-emphasize association in the public mind with the violence-prone American Klan. In any event, in its public rallying the Klan was a bare-faced and uncostumed operation in Saskatchewan.

In plain fact, all this made the Canadian Klan no Ku Klux Klan at all. With the real Ku Kluxers, the preservation of anonymity was the *sine qua non* of the organization. What was the point of being a Ku Kluxer if one could not gang up on defenceless people, wreak violence upon them, and depart in the sure knowledge that one would never be caught? What, indeed, was the point? Without the paraphernalia that went with it, the Klan induced as much terror as a Rotary Club. It was this kind of a crazy excuse for a Ku Klux Klan that Scott and Emmons thought they could promote in Saskatchewan. Yet promote it they did.

While Scott remained in Regina parcelling out charters to local Klans around the province, Emmons undertook the cultivation of Moose Jaw. He was happy to discover a most friendly populace that was generous in its verbal support but more than a little reluctant to part with $13 a head in cash. In a desperate mood he notified Scott that he would have to have a better deal to make continuation of the campaign possible. He suggested he be allowed to keep the entire $13 along with a cut of $2 per head on all the members who joined as a result of his evangelical oratory at the organization of other Klans in the hinterlands. While Scott was consulting with Toronto, Emmons went home to Indiana. He did not have long to wait. He got acceptance of his proposal and returned to Moose Jaw with renewed strength for the cause.

In order to attract "prestige" members he began to hand out complimentary memberships to clergymen and prominent local businessmen. Of the 2,000 Klansmen he enrolled in Moose Jaw, he estimated that about 600 came in via the free-admission route. With the business leaders of the city on the bandwagon, it was easier to attract the smaller fry. Moose Jaw, of all the Saskatchewan communities, was the most susceptible to the Ku Klux gospel of moral rectitude. The city businessmen, who had shown little interest in all other aspects of the Klan message, were instant converts to its promise to clean up River Street and joined enthusiastically in its intimidating parade down that street of ill repute.

Moose Jaw, Regina, and Saskatchewan generally were peculiarly ripe for exposure to the Klan slogan of "One Flag, One Language, One School, One Race, One Religion" when Scott and Emmons arrived in the winter of 1927. No less than Manitoba, the people were caught up in the bitter controversy over Catholic versus public schools and the use of French as a language of instruction. A decade before the first Klansman hit the province, Premier Walter Scott was subjected to bitter personal abuse from the pulpit of his own Presbyterian church in Regina because his government was proposing that tax money could be allocated to Catholic schools in districts where the Catholic minority organized them. The Liberal government also proposed to provide a university French-language course for a handful of French-language teachers. So bitter was the campaign of personal vituperation directed against Scott that his health broke and he retired from politics and moved to British Columbia in 1916. In the decade that followed, the angry factions never allowed the boiling cauldron of religious disputation to subside. When, in 1921, the Martin government amended the school act to permit French to be used as the language of instruction in the first grade, and French to be taught as a subject in the public schools, the seething unrest increased rather than diminished.

When the Kluxers arrived, less than one resident of Saskatchewan in five was a Catholic, less than one in twenty was of French origin. Unhappily, the French minority also accounted for a quarter of all the Roman Catholics in the province, while the balance was made up mainly of Germans and Austrians. So the French Canadians got it with both barrels from the Klan — because they wanted to speak French and because they were Catholics. The Germans and Austrians likewise were targets for double whammies, because they were enemy aliens and because they were Catholics. Nobody bothered about the religion of the Ukrainians, Russians, and Poles. It was enough that they came upon the scene as "garlic-eating foreigners so ox-dumb that they had to go about with identification tags pinned to their clothing".

The hard-shell Protestant Anglo-Saxons of the prairies carried an inborn distrust of and antagonism toward the Church of Rome that was nurtured and encouraged by familial commitments to the Loyal Orange Lodge, the Knights of Pythias, the Masonic Order, and other Protestant fraternal societies which were all taken with a deathly seriousness at the time. It did not follow that Saskatchewan was a wasteland of bigots in which everybody went around making nasty gestures at the objects of their bigotry. The great majority, as events would prove, were ordinarily tolerant, decent people who minded their own business and were usually willing to take people at their face value. Nevertheless, religious, racial, and national prejudice bobbed along, sometimes on the surface and sometimes partially submerged, bruising human relations wherever it touched them.

In all the flotsam and jetsam of bigotry mucking the surface of

Saskatchewan in the mid-Twenties, none was more productive of mischief than that which befouled all discussion of immigration policy. Immigration from all sources into Canada, and particularly into western Canada, dropped far below the pre-war level during the 1920s. The sharpest drop of all, however, was in British immigration—from 158,000 in 1913 to 58,000 in 1926. During the same period the inflow from northwestern, central, and eastern Europe declined from 92,000 to 69,000. Many in the latter category were refugees from the Russian and German revolutions and relatives of early incomers being brought over. A comparison of these crude figures was enough to convince the nativistic extremists that both the federal and the Saskatchewan governments were discriminating against British immigrants and favoring the immigration of foreigners.

Ottawa, during this period, was being pushed and shoved by contradictory pressures. The labor unions wanted immigration reduced and Oriental immigration stopped entirely. Farmers and business leaders generally opted for a steady inflow of useful workers from abroad. The government sought to avoid trouble by being restrictively selective about whom it would let in. In one area, trying to lure Canadians who had settled in the United States back to Canada, Ottawa decided on a step that was both bold and imaginative. It enlisted the services of clergymen to visit Canadian enclaves south of the border and try to persuade the expatriates that it would be worth while to give Canada another chance. To encourage the clergymen the government subsidized their travels. Because of the large population of emigré French Canadians in what was called "the Boston states", a large number of priests from Quebec became involved in the program. That fact was trumpeted about as proof that Ottawa was trying to bring back French Catholics as part of a scheme to submerge Anglo-Saxon influence in Canada.

One of the most dedicated force-feeders of prejudice against non-Anglo-Saxons was George Exton Lloyd, Anglican Bishop of Saskatchewan and the province's resident bigot of the 1920s. For thirty years Lloyd had been preaching the dire necessity of peopling the west with the purest of Anglo-Saxon stock. He had been a leading figure in the promotion of the ill-starred Barr Colony at Lloydminster at the turn of the century. In the 1920s he began developing a phobia against foreigners and the immigration of non-Anglo-Saxons. In letters to the newspapers he became a persistent denouncer of such immigrants. When he discovered that the C.P.R. was paying a higher commission to European than to British immigration agencies he blistered it with an open letter accusing it of trying to mongrelize the country for its own profit. His vituperation reached its peak in May 1929 when he called the immigrants dirty, ignorant, garlic-smelling continentals. Each Lloyd epistle naturally stirred up a barrage of pro and con responses.

There was, clearly, a predisposition throughout the province, in which more than half the population was Anglo-Saxon and overwhelmingly Protestant, to look upon the foreigners in their midst with jaundiced eyes, even though the flow of European immigrants into the west in the 1920s was never more than the merest trickle. When Saskatchewaners came upon the Ku Klux Klan's articles of faith, many discovered they could freely, even enthusiastically, subscribe to most of them. Many of the tenets of the Klan platform were already deeply held articles of faith of the Loyal Orange Lodge, which was at its peak of popularity about that time. The Orangemen had been "having at" the Roman Catholics and their Papist conspiracies long before the Klan arrived. The Klan's code, variously defined from time to time, might be summarized as a belief in Protestantism, racial purity, separation of church and state, one language, one public school, allegiance to one flag, gentile economic freedom, immigration restricted to British races, and high moral standards rigidly enforced.

The Klan regarded Roman Catholics as a subversive minority because of the alleged priority of their allegiance to the Pope over allegiance to Canada. It charged that the Catholics were conspiring with the Liberal government to deliver the country into the control of the Vatican. It regarded the foreign immigrants as unassimilable and as mongrelizing to the race if assimilation was permitted.

In addition to its catch-all appeal to the Anglo-Saxon Protestants, the Klan had specifics that attracted the working class and the merchants in particular. The despised foreigners were an omnipresent threat to the wages of "white people". Look at what was happening in Yorkton where the foreigners were offering to take any job for 10 cents an hour less than the Canadians were willing to work for! And why wouldn't they? They lived like a bunch of rats doubled up in houses nobody else would rent and seemed to survive on a diet of garlic, onions and rye bread! What to do about it? Restrict immigration into Canada to Anglo-Saxons alone and send the immigrants back to where they came from if they refused to conform to Canadian ways!

For the merchants they had similar arguments: Were the clothiers having difficulty competing with the Jewish merchant down the street? Did they object to the way the Jews exploited their children in their stores? Then give all the Jews a choice of conforming to "gentile standards of business ethics" or be sent back to where they came from. Occidental restaurant operators who were feeling the pinch from Chinese competition understandably looked with favor on proposals to deport all Chinese convicted of any offence against Canadian law.

It was small wonder that by May 22, 1927, when Emmons packed the Grand Theatre in Regina and turned several hundred away, he could boast that in four months the Klan's Saskatchewan membership had grown from less than 50 to more than 15,000. It was later estimated that the Klan had more than 100 branches in rural Saskatchewan. Nor was it surprising that much of the steam behind the recruiting drive was supplied by influential Protestant clergymen. The Baptists—Hind in Moose Jaw, Surman in Regina, and Rev. David Nygren, the Baptist revivalist and Klansman from Chicago—spearheaded the preliminary organization phase. They were quickly joined by other Protestant ministers, the most prominent and enthusiastic of whom was the Rev. S. F. Rondeau, who had been the moderator of the Presbyterian Church in Saskatchewan before church union. William Calderwood, in his Master's thesis on the Klan, turned up half a dozen prominent United Churchmen on the Klan bandwagon, along with a like number of Anglicans.

The strength of United Church support of the Klan is best illustrated not by names but by deeds. On June 3, 1928, the United Church ministers of Saskatchewan attended a provincial convention in Regina. Many of them were deeply concerned over the claims being made that their church was solidly behind the Klan. In order to repudiate the claim, several ministers from Saskatoon got together and drafted a resolution which they submitted to the convention. It read: "This presbytery believes that the principles of the Ku Klux Klan are in opposition to the teachings of Jesus Christ and the United Church cannot in any way support the Ku Klux Klan." The resolution evoked an immediate objection from an unidentified Klan adherent who rose to put forth an amendment which stated that the church, however, was not opposed to or fighting the Klan in any way. His objection drew such a round of applause that the Saskatoon resolution was shifted to a committee, where it was quietly buried.

Among the smaller sects, the Klan had most enthusiastic support. Most vociferously active was an unfrocked Roman Catholic named J. J. Maloney, who lived in the town of Cabri and toured the province for the Klan. Ultimately, he was jailed in Edmonton for pocketing funds belonging to Klan members.

Where the Klan was concerned, there was no hesitation among Saskatchewan residents in standing up to be counted among its supporters, particularly in letters to the editors. One prominent letter-writer was E. W. Painter, a well-known Anglican layman. In May 1927 he wrote to the *Regina Leader*:

As Regina's representative of the British Israel World Federation (the greatest unifying force in the British Commonwealth of Nations) I have thoroughly investigated, and thanks to the organizers of the Ku Klux Klan in Regina and Moose Jaw, have been afforded every opportunity to obtain a very complete knowledge of the aims and objects of the K.K.K. movement, and am perfectly satisfied that these are worthy of the acceptance and support of every Protestant minister and member of the Christian Church and have no hesitation in urging these and also the members of our

British Israel Movement, Masons, Orangemen, and Daughters of England, Scotland and the Empire and every patriotic Protestant organization, men and women, to unite with this great and glorious movement which is law abiding and anti-nothing except anti-wrong.

After several more similarly non-stop sentences, he closed with "Yours most sincerely in the interest in truth and righteousness, E. W. Painter."

The summer of 1927 was enlivened by the flowering of Klan branches all over the province, complete with initiation rituals and the burning of crosses. But with the coming of fall the Klan was almost wiped out by the departure of Emmons and Scott with the organization's funds just as the frost was coating the pumpkins. Yet phoenix-like it was able to rise quickly from the ashes of near bankruptcy on the wings of its involvement in Saskatchewan politics.

Whether the Klan infiltrated the Conservative Party and what remained of the Progressives, or whether it was infiltrated by them, can be argued either way. What is beyond cavil is that a liaison was established between the Conservative Party and the Ku Klux Klan, and that it played a part in the defeat of the Liberals in the 1929 election in Saskatchewan. Emmons took an affidavit that Dr. J. T. M. Anderson, the Conservative leader, had approached him with a request for Klan support in the oncoming provincial election. And during his trial in Regina Emmons insisted that the reason he had left Canada was that the Klan had been taken over by the Conservatives, headed by Anderson, Dr. Smith of Moose Jaw, and Dr. W. D. Cowan, a leading Regina Tory and treasurer of the Klan. Several weekly newspapers which supported the Conservatives also supported the Klan, and others, while maintaining an impartial editorial stance, reported Klan rallies in their news columns with ill-concealed enthusiasm.

The Liberal Premier, the Hon. James G. Gardiner, seems to have paid little attention to the Klan in its early stages, until word came up that it was recruiting members among the civil servants of the province. He then took off after it with all guns blazing, and he kept them blazing for the next two years, until the battle lost all relevance with the onset of the Great Depression. Being Jimmy Gardiner, he was always careful to look for opportunities to tie in the Klan with both the Conservatives and the Progressives, although his main target at all times was the Conservatives. The barrage began with the opening of the legislature in 1928, when he accused Anderson of seeking Klan support in a recent by-election in Maple Creek.

The Klan, meanwhile, was back in business, with a new Imperial Wizard for all Canada and a new set of officers and organizers for Saskatchewan. The new Imperial Wizard and Emperor of the Knights of the Ku Klux Klan for Canada was J. H. Hawkins, an optometrist from Dallas, Texas, who had moved to Toronto. His aides in Saskatchewan were Imperial Wizard (Saskatchewan) J. W. Rosborough and Imperial Kligrap J. H. Ellis. The Exalted Cyclops was R. C. Snelgrove. Ellis and Rosborough were delegates to the Conservative party convention in Saskatchewan in 1928 and Hawkins was a regular attender. Rosborough, a chartered accountant, was the auditor for the City of Regina. Hawkins became firmly established in Saskatchewan, and when spring came in 1928 he and Premier Gardiner followed each other around the province exchanging insults, charges, and countercharges. In this contest the advantage was all Gardiner's, for he had the former Imperial Wizard, Emmons, providing the ammunition. This unlikely teaming-up produced the most intriguing political conundrum in Saskatchewan history: Did the Liberals bring Emmons back to Saskatchewan to destroy the Tories, as the Conservatives claimed? Or was Emmons swearing to the truth when he testified that he had lost control of the Klan to Drs. Anderson, Smith, and Cowan.

Certainly, the appearance of Emmons in police court in Regina and Moose Jaw was manna from heaven for Jimmy Gardiner. Arranging for the delivery of that sort of manna was just the kind of ploy one might have expected from the no-holds-barred tactical approach to politics of the Saskatchewan Liberal machine. Adding credence to the Conservative charge was the fact that the prosecution of Emmons was incredibly cavalier in all its essentials, and based on charges so trivial that they could hardly have justified having him return from Indiana. And he did return without extradition. The first charge—of embezzling Klan funds — failed to establish that the money collected even belonged to the Klan and not to Scott and Emmons. The second charge — of obtaining $6.50 from a Moose Jaw woman under false pretences — was ridiculously trivial and failed on the testimony of the complainant alone. Emmons' testimony in Regina and Moose Jaw followed the pattern he had established in his appearance before the United States Senate. He seemed under some compulsion to expose the innermost workings of the order, despite the Klan oath that required its members to deny, under oath, that they belonged to the Klan. He so antagonized his former associates by his testimony that they reacted angrily when he hired the City Hall auditorium in Regina to deliver an in-person exposé to Klan members. The Klan leaders packed the hall with their supporters, who howled Emmons down when he tried to speak. He departed the hall, Regina, and Canada, and was never heard from again.

But did the Tories, as Emmons swore, take over the Klan in Saskatchewan?

Hawkins himself vociferously denied that Anderson had ever sought the support of the Klan, or was a member of the order. On the other hand, Charles Puckering, a sometime organizer with Emmons, gave J. H. Ulrich, the Liberal Minister of Health, a sworn statement that he had introduced Anderson to Emmons in Moose Jaw in May 1927, and that Anderson had asked Emmons to organize a Klan in Saskatoon and had offered to provide a list of prospective members. Emmons, in turn, swore that he met Anderson at the Western and Flanagan hotels in Saskatoon and got such a list from him.

Proving any negative proposition is always next to impossible. Denial that the Klan was in cahoots with the Tories was just that —impossible to prove—for the Saskatchewan Conservatives. M. J. Coldwell, for example, who was knee-deep in Saskatchewan politics at the time, was far from convinced. A lifetime political opponent of J. G. Gardiner and a veteran critic of the Liberal machine, Coldwell none the less gave Gardiner the highest marks for his forthright and vigorous campaign against the Klan in Saskatchewan. Coldwell himself recalled being introduced to Hawkins at the Kitchener Hotel during the 1929 election campaign. He was leaving a radio studio in the hotel when Anderson and Hawkins were coming in, and after the introduction they chatted about the campaign for a while. It was only later that Coldwell learned that Hawkins was the Imperial Wizard of the Klan.

Actual proof of the involvement of the Klan and the Conservatives did not come to Coldwell until after the election. The Progressive Party, with which Coldwell was then allied, threw its support to the Conservatives, which along with that of the independents enabled Anderson to take over the government. The price of Progressive support was a commitment by Anderson that a royal commission would be established to investigate the relationship of the civil servants with the Liberal Party machine. Anderson also gave his assurance that none of the government's employees would be fired while the inquiry was proceeding. Coldwell was appointed chairman of the commission. Two employees were fired and the wife of one appealed to Coldwell to get her husband's job back. He had, she said, joined the Ku Klux Klan on instructions from the government to provide it with inside information. She gave Coldwell a complete membership list of the Regina organization. "I was astounded at the number of highly placed Conservatives who were on that list," Coldwell said, adding that he had destroyed the list when he left Regina for Ottawa twenty years later.

Aside from palling around with the Tories, Hawkins spent the summer of 1928 trying to recapture the momentum and the dollar inflow that the Klan had generated the previous year when Emmons was running the show. But Emmons did not have Jimmy Gardiner to contend with, and as a result the first Klan membership drive had snowballed along with only an occasional United Church minister taking a pot-shot at it. As a result of this lack of opposition, it was possible for the Klan to claim far greater strength than it had actually developed. Gardiner's vigorous campaign against it awakened the hitherto silent majority to the kind of bigotry that was being peddled, and the glamor of the Klan began to tarnish. It was a campaign that Gardiner enjoyed to the utmost, for he wasn't really fighting the Klan as much as he was using it to attack his Conservative and Progressive opponents.

Gardiner's agents were busy watching every movement of the Klan and collecting names of those who were joining. With the flood of material that reached him in correspondence from Liberals throughout the province, it was not long before Gardiner knew more about the activities of the Klansmen, and who they were, than the Klan itself. The Gardiner papers contain many hundreds of references to every aspect of the Klan, including membership lists that contain not only the names of prominent Conservatives and Progressives, but also a sprinkling of Liberal names as well. So deep-rooted was Gardiner's phobia where the Klan was concerned that almost twenty years later a casual reference to the Klan in conversation would set him off on a torrent of reminiscences.

The Klan, as an organization, never really recovered from the defection of Emmons, despite the frantic efforts of Hawkins. Nevertheless, the Gardiner attacks, coupled with Hawkins' denunciations of Gardiner, undoubtedly drew many dedicated anti-Liberals from both the Conservatives and Progressives into the organization. Anything Jimmy Gardiner attacked they automatically had to support, just as they opposed anything he supported. The Klan, by the end of 1928, claimed a membership of 70,000, although it is doubtful if in reality it had more than a fifth of that number. Hawkins managed to harvest $40,000 in fees and another $8,000 in donations in 1928, a fair indication that it was losing its attraction. Emmons and Scott, by most accounts, had milked twice that much from their campaigns the year before.

As an organization the Klan may have been a diminishing force, but as a state of mind it was far from through as a power to be reckoned with in Saskatchewan. And it was as a state of mind, more than as an organization, that it surfaced in the Arm River provincial by-election in October 1928. Traditionally a solid Liberal seat, it would ordinarily have been an easy win for the Gardiner government's candidate. One of the bitter issues of the campaign was one that was dear to the heart of every Klansman —Protestant children being taught by Catholic nuns in Catholic school districts. It so happened that in all Saskatchewan there were precisely 117 such children, but espousers of the Klan doctrine made it sound like a monumental threat to the existence of the public schools.

In addition to the schools issue, the Tories raised another racial question—the failure of the Liberal government to prosecute Harry Bronfman on two charges that had been hanging fire against him for many years. One was of trying to bribe a customs official, and the other was of spiriting out of Moose Jaw a couple of witnesses in a prosecution involving one of his export warehouses. The refusal of Liberal administrations in both Regina and Ottawa to act had been a needle in the hands of the Conservatives in both places. Bronfman had dominated the liquor export trade in Saskatchewan, and the thrust of the Tory needle was that the Liberals were so corruptly indebted to the Bronfmans that they could not afford to prosecute. Adding anti-Semitism to anti-Catholicism became such a factor in the Arm River constituency that T. C. Davis, the newly appointed Attorney General, promised he would personally guarantee the prosecution of Bronfman. The Liberal was elected, but by only a 60-vote majority, when a margin ten times that size might have been expected.

The emotionally charged Arm River campaign of October 1928 was only a prelude to the emotionally supercharged provincial election campaign of 1929. All the Arm River issues—the Catholic influence, the school system, Bronfman, and immigration — were intensified. In Regina, Saskatoon, and Moose Jaw in particular, the Bronfman issue was prosecuted with great vigor by the Conservative press.

If Gardiner's vigorous attack on the Klan solidified Liberal support in constituencies with large foreign or French-Canadian populations—and it did—it can also be argued that it cost him the election. Numerical support for the Klan was heavily concentrated in the cities, although it had blanketed the province with its Klaverns. The Tories all but swept the urban ridings. Moose Jaw, Regina, and Saskatoon had two seats each; all six went Conservative, as did Swift Current, which was a single-seat riding. Yorkton elected an independent, who joined the Conservative cabinet. The only city to vote Liberal was Prince Albert. In that election the Liberals polled 28 seats to the Conservatives' 24. If the Liberals had kept their urban seats they would have emerged with a clear majority in the House of 63. As it was, Dr. J. T. M. Anderson was able to persuade the eleven Progressive and Independent members to support his group government, and thus ended twenty-four years of Liberal rule in Saskatchewan.

Dr. Hawkins folded his tent, pocketed his profit, and disappeared from Saskatchewan in the fall of 1928, but two of his henchmen, R. C. Snelgrove and D. C. Grant of Moose Jaw, tried to carry the message into Alberta and Manitoba. Snelgrove chose Drumheller as the most likely spot in which to set a fiery cross ablaze because the town had been tormented by racial strife for almost a decade. Its coal miners were largely foreign-born, the business community and the coal-mine owners were predominantly Anglo-Saxon, and the two had been at each other's throats for years. The miners had staged a series of bitter strikes against both the mine owners and their "white" union leaders. The establishment had organized vigilantes and visited gang violence upon the miners. Best of all, the town had two gambling joints, running more or less wide-openly, and two of the busiest brothels in western Canada—great targets for a Ku Klux morality crusader.

Drumheller was such a natural for the Ku Klux Klan that Snelgrove had little difficulty in persuading bank managers, merchants, Legionnaires, and a sprinkling of lawyers to join up. The local newspaper, the *Drumheller Mail*, was edited at the time by Archie Key, who denounced the Klan in his editorial column in language seldom used by country papers where the Klan was concerned. When his publisher mildly expostulated, Key winked and said he was aware the publisher was a member. That ended the conversation. Following Key's next editorial the Klan reacted by burning a cross in front of his house. Later somebody fired a shot over his head as he stood on his front step. Aside from burning a cross or two on the hills outside town, that was about all the Klan in Drumheller ever amounted to.

Elsewhere in Alberta, however, the Klan managed to survive in a nebulous fashion for almost a decade. Branches were established at Red Deer, Vulcan, Milo, Rosebud, Taber, and Edmonton. In all, about 1,000 memberships were sold for $10 each. The original organizers, according to the *Calgary Herald*, which did not name them, absconded with the funds, and the organization languished until Snelgrove and J. J. Maloney came in from Saskatchewan. Maloney first established his headquarters in Calgary and then moved to Edmonton. Although jailed once for misappropriation of funds, he operated his anti-Catholic campaign under one guise or another until well into the Depression. For reasons unknown, he actually had the Klan incorporated under the Companies Act. Then he dropped the name and turned to publishing *The Liberator*, a monthly magazine, as official organ of the J. J. Maloney Free Speech Movement. In abandoning the Klan, Maloney was guilty of behavior unbecoming a Klan organizer. He neglected to clean out its bank account, and in 1952 a list of dormant bank accounts listed the Klan as having $40.19 to its credit.

The Klan made a much bigger first splash in Winnipeg than it did in Alberta, but it died even more quickly. It hit the front page of the *Manitoba Free Press* with a banner headline on October 17, 1928, quite unexpectedly as far as its organizers were concerned. They were Puckering and Grant of Moose Jaw, and Andrew Wright of Winnipeg, a local organizer. Grant had been a Klan organizer under Emmons and, for some completely obscure reason, in Winnipeg he insisted he was from Brandon and refused to disclose any information about his origins or background. The trio had quietly spread the word through their fraternal affiliations and rented the Norman Dance Hall on Sherbrook Street for their first meeting. Some 150 were invited, including thirty women, but not including a shorthand reporter of the *Free Press*, who got wind of the meeting and secreted himself within earshot of the speakers' table. It was well that he had, because nobody got into the hall except those who passed an extensive questioning at the door. No one was as surprised as Grant when the *Free Press* appeared the next morning with an eight-column front-page headline and a two-column sub-head:

Ku Klux Klan Plans to Clean Up Winnipeg

Organizer Tells Meeting
Vice is Rampant in City

The body of the report ran to better than two columns and included such direct quotations from Grant as these:

"We strive for racial purity. We fight against intermarrying of negroes and whites, Japs and whites, Chinese and whites. This intermarriage is a menace to the world. If I am walking down the street and a negro doesn't give me half the sidewalk I know what to do," Grant cried, so loudly that someone rushed to the table to urge him to keep his voice down. The landlord, apparently, had been fearful of the noise the Klan might make and made quietness a condition of the rental agreement. It was a plea that had to be repeated many times during the evening.

After a lengthy discourse on racial purity, Grant turned to "Gentile Economic Freedom", and an attack on the Jews. "The Jews are too powerful and are throttling the throats of white persons to enrich themselves." He described Jews as "slave masters" and urged his listeners to concentrate on the fact that while the Jews were all-powerful the Ku Klux Klan was more all-powerful. After the Jews he turned his attention to the "scum of Papist Europe" which the Liberal government was allowing to flood into the country while refusing to allow the entry of immigrants who were not Roman Catholic.

Ultimately, toward the 90-minute mark, Grant reached the "Ninth Principle of the Ku Klux Klan—Law, Order, and Higher Moral Standards". "We've cleaned up Moose Jaw, Saskatchewan," he shouted. "We have made it half decent to live in. Vice was wild in Moose Jaw and wantonness was not unknown before the Ku Klux Klan abolished it. Winnipeg is next," Grant promised. "Vice, wantonness, graft and corruption walk hand in hand in this city and the Ku Klux Klan is going to abolish all this." With that he launched into an attack on Chief of Police Chris Newton and Morality Inspector Bill Eddy. These references evoked further shushing and a warning call that there was a policeman downstairs. "The Ku Klux Klan is not afraid of the police," Grant shouted, to set off another outbreak of shushing.

In the end, as always, Grant got down to money. The dues in Winnipeg were $13 cash in advance and 50 cents a month. Women got in for half-price, $6.50 for the first three months and 25 cents a month thereafter.

Grant was awakened the following morning by the shouts of newsboys heralding his promise to clean up their city. He was both astounded and distressed by the lengthy report of his speech — astounded at how the *Free Press* had discovered his meeting and managed to get a reporter onto the premises; distressed because the publicity was premature. Grant spent the next couple of days challenging the accuracy of the news report and denying that he had criticized the Winnipeg police officials or demanded their dismissal.

Embarrassing though the premature publicity may have been, Grant made the best of it, and as an attention-getter he came down hard on the wide-open vice in Winnipeg and St. Boniface. But in the latter case he did it from afar. Save for its Norwood Anglo-Saxon Protestant enclave, St. Boniface was a predominantly French-Belgian city across the Red River from Winnipeg. In triggering his attack on St. Boniface morality, and ridiculing the "petticoat"-wearing priests of St. Boniface College, Grant circumspectly did it from Norwood. This got him accused of cowardice by Monseigneur Jubinville, who warned him that the Klan had better stay out of St. Boniface. But even in his defence of his community, Mgr. Jubinville's very tone indicated that all was not right within St. Boniface.

"We all want a clean city," he said, "and we all know too well that it is not exactly as clean as it might be, but there is no excuse for Mr. Grant's charges against our police department. Some of the officers, perhaps, do not do their duty as well as they might, but that does not implicate the whole force. It must be remembered that keeping a city spotlessly clean is a very difficult task."

The last sentence was the understatement of 1928, if not of the ages. With or without the publicity barrage laid down by the Ku Klux Klan, St. Boniface a month later elected a new city council, which fired the police chief and hired a new police force. But it, like Moose Jaw, never did get a "spotlessly clean city". And as for Winnipeg, it simply couldn't be bothered, either with the Ku Klux Klan or with Annabella Street. When only a highly unprofitable corporal's guard could be attracted to membership, the Klan organizers gave up and vanished as suddenly as they had appeared.

Grant clearly lacked both the oratorial fire and the organizing flair of Emmons or Hawkins. Where they had promoted mass meetings of followers, Grant, after the first meeting, seemed afraid that his movement might become infiltrated by secret agents of the Catholic Church, the Jews, or perhaps the police departments. The screening of meeting attenders at the door was reduced to absurdity. At the Norwood meeting they even asked some people if they could produce letters of reference from acceptable and responsible people. They demanded to know whether the attenders intended to join the Klan at the meeting, and whether they had the $13 admission fee. At one meeting Grant read off a condensed version of the Klan principles. Then he asked all those who subscribed to them to stand up. Those who remained seated were ordered out of the meeting, and it did not proceed until they left. Then, halfway through, Grant stopped and ordered all press representatives to leave because the rest of his message was confidential, for the ears of the audience only.

The truth was, that by the time Grant got to Winnipeg in October 1928, trying to promote the Klan in the city was like flogging a dead horse. When he realized that fact, Grant returned to Saskatchewan and obscurity until 1935, when he reappeared as the C.C.F. organizer for T. C. Douglas in the Weyburn constituency. He had better luck there, or better skills, than he had in Winnipeg. He managed to get Mr. Douglas elected to Parliament.

14. Take My Money — Please!

Aside from their simultaneous appearances in the Winnipeg criminal court docks in April of 1926, Joseph Xavier Hearst and Joseph Myers had little in common, in appearance or in modes of operation. A police circular issued following his disappearance described Hearst as "5′ 3″ tall, 33 years of age, weighing 110 pounds. He plays the piano and neither smokes nor drinks. He is shifty in manner, slovenly in appearance, cannot sit still, walks about when talking, is pompous, egotistical and argumentative and gives the impression of being a dope addict." That reads more like the description one might expect to see on a "wanted" circular for a pickpocket or a sneak thief, not for the most consummate swindler in the history of western Canada. And, until John A. Machray, that unctuous, pious fraud, was unmasked in 1932, Hearst was also the most unscrupulously successful and the most heartless. Both preyed on widows and orphans and on wealthy tycoons with equal enthusiasm. Machray spread his defalcations over a lifetime. Hearst's career as an embezzler-extraordinary spanned less than two years. But in those twenty-four months, he managed to mulct the people of western Canada of better than $500,000.

Myers was physically a bigger man than Hearst. If he could have been described as a "consummate" anything it would have been the "consummate mining promoter who had struck it rich". Compared with the scores of charges against Hearst, Myers faced only four charges of issuing false information with the intention to defraud.

Two more disparate characters than Myers and Hearst could hardly have been found. But placed in juxtaposition they provide a sort of prismatic refraction of the outstanding qualities of the people of the Canadian west in the 1920s. It was an age of monumental gullibility when the will to believe ran rampant. Only people utterly devoid of any kind of critical faculty could have been taken in by either Hearst or Myers. It was, moreover, an era before prospectuses were invented, before there was any real protection for investors, and before there were any curbs on the freedom of stock promoters to work the most outrageous, within-the-law frauds upon the public. A few thousand dollars invested in mining claims was easily transmuted into a controlling interest in a 1,000,000-share mining company whose stock was then sold on the basis of assay reports. In Alberta, oil stock replaced mining shares as the prime bait on the promoters' hooks, but nothing else changed, save that the public appetite for get-rich-quick promotions seemed to become more insatiable as time went by.

The very name that Hearst chose for the vehicle for his swindle ought to have been warning enough for the unwary to step back and take another look. It was the Hearst Music Publishing Company Limited, whose business would be to print sheet music composed by Hearst and other American composers and sell it through music stores on both sides of the border. Indeed, one of Hearst's first proposals was to set up his own chain of sheet-music stores all across Canada. A sheet-music publishing business? In Winnipeg? A thousand miles from nowhere?

To an easy mark for a fast sales pitch, the idea, curiously enough, could be dressed up to appear less lunatic than it sounded at first hearing. Winnipeg was the Eisteddfod *cum* Bayreuth of Musical Canada, thanks to its concentration of music-mad Ukrainians, Jews, Scots, and Welshmen. The month-long Winnipeg musical festival was an annual harbinger of spring. The city boasted more music teachers per square yard than the other prairie cities put together. Its Male Voice Choir made annual forays to the music halls of Minneapolis and Chicago. The San Carlos and D'Oyly Carte opera companies

played week-long engagements to capacity crowds in the luxuri-
ous Walker Theatre. Touring stars of the Metropolitan Opera
Company and the American concert stage made Winnipeg a
regular port of call. The *Manitoba Free Press*'s special annual
music section reached eight pages in length in 1920, which was
more space than was needed to review western agricultural
progress, church activities, or the booming automobile business
in the city and its environs. Indeed, it was not until late on in the
1920s that the automobile displaced the piano as the prestige
symbol of the Winnipeg middle class.

By the time a Hearst stock salesman got through his spiel, a
music publishing business in Winnipeg did not seem such a
far-out proposition after all. Indeed, so august a body as the
newly elected Progressive Party's Utilities Commission was
quickly convinced that a music publishing business was just the
kind of a business Manitoba needed at the moment. At the outset
of his promotional career Hearst had applied to Utilities Commissioner P. A. Macdonald for permission to sell $175,000 worth
of stock to Manitobans for the purpose of establishing a music
printing plant. Unimpressed with the financial statements and
other data presented by Hearst, he refused to permit the stock
offering. Hearst sent his lawyer over the head of the official to
the commission itself and it issued the licence that put Hearst in
business.

Whether Hearst launched the publishing business with lar-
ceny aforethought was never completely proven, but all the
evidence pointed to that conclusion. The jittery little piano
player landed in Winnipeg some time in 1920, probably from
New York. Whether he had been a denizen of Tin Pan Alley is
likewise a matter of conjecture. But in the catch-phrase of the
times, "he sure could rattle the ivories", and in a number of the
songs he did market credited the words and music to himself.
The most memorable in an easily forgotten lot was "You Can
Take Me Away from Dixie, but You Can't Take Dixie from Me".
Prospective purchasers of Hearst Music stock were assured that
it was an Al Jolson standard. They were also given a free bonus
of a dozen sheet-music numbers with the $100 shares and were

urged to listen in on their crystal sets for *their* songs to be played on the proliferating American radio stations.

From a never-identified source, Hearst seemed to have got enough money together by the middle of 1921 to bring his company to life. John Anderson, who became a sort of non-directing director and supernumerary secretary of the Hearst Company in 1921, said Hearst showed him a cheque he had received for $7,000 as payment of royalties on songs he had written.

Anderson's function in the enterprise was never very clearly defined, either for him or for the courts. He seemed to be a part-time bookkeeper, but only to the extent that Hearst told him what entries to make in the books. On two occasions he visited a branch office Hearst had established in Chicago, but the reasons for the trips remained forever vague in his mind. From time to time he collaborated with Hearst in fitting words to Hearst's music. While he said he had provided hundreds of lyrics, he could not remember the title of any of the songs so written.

In addition to writing the company's songs, Hearst was also active both as a stock salesman and as a supervisor of the salesmen he had on the road. The system seemed to be that, when a salesman working the boondocks came up with a live prospect with enough resources to make an extra effort advisable, Hearst went out to assist in closing the deal. He was as adept at persuading retired farmers and merchants in western Manitoba to entrust their life savings to him as he was in sweet-talking widows of Killarney and Boissevain into exchanging their Victory Bonds for blocks of his company's shares. Certainly, when it came to belling the fat cats of Winnipeg, Hearst had exclusive rights to the territory. In the meantime he kept the books, all other records, and the banking of the company very tightly under his own control. Anderson seemingly spent three years as one of Hearst's directors and officers without discovering anything about his operations — or so he indicated at Hearst's trial. Neither did the company auditor who provided the financial statements that were the basis of Hearst's stock-selling campaign.

Hearst's books showed that in 1921 he had $250,000 on deposit in the Chase National Bank in New York. Where it came from or how it got there was never recorded. In the first ten months of 1922 he claimed the company had done $290,000 in business and earned $140,000 net profits. Shareholders who had subscribed for their shares in the first drive and had paid $100 a share for them, were paid a dividend of 30 per cent for the first year. Such was the state of credulity of the populace that this dividend became, not a cause for suspicion, but the lubricant on the slide to disaster for all who came after. Far from becoming suspicious about any company which could earn 50 per cent net profit on sales and pay an annual dividend of 30 per cent, they rushed to put their pens to the salesmen's dotted lines. One retired farmer drew out his entire life savings of $48,000 and handed them over to Hearst.

Whether it was fascination with the song-writing business or the eloquence of Hearst himself, his appeal was irresistible. Nor were his sales confined to the unsophisticated. His shareholder lists included some of the sharpest money-men in Manitoba. One was E. S. Parker, a wealthy grain broker from the Winnipeg Grain Exchange. He went for $45,000, and there were reports that other grain men had invested even more. Parker took his loss, not with a sickly smile of chagrin, but with a broad grin. It wasn't the first time he had lost $45,000 and he hoped it would not be the last either. He was attracted by the long-shot nature of the popular-song gamble. It didn't matter to him that few of Hearst's songs had achieved best-seller status. One hit that would sell 1,000,000 copies would make up for a lot of losers. And any man who could not take his losses with a smile was no man in Parker's estimation. The last thing he ever wanted was a reputation as a groucher.

There was, indeed, a certain specious logic to Parker's preoccupation with the possibility of collecting on a long-shot winner. North America was moving rapidly into the age of music. The radio rage was in full flight and more than 400 stations were battling for the listeners' ears from 8 to 10 each evening. In addition, the phonograph was reaching new levels of popularity as the first electrically driven models were soon to be placed upon the market. The shape of things to come for Hearst's commodity was plainly visible in the way in which the public was turning new songs into overnight smash hits. "Yes, We Have No Bananas" had started it all, but sales for "Three O'Clock in the Morning" passed 3,000,000 in little over a year, and "Yes, Sir, That's My Baby" had more than 1,000,000 sales in a matter of months. When such things as "Do wacka do wacka do" and "The Wang Wang Blues" made it to the top, who could say that the next Joe Hearst song would not ring all the bells?

D. R. Finkelstein, a real-estate developer, seems to have been one of the very few of Hearst's victims who was immune to glamor, if not to 30-per-cent dividends. He subscribed for 150 shares of Hearst stock in 1923 at $175 a share, but only with a hard-fisted determination to protect his investment. Not only did he get a written guarantee from Hearst that his shares would earn 30 per cent a year for five years, he insisted that Hearst buy and set aside in a trust company $25,000 in Victory Bonds to safeguard the investment. Obviously this was a heads-you-win, tails-I-lose transaction for Hearst. What use could he make of Finkelstein's $25,000 investment, on which he was committed to pay 30-per-cent annual dividends, if he had to invest it in Victory Bonds earning only 5 per cent? Here was a citizen whose business was finance, who had been smart enough to survive the real-estate collapse of 1913, and who was still in business as a subdivision developer. Indeed, he was the only important real-estate developer still active in 1923. Yet he had failed to have his suspicions aroused by Hearst's acceptance of his impossible deal. Or had he? Was he so intrigued by the complexity of the deal he had concocted that he had to become involved — if only to see how Hearst would ever work himself out of it? It probably never occurred to him that it was the D. R. Finkelstein signature and not his money that Hearst was after. With that signature on a cheque, a lot of other wavering investors could be expected to drop their nest-eggs into Hearst's basket. E. S. Parker thought of that. To make sure that Hearst did not use his name as a sales gimmick, he channelled his purchase through another Grain Exchange broker.

In any event, Hearst was not restricted to selling the glamor of the music business, or even forced to rely only on the fabulous dividends his company was paying. Hearst had a real clincher, a letter from the Chase National Bank of New York that confirmed his status as a man of great wealth whose presence on the board of directors of this great institution would have been welcomed. The letter was a forgery, but reading it must have given many a retired farmer a pleasant glow of satisfaction at being privileged to be associated with so eminent a personage. It was almost like being invited to Buckingham Palace.

The forged letter was a prime example of Hearst's monumental gall. He wrote to the Chase National to inquire about placing the sum of $250,000 on deposit, against which his company could draw for the payment of its accounts in the United States. When the answer came back, Hearst cut off the body of the letter and took the letterhead to a local printer who made an engraving of it and used it to run off fifty letterheads for Hearst. Then he took the signature of G. H. Gates, the assistant cashier of Chase National, to a stamp-making shop and had a rubber stamp made. Thereafter, whenever the need arose to document any fictitious transaction with the Chase National Bank, he had the letterheads handy.

The Chase National Bank letter, which Hearst concocted to show doubters of his financial competence, read like a cross between the plot of an Italian opera and the farthest-fetched of the Kingfish's outlandish plots in the "Amos 'n' Andy" radio series. The letter began sensibly enough with a statement that Hearst's $250,000 deposit was acknowledged and a loan of $150,000 on which he could draw as required had been approved. Then it took off on a series of flights of fancy.

Hearst's ownership of seventeen flowing oil wells was confirmed, along with the fact that he had 25,000,000 barrels of oil in storage which was to be moved to refineries in 140 tank-cars on Hearst's instructions. (Based on the largest tank-car in existence in 1924, it would have taken more than 15,000 of them to move that much oil, or each of the 140 cars would have had to make 100 trips.) Several officials of Chase National were mentioned as being particularly anxious to participate in Hearst's oil syndicate. Then came the clincher. The directors of Chase National Bank were most disappointed that Mr. Hearst had not accepted the invitation to join its board of directors. It was hoped he would see his way clear to reconsider.

Could anyone reading such a letter do other than clasp both hands over his pocketbook? They could indeed. The only question anyone ever raised was to ask about the rubber-stamped signature. "Oh, didn't you know," Hearst came back, "Mr. Gates had his right arm shot off in the war and finds writing a terrible ordeal."

During the summer and fall of 1923 the money poured into the Hearst treasury. Hearst's problem was to get it out. For the bulk of the money coming in this was relatively simple: he transferred it to himself, because it was his own stock in the company that was being sold, not Hearst Music Company Limited treasury shares. Between June of 1923 and August of 1924, $414,787 was deposited in Hearst's private account.

Hearst had also to demonstrate that the company was doing a large volume of business in order to make the kind of profit which would justify 30-per-cent annual dividends. Dividends at that rate were in fact paid to all the people who had bought stock in 1922. In the small towns of western Manitoba, no less than in the Winnipeg Grain Exchange, these dividends were accepted as demonstrable proof of the soundness of the company. Hearst and his salesmen naturally moved quickly to talk the shareholders into reinvesting their dividends in more Hearst shares, at $175 a share instead of the $100 originally charged. The money with which to pay the dividends came, of course, from the new money flowing in from the sales of shares. The books of the Hearst Music Company were noteworthy because any accurate entry made in them was purely accidental. It must have been the only set of books in Canada that contained nary a legitimate entry.

The T. Eaton Company was recorded as having made a $1,350 purchase and paid for it by cheque. It had done neither. Scores of other Canadian retailers were down for similar fictitious purchases and payments. Such noted American firms as McKinley Music Company, Jerome H. Remick, Richmond, Robbins Music Corporation, and a score of others were accounted regular purchasers of Hearst sheet music, up to $10,000-worth at a time. The Hearst ledger read like a catalogue of the American music-publishing industry. Everybody who was anybody was in it, for purchases of from 15,000 to 60,000 sheets at a time. And, of course, all were credited with paying promptly for their purchases. That ledger was a complete work of fiction.

So, indeed, were the royalty account and the advertising account. To have earned the royalties paid to fictional American composers, the Hearst Company would have to have been the world's largest sheet-music publisher. It had one New York composer down for $125,000 in royalties which, at 2 cents a copy, would have meant sales of 6,250,000 copies. That figure was more than Gus Kahn, Irving Berlin, and Jerome Kern together were collecting from their sheet-music sales in 1923. It listed $80,000 as being paid to a Chicago advertising agency whose largest client paid it less than $5,000 a year. Ultimately, all these sums wound up in Hearst's American bank accounts, along with almost $100,000 he collected personally as dividends on his own stock. Unlike his shareholders, he was not sold on reinvesting his dividends in more company stock. When it was only walking-around money he needed, Hearst simply dipped into the petty cash, "petty", of course, by his standards. He once charged up the purchase of $5,000 in 1-cent stamps to the company.

And how was all this possible, even in the wacky era of the 1920s? The answer in the main is that Hearst surrounded himself with as clueless an assemblage of dunderheads as was ever collected under one roof. Keeping the company's bank account in New York was, of course, a help. And having an auditor who was satisfied with Hearst's explanations and with letters on Hearst's forged Chase National Bank letterheads instead of bank statements also helped.

The general mental attitude surrounding Hearst is illustrated by the behavior of John Anderson, his quondam company secretary. When Hearst took off for the States in August 1924 and failed to return, Anderson decided to quit. He sent his resignation to Hearst who wired him to come to Chicago to see him. Hearst explained that he was deep in negotiations to buy out a large New York music-publishing firm, M. Witmark and Company, which had been having a run of bad luck in its song selections. He shepherded Anderson off to New York, where the general manager of the company indicated that control could be obtained for $50,000. The company in fact was close to bankruptcy. In the never-never land of Hearst finance, this became a million-dollar deal, and he escorted Anderson out to the Long Island home of the senior partner of the brokerage firm of Cardin and Green who was prepared to advance the million needed to complete the transaction.

Hearst flitted from one brokerage office to another for the better part of a week, from Hornblower and Weeks to Cardin and Green to Harriman and Company to Werriner and Company. Somewhere en route Hearst had picked up a $10,000 United States Treasury note — a $10,000 bill. "Here," he said, casually handing the bank note to Anderson, "keep this for me as I may need it in a day or two." Anderson took the bill without question and stuck it in his pocket. Three or four hours later Hearst retrieved the note and that was the end of the episode. Did this director of Hearst Music Publishers Limited not think that all this was somewhat strange? No, he later testified, he just thought that perhaps Hearst might have had a hole in his pocket.

His confidence in Hearst fully restored, Anderson returned home, and a couple of weeks later local creditors put the company into bankruptcy. By then Hearst was off on a holiday in Europe and he disappeared completely from circulation until July 28, 1925, when he returned to Winnipeg and surrendered to the police.

And what had become of the $500,000 Hearst had lifted from the pockets of the people of Manitoba? Nobody ever knew. From Anderson's testimony Hearst seemed to have been heavily committed in the New York stock market. Some of his victims reported that he had discussed the stock market in sophisticated terms. At his trial Hearst admitted nothing, claiming to have acted only as an employee of a mysterious stranger who was trying to bring all American song publishers into a single company. His story drew only gasps of disbelief from the bench.

If he had taken his plunder into the stock market, it was most unlikely that he would have lost the money. The market was boiling and churning upward all through 1924 and 1925, and it was not until November 10, 1925, that a crash of historic proportions occurred. By then Hearst was back in Winnipeg, out on bail, and putting in his time playing snooker in a Fort Street pool hall while awaiting the beginning of his preliminary hearing. He was also capitalizing on the front-page publicity he had received by playing the piano in a local vaudeville house.

Hearst had considerable difficulty raising bail, and his defence was handled by a lawyer of something less than first-flight rating. Such were the ramifications of the Hearst swindles that it took the Crown four months of almost continuous sitting to complete its case at the preliminary hearing. A total of 1,158 exhibits was entered at the trial, and when the wordage of more than 100 witnesses approached 1,000,000, the reporters stopped counting. To prevent the case from jamming up ordinary police-court business, the Hearst sittings were delayed until late in the afternoon and frequently ran until 11 p.m. The Hearst trial may still hold the record in the history of prairie jurisprudence for exhibits, wordage, and time consumed. In the end Hearst was convicted of embezzling $385,000, was sentenced to seven years in the penetentiary, served four years, and disappeared into the American cultural backwash from which he had emerged.

Unlike Hearst, Joe Myers was never convicted of anything. The four charges on which he was tried shook down into one basic accusation—that he had "salted" the ore of the Bingo Gold Mines, of which he was managing director, so that near-worthless ore samples assayed over $100 a ton. Among other things, the Crown contended that Myers had hired a Winnipeg plumber to file down two little chunks of what he said was brass into small flakes. Small flakes of filed-down gold turned up in the Bingo samples that went to the assayers. Thus improved, the samples gave such spectacular assay results that some British investors bought the property for £5,000 in cash and £185,000 in shares in a new company. While Myers was off in England, the mine manager and the directors did some routine rechecking of assays and discovered that gold values were so low that production eventually had to be abandoned. Further investigation indicated that assay samples had been "salted". The finger of suspicion pointed toward Myers.

The Bingo Gold Mines were launched on the sea of mining promotion in 1920, under the imprimatur of a half-dozen member firms of the Winnipeg Stock Exchange, in a manner that P. T. Barnum himself might have envied. Bingo was heralded in a series of three-column newspaper ads as:

The Richest Vein
in the richest camp
since Cripple Creek

That not one Manitoban in 10,000 had ever heard of Cripple Creek, or had the slightest notion of the significance of the claim, hardly altered the fact that when it came to making claims Myers and his partners went first class. The discoverer of gold at Cripple Creek in Colorado in 1891 died broke, but it turned out to be one of the richest and longest-producing gold camps in the western world.

The Bingo promoters claimed, in bold-face type, that they had proof that it was the best gold-mining proposition being offered. Gold had been discovered not in just one spot but all over the property. Everywhere excavations had been made gold was found to be present, and the deeper the holes the bigger the find. The average value of the gold ore was $135 a ton and they quoted the Department of Mines, Ottawa, which had made the assays, as authority for that statement. This was the chance of a lifetime! The promoters even offered a money-back guarantee to everybody who subscribed to Bingo shares at 50 cents apiece. Naturally, the supply of shares was limited and purchasers were urged to buy early while the offer lasted.

How much money they raised is probably lost to history.

During the next three years a camp was established at the mine, seventy-five miles northeast of The Pas, a shaft was sunk, and several cross-cuts were driven across the ore-bearing veins. Then Bingo drifted into the doldrums until 1924, when it was sold to British financial interests. This sale was followed all too quickly by the charges that the mine had been salted.

When a warrant was sworn out against him, Myers returned voluntarily to Canada, after friends in Winnipeg posted a $50,000 bond to guarantee his appearance. Louis Morosnick, a Winnipeg criminal lawyer, journeyed all the way to Halifax to greet Myers when he got off the boat. In Winnipeg a large delegation was on the platform to give aid and comfort to the promoter on his arrival, and he was escorted like a returning hero to the police station where the formalities of laying charges were completed. For his preliminary hearing a top-drawer Winnipeg barrister, H. P. Blackwood, joined the firm of Shinbane and Morosnick at his counsel table. For the trial itself, the defence panel was further reinforced by the retention as chief counsel of the most eminent prairie criminal lawyer of his generation, R. A. Bonner, K.C. Between his preliminary hearing and trial, Myers obtained the Conservative Party nomination for the Nelson constituency of northern Manitoba, where the Bingo mine was located. As a candidate in the 1925 federal election, he polled almost 3,000 votes and was beaten by only 700.

The case against Myers collapsed when the presiding judge at his trial, a Mr. Justice Curran, ruled that a mass of evidence presented to the preliminary hearing was inadmissible, along with the testimony of key witnesses. Included in the material that was ruled out were the results of the assays which the directors of Bingo had obtained from the mine. They would be relevant, he ruled, only if it could be proved that they were taken from the exact same spot along the veins where the samples for Myers' tests had been taken. That obviously would have been physically impossible because once a chunk of rock was removed from a vein the "exact same" spot went with it. When the prosecution threw up its hands at the court's rulings, Myers was given an honorable discharge and "walked from the court to the arms of his friends without a blemish on his character."

Of the fact that the Bingo mine samples were salted, however, there can be not a sliver of doubt. Even the shareholders of the company accepted that conclusion. In the hiatus between Myers' preliminary hearing and his trial, a general meeting of the shareholders overrode Myers' stormy objections and vituperative attacks on his fellow directors and voted overwhelmingly to abandon the mine, wind up the company, and surrender its charter.

Salted the mine was. By whom, if not by Myers, who went to his grave within the year? By almost anybody. It could have been done by somebody who never went within a hundred miles of the mine. The salter might have proceeded precisely as the Crown claimed Myers had done. First, some refined gold had to be reduced to mere specks and shavings. Then the flakes of refined gold had only to be sprinkled sparingly into the hip-pocket-sized canvas bags in which the samples were gathered for dispatch to the assayers.

As a mine worker testified at the preliminary hearing, there was gold dust everywhere — on book covers, or mixed with the dirt on the floor. One employee had used a sample bag to replace a pants pocket that was worn out. When that pocket was turned inside out it yielded flakes of refined gold, along with accumulated dust and bits of tobacco. So did scrapings from the blacksmith shop floor and from the root cellar. So did several of the sample bags the police had taken from a trunk owned by Joe Myers. Dr. R. C. Wallace, a former commissioner for northern Manitoba, brought his comparison microscope along to the preliminary hearing and pointed out how these, and a host of other samples of refined gold, differed in form from natural gold. The marks of the files used to reduce a piece of refined gold to specks and flakes were plainly visible under the microscope. Refined gold bore little resemblance to rough-textured gold in its natural state.

The importance of the salting of the Bingo mine lay not in who had done the job, but in its impact on the people of Manitoba. The Bingo mine salting had been on the front pages of the newspapers for weeks. Anyone who walked could read of how easy it was to salt a gold mine. At a time when such intelligence was being trumpeted from the housetops, the Red Lake mining boom was taking off just across the border in Ontario. Following the discovery of gold on several rather widely separated claims, the moose pasture was being staked for miles and miles in all directions. Every week brought new and gaudier promotions onto the market. Because of the greed of the promoters, even the best of these raw prospects would have to go through three or four reorganizations before perhaps one in fifty would be developed into a successful mine. But did the Bingo revelations or the Joe Hearst scandal in any way impede the urge of Manitobans to part with their hard-earned savings at the behests of peddlers of mining stock? It did not, and the promotional techniques which were used with cavalier disregard for the truth in the early Bingo promotional advertising became the order of the day.

Off in Alberta, where the Royalite #4 well had blown in and blew wild in October 1924, the stage was being set for an oil boom that would put additional strain on the critical faculties of prairie people, and find them wanting. The possession of a well-oiled critical faculty was alien to the very nature of prairie people. They were a simple, direct, and moral people, with a case-hardened, nickel-plated will to believe and an incurable optimism. If they had not believed that everything would work out for the best, in what could become the best of all possible worlds, they would not have been on the western prairies. They would have been back in Ontario, the United States, the United Kingdom, or Central Europe. They had to be that kind of people or they would never have planted a crop, built a warehouse, opened a store, or hung out a shingle.

Nobody ever came to western Canada just to be what they had been at home. They came to a land ripe with the opportunity to better their status materially and socially. The attraction for the peasants of Europe was freedom, on land of their own, on which they could become rich landowners and send their sons to college instead of having them conscripted into the armies of the Czar or the Emperor. For the Jews there was to be security of their persons and property for the first time in 2,000 years, and freedom of enterprise in fields previously fenced off from them. For the young farmers of Ontario there was available land on which to settle. For the Americans this was the last frontier which starved for their initiative, their drive, and their know-how.

And it was a land of opportunity for all who had developed the sense to recognize opportunities when they arose. If one opportunity soured, another would always turn up. Examples were everywhere. There was Jimmy Ashdown, who had come west with some lead and a soldering iron and had parlayed his tinker's skills into a chain of hardware stores that was making him the richest man in Manitoba. Or there was Pat Burns, who achieved the same status in Alberta after trying and failing several times. Indeed, a newcomer could walk down any street in the west and read the names on the store windows, office buildings, and factories and be impressed with the legions of bootstrappers who had arrived with nothing and had made it on their own.

Inside every enterprise were other bootstrappers working toward "making it on their own". They were the clerks and straw bosses who had started as sweepers and worked their way up to a point where they would soon be able to "get into business for themselves". And any chance to hasten the arrival of that day, like investing a hard-earned $1,000 in such an enterprise as the Hearst Music Company Limited, was not to be passed over lightly.

Even in the 1920s, after a decade in which everything that could go wrong had gone wrong, the people of the prairies still exuded confidence in the future. Being alert to opportunities was part of that confidence. So was taking a man at his word. As E. S. Parker testified, millions of dollars' worth of grain business was done daily on the basis of a man's word alone. So were other millions of dollars of business in every line of endeavor on the prairies, from the hiring of labor, to the negotiation of contracts, down to trade in the corner butcher shop. In the universal eagerness to seize opportunity when it arose, some things always had to be taken for granted. As one investor put it, you assumed the man and looked only at the deal. To the unsophisticated investors of the prairies, Hearst's deal looked so good they never looked at Hearst himself. "Mr. Hearst recommended it so strong that we bought it" was the oft-repeated chorus of the mulcted at his trial in Winnipeg. Assuming the man was a fatal mistake, and it was one that would be repeated many times as the latter-day Hearsts of the mining-stock and oil-stock pushers descended on the prairies. Mistakes they were, but it was the state of mind, the character quirk, which made the making of such mistakes inevitable, which built the west.

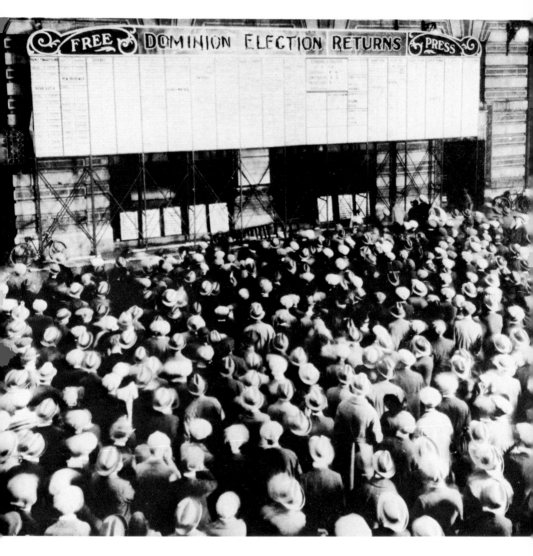

34. Even after the advent of radio, crowds would still congregate outside newspaper offices for news of special events. Here the crowd watches the returns for the federal election of 1926 in front of the *Manitoba Free Press* building.

35. *(Left)* The designs of Emmanuel Hahn and Elizabeth Wyn Wood were the first-prize winners in two successive competitions to choose a design for the Winnipeg Cenotaph. As a result of popular prejudice neither was accepted.

36. In the 1920s the Manitoba Medical College *(above)* was a stronghold of Anglo-Saxon Protestant prejudice, and its admission policies were heavily weighted against Jews, Slavs, and women.

37, 38, & 39. Isaac William Solloway brought a revolution to the brokerage business in western Canada. *(Above)* There was standing room only in Solloway, Mills brokerage offices in the west like this one in Vancouver. Solloway himself was equally at home with prospectors *(right)* and in society *(opposite page).*

40. This midnight photograph taken in Calgary in 1928 shows how the gas flares from the Turner Valley, thirty miles away, lit up the southwestern sky. At night settlers living within two miles of the burning gas could read their newspapers by the light from "Hell's Half-Acre".

41 & 42. Whether in 1920 or in 1930, in a Model T or in a Model A, prairie roads after a rain were a nightmare.

15. The Glow from Hell's Half-Acre

The fastest-acting stimulant that ever hit western Canada, indeed one of the most stimulating characters in all Canada in the 1920s, was Isaac William Cannon Solloway. An English laborer turned prospector, I. W. C. Solloway emerged from the north woods of Ontario in 1925-6 and lit the fuse that blasted the Canadian stock-brokerage business out of its lethargy, revolutionized the financing of mining and oil properties, became a one-man Committee for an Independent Canada, amassed a fortune estimated at $20,000,000, and wound up in jail. And all within a period of four years.

Though he had neither seen nor heard of western Canada until 1928 when he began looking around for more places to put brokerage offices, Solloway came closer to epitomizing the image westerners have built of themselves than any of the natives. He was brash, outgoing, and a born gambler. His conviction that Canada's destiny to become one of the great nations of the world could only be achieved by the development of its natural resources with Canadian capital, was as deep-running as his boundless faith in himself. He was a risk-taking enterpriser with a gambler's eagerness to put his money where his mouth was. His trouble, when he descended on Toronto in search of development money for a mining prospect, was that he was fresh out of funds.

Toronto's financial establishment had little interest in developing sources of equity capital for Canadian enterprise of any kind, least of all for mineral development. It was engaged exclusively in trading in stocks listed in New York and on the moribund Toronto and Montreal Stock Exchanges.

The mining brokers, on the other hand, were hived away in back rooms of decaying walk-up office buildings, peddling moose-pasture mining shares which they had taken under option. So small a portion of the funds milked from the public by these brokers reached the treasuries of the companies that the failure of the mines to reach production was almost guaranteed. If a customer approached them to buy shares in an existing company at 75 cents a share, the practice was for the brokers to shop around in an effort to make the purchase at 50 cents and pocket the difference.

The entire system offended Solloway's sense of the fitness of things. He was outraged at the thought of exporting Canadian funds for investment in New York securities, and he remained so throughout his life. He was convinced that the Canadian public was thirsting for a chance to participate in resources development. The more he pondered the situation, the more ambitious he became to take the mining brokerage business out of the musty back rooms and bring it down to street level like all other retail establishments.

The Canadian financial woods, of course, have always been full of imaginative enthusiasts without money. Solloway, however, had a fishing-companion living in Buffalo, N.Y., who vacationed around Kirkland Lake and who had occasionally grub-staked a Canadian prospector. His name was Harvey Mills, and he owned a cigar store that he had boasted yielded him an income of $15,000 a year. Solloway carried his vision to Buffalo and talked Mills into providing the $17,000 needed to establish the firm of Solloway, Mills and Company in the mining-stock brokerage business.

A 25' × 30' ground-floor office was located in the Metropolitan Building in downtown Toronto. The office was directly opposite the elevators, separated from the corridor by large glass partitions. Everybody entering this busy office building had a full view of the quotation board being marked by an office boy. When they eventually dropped in to buy some shares, Solloway himself took the order, telephoned it to the Standard Stock Exchange, and confirmed the trade to the customer in short order. If the purchase was made below the figure set by the customer, the buyer and not the broker got the benefit. Within a matter of weeks the partnership was so busy that Solloway had to hire a clerk to do nothing but handle orders. He put the order desk in the centre of the room where the customers could hear their orders being handled.

That first office became the model for all the other Solloway offices. Wherever he went he searched out and got the busiest locations in town. In Winnipeg it was hard by the corner of Portage and Main, in Calgary it was on Eighth Avenue in the heart of the shopping district, in Edmonton it was similarly located on Jasper Avenue near First Street. In all cases, both the king-sized quotation boards and the order desks were focal points of customer attention. As business developed, Solloway poured much of his weekly profits into advertising and into hiring prospector friends to keep track of developments at the northern mines.

It was this latter step that almost ruined the firm in its first year. Solloway got some exceedingly good news from the Amulet mine when the stock was selling for $1 a share. He urged his customers to buy the stock and they made huge profits when the price rose to $7. He then put them into Bidgood-Kirkland at $1.50 which, after moving to $1.80, dropped sharply to below $1 and his customers lost money. That cured Solloway of recommending purchases or sales. Thereafter he published his prospectors' reports in a weekly newsletter and let the customers make up their own minds. Within three years Solloway and Mills had a staff of 225 in the Toronto office alone and was occupying two full floors of the Metropolitan Building.

But all that was to come later, after Solloway discovered western Canada. That discovery was made after word reached Toronto in 1927 that some wild things were happening in Winnipeg and Calgary. A dozen attractive mining prospects had appeared in eastern and northern Manitoba. The Whitney interests in New York paid Mining Corporation $860,000 in cash plus a 15-per-cent equity for the base-metal claims which they would develop into the gigantic Hudson's Bay mine at Flin Flon. The Sherritt-Gordon copper-nickel claims were being proved up, and ore bodies were being drilled at Callinan Flin Flon, Jackson Manion, Central Manitoba, and San Antonio. The Manitoba Chamber of Mines could see the province eventually rivalling Ontario in the wealth it would produce from the Canadian Shield.

Solloway's impact on Manitoba was fated to be minimal for several reasons. The stock-brokerage business in Winnipeg was already sustaining about as many brokers as it could afford. Stobie Forlong and D. S. Paterson were already in from Toronto, Clark and Martin were established from Montreal, and Miller Court from Vancouver. All were in competition with a dozen old-fashioned local houses.

By the end of 1927 the bloom was fading from the Manitoba mining stocks. Central Manitoba had gone from raw prospect to producing mine and its shares had risen from 25 cents to $2.10, but with little favorable news it was beginning the slide that would end at zero. San Antonio had gone from 10 cents to 65 cents and was likewise on the way down. Callinan Flin Flon and the others had flashed briefly in the pan and lapsed into dullness. And although the prospectors were out in force, they were finding nothing worth trying to promote.

Mining developments, particularly those in Manitoba, did not lend themselves to fast-action promotion. Mining claims grew out of long spells in the remote bush by grub-staked prospectors. Then geologists had to visit the properties, and diamond drillers had to be hauled in and left for months. In all this, tens of thousands of dollars could be required before a promotable prospect came into being. While Solloway got his Winnipeg office open, it never cut the swath his Calgary operation did, perhaps because it never got so much of his personal attention. Perhaps because Winnipeg had nothing like Royalite #4 to attract his attention.

Royalite #4 was the lineal descendant of the famous Dingman

oil well which had come into production in July of 1914. That discovery had spawned oil companies like mushrooms. A month after Dingman there were more newly formed oil companies clamoring for public attention along Calgary's Ninth Avenue than there had been land offices in 1912. Every real-estate agent who could scrape $100 together to acquire a mineral lease from the federal government was into the oil business, regardless of the location of the leases.

Though the original discovery well in Turner Valley perpetuated the name of Archibald W. Dingman, the professional geologist who supervised its drilling, the moving force in promotion of Calgary Petroleum Products was William Stewart Herron, an Okotoks coal-hauler who had a cattle ranch west of Turner Valley. He had very early become entranced by gas seepage along Sheep Creek which he had to cross coming and going from town. When conditions were right he could touch a match to the seeping gas and set it afire. Eventually Herron caught some of the gas in a bottle and sent it off to the University of California for analysis. It proved to be petroleum gas, so Herron acquired 700 acres of mineral rights and went out to get somebody to help finance the drilling of a well. Among those who became interested in putting up some money were a coterie of Calgary businessmen headed by William Elder, A. W. Dingman, Eric Harvey, and T. A. P. "Tappy" Frost.

According to legend, after the Dingman well came in and money was needed for a second well, Frost took several jugs of the oil to Toronto to prove to the brokers that there was oil in Alberta. They scoffed at the idea, so Frost took his samples out onto Bay Street and invited passers-by to sample the stuff from a tablespoon. They too exhibited a monumental Toronto indifference toward Tappy Frost, his crude oil, and his Calgary Petroleum Products stock certificates.

Albertans, however, had been fascinated by the possibilities of finding oil ever since the discovery of natural gas in commercial quantities was made near Medicine Hat in 1890. Showings of crude oil were reported from Pincher Creek at the turn of the century. A natural gas well was successfully completed on the outskirts of Calgary in 1909 and gas was piped into Calgary the following year. The Dingman well was a confirmation of everything the optimists had believed. Oil could be found, and people could get rich. The company drilled a second and a third well close to the first, and over the next five years took better than 48,000 barrels out of the ground.

How many thousands of dollars were extracted from the pockets of Albertans by the promoters of other oil companies has never been determined, but it must have run into the millions. The Calgary City Directory of 1914 listed 226 "oil mining companies", 32 oil brokers, and four competing oil-stock exchanges. A four-inch pipeline was soon built to carry the natural gas being produced into Calgary. Despite the Dingman successes with two other drillers, the total failure of all the other promoters to get even a smell of oil, coupled with the Great War emergency, dampened the oil boom. By 1917, the City Directory listed only 21 oil companies, two brokers, and one oil-stock exchange.

At the end of the war, Turner Valley was still producing some oil and gas from the discovery wells. Unfortunately, in 1920 the absorption plant, which separated the gas from the oil, was destroyed by fire. This led to the sale of the company's properties to Imperial Oil for roughly 16 per cent of the share capital of Royalite Oil Company, which Imperial formed to take over. Royalite rebuilt the plant, and in 1922 decided to drill a fourth well a half-mile northwest of the discovery well. For a well that would set Alberta afire with delayed-action oil fever, Royalite #4 provided its drillers with disappointment after disappointment.

The original Dingman well had encountered encouraging bursts of gas and a show of oil at 1,557 feet. At 2,718 feet came the blast of gas that blew oil wildly over the top of the derrick. Eventually the well was taken down another 1,000 feet into the lower Cretaceous, the production zone for it and the two succeeding wells. None of these positive signs were repeated at Royalite #4. Instead the bit found the dense black Fernie shale which was devoid of reservoir rock. Eventually, it reached the top of the Devonian limestone which had been barren everywhere else in Alberta. Nevertheless, drilling was continued into the lime, for no better reason than that the drilling crew had nothing else to do, while Imperial Oil geologists made up their minds about what to do next. The limestone seemed to go clear down to China and the hole was slowly, slowly driven down 100 feet into it, then 200 feet, then almost 300 feet. On October 17, 1924, the crew was at last getting ready to abandon the well when the derrick floor became permeated with the odor of sour gas. The crew let the bit pound ahead for another ten feet and there was a burst of gas. They closed the valve and watched the gauge rising at the rate of 100 pounds a minute. When it reached 500 pounds to the square inch they retired to a safe distance to await developments. At the end of fifteen minutes the 92-ton string of casing was slowly blown out of the well to the top of the 100-foot derrick. As the gas began to escape around the outside of the casing, the casing dropped back into place. Then the well caught fire, quickly consumed the wooden drilling rig, and sent flames roaring 100 feet into the air.

Royalite #4 burned for weeks, consuming upwards of 20,000,000 cubic feet of gas and over 500 barrels of oil a day. It took the company three months to put out the fire, bring the flow under control, and install a separator to extract the oil from the natural gas. The oil was of such light gravity that it was akin to natural gasoline. Getting it to market required that it be hauled in tank trucks over dirt roads from the well-site to Okotoks, a small town on the C.P.R. twenty miles south of Calgary. Though the oil brought $4.40 a barrel at Okotoks, high transportation costs caused the company to wonder whether the whole exercise had been worth while. Almost half a year passed after the Royalite #4 came in before Royalite made up its mind to drill a follow-up well.

The first reaction of Calgarians to Royalite #4 was to start rummaging through dresser drawers in search of oil shares acquired during the 1914 madness, to see whether Royalite would bring their shares back from the dead. For most of the 1914 share purchasers, it was a disappointing search. Half the companies organized that year had gone bankrupt. Another score had simply given up and surrendered their charters. But there were still about 100 dormant companies in existence and Royalite #4 was a signal for the directors of most of them to go into executive session to decide what to do next. The unanimous decision of everybody in sight was to grab up some leases and get back into the oil business.

Stewart Herron organized his Okalta Oils with the most prestigious board of directors in the business. W.E. McLeod resuscitated McLeod Oils, and Robert Spooner and O. G. Devenish did the same for their companies. Two physicians and a shoe merchant, Drs. Singleton and Hackney and Harry Glass, molded a handful of small companies into Alberta Pacific Consolidated. A dozen other companies, with Turner Valley leases still intact, were likewise brought back to life. But that was the easy first step. The second and far more difficult one was to interest the public and raise money.

Southern Alberta in 1925 was still being tightly held in the grip of the post-war depression. The cattle industry was brought near to ruin by the U.S. tariff on Canadian livestock. The coal mines were caught up in prolonged and costly labor disputes, and winter unemployment was a recurrent problem. In Calgary itself, there was little public enthusiasm for spending money on anything, least of all on oil stocks. The mood was reflected by the *Calgary Herald,* which in its year-end review of the highlights of 1925 found nothing interesting enough about the oil business to merit even a short paragraph.

Elsewhere the pyrotechnics of Royalite #4 got photographic reproduction in the newspapers across the country. But that was all. It attracted no more capital to Calgary than had Tappy Frost with his oil samples. That capital, for the next two years, had to come from Calgary itself and from Edmonton and Vancouver. Even in Calgary the public interest developed slowly, in contrast to 1914. In 1925 the best the City Directory compilers could do was locate a dozen oil companies. These, however, were authentic oil companies which were in the business of drilling for oil, not disguises for promoters only digging for money in the pockets of investors. It cost around $100,000 to complete a well in

Turner Valley, and a great deal of this money was put up by the directors themselves.

By the end of 1925 production from Royalite #4 was being piped through a new line to the Imperial Oil refinery in Calgary. But because the drilling of a well to 4,000 feet was a tedious and costly process that could take a year to complete, maintaining public interest in the shares of a company which was pounding away for weeks on end was almost impossible.

The wells used up carloads of well-casing before they neared completion, and it had to be imported all the way from Pittsburgh. The first step was to drill a 24-inch hole through the overburden to bedrock at about forty feet. A string of 24-inch surface casing was cemented into the hole. A 20-inch bit was then used to pound the hole down another 200 feet, where a string of 20-inch casing was cemented in. The next bit would take the hole down to 1,200 feet and a string of 16-inch casing would be inserted. A still smaller bit would be used down to 3,500 feet, and a string of 10-inch steel pipe would be used. Then, if the hole was going to 4,000 feet, the final string would be 4,000 feet of 6-inch pipe. Thus, when a well reached production it could contain five strings of pipe, one inside the other. Using the old cable-tool system of dropping and raising a heavy steel bit was fraught with problems. As the hole deepened, running a bailer into the hole to remove the rock fragments consumed hours, and fishing out broken-off drilling bits from the bottom of the hole could take days. Holes frequently had to be abandoned when the bit wandered too far from the perpendicular. In the nature of things, putting money into an oil company in Turner Valley was about as slow a gamble as an investor could take in 1925.

Paradoxically, it was the slow pace of making a hole that really ignited the wild local boom in Turner Valley oil stock as 1925 turned into 1926. Independent oil companies had surrounded the Royalite #4 with their drilling rigs, some on leases only twenty acres in size. A half-dozen of them had drilled away during 1925 and by the end of the year were well down below 3,000 feet and getting close to the Royalite pay-zone. As the wells went down they passed through a thin sand formation, which contained small amounts of oil and gas like those in the Dingman discovery. As it puffed to the surface it would set off a wave of excitement. Ultimately, it would be proven to be non-commercial and drilling would continue. There would be inter-mittent build-ups of pockets of pressure, and when these too burst there would be more excitement at the surface.

The winter of 1925-6 was the mildest in Alberta history, and a Sunday safari to Turner Valley by car or truck was the most popular winter pastime for Calgarians. They could hear the waste gas from Royalite #4 being burned in a flare-pit 250 yards from the well. It was a spot that would become famous as "Hell's Half-Acre" when the gas from three other wells was added to the flames. A half-mile to the south, McLeod #2 had gone through several zones, from one of which crude oil rose 500 feet in the bottom of the hole. A half-mile west, the Illinois Alberta well had similar showings. A mile and a half northwest of Royalite #4, the Vulcan well was nearing the limestone. It would have taken thicker hides than the picnickers possessed to traipse around the drilling wells in Turner Valley that winter and not succumb to an urge to have a piece of the action. Hundreds made the trip every week and everyone who had a few dollars to spare became vulnerable to the floods of rumors that flowed into Calgary.

The beautiful thing about the oil boom that developed was that anybody could participate, for shares in the Turner Valley companies were available for less than $1 a share and in de-nominations down to as little as five shares. It was probably the first boom on record in which a ribbon clerk could qualify as an "oilman" with the investment of $5.

The unsavory side of the boom was that most of the companies that were organized were doomed to lose their shareholders' investments. Some, indeed, were organized with that intention. Promoters could gather up petroleum leases on a few thousand acres for a few thousand dollars. The next step was to incorpo-rate a 500,000-share company, issue 300,000 shares to them-selves for the leases, and get a broker to underwrite 200,000 shares for sale to the public at 25 cents per share, and 15 cents net to the company. Such promotions, if they ever actually got around to trying seriously to drill a well, were sure to run out of money long before production zones were reached.

In mid-February, 1926, the most conservative financial house in Calgary, Lougheed and Taylor, took advertising space in the *Herald* to warn the public against the fly-by-nights who were pushing oil shares. It said that investment in moderately capitalized companies on good locations might make investors a lot of money in a very few years. Lougheed and Taylor expected to have such opportunities available from time to time. "But we wish to emphasize that unsound speculation in shares of companies not properly financed, in charge of inexperienced men, may carry very harmful affects. The utmost caution should be exercised."

It was a warning nobody in Calgary was prepared to heed, least of all the "inexperienced men" who were then organizing oil companies right and left. Royalite Oil Company, with the Hon. R. B. Bennett at its head and Imperial Oil supplying the financial sinews and expertise, was an oil company. So was Okalta Oils, whose directorate included John I. McFarland, Eric Harvie, G. F. Tull, A. H. Mayland, and Stewart Herron, all men of substantial wealth whose oil-industry experience went back to the Dingman well. But for every Okalta there were a dozen lawyers' oil companies, doctors' oil companies, merchants' oil companies, farm implement dealers' companies, ranchers' oil companies, car dealers' oil companies, officers corps's oil companies, and school teachers' oil companies. There were even a couple of companies with senators as their guiding lights. A typical board of directors of an Alberta oil company might include a doctor, a lawyer, a broker, a trust company manager, an insurance man, and a merchant. Some of them were organized with as little as 40 acres of leases on which to drill, some with less than half as much cash in the treasury as it would take to drill a well.

Calgary broke out in a rash of oil-stock brokers who paid the city $50 for a licence to hang out a shingle. They went "bird-dogging" through the community looking for people who had shares to sell and for people who wanted to buy them. At any given January or February hour in Calgary in 1926, there might be a dozen different prices prevailing for any of the oil companies with active drilling rigs. There was no regular stock exchange, so Calgarians invented the next best thing—auction rooms where stock certificates could be auctioned off for cash.

Advertising their "Original Oil and Stock Exchange" at 109 Seventh Avenue East, W. A. Murphy and R. A. Johnson offered a "grand opening special" for their first night session — a flat commission of 25 cents per certificate for all share certificates sold. By March 1, 1926, there were no fewer than five such establishments. Many of the licensed brokers attended the auction sales on the chance of unloading some shares they had bought cheaply that morning, or of buying some shares they knew could be sold expensively the next day.

The brokers and the auctioneers lived off the rumors that flowed in a steady stream from Turner Valley to Calgary. One day the city was shaken by a rumor that the Vulcan well had struck sulphur water, and the next that it was gushing oil. On one report the shares dropped 50 per cent in value, on the other they jumped 200 per cent. Rumor-mongering became so prevalent and erratic that the police announced an impending crack-down on spreaders of false reports from the Valley.

In late January a group of brokers in Calgary got together to discuss reactivating an old Calgary Stock Exchange charter that had been lying dormant since the 1914 boom. The business was becoming so cluttered with brokers that oil-share prices not only fluctuated from day to day, they fluctuated from block to block within the city. Shares that an Eighth Avenue broker was buying for 25 cents might be selling for 35 cents on Seventh Avenue, and for 18 or 40 cents on First Street West.

While the brokers were talking, the McLeod #2 well spewed oil to the surface on February 27, and after the story hit the front page of the *Calgary Herald* there was hardly a sane man left between the Bow and the Elbow. McLeod Oil stock, which had been selling for $3 at Christmas, was at $4.50 that morning. By one o'clock it was being traded at $7.50. Two days later it was up to $15. Royalite shares, which had been selling for $150 a share, zoomed to $250. United Oils, which was not even drilling a well, jumped from $1.50 to $3.50.

Secondary shocks from the McLeod gusher were felt as far away as Winnipeg and into Montana. A group of Winnipeg grain brokers headed by George Cathcart joined the Kyle and Hart-Green syndicate and drilled a well across the border in Montana south of Coutts, Alberta. They struck it rich in the form of a 100-barrel-a-day potential producer. Hopes were dashed, however, when it was discovered that the inside diameter of the casing in the well was too small to permit a pump to be installed. So they had to abandon the well and drill another one. It turned out to be dry. Another syndicate drilled a well at Grandview, Manitoba, and great was the excitement when reports circulated that the well had struck oil at 800 feet. Those hopes aroused turned to ashes when investigation proved that the oil in the well came from barrels brought from town, that the well was down less than 200 feet, not 800.

It was the McLeod gusher, more than the Royalite #4, that convinced William J. Stokes, a Calgary hotelman, that Turner Valley was for real. In fact he was so bowled over by it that he began un-papering the rooms of the Imperial Hotel on Ninth Avenue. In 1914 Stokes had been Alberta's most compulsive buyer of oil stocks. When that boom collapsed he was left with a steamer-trunkful of worthless share certificates. As a warning to himself, and to his guests, he picked out several colorful bundles and used them to paper the walls of several of his suites. Some time shortly afterward his hotel burned down with little saved except the hotel safe which, when opened, contained even more bundles of stock certificates and not much else. Stokes saved the certificates and, when he rebuilt the hotel, used them to paper several walls and a couple of ceilings. In February 1926 he started checking the names on the certificates with the names of the companies announcing they were going to drill in Turner Valley. The unpapering yielded certificates worth several thousand dollars, including one for McDougall-Segur Exploration which alone brought him $1,000.

The brokers stopped arguing about whether a stock exchange

was needed or not and got one into business in the basement of the Lougheed Building immediately. The membership fee was set at $200, a price calculated to keep out the riffraff. Within three years the price of those seats would touch $4,000. The Calgary Stock Exchange did not put an end to bird-dogging brokers scalping profits for themselves from transactions made on behalf of their customers rather than relying on commission. But the Exchange did provide a convenient meeting-ground for brokers with orders to buy and orders to sell. It did establish a scale of commission—$2^1/_2$ per cent on orders worth less than $500, one per cent on orders worth more than $1,000. Most of all, it provided some sort of valuation centre where the public could get some idea as to the worth of their shares.

The wild enthusiasm of Calgarians for oil stocks evaporated almost as quickly as it had developed. The wells that followed McLeod into the headlines shared with that company all the problems of bringing the wells into actual production. The wet gas froze in the well-bores and sealed off production. Strings of casing got stuck in holes. Ropes broke and dropped bailers and bits to the bottom of the holes. Formations full of water were drilled into and had to be sealed off. Other formations caused so much caving that progress was almost impossible. Wells reported as being about to penetrate the Royalite pay-zone in March were still about to penetrate it in October.

Trouble in the field and the snail's pace of drilling were only part of the cause for the end of the boom. There simply were not nearly enough Calgarians to put up the money needed to bring all the wells into production and to buy all the shares that were for sale on Eighth Avenue, particularly when so many of those riding the boom were doing so with investments ranging between $10 and $100. At the height of the boom on the Exchange, many more sales of 5- and 10-share certificates were recorded than sales of 100 shares, and the sale of 1,000-share blocks was a rarity, even in stocks selling well below $1. On one day, when the sale of 150,000 shares in a session broke a record, the gross value of the shares was only $60,000. As Solloway himself once noted, many investors in oil stocks bought shares the way they bought groceries. Shares being offered at 25 cents each were better value than those being sold at 50 cents. The whole business of setting par values for oil shares was reduced to absurdity by a British Columbia company—Capital Oil and Natural Gas Company Limited, which was capitalized at $2,500,000, divided into 250,000,000 shares of 1 cent par value.

It was not long before the Cleopatra syndrome began to operate in the oil business. She blamed the messenger who brought bad news for that bad news. The oil investors who saw the stocks they bought in 1926 for 90 cents, $5.00, and $1.60 sink to 16 cents, $1.70, and 38 cents a year later began blaming the existence of the Calgary Stock Exchange for their losses. Cleopatra had the messengers beheaded, and there were mutterings in Calgary that a similar fate should be visited upon the Stock Exchange. Some of the brokers may well have agreed, for interest in oil stocks had dropped so low that trading was reduced to sessions a half-hour long in the mornings.

That was about where everything stood when I. W. C. Solloway embarked on his voyage of discovery to the west in the fall of 1927. It took some kind of genius to recognize the potential of Turner Valley under such circumstances. Either Solloway was that kind of genius or, from his Palliser Hotel window, he was mesmerized by the spectacular way the glow from Hell's Half-Acre lit up the whole southwestern sky. When he followed the flares to Turner Valley he discovered that he could read the stock quotations in his newspaper at midnight two miles from the flare pit. The more he talked to the oilmen the more convinced he became that this was not only his kind of country, these were his kind of people. In Winnipeg he discovered the Winnipeg Grain Exchange futures market, then in the doldrums, which could add an exciting new dimension to the brokerage business. There, too, were the dedicated mining men—people like Hurst, Drysburgh, Drummond-Hay, Brown, Anderson, Dickson, and the Perrins—who were trying to make mines out of raw and remote prospects.

In Calgary he was mobbed by a euphoric crew who ate, slept, and drank oil and lived off the glow of the future despite the depressed state of the stock market. It was a mood Solloway knew well from his own experiences as a prospector in northern Ontario. In Edmonton a smaller contingent was going equally wild over the prospects of future wealth in the development of the heavy oil at Wainwright. In Vancouver there was an army of mining enthusiasts who were pouring their own money into the development of prospects he had never heard of.

Over all the mine developers and oil-field developers lay a thick overburden of promotional highbinding. For every well-managed and adequately financed oil or mining prospect there were a dozen promotions that were doomed to failure from the start. Less than a quarter of the money raised from the public ever reached the mines or oil wells, as brokers, stock salesmen, and vendors of claims and leases grabbed off the lion's share. But such was the pioneer status of resource development financing that some of the leading figures had their feet in both camps. Some of the best oil developers were also great promoters, some of the promoters actually believed they were oilmen, and by some miracle some of the wildest promotions evolved into oil companies. Solloway saw all this at a glance, and in seeing recognized that there would be profits to be made from the promotional overburden as well as from the legitimate developments.

The promotional technique was as old as the hills. The brokers with chunks of optioned stock to unload stirred up the market with a flurry of washed sales—buying and selling stock from and to themselves in large quantities and at slowly advancing prices. This attracted public attention and triggered the rumor mill, and as the market rose, public buying always came in. The brokers fed out their stock carefully to the public and then often sold the shares short after they disposed of all their optioned stock. The shares gradually sank back to the original level as the broker lost interest and went looking for other stock to get under option. A well-financed broker like Solloway could get rich on the short side of the promotional market—all he needed was a market and the volume of promotions that had developed in the oil and mining industries. Which is precisely what Solloway proceeded to do. He got rich working both sides of the street.

Instead of sending out employees from Toronto to establish Solloway and Mills offices from scratch in the western cities, Solloway canvassed the field of brokers already in business in order to buy out one of the top five or six. Using Mills' cigar-store experience, the partners walked the sidewalks of the cities to find the best available locations — as close to the heart of the financial district as possible with the maximum pedestrian traffic past the front door. In both Winnipeg and Calgary, the best available sites were occupied by retail stores. They bought up the leases. In Calgary a temporary office was opened in a small store next to the Palace Theatre on Eighth Avenue to serve until they could get into larger quarters at the other end of the block.

The stock-brokerage offices Solloway opened were unlike anything the natives had ever seen before. The stock-quotation boards covered an entire wall and were lighted indirectly from behind a polished mahogany canopy. A three-foot-high platform extended the length of the wall, and a telegraph sounder at one end clicked out the quotations from Toronto, Montreal, New York, and Winnipeg. A telegrapher with a chamois in one hand and chalk in the other raced back and forth erasing and changing the figures he had previously chalked on the board. Within months the telegraph sounder was displaced by tickers which spewed out quotations on endless streams of ticker tape.

The Solloway offices opened everywhere with an established clientele. This was augmented instantly when it was discovered that at Solloway and Mills customers could buy mining and oil stocks on 50-per-cent margin. That meant that the people who had been buying oil stocks for cash in Calgary, or mining stocks in Winnipeg and Vancouver, could take the certificates into Solloway and mills and use them as collateral with which to buy additional shares. It was hardly a coincidence that, with the opening of the string of Solloway offices in western Canada in the early winter of 1928, the oil-stock market came roaring back to life.

Once again the road between Calgary and Turner Valley became choked on weekends with sightseeing investors eager to obtain first-hand information from the drillers on the well-sites. A safari to Turner Valley, despite the fact that hundreds made it every weekend, was not a journey to be undertaken lightly. The road south of Calgary was gravelled, after a fashion, as far as Okotoks. The 20-mile stretch from there to the oilfield was unimproved mud into which vehicles sank hub-deep with the onset of the spring thaw or the April showers. At other times the churned-up dust reduced visibility to a couple of car-lengths.

It was the uncertain condition of the road south that provided Pearl Miller with the inspiration that led to the establishment of Calgary's most famous roadhouse, which in turn became the springboard for propelling her on her way to becoming Calgary's most famous madam. Midway between Calgary and Midnapore, where the C.P.R. Lethbridge branch crossed the Macleod Trail, was a tiny station known as Turner Siding. Some distance back from the road, and a half-mile north of Turner Siding, stood a large fieldstone house, a landmark on a treeless plain. Mrs. Miller persuaded her current inamorato, a prominent police-court lawyer, to lease the house for her, and into it she moved her brothel from Ninth Avenue.

Pearl's Place became, if not a home-from-home, at least a port of call for many of the Turner Valley-bound rubbernecks. They could stop in at Pearl's on their way out to obtain reliable road information from returnees from the valley. Many of the latter found her place a welcome refuge after a day spent fighting their way out of the mud holes between the oilfield and Okotoks. Out of these encounters between travellers evolved something more than a mere brothel. Pearl's Place became a sort of information exchange, as the northbounders who had been to the oilfields became spreaders of news and gossip from the rigs. Gradually it became comparatively easy for the curious of Calgary to hole up at Pearl's Place for the day and pick up as much information as if they had made the complete journey. In short order the phrase "going to Turner Valley" became a popular double-entendre for errant Calgary husbands-cum-oilmen. It could mean just that, or the sampling of the services in Pearl Miller's bordello.

Sex, booze, road information, oil-well scuttlebutt, an occasional meal, and even a bed for the night were available around the clock at Pearl's Place. So mightily did she profit from the enterprise that she was able to finance the purchase of a posher house in Calgary's poshest neighborhood, at the foot of Mount Royal on Ninth Street West. The move was a mistake. It brought her house and girls too close to the home grounds of the oil promoters and too far from the flight paths of the Turner Valley roughnecks en route north for a night on the town. Their rowdy behavior when they located Pearl's new palace of joy set the neighbors to calling in the police, and Pearl was forced back to the friendlier environment of Ninth Avenue East.

For I. W. C. Solloway, opening stock-brokerage offices was only the beginning, for it was not long before he was into oil exploration with both feet. He not only took down treasury shares of a dozen companies, he became an important lease holder in Turner Valley. His oil financing differed radically from the Toronto practice in that he was both highly selective in the choice of people to finance and careful always to take down his blocks of treasury shares at par. The universal practice in Toronto was to insist that the vendors offer their treasury shares at substantial discounts. One of the most successful of Solloway investments was in Mayland Oil Company, which was promoted by E. H. Mayland, a prominent Alberta rancher. Solloway subscribed for 150,000 shares of its $1 par stock. Within a year the shares were selling for better than $7, and the company went on to become one of the most successful and longest-surviving in Turner Valley.

J. R. Lowery, the colorful president of Home Oil Company, crossed paths with Solloway on one of the latter's early visits to Calgary. Home Oil had been promoted by a group of Vancouver businessmen and in early 1928 was running out of money trying to complete its first Turner Valley well. Lowery needed $50,000 and told Solloway he was sure he could get $25,000 out of Pat Burns, the meat-packing tycoon, if Solloway could take 25,000 shares of Home stock. Solloway did so, and Home Oil eventually became the medium of one of the greatest coups of oil industry history.

Despite the impact of the Solloway establishment on the volume of oil stocks traded, 1928 saw little sustained increase in the value of the shares, even though several substantial new successes had been scored in the field. Between March and late May, most of the Turner Valley shares had at least doubled in price, and a good many of them had tripled. But much of the gain was lost by the end of the year, and the consensus of the Palliser Hotel palavers was that something unusually striking was needed to get a real bull market going and to keep it going.

To whom the credit should go for devising the propellant that put the shares of Home Oil Company into orbit depends to some extent on the source consulted. The late Robert A. Brown, Jr., always claimed that it was his father's idea, and the Brown version probably comes very close to the truth. Corroboration of a sort is provided by A. P. McDonald, K.C., an oil-wise Calgary lawyer, who once recalled having met Brown on the street a few days after the coup. Brown flourished a $50,000 cheque he had received from United Oils as a finder's fee and said he was headed for the office of William Connacher to buy an annuity with it before he yielded to the temptation to put it into the oil market. In any event, the Brown version of the legend goes like this:

Brown, senior, was electrical superintendent for the city of Calgary and became infected by the oil bug with the Dingman discovery. In the 1920s he was a director of one dormant oil company, a shareholder in several more, and a free-lance geological theorizer. It was universally believed in Calgary that a huge pool of crude oil would one day be discovered in Turner Valley. Brown shared one theory with a score of others that the location would be down-flank from Royalite #4 and at considerably greater depths.

When Solloway was in town his Palliser Hotel suite was usually the site for prolonged and well-lubricated bull sessions with local oil promoters. On other occasions the locale would be Jim Lowery's suite, or Jack Dallas's suite. On this particular occasion the participants in the Solloway suite were — in addition to the host — R. A. Brown, Fred Green, who was president of United Oils, Jim Lowery, perhaps W. M. Connacher, and several others.

Home Oil had brought in two successful wells in Turner Valley and conversation drifted around to why it was not doing better in the market. Solloway said he hoped it would do much better now that it was listed in Toronto. Certainly it was a stock being highly recommended by Solloway and Mills. Brown suggested that what Home Oil needed was news of some kind that would capture newspaper attention all across the country. It so happened that Fred Green's company owned a quarter-section lease southeast of the lease on which Home had brought in its successful wells. Along toward dawn the consensus emerged through the alcoholic haze and cigar smoke that one head-grabbing story would be for Home Oil to buy the United Oils lease for $1,000,000. On a dollars-per-acre basis it was by no means a far-out deal. Only a few weeks previously a 20-acre tract had sold for $10,000 an acre. At that price, United Oils' 160-acre quarter would have been worth $1,600,000. However, $1,000,000 was a number with special intrinsic qualities and would be a real headline-maker.

There was one flaw in the plan, as there usually is with schemes hatched in such circumstances. Home Oil did not have $1,000,000. But Solloway did, and Brown was delegated to try to work out some kind of a deal with him on behalf of both Home and United. The details of the deal were never spelled out, but Solloway did eventually put up the $1,000,000 and unquestionably took a large position in the shares of both companies.

At the beginning of February 1929, Home Oil was selling quietly at around $3.50 a share in Toronto and United was trading at $1.65 to $1.70 in Calgary. During the week of February 10, Home jumped to $5.25, to $6.25, and to $7.95, and the whole oil market blew out of control. Records for share volume were established everywhere almost daily. United Oils was sluggish in following the market and was still selling at $1.80 the day Home hit $7.95. Then it too became active, and by month-end it touched $3.50 while Home zoomed to $15.75. And all this without hard news of any kind coming out — only great rumors of impending big deals.

So frantic was the buying surge for all oil shares that the

Calgary Stock Exchange had to hire a night staff to catch up with the clearing-house bookkeeping. New records in sales were made daily, and on Thursday, March 14, the Calgary Exchange shut down completely to enable the brokers' staffs to catch up with their bookwork. There wasn't a brokerage office in town that was not jammed to the doors. Even on Saturdays, when the markets were closed, they were so congested with throngs of customers that there was no working space for the staff. Prices all down the quotation boards were setting new highs every day. Royalite, which had been selling for $65 eight weeks before, soared above $200. Okalta, which had been $30, went bounding over $300. Mayland was $13.75. Advance, which was $4, jumped to $7 overnight and then quickly leaped to $15.

On March 19, 1929, Lowery officially announced the completion of the $1,000,000 deal with United Oils for the quarter section which adjoined Home's property to the southeast. Home that day sold for $25 dollars a share, and when United Oils announced that it was going to declare a $4-per-share dividend on its 200,000 shares they jumped to $14 each. Ironically that deal, far from sending the market off into much higher levels, signalized the end of the great bull-market in oil stocks, though this went unrecognized at the time. The pace of trading continued unabated, but the highs for everything had been reached and, as spring moved into summer, prices levelled off and then slipped back, as if in anticipation of the disaster that would strike from Wall Street that October.

Solloway and Mills were not, of course, solely responsible for the wild markets that developed after the firm opened its western offices in 1928. The land-office business it was doing in the west quickly attracted other Toronto brokers to the area. Within a very few weeks several other prominent mining stock brokers opened offices as close to Solloway's as they could get. Paradoxically, the volume of business that Solloway and Mills did posed a real hazard to the solvency of the company. Because few oil or mining shares were acceptable to the banks as security for loans, financing their customers' margins might quickly have drained off the company's financial resources. All securities purchased through stock exchanges had to be paid for in cash at time of delivery. Solloway and Mills, therefore, had to find the other half of the purchase price the customers were not putting up.

A much greater hazard was the size of the "long" line carried in many company shares by Solloway and Mills' customers. If 60 or 70 per cent of the floating shares of an oil company were owned by Solloway and Mills' customers, and if a severe market break occurred, the sheer volume of the liquidation by Solloway customers would find insufficient buyers and would cause the price to drop to near nothing. A general market decline could ruin the company. For example: A customer buying 1,000 shares of $1 stock would put up $500. In a severe market decline, the price of that stock could drop to 30 cents a share or less before a purchaser might be found. The customer would be wiped out and Solloway and Mills would also have lost $200 or more.

To finance the margining of customer surpluses, and to protect itself from the consequences of severe market drops, Solloway and Mills adopted the policy which would ultimately land the partners in jail. They sold "short" against their clients' purchases. The charge against them was "bucketing"—accepting orders from customers and then not putting them through the stock exchange. Solloway vigorously denied the charge and claimed that he was engaged in legitimate short selling, even though it was done on a massive scale; that any failure of his offices to put sales through stock exchanges was unintentional and attributable to the rush of business and human error. His employees corroborated his story.

Running a "bucket shop" is everywhere against the law. A "bucket shop" has been defined as a broker's office in which the "house" takes the opposite side to that taken by the customer. Since most people buy or go "long" on stocks, the house, in taking the opposite side, goes "short" by agreeing to deliver the stocks at a later date.

Short selling, however, has been recognized as an integral part of all stock and commodity markets. It is generally accepted that the short-sellers provide an essential function in creating market liquidity. In this connection the line which divides "legitimate" short selling from "bucketing" is of gossamer thinness. On the New York Stock Exchange, where the minimum trading unit or "board lot" is 100 shares, "odd-lot specialists" exist to provide markets for shareholders trading smaller numbers of shares. Under New York regulations, odd-lot specialists are required to take the opposite side to another broker's customer, to buy when the customer wants to sell, and to sell short when the customer wants to buy. When the specialist has done that often enough to build up a "board lot" of 100 shares, he can dispose of it as a unit. The difference between what the New York brokers do and what Solloway did is represented by a broker go-between. That is, instead of the customer's broker going "short" on the stock the customer is buying, he deals with a specialist who goes "short". The result is the same, a customer is "long" and a broker is "short".

While Solloway was taking a strong "long" position in the oil and mining companies he favored, he was taking an even stronger position on the "short" side of other companies—even those companies in which his customers were buying heavily. At one time he was "short" more than $4,000,000-worth of the stocks in which his customers were "long". But this, he insisted, was not "bucketing". In his book *Speculators and Politicians,* which he published privately in 1933, he wrote:

> Naturally . . . we expected to make money on the short side of the markets in the same manner that we expected to make money on the long side of the market. I believe that if an individual or corporation exercises reasonable intelligence and judgement, money can be made . . . both in buying for a long account and selling for a short account. . . .
> But it would be absolutely impossible for any broker in any stock market in the world, carrying millions of dollars in securities on margin for his customers to protect his solvency unless he had a short position. . . . On a falling market the equity in securities carried by a broker for his customers decreases and the broker's financial responsibility increases. The danger which can appear almost overnight is

—where is the broker going to sell large quantities of securities during times of panic or violent depreciation of security prices? Ninety per cent of his customers have no further monies with which to margin their accounts once the securities held have depreciated by the full amount of their original equities with the result than unless he takes the precaution to protect his own solvency and his own financial responsibilities, every broker carrying large quantities of securities for his customers would go into liquidation during periods of financial depression, particularly in time of panic. . . .

. . . The main reason for the firm's short position was to insure solvency and place the firm in the position of being purchasers of speculative securities when there would be no other market or purchaser for them. . . .

In the collapse of Canada's financial markets that followed the October 1929 crashes in New York, thousands of Canadian speculators went broke, and in the going set up a hue and cry for scapegoats.

In Edmonton, on January 3, 1930, Premier J. E. Brownlee was the principal speaker at a testimonial dinner which the Aero Club of Edmonton gave for I. W. C. Solloway as president of Commercial Airlines. With Captain W. R. "Wop" May at the controls, one of Commercial's planes had just made Canadian aviation history with the first airmail flight from Edmonton to Aklavik and back. The crowd cheered Brownlee's tribute to Solloway as one of those responsible for putting the Canadian North on the aviation map of Canada. A week later, Brownlee selected Solloway as his scapegoat for the collapse of the oil-stock market, had him arrested in Vancouver and returned under police escort to Calgary, and launched him on an eight-year career as the sugar daddy of the Canadian legal profession.

The arrest of Solloway had the immediate effect of sending another wave of panic through the Canadian security markets, and Brownlee got a great deal of flack from eastern newspapers for his role in the case. However, he put Solloway on trial and got a conviction on a charge of conspiring with Mills to defraud their customers. Solloway was sentenced to four months in jail and fined $200,000, while Mills was fined $50,000 and given one month in jail. After the deduction of legal expenses, the trial yielded the government of Alberta a clear profit of better than $178,000, as Premier Brownlee boasted to the legislature.

Solloway's reaction to his arrest was to shut down his entire chain of thirty-eight brokerage offices and to retire completely from the purlieus of finance. The closings cost 1,500 employees their jobs and $60,000 a week in wages. Solloway was then launched upon a career as the star attraction in a whole series of trials as attorneys general in Ontario and British Columbia hauled him into court. He paid additional whopping fines for technical breaches of the law, but when Ontario tried to duplicate Alberta's jailing of Solloway, on the identical charge on which he was convicted in Alberta, the newspapers shouted foul and he was acquitted. In these trials, and in the other suits that he had to carry to the Privy Council to win, Solloway had to pay out several millions of dollars in legal fees.

While he and Mills were in jail in Lethbridge, a quaintly significant footnote was added to his thesis that bankruptcy was the inevitable fate of brokers who did not protect themselves against market disasters by selling short. Two of his largest competitors, Stobie-Forlong and Company and D. S. Paterson and Company, went broke. Their four principal partners were sentenced to a total of twenty-two years in the penitentiary for theft of their customers' securities, which they sold in an effort to keep their firms afloat amidst the crashing markets. None of Solloway's customers ever lost a dollar on that score, and Solloway himself retired to Vancouver where he died, still a wealthy man, in 1965.

With the disappearance of Solloway, speculative interest in Turner Valley vanished, along with employment in the drilling industry and in the brokerage business. The brokers disappeared from Portage and Main, and Eighth Avenue, and Jasper Avenue, and those who survived moved back into walk-up offices that could be had for rents they could afford to pay. From the 240,000 feet of hole that was drilled in Turner Valley in 1929, activity dropped to only 13,000 feet in 1932.

16. Downward to Disaster

For the sake of convenient identification it is generally accepted that the Twenties ended, and the Great Depression era began, with the Wall Street crash on Black Tuesday, October 29, 1929. On that day more than 23,500,000 shares were traded on the New York and the Curb exchanges. The ticker fell four hours behind the market. Losses up to $60 a share were recorded for a number of stocks. Shares that had been selling for hundreds of dollars were down 60 per cent and more from their high points. The *New York Times* average of fifty blue-chip stocks, which had dropped more than 20 points on Monday, plummeted another 40 points on Black Tuesday. While that was certainly some crash, it was in fact the culmination of a whole series of crashes.

Attention focussed so sharply on historical bench marks inevitably distorts perspectives. This is particularly true of the stock-market crashes of October 1929. During the previous two years, billions of dollars in bank credit had been diverted from ordinary commercial channels into stock-exchange call loans that enabled speculators to gamble even more heavily in the stock market. Where common stocks had once been bought for cash at prices largely established by earnings and dividends paid, the availability of call loans stood the securities business on its head. By putting up only a third to a half of the market price, speculators could buy twice as many shares as they could on a cash basis. The result was to double the demand for shares and to push the prices upward. As prices rose, the speculators then used their "paper profits" as margin with which to buy more stocks—and more stocks and more stocks. Share prices were forced to outrageous levels. In a little more than a year, Radio Corporation stock rose from $100 to $500 a share, Westinghouse from $92 to $313, Montgomery Ward from $130 to $466, and General Electric from $130 to $396. From Labor Day onward in 1929, however, the market was running out of steam. Quotations slipped steadily downward from the high points, and a rather vigorous shake-out was going on for some weeks prior to the big breaks. At first the sharp drops were interpreted as normal profit-taking, and analysts rushed out predictions that the market would soon recover its poise and that the onward and upward march of stock prices would be resumed. American prosperity was so fundamentally sound, America's financial wizardry, industrial might, and technical expertise were of such monumental superiority to anything the world had known, that nothing could impede the progress of the United States for long!

On Monday, October 21, after the New York market had suffered its worst shake-out of the decade, the financial editor of the United Press polled the heads of Wall Street financial houses for their analyses of the situation. It was their consensus that the day's drop might be the dying spasm of the two-month-long bear-market. On Tuesday the market rallied moderately, only to take an even sharper drop on Wednesday that carried prices well below Monday's lows. Then Black Thursday demolished what was left of the "dying spasm" theory.

Margin speculation in industrial securities had never reached the frenzied pace in Canada that it had south of the line. But because a number of Canadian companies listed their shares in New York as well as on the Toronto and Montreal exchanges, when New York shuddered and shook, Canadian markets shivered in sympathy. Fluctuations were always wildest in the interlisted issues, and Canadians who had developed a passion for faster action did their trading in New York rather than in Canadian markets. They paid dearly for the preference. Between Black Thursday and Blue Monday, when interlisted issues were particularly hard hit, International Nickel dropped $14 a share and Brazilian Traction was down $17 a share. The next day they dropped another $8. Over all, the interlisted issues lost about three times as heavily as shares listed only in Canada. Then came Tuesday, October 29.

Yet, for the people of the Canadian prairies, Wall Street's Black Tuesday was something they could take in stride because they had been through it all before on their own Black Thursday, October 24, when the price of wheat dropped 11 cents a bushel in less than twenty minutes on the Winnipeg Grain Exchange. The Thursday disasters tempted the editor of the *Manitoba Free Press* into a prophecy that immediately returned to haunt him. In a short editorial animadversion on the deleterious effects on the economy of unrestrained speculation, the *Free Press* predicted "it will be a long time before followers of the stock market forget October 24, 1929." Five days later the shambles of Black Tuesday made it very forgettable indeed.

The United Press poll and the *Free Press* editorial were not only examples of how wrong the experts could be, they also marked the beginning of a ten-year stretch in which experts in every field would be consistently wrong whenever they hazarded a guess about anything.

In western Canada, interest in eastern stock markets had only begun to pick up steam in 1928 following the arrival of I. W. C. Solloway and the introduction of margin trading in oil and mining shares. Until then Manitobans had confined most of their speculative flings to the grain market and to home-grown mining developments. Albertans had favored the grain market and oil stocks. Speculation by residents of Saskatchewan was almost entirely in wheat futures. So it was hardly surprising that when the first sharp drops in New York and Montreal occurred on October 21 and 23 they went unnoticed by the news editors of prairie newspapers, save for the usual brief financial-page stories. The *Edmonton Journal* was far more interested in the upcoming dinner the Prince of Wales was putting on in London for the Empire's Victoria Cross winners. The Winnipeg and Calgary papers gave their banner headlines to the storm raging on the Great Lakes which would take more than fifty lives before subsiding.

Invisible though they were journalistically, the shock waves from what was happening in New York, bouncing off Toronto and Montreal, were being felt in all the brokerage offices across the prairies. Business and professional offices were frequently deserted that week as the managers, doctors, dentists, and lawyers found excuses for dropping into and out of their brokers' offices half a dozen times each morning. By some process of psychic osmosis everybody who was "in the market" seemed to have become privy to what was about to happen in New York on Black Thursday morning. Long before noon, Winnipeg time, and before breakfast time in Calgary and Edmonton, there was not a square foot of standing-room left in the board rooms of the land as the assemblage watched sweating ballets of board-markers chalking away the ruination of the speculating world on the quotation boards.

The atmosphere that morning was different from anything it had been before. Gone were the hum of voices and the small talk. Gone was the rippling laughter that erupted from the retelling of the Amos 'n' Andy radio routines of the night before. The telephones never stopped ringing, until clerks gave up and left the receivers off the hooks. The clattering of the telegraph sounders seemed more imperious than before. The customers stood in unseeing trances for minutes on end, and struggled through the crowd to get out of the board rooms; a few minutes later they were struggling to get back in.

On that Thursday the front pages of every prairie newspaper caught up with the collapsing financial markets, but in doing so they all kept things in a prairie perspective. Emphasis was not on Wall Street but on the Winnipeg wheat pit. Thus the *Edmonton Journal*'s 8-column front-page heading read: "Mad Rush of Selling Sends Winnipeg Wheat Down 14 cents". The *Calgary Herald* heading almost duplicated the *Journal*'s. The *Manitoba Free Press* managed equal billing for the wheat market and the stock market under a four-column two-line heading: "Millions in Paper Profits Are Swept Away as Prices Crash".

Unlike the collapse in Wall Street, where the market opened lower and kept dropping throughout the day, wheat prices in

Chicago and Winnipeg, though forced down in sympathy with New York, were only moderately lower at the close. The market had closed strongly on October 23 with May wheat at $1.45 ¹/₂. At 11 a.m. on Thursday it was down to $1.42 when a wave of selling set in, and by 11:12 the price touched $1.40. Then a bear-raid hit the Winnipeg Grain Exchange like a summer tornado and within six minutes selling orders for millions of bushels of wheat drove the May option to $1.31 a bushel. Never in the history of the Exchange had there been so sharp and deep a break in so short a time.

The sharpness of that break spelled ruin for thousands of grain speculators who were "long" on wheat futures on 10-cent margins. Stop-loss orders, which brokers normally entered a cent or two above the point where a market drop would wipe out the margin, were filled automatically before margin clerks were able to notify their customers of the disaster that was occurring. From its extreme lows the wheat market slowly recovered until, at the close of trading on Black Thursday, the May future was back to $1.39 ¹/₄ for a loss of roughly six cents a bushel from the previous day.

The quick drop of the wheat market brought financial disaster to even the well-heeled speculators who had survived the August debacle. Many of them might well have been able to put up more margin if they could have been notified in time. But the dumping of millions of bushels on both Chicago and Winnipeg sent prices down so far, so sharply, that stop-loss selling orders were filled before the order clerks in the brokerage offices became aware of what was happening on the trading floor.

As poignant a tale as any to be told of that day concerned a Winnipeg broker who that very morning began his appointment as manager of the grain department of a large Toronto brokerage house. After eking out a modest living as a freelance wheat-pit trader for a decade, he had sold his Grain Exchange membership to his new employer for $25,000 and a $10,000-a-year salary. He, like most of the other traders in that wheat-pit-that-became-a-maelstrom, was overwhelmed with orders to sell wheat. As the market was touching bottom he was handed an order for 100,000 bushels. It, however, was an order to buy, not to sell. In his exhausted condition, he sold 100,000 bushels of May wheat at $1.32 instead of buying, and did not discover his error until after the market closed. The mistake cost the firm $14,000 to correct. The new manager was faced with the alternative of absorbing the loss or losing his job. He opted to absorb the loss. That was his second mistake. Six months later the firm went into receivership and he lost his job anyway.

What differentiated the wheat market from the stock market was that the wheat market recovered that Thursday, even if hordes of speculators were wiped out. The stock market never did. After Black Thursday was followed by Blue Monday and Black Tuesday, a slower but steady slide developed through the first half of November. The wheat market struggled back above $1.40 on Friday, and though it took another beating the following week it bounced back again. In doing so it made the reassurances being issued in Canada sound more sensible than those coming out of the United States.

The Hon. J. A. Robb, Canada's mortally ill Minister of Finance, was roused briefly after the Thursday disaster to reaffirm official faith in the fundamental soundness of the Canadian economy and to express confidence in its financial institutions. While the dust was still settling on the following Black Tuesday, Prime Minister Mackenzie King called newspaper reporters to his office for a statement. Economic conditions in Canada, he said, were never sounder, nor was faith in the development of the Dominion ever greater. He pointed with pride to the growth of Canadian primary and secondary industries and noted that the confidence that the world had in Canada was best illustrated by its willingness to provide Canada with investment capital. If there were any nay-sayers in the land willing to dispute these sentiments, they did not surface that autumn. On the contrary, one business leader pretty well summed everything up with a statement which noted that things had been so extraordinarily good for Canadian business that, if they just reverted to what was once considered normal, the future was assured.

Not only did the price of wheat hold firm for the rest of 1929, export sales, which had been lagging all year, perked up. Sales, moreover, were being made at prices fully 30 cents higher than those that prevailed in 1928. There was even hope that the 1928 carry-over would be quickly liquidated, and a return of $1.50 per bushel for the 1929 crop was a distinct possibility. So the farmers faced the new year so full of confidence that they went on a shopping spree for the fancy new tractors they had been coveting for so long.

The steady recovery of wheat prices was taken as proof that the wheat pools were succeeding in stabilizing wheat prices at levels that would yield a profit to the producers. Railway construction spread extra purchasing power far and wide in rural areas as the branch lines were extended. In the cities a mild house-building boom spurred the recovery of the construction industry, which also had the benefit of some large railway-hotel buildings and retail-store expansion. With better times came an improvement in wage rates and a gradual shortening of working hours.

In Alberta, though the oil stocks sank to dismal depths, confidence in the future of the industry was never greater. Home Oil, which had dropped to $14 a share from a high of $27 during the stock-market crashes, was down to $8.20 at the year end. Mayland, which had topped at $15, was down to $1; Calmont had sold at $6 and was at $1.20. But the Turner Valley wells were producing at a record 100,000 barrels of oil a month for the Calgary refineries. Production for the year just missed reaching 1,000,000 barrels, and every forecast was for an increase of at least 50 per cent in the year to follow.

For the urban citizenry all the portents were favorable. The retail trade had been notably on the upswing for two years, and was enjoying its best Christmas-shopping season in a decade. The "electronics" revolution was on, though the word itself had not yet been coined. Giant strides in radio engineering, coupled with the development of small motors and improved sound reproduction systems, gave merchants two hot new items for the Christmas trade. The new "all-electric plug-in" radios made all the battery sets then in use obsolete. The Victor Orthophonic

Victrola, which also used electric currents, did the same for all the crank-up gramophones in the land. For upper-bracket shoppers, combination radio-gramophones were beginning to appear.

Radio broadcasting itself was reaching maturity with the development of regularly transmitted feature programs carried by telephone lines to scores of stations across the United States and easily picked up on Canadian sets. Amos 'n' Andy had become the first of the radio rages and were soon facing competition from Moran and Mack—the Two Black Crows, Rudy Vallee and his Connecticut Yankees, Paul Whiteman, Ben Bernie, Joe Penner, and a host of others, including Gene Austin, Frank Crumit, and The Happiness Boys. The advertising industry was on the verge of discovering the pulling power of what had once been merely a fad.

That December there were even signs that long-dormant interest in social betterment was reviving. The prairie governments were all participating in the federal old-age-pension scheme, under which indigents over seventy years of age became eligible for a pension of $20 a month. Provincial health departments were in existence, and health services were being substantially improved everywhere. So was education—particularly in Manitoba.

The long and socially divisive debate over Prohibition seemed to be over. Booze was conveniently available through government stores and beer by the glass was on tap in Alberta, and more recently in Manitoba, in taverns of rigidly puritanical decor. Government liquor profits were quietly moving upward from the $2,000,000-a-year mark, though bootlegging and prostitution, which government control was supposed to abolish, still constituted the most publicized moral issues in the major cities.

Three years of better-than-average times seemed to have at last brought everything together for the people of the prairies. As the last page of the calendar of the era fluttered to the floor, a look backward over the decade naturally enough lighted, not on the troughs and valleys, but on the peaks. It had seen the completion of the radio revolution, the automobile revolution, the farm-machinery revolution, the electrical revolution, and even the entertainment revolution, which introduced such a miraculous invention as talking movies.

Mesmerized as everybody had to be by such wonders, it was hardly surprising that nobody caught a glimpse of the far horizon where the economic clouds were gathering for a storm that would send the whole world careening downward to disaster.

Mercifully, the future was unforeseeable.

If the Twenties brought to the western Canadian prairies much that was new and different, good, beautiful, gauche, rococo, and just plain outlandish, it was also — as much as anything — a period of alarums and excursions, and the culmination of crusades and upsurges that had enlivened the preceding decades.

As such it may have been part of an immutable process in nature that W. R. Leslie, the superintendent of the Morden Experimental Farm, once noticed in an old apple tree, one of the earliest planted on the farm. The tree was dying, and as Leslie contemplated it ruefully, he said:* "It's a funny thing about that tree. It was a good bearer until recently. Then it began to show signs of rapid decline and we marked it for replacement. But last spring it was just covered with blossoms and one of the boys said, 'Maybe it heard us talking about cutting it out and put on a special show to demonstrate that there is life in the old trunk yet.' He said he'd noticed previously that trees often put on a great spurt of blossoming just before they die.

"It's not something I've paid too much attention to myself," Leslie continued. "If there is anything in it I suppose it's a survival factor in nature — nature's way of assuring the survival of the species with the death of the individual. However, while this old tree did set a lot of fruit, there'll only be a handful of apples to pick because they fell off long before maturity. Maybe this old tree was like the old man shovelling snow. It overtaxes its strength and reached its fullest flower on the day of its death, as it were."

*as the author recalls the conversation, thirty years later.

Perhaps, like Leslie's tree, the great crusades that carried into the 1920s overtaxed their strength. Certainly the decade saw the "last flowering" of the great moral-uplift campaigns that had sought for forty years to elevate human behavior — by the full force of the law if moral suasion failed. As the decade began, the forces of righteousness were uniting for the last time to rescue mankind from addiction to beverage alcohol by the reimposition of Prohibition. They carried everything before them, then they relaxed, their zeal withered away; they were routed by the Moderationists four years later.

It was also the last flowering of a concerted ecumenical movement that produced the United Church of Canada. This movement fell short of its goal when the Presbyterians split into two warring factions and the other Protestant denominations and sects spurned the union and stoked up their determination to continue in their separate ways.

Equally spectacular was the way in which the trades union movement peaked and declined after the disaster of 1919. The unions, which had carried everything before them, watched impotently as the prairies turned into a depressed-wage area. The once-militant unions drifted under the control of craft union bureaucrats; the One Big Union, which had come on like the power and the glory immediately after the strike, was quickly lost in a cloud of ideological bickering.

The major difference between the urban workers' movement and the prairie farmers' was that the last flowering of the farmers' ended quicker. Their angry, aggressive, and superbly stage-managed agrarian revolt destroyed overnight the two-party political system in the west. Their Progressive movement seemed to sweep everything before it, yet it disappeared into nothingness in half a decade.

The last flowering was not limited to the constructive efforts of mankind. Its impact on the fimetarious weed-growth of racism was equally devastating. It was at least the *beginning* of the last flowering of Anglo-Saxon bigotry, which insisted throughout the decade that a man's religious persuasion, his race, and his national origin must count for more in prairie society than the man himself.

But if the decade saw the ending of much that was true and good and beautiful — and of much that was false and foul and frightful — it was also the beginning of developments that would send prairie people off in exciting new directions. After the failure of the Progressive political movement came the agitation that led to the birth of the prairie wheat pools, as exciting and far-reaching an agitation as ever hit the west. The dawning of the electrical age saw the planting of the first seeds of women's liberation — liberation from the kitchens and sculleries of the urban west. Out went the wood-burning kitchen ranges, iceboxes, scrubbing boards, and clothes boilers. In came electrical stoves, refrigerators, water heaters, and washing machines.

Powering the electrical revolution were two recently developed devices — not unmixed blessings — that rapidly accelerated its pace: advertising and the instalment plan. Under the beguiling pressure of easy-payment advertising, prairie dwellers seldom waited for one gadget to be paid for before assuming the easy payments for a second and a third. But, as they told each other, "It's the only way we'll ever be able to get them because if we don't have to make the payments we'll never save enough to buy them." Advertising and easy credit washed away the dividing line between luxury and necessity.

Although the decade had its periods of excitement, these years were by no means the "Roaring Twenties" in the American sense of the term. None of the fanciful catch-phrases they coined to label the decade — the jazz age, the flapper era, the flaming-youth decade, the ballyhoo years — had more than the most limited application to western Canada — if, indeed, they had any real application to the United States outside New York, Chicago, and Los Angeles.

That the prairies did not roar in the American sense does not mean that they did not roar in the Canadian sense. It took the American labor movement fifteen years to catch up with the ferment that typified the Canadian movement in 1920. The uproar that accompanied the organization of the wheat pools kept the farmers in a turmoil. The impact of the Alberta oil boom and the Manitoba mining boom could hardly be exaggerated. Politics were never as exciting, before or since, as when the

Progressives were tearing everything apart. If the Ku Klux Klan could stir up no lynchings, it nevertheless set the province of Saskatchewan on its ear for two years.

It cannot be denied that many of the great agitations of the 1920s shared a common weakness. Once they had achieved their immediate goals, their outward enthusiasm and inner drive disappeared, making them vulnerable to the inevitable reaction. Their "last flowering" seemed to embody the Marx-Engels axiom that all human institutions have within them the seeds of their own destruction. But until that process began, the onward, upward, and outward rush of these movements of the 1920s turned it into the west's most exciting decade, which, almost by definition, made it more exciting than anything that happened anywhere else in the country.

A Note on Sources

The purpose of this book is to do for the people of the Prairie provinces what Frederick Lewis Allen did for the United States with his book *Only Yesterday: An Informal History of the 1920s*, but to do it with the politics left out, to the extent that that is ever possible. For that reason alone it is less detailed than Allen's work. In addition, several aspects have been covered *in extenso* in the author's previous works, *Booze, Red Lights on the Prairies*, and *The Boy from Winnipeg*.

The absence of footnotes is explained by the fact that the authority for much of the narrative is the author himself. Because it was my great good fortune to be born at the right time, I was there or thereabouts when most of the events described were happening. I was a short-pants spear-carrier in the 1915-16 Prohibition crusade, a newsboy for the O.B.U. *Bulletin*, an urban teen-ager frequently rousted from his bed by visiting country cousins, an unskilled harvest-time stooker, an office boy in the Grain Exchange, a grain-brokerage ledger-keeper, stock-market margin clerk, sometime buyer of oil and mining stock, Model T owner, race-horse trainer, failed pool-shark, and a communicant of Marshall Gauvin's. For the fleshing out of remembered and half-remembered episodes, I relied on two main sources. The first was interviews with people who were directly involved. The second was the newspapers and periodicals of the era, in particular the back files of the *Manitoba Free Press, Winnipeg Tribune, Brandon Sun, Regina Leader, Regina Star, Saskatoon*

Phoenix, Saskatoon Star, Moose Jaw Times, Grain Growers Guide, Farm and Ranch Review, and *Western Producer.*

1. Going For Broke

For much of the material on R. James Speers I am indebted to W. E. Osler, who generously provided access to transcriptions of interviews he conducted with a number of former associates and employees of the colorful gambler, and to Jim Coleman's *A Hoofprint on My Heart.*

2. Down on the Farm

The material on the rural life-styles of the 1920s will be familiar to every farm resident and former itinerant harvester over sixty. So will the examples used in the scores of community histories produced by women's groups and community associations since 1967.

3. After the Strike Was Over

A good deal of factual material was mined from the *Labour Gazette,* the publications of the Dominion Bureau of Statistics, the *Canadian Annual Review,* and the daily newspapers. Anne B. Woywitka's article "The Drumheller Strike, 1919" in the *Alberta Historical Review,* Winter 1973, and the Estevan kidnapping trials reports of 1920 in the O.B.U. *Bulletin* were sources for the discussion of vigilante terror in the mining towns.

6. The Gospel of Co-operation

A definitive history of the three prairie wheat pools has yet to be written, but Leonard Nesbitt's *Tides of the West* is a useful popular history of the Alberta Wheat Pool. Paul Sharp's *Agrarian Revolt in Western Canada* is required reading for its delineation of the impact on western Canadian farm movements of the ideas imported from the United States by incoming American settlers. The immense literature on the Populists is well summarized in R. J. Cunningham's pamphlet *The Populists in Historic Perspective.* Aaron Sapiro got a tremendously favorable press in Alberta and a boisterously antagonistic reception from Saskatchewan city newspapers. His ultimate fall from grace in the United States is reported obliquely in Charles P. Larrowe's *Harry Bridges.*

7. Back to the Booze

The material for this chapter is drawn in part from the Senate and House of Commons *Debates* for 1919, and the previously mentioned works of the author.

10. Almost United

The final debates on church union were covered extensively in the Winnipeg, Edmonton, and Regina newspapers. So extensive is the United Church Archives material that no listing is needed. The social conditions underlying the movement toward union are well detailed in such books as Richard Allen's *The Social Passion*, Donald Swainson's *Historical Essays on the Prairie Provinces*, J. S. Woodsworth's *Strangers Within Our Gates* and *My Neighbour*. W. E. Mann's *Sect, Cult and Church in Alberta* probes the depths of the sectarian fervor that existed outside the Presbyterian-Methodist ambit. The case for the more restrained and reasonable opponents of church union is well stated in E. A. Corbett's biography of Dr. D. G. McQueen—*McQueen of Edmonton*.

11. The Sting of the WASP

There are shelves of books in the Glenbow-Alberta Institute library dealing with the ethnic settlement of western Canada. Almost without exception they are more concerned with vital statistics and material achievement than with the treatment meted out to them by the Anglo-Saxon majority. An exception is Howard Palmer's *Land of the Second Chance*. In his *The Jews in Manitoba*, Rabbi Arthur M. Schiel notes the physical assaults made by Anglo-Saxon workers on Jewish refugees brought into Manitoba to work on railway construction in 1882. Otherwise, it is difficult to locate examples of overt discrimination in any of the ethnic publications. Not only is there reluctance to raise the subject in print, it is one that immigrants hesitate to discuss even in private. One Ukrainian doctor, who suffered more than most at the hands of the Manitoba Medical College racists, refused even to be interviewed because "their sons and daughters are still here and why should they be hurt by what their fathers did?" Jewish doctors in Winnipeg, Calgary, and Vancouver who were interviewed hesitated to disclose the names of their tormentors, even in confidence. The author, who was an editorial writer on the *Winnipeg Free Press* at the time, was personally involved in the agitation that led to the ending of discrimination in the Medical College in 1944.

13. Jimmy Gardiner *v.* the Ku Klux Klan

All Saskatchewan newspapers carried extensive reports of the Ku Klux Klan invasion, including almost verbatim reports of the long-distance debates between Premier J. G. Gardiner and the Klan leaders. Much new material is now being brought to light from the Gardiner papers. Two excellent research jobs have been done on the subject, one by William Calderwood in his M.A. thesis, "The Rise and Fall of the Ku Klux Klan in Saskatchewan", and the other by Paul Kyba in his chapter on the Klan in *Politics in Saskatchewan*, edited by Norman Ward and Duff Spafford. M. J. Coldwell contributed his recollections of the Klan in Regina, and former members explained their motivation in becoming members.

15. The Glow from Hell's Half-Acre

While I. W. C. Solloway was still being dragged through the courts by provincial governments, he took time out to write two books. The first was his apologia, *Speculators and Politicians*; the second was *Canada's Destiny*. Some of his ideas were as preposterous as others were imaginatively sensible. Taken together, the books provide a detailed explanation of the Solloway operations and an insight into the man himself, and in addition throw light on some of the darker passages of Canadian financial history.

Index